Cheap Sleep Guide

GW01017793

KATIE WOOD was bc
Edinburgh, reading Communications then
English at Edinburgh University. Interspersed
with working as a freelance journalist, she trav-
elled extensively in Europe and North Africa in
the late 1970s and 80s, and this resulted in the
bestselling guide *Europe by Train* (published
by Fontana). Since then she has worked
as a full-time travel writer and journalist,
travelling to over 60 countries worldwide.
She has now written eighteen guides covering
every aspect of travel, and writes freelance for
many national papers and magazines, including the *Daily Telegraph*, *Observer*, *Independent*
and *Guardian*, and regularly contributes to
radio and TV travel programmes on the BBC
and ITV. She is currently involved heavily in
the issues of green tourism. Following her
book *The Good Tourist Guide* she is actively
writing and working in this field, acting
as a consultant to many organizations and
agencies on greening their tourist activities.

Katie lives in Perth, Scotland, with her
husband, and has two young sons who frequently don their backpacks and take to the
road with Mum.

Available by Katie Wood

Europe By Train
The Round the World Air Guide
The Best of British Country House Hotels
European City Breaks
Holiday Ireland
Holiday Scotland
The 100 Greatest Holidays in the World
The 1992 Business Travel Guide
The Good Tourist Guide
The Good Tourist in France
The Good Tourist in the UK

Cheap Sleep Guide to Europe 1992

KATIE WOOD

Editorial Assistant and
1991–2 Head Researcher: Craig Aitken

Fontana
An Imprint of HarperCollins*Publishers*

To Craig Aitken, editorial assistant and 1991–2 head researcher, a large debt is owed for his last-minute burning of the midnight oil. Also for his checking, double-checking and checking again. Sorry about the fleas in the various pits, Craig. By the time you stop scratching, you'll be on the road again.

Fontana
An Imprint of HarperCollins*Publishers*,
77–85 Fulham Palace Road,
Hammersmith, London W6 8JB

A Fontana Original 1992

9 8 7 6 5 4 3 2 1

Copyright © Katie Wood 1992

The Author asserts the moral right to be identified as the author of this work

A catalogue record for this book is available from the British Library

ISBN 0 00 637728 9

Set in Linotron Palatino by
The Midlands Book Typesetting Company

Printed in Great Britain by
HarperCollins Manufacturing Glasgow

All rights reserved. No part of this publication may be reproduced, stored in a retrieval system, or transmitted, in any form or by any means, electronic, mechanical, photocopying, recording or otherwise, without the prior permission of the publishers.

This book is sold subject to the condition that it shall not, by way of trade or otherwise, be lent, re-sold, hired out or otherwise circulated without the publisher's prior consent in any form of binding or cover other than that in which it is published and without a similar condition including this condition being imposed on the subsequent purchaser.

Contents

Introduction

The single most difficult thing when travelling round Europe
on a budget is to find a clean, safe and comfortable place
to lay your head come nightfall. Whether you're Inter
Railing, hitching, cycling, bussing or driving round the
continent, unless you want to follow a strict timetable
and book beds ahead (and you can rarely book the real
budget ones anyway), your main headache is going to be
getting accommodation sorted out.

In the main cities and resorts in high season, you'll soon
begin to feel as if you're back in the school nativity play
again – the Mary and Joseph 'no room at the inn' syndrome
really gets to you after a while, as you trail round the streets
looking for a suitable pensione, hostel or campsite. Rather
than being 'great with child', of course, you're great with
rucksack – almost as uncomfortable after a few miles in high
temperatures. It's not much to ask, you grumble to anyone
who'll listen, a bed for under £10 a night, preferably nearer
£5. But the trouble these days is that so many people are
'doing Europe' using the same guidebooks, that supply
never meets the demand. Or does it? Well, there actually
are enough places, it's all a matter of knowing where to
look. In your home town, you could probably find beds
for £5–8 without a problem. But that's because you would
know where to look, whereas a tourist in your town would
never find it so simple. And that's the position, a stranger,
that you will be in many times in Europe.

This book can be your guide to the 'inside knowledge'
that a local has. I've stayed in more than my fair share of
dives, from a house of ill-repute in Casablanca (not a lot of
sleep that night!) to what turned out to be a hippy commune
in Denmark (you thought no one said 'far-out, man' any

longer?). Neither were experiences I'd repeat, but as the wrinklies say, 'If I'd known then what I know now . . .' So as I slap on the vitamin E cream, you might as well have the benefit of my good and bad experiences now.

This guide is written as a reaction to the literally hundreds of letters I receive each year from readers of my *Europe by Train* guide. You asked for more accommodation suggestions – well, now you've got them, in a book dedicated exclusively to this subject. And as I've listed so many, it should spread *Cheap Sleep* readers more thinly and at least give each of you a chance of getting that pack off your back and putting your feet up, after a long day's travelling. I know, after a couple of hours searching, in true biblical style, you'd even settle for a stable.

This guide covers all types of cheap accommodation: pensiones; hostels – both IYHF and independent; campsites; sleep-ins; student hostels; campus accommodation; private accommodation with families; and, if all else fails, 'safe' places to sleep rough. The recommendations will obviously vary in quality and price, but they are all the cheapest around in that country – it's just a fact that a 'cheap sleep' in Norway will cost you three times what it will in Turkey.

In terms of hierarchy and which type of accommodation suits who, basically, **hotels**, **pensiones** and **B&Bs** are usually the most expensive, but they are also one of the most comfortable options. About the same price, and an excellent way of finding out more about the locals is to stay with them direct: **private accommodation** is generally arranged through Tourist Offices. Effectively you become a paying guest, mixing with the family and getting the opportunity to ask all the questions about their lifestyle and culture that you otherwise might not have had the chance to. **Private** and **IYHF hostels** are pretty much on a par in terms of price. If a private hostel is offering rates half that of the local IYHF, it's generally because standards are extremely low.

Sleep-Ins and **YMCA/YWCA Inter Rail points** are fairly recent developments. Very reasonably priced, and an excellent way to meet other travellers, the only problem is that they're limited to certain locations in Europe. **Camping** is fine if you're the outdoor type and are experienced in pitching a tent and cooking over a camping stove. An International Camping Carnet is a good idea if you plan doing a good deal of camping and these Carnets can be bought at most sites. Official camping is obviously more regimented than 'freelance' camping, but as the latter is illegal in some countries (I state which in the guide), the choice is often made for you. Always clean up after yourself and seek permission from the landowner, wherever you are. Using **student halls of residence** is a good way to get round Europe. It's cheap, they're well equipped, and you meet other travellers. Tourist Offices have details.

If you want further information to that provided in this book, and if you're very organized, you could write ahead to the individual country's Tourist Boards, located in your capital city (London in our case).

If you come across a place suggested in this guide that has dropped standards, upped prices or is definitely not worth recommending any longer, please drop me a line and let me know. Likewise, if you find a little gem, pass on the info so we can all benefit. Particularly in Eastern Europe, where the demand for cheap beds now exceeds supply ten times over, we could all do with other travellers' hints and help.

However you do it, wherever you get to, I sincerely hope this much-requested guide will help you.

KATIE WOOD
Perth, Scotland
December 1991

Note to readers

The exchange rate used in this guide is £1=$1.90=DM2.90

Be a Good Tourist

As this edition of *Cheap Sleep* goes to press the second edition of my latest project is about to be published; it's something very close to my heart; something I believe in very strongly, and not since the launch of *Europe by Train* have I felt that there was such a great need for a book like this. It should be of interest to many of *Cheap Sleep*'s and *Europe by Train*'s intrepid types, and the theory behind the book is of relevance to all of us who travel, in any way, at any time. Called *The Good Tourist – A Guide to Green Travel Worldwide* – the book addresses the issues of the impact of tourism on the environment and society. It's about what you are on the point of doing – travelling to a foreign country; any country. What you do; where you go; how you go; where you sleep; what you eat – it all has a great impact on that country. You can make this a positive or negative experience. For too many countries, for too many years now, the impact has been increasingly negative, and it's up to every one of us to take account of our actions.

Traditionally, travel has been seen as a good thing. Tourism generates valuable income for a country (indeed, more money is made through tourism and its related services than any other industry in the world!), and broadening the horizons and experiencing other cultures can only do good, can't it? Well, it can be good for the guest, but what of the host in this relationship? How much income goes back into the pockets of the waiters and taxi drivers in Third World countries such as Thailand and Gambia from all the mass tourism in their country? How much land is given over to developments for wealthy tourists? What control do any of us as individuals have on the mass developments going on the world over in the name of tourism?

We are destroying the very things we set out to see.

Europe is a classic case, and travelling through it is a good way to discover the truth about the tourist industry. Venice is sinking under the weight of tourists' feet; the Acropolis is being eroded by pollution and over-visiting; the once-beautiful beaches of the Spanish costas and the Med are polluted and ugly; the Alps are crumbling under the pressure of skiing.

Fortunately, the current wave of 'green thinking' is also percolating into tourism and travel. But is enough being done? Where is the mass industry going? Are you leaving your conscience at home when you travel? Have you really questioned why you are making this trip? Do you truly respect the country you are visiting? What do you hope to gain from this trip? Do you make an effort to meet the locals and to get to know the real culture of the place? Are you staying in appropriate accommodation; are you adding to the litter and pollution? The chances are, you, like most educated independent travellers, are among the few who try to be as 'green' as possible in your travel. Staying in locals' houses, or hostels or camping makes sense, and having a caring and aware attitude, you will probably be contributing as little as possible to the deterioration of our world.

My husband (an ecologist) and I have written a book which looks in detail at how to be a good tourist; it looks at the impact of all different types of holidays; it tells you which companies to travel with (and which not to). Now that being green is so trendy, it's good to separate the wheat from the chaff. Reading this may make your European wanderings all the more pertinent and give you more of an idea of the overall plan of things. The book aims to take a balanced approach between tourism and related development, and the need to conserve the very things that most of us as tourists want to enjoy. Knowing so many of you from your letters as I do, I feel sure it's the sort of read you'll enjoy. I welcome your comments.

The Good Tourist Guide is reissued in 1992 along with the first two in a new series, *The Good Tourist in the UK* and *The Good Tourist in France*.

AUSTRIA

Despite being one of the most expensive places to visit, it is still possible to find reasonably cheap accommodation in Austria. Hotels, admittedly, are probably going to be outside your budget, but there are a number of other possibilities. In general, prices are higher in the cities (Vienna, especially) and in the alpine resorts. As the student hostels and temporary IYHF hostels in the cities do not open until July, late June can be a particularly bad time for those looking for budget accommodation. Finding somewhere cheap to stay in Vienna can be tricky at any time of the year, while Salzburg becomes very crowded during its summer festival (late July–August). With this in mind, it might be advisable to take a tent, even if only for use in emergencies. One bonus is that no matter where you stay, impeccable standards of cleanliness are virtually guaranteed.

Hotels are graded from one star up to five stars. Outside the main tourist towns and resorts, a double in a one-star hotel generally costs from 200AS upwards per person (£10; $19; DM29), but in the more popular tourist areas prices for a similar room start around 350AS p.p. (£17.50; $33.50; DM51). Prices may be reduced outside the peak-season months of July to August, as hoteliers try to fill their hotels; in May, June and September by 15–25 per cent, and by up to 40 per cent for the rest of the year. Pensions, seasonal hotels and *gasthaüser* are cheaper than hotels. These are graded from one star up to four stars, with a two-star pension being the rough equivalent of a one-star hotel. Outside Vienna prices are normally under 200AS p.p. (£10; $19; DM29). Unfortunately, these tend to fill up quickly during the busy periods mentioned above.

Private rooms and **gasthaüser** can be booked through

Tourist Offices, or through private organizations which control a number of rooms. Alternatively, simply approach the owner of any house or farmhouse displaying a sign saying 'zimmer frei', or showing a stylized white bed on a green background. In the cities and resorts expect to pay from 150–200AS p.p. in doubles (£7.50–10.00; $14.50–19.00; DM22–29). Elsewhere, 100–160AS for a single (£5–8; $9.50–15.50; DM14.50–23.50), 70–120AS each in doubles (£3.50–6.00; $6.50–11.50; DM10.00–17.50) is the normal price range. Travellers staying only one night may be liable to a small surcharge. The overnight price usually includes a continental breakfast.

At some **farms** it is possible to rent apartments. Most sleep from three to five people, but occasionally larger apartments are available. Assuming you fill all the bed space, you can expect to pay from 60–120AS each per night (£3–6; $6.00–11.50; DM9.00–17.50) in the summer. During the winter months prices rise slightly, adding perhaps another 20AS p.p. per night to the bill (£1; $2; DM3). The minimum length of stay permissible in farm accommodation seems to vary between regions. In the Tyrol it is only possible to pre-book for a week at a time, but in other areas stays of one night seem quite acceptable. If there is a train station nearby, farm accommodation can make a good base for exploring the surrounding area.

There are about a hundred **IYHF** hostels spread over the country, covering all the main places of interest. Many are only open for the period between April/May and September/October, while some open only during July and August. Provided there is space, stays of longer than three days are allowed. The large city hostels can be very institutional, but in the rural areas hostels can be a bit more easy-going, although the 10 p.m. curfew will probably be strictly enforced. In city hostels there is usually a midnight curfew. In general, prices vary from 80–130AS (£4.00–6.50; $7.50–12.25; DM11.50–18.75), usually with breakfast. Higher prices are sometimes charged at the large city hostels, which seek to attract groups by providing a range of facilities that may be of little interest to the budget traveller, and as a result tend to be monopolized by visiting groups. It is advisable to have an IYHF card. While some hostels may let you stay for a 20AS surcharge (£1; $2; DM3), the hostels in Vienna are for members only, as is the main hostel in Innsbruck.

You will also find a few **independent hostels** in the main towns. These are mainly seasonal (May/June to September/October). Unfortunately, curfews are usually just as restrictive as those of their IYHF counterparts. Prices for dormitory accommodation are similar to the IYHF hostels, but some of the independent hostels also offer singles and doubles, with prices ranging from 120–200AS p.p. (£6–10; $11.50–19.00; DM17.50–29.00). Similar prices are charged for accommodation in the various **student residences** that are let out for periods between July and September. Some are run by students themselves, and a much more relaxed atmosphere usually prevails in these establishments.

It is easy to recommend **camping** in Austria, as the campsites are among the best in Europe. Charges at the 450 sites are reasonable, given that they are immaculately maintained, and have all the necessary facilities. Pitching a tent costs 30–50AS (£1.50–2.50; $3.00–4.75; DM4.50–7.50), with a similar fee per occupant. The International Camping Carnet is not obligatory, but holders qualify for reductions at most sites. All the main towns have at least one campsite, and there are plenty of sites in the countryside. Except in Vienna and Linz, the city sites are all within walking distance of the centre. One site in Vienna stays open all year round, but elsewhere even the city sites only open for a period between Easter/May and September/October.

Freelance camping is allowed, but you must first obtain the consent of the local *Bürgermeister*, or the landowner. Avoid lighting fires in or around woodland. Camping rough is a useful option for those planning to do a bit of walking along the excellent network of hiking trails. Be sure to have a good quality sleeping bag, as it gets very cold at night. For anyone planning to hike extensively in the Alps, there are about seven hundred mountain huts, with 25,000 sleeping places (beds, or mattresses on the floor to put your sleeping bag on). Even if all the places are filled, it is unlikely that you will be turned away. All the huts have at least rudimentary kitchen facilities, and many serve meals. Joining one of the clubs might save you money in the long run. The largest is the Österreichischer Alpenverein, which offers its members discounts of 30–60 per cent on the normal overnight prices of 50–160AS (£2.50–8.00; $4.75–15.50; DM7.50–23.50), plus reduced prices on various cable car trips and organized outings. Membership costs about 300AS (£15; $28.50; DM44) for under 26s, 400AS otherwise (£20; $38; DM58). If you are going hiking in the east of the country, it might be better to get in touch with the Österreichischer Touristenklub.

ADDRESSES

Austrian YHA	Österreichischer Jugendherbergsverband, Schottenring 28, 1010 Wien (tel. 0222 5335353). List from National Tourist Office, London or your capital city.
Camping	Österreichischer Camping Club, Johannesgasse 20, 1010 Wien. List from NTO in London or your capital city.
Farm accommodation	Various regional lists available from NTO, London.
Mountain huts	Österreichischer Alpenverein, Wilhelm-Greil-strasse 15, Innsbruck 6020 (tel. 05222 584107). Austrian Alpine Club, Getreidemarkt 3, 1060 Wien (tel. 0222 5638673). The UK branch is at Longcroft House, Fretherne Road, Welwyn Garden City, Herts., AL8 6PQ (tel. 0707 324835).

Österreichischer Touristenklub
(ÖTK), 1 Backerstrasse 16, Wien
(tel. 0222 523844).

Graz (tel. code 0316)

HOTELS

Cheapest doubles 200–250AS (£10.00–12.50; $19.00–23.75; DM29.00–36.25) per person, including breakfast.

Saringer, Gaisbergweg 7 (tel. 53514). One of the cheapest. Singles for the prices quoted above for doubles.

Wagenhofer, Baiernstrasse 3 (tel. 56615).

Doktorbauer, Krottendorferstrasse 91 (tel. 284235).

'Spitzwirt', Triesterstrasse 330 (tel. 291682). Another with relatively cheap singles.

'Zur Stadt Feldbach', C.-von-Hötzendorf-Strasse 58 (tel. 829468).

Dorrer, Steinbergstrasse 41 (tel. 52647). Rooms with private bath/shower, unlike most of the places listed.

Schmid, Grabenstrasse 64 (tel. 61482).

'Kehlberghof', Kehlbergstrasse 83 (tel. 284125). Rooms with shower/bath.

WIFI-Gästehaus, Grottenhofstrasse 5 (tel. 292242). Entrance on Harterstrasse. For similar prices you can get a room with a private bath/shower here.

IYHF HOSTEL

Idlhofgasse 74 (tel. 914876). Five minutes' walk from the train station. On leaving the station turn right along Bahnhofgurtel, left up Josef-Huber-Gasse, then right into Idlhofgasse.

CAMPING

Graz-Nord (tel. 627622) (1 May–30 Sept.)

Central, Graz-Strassgang (tel. 281831) (1 April–31 Oct.)

Austria 7

Innsbruck (tel. code 0512)

HOTELS

Prices quoted are per person. However, a supplement is usually added if you stay in a single room.

Cheapest prices 170–190AS (£8.50–9.50; $16.25–18.00; DM24.75–27.50)

Ferrarihof, Brennerstrasse 8 (tel. 580968). Ten minutes from the train station. Bergisel area.

Möslheim, Oberkoflerweg 8 (tel. 67134). In Mühlau, about 25 minutes' walk from the centre.

Innrain, Innrain 38 (tel. 588981). A few minutes from the centre.

Rimmi, Harterhofweg 82 (tel. 84726). Quite far from the centre. Closest station Hötting.

Cheapest prices 200–220AS (£10–11; $19–21; DM29–32)

Gartenhotel Putzker, Layrstrasse 2 (tel. 81912). About 15 minutes from the centre, across the River Inn.

Goldenes Brünnl, St Nikolaus-Gasse 1 (tel. 83519). Across the Inn, five minutes from the centre.

Laurin, Gumppstrasse 19 (tel. 41104). In the area just behind the station.

Eckenried, Eckenried 9 (tel. 67319). In Mühlau, about 25 minutes' walk from the centre.

Heis, Dorfgasse 11 (tel. 85345). In Hötting, about 15 minutes from the centre, across the Inn.

Paula, Weiherburggasse 15 (tel. 892262). About 10 minutes from the centre, across the Inn on the way to the zoo.

Stoi, Salurnerstrasse 7 (tel. 585434). A hundred metres from the train station.

Ölberg, Höhenstrasse 52 (tel. 86125). Twenty minutes from the centre, across the Inn.

Bistro, Pradlerstrasse 2 (tel. 46319). In the area just behind the station.

Cheapest prices 220–240AS (£11–12; $21.00–22.75; DM32.00–34.75)

Innbrücke, Innstrasse 1 (tel. 81934). Five minutes from the centre, across the Inn.

Menghini, Beda-Weber-Gasse 29 (tel. 41243). Twenty minutes from the station, in the area between the Olympiabrücke and Schloss Ambras.

Oberrauch, Leopoldstrasse 35 (tel. 587881). About five minutes' walk from the station. Head left, then third right on to Leopoldstrasse.

Glockenhaus, Weiherburggasse 3 (tel. 85563). Ten minutes from the centre, across the Inn on the way to the zoo.

Lisbeth, Dr Glatz-Strasse 24 (tel. 41107). In the area behind the station, left off Amraserstrasse. Fifteen minutes' walk.

Hotel-Pension Binder, Dr Glatz-Strasse 20 (tel. 42236).

Bergisel, Bergisel 2 (tel. 581912). A three-star hotel, 10 minutes' walk from the station.

Cheapest price 290AS (£14.50; $27.50; DM42)

Tautermann, Stamser Feld 5 (tel. 83715). Ten minutes from the centre, across the Inn, and left off Hottinger Gasse.

STUDENT RESIDENCES

Technikerhaus, Fischnalerstrasse 26 (tel. 82110). By the riverside, about 15 minutes from the centre, across the Inn. Prices start from 190AS (£9.50; $18; DM27.50). Open July–Sept. 90 beds.

Internationales Studentenhaus, Rechengasse 7 (tel. 59477). Ten minutes from the centre. Prices start from 200AS (£10; $19; DM29). Open July–Sept. 400 beds.

IYHF HOSTELS

Jugendherberge Innsbruck, Reichenauerstrasse 147 (tel. 46179/46180). No phone reservations taken. 15 minutes from the station. Bus R or O to Campingplatz-Jugendherberge. From 10 July to 31 Aug. a temporary hostel operates at the same address (Studentenheim). Both charge around 130AS (£6.50; $12.25; DM18.75) for the first night, 100AS (£5; $9.50; DM14.50) thereafter. Price includes breakfast and bed linen. Members only.

Torsten-Arneus-Schwedenhaus, Rennweg 17b (tel. 585814). Open 1 July–31 Aug. Curfew 10 p.m. By the riverside about 5 minutes' walk from the centre, 15 minutes from the station. Bus C to Handelsakademie from the station. 80AS (£4; $7.50; DM11.50). Breakfast and sheets extra. Members only.

Glockenhaus, Weiherburggasse 3 (tel. 85563). Ten minutes from the centre, across the Inn on the way to the zoo. Bus K to St Nikolaus, walk uphill and right where the road splits. Doubles and quads. 125–180AS (£6.25–9.00; $12–17; DM18–26). Anyone looking for dormitory accommodation is sent to the St Nikolaus hostel.

Jugendherberge St Nikolaus, Innstrasse 95 (tel. 86515). Ten minutes from the centre, across the Inn. Same management as the Glockenhaus hostel. There have been complaints about this hostel. 110AS (£5.50; $10.50; DM16) first night, slightly cheaper for subsequent nights.

Volkshaus Reichenau, Radetzkystrasse 47 (tel. 466682). Same area as the hostel in Reichenauerstrasse. Follow Reichenauerstrasse away from the centre, turn left into Radetzkystrasse.

HOSTELS

St Paulus, Reichenauerstrasse 72 (tel. 44291). Open mid June–mid Aug. Curfew 10 p.m. Fifteen minutes from the station. Bus R to Pauluskirche. Dorms 60AS (£3; $5.75; DM8.75).

MK-Jugendzentrum, Sillgasse 8a (tel. 571311). Open July–mid Sept. Curfew 11 p.m. Five minutes' walk from the station. 100AS (£5; $9.50; DM14.50) first night, then price falls slightly. Good bar.

CAMPING

Reichenau, Reichenauerstrasse (tel. 46252). Open Easter–Oct. 70AS (£3.50; $6.75; DM10) p.p. (includes tent). Small reduction for students. Bus O or R from the station. Closest site to the town centre.

Seewirt, Geyrstrasse 25 (tel. 46153). Open all year. In the Amras district behind the station. Twenty to twenty-five minutes' walk. Turn right on leaving the station, right under the tracks, follow Amraserstrasse, left on Amraser-See-Strasse, right on Geyrstrasse.

Innsbruck Kranebitten, Kranebitter Allee 214 (tel. 84180). Far from the centre off the road to Seefeld. Open May–Sept.

Kitzbühel (tel. code 05356)

HOTELS

All prices are for high season (July and August).

Cheapest doubles for under 150AS (£7.50; $14.25; DM21.75) p.p. with breakfast.

Schmidinger, Ehrensbachgasse 13 (tel. 3134).

Cheapest doubles 150–200AS (£7.50–10.00; $14.25–19.00; DM21.75–29.00) p.p. with breakfast.

With singles:
 Hörl, Josef-Pirchl-Strasse 60 (tel. 3144). Price includes half
  board, provided you stay at least three days.
 Traunstein, Traunsteinerweg 22 (tel. 2246).
 Haus am Sandhügel, Am Sandhügel 2 (tel. 2341).
 Gary, Jochbergerstrasse 26 (tel. 2331).
 Hinterholzer, Walsenbachweg 25 (tel. 49883).
 Eugenie, Pulverturmweg 3 (tel. 2820).
Without singles:
 Astlingerhof, Bichinweg 11 (tel. 2775). One of the cheap-
  est in town.
 Rosengarten, Maurachfeld 6 (tel. 2528).
 Burgstallhof, Burgstallstrasse 41 (tel. 2529).
 Entstrasser, Jochbergerstrasse 93 (tel. 4884/2328).
 Erlenhof, Burgstallstrasse 27 (tel. 2828).
 Hauser, Ehrenbachgasse 29 (tel. 2852).
 Hebenstreit, Jodlfeld 1 (tel. 3022).
 Jodlhof, Aschbachweg 17 (tel. 3004).

**Cheapest prices around 200–250AS (£10.00–12.50;
$19.00–23.75; DM29.00–36.25) p.p. for doubles with half
board.**

 Schwabl, Knappengasse 17c (tel. 4097).
 Christl, Webergasse 21 (tel. 2145).
 Karlberger, Hahnenkammstrasse 9 (tel. 4003).
 Rainer, Wegscheidgasse 11 (tel. 2454).
 Hochfilzer, Maurachfeld 17 (tel. 2217).
 Maria Hilde, Faistenbergweg 3 (tel. 3130).
 Maria, Malernweg 3 (tel. 3174).

CAMPING

 Schwarzsee (tel. 2806/4479). Open all year round.

Salzburg (tel. code 0662)

Accommodation can be very difficult to find during the summer festival (late July–Aug.). Hostels fill rapidly around this time. Unless you have a tent you will have to spend the best part of 200AS (£10; $20; DM30) on a private room (assuming there are any available) or even more on a hotel room.

HOTELS

Cheapest doubles around 175–185AS (£8.75–9.25; $16.75–17.50; DM25.25–26.75) p.p. These rooms are comparable in price to private rooms.

> Hämmerle, Innsbrucker Bundesstrasse 57a (tel. 845404 or 827647). Closed 15–29 June and Fri. and Sat. Line 77 from the train station.
>
> Noisternig, Innsbrucker Bundesstrasse 57 (tel. 845454 or 827646). Closed 15–29 June and Fri. and Sat. Line 77.
>
> Junger Fuchs, Linzer Gasse 54 (tel. (8)75496). Line 51, 55, 1, 2, 5 or 6 from the station to the Staatsbrücke bridge, or a 10–15 minute walk. Linzer Gasse runs away to the left just before the bridge.
>
> Sandwirt, Lastenstrasse 6a (tel. (8)74351). Out the rear entrance of the station on to Lastenstrasse, then right down the street. Alternatively, left out the main exit, left under the tunnel, left again (slightly longer, but still only five-minute walk).
>
> Elisabeth, Vogelweiderstrasse 52 (tel. (8)71664). Rear exit of the train station, left along Lastenstr, which leads into Gniglerstr. Right when you join Vogelweiderstr.

Cheapest doubles around 200AS (£10; $19; DM29) p.p.

> Samhof, Negrellistrasse 19 (tel. (8)74622). Line 33 from the station.

Cheapest doubles 210–230AS (£10.50–11.50; $20–22; DM30.50–36.25) p.p.

Dietmann, Ignaz-Harrer-Strasse 13 (tel. (4)31364). Line 77 from the station. Closed Sun.

Hölle, Dr.-Adolf-Altmann-Strasse 2 (tel. 820760). Line 5 to the coach park in Berchtesgadenerstrasse. Closed Fri.

Leopoldskronerhof, Firmianstrasse 10 (tel. 848144). Five-minute walk from the station to Mirabellplatz to catch line 15 to Firmianstrasse.

Lilienhof, Siezenheimerstrasse 62 (tel. (4)33630). Line 77 to Innsbrucker Bundesstr. then line 80 to Siezenheimerstr.

Merian, Merianstrasse 40 (tel. 740060). Rear exit of station, left Lastenstr., sharp right Weiserhofstr., left Breitenstr., right Bayernhamerstr., left Merianstr. 10–15 minutes.

Wastlwirt, Rochusgasse 15 (tel. 845483). Line 27 from Mirabellplatz, five minutes on foot from the station. Closed Mon.

Teufl-Überfuhr, Franz-Hinterholzer-Kai 38 (tel. 21213). Closed Thurs. Line 51 from the station.

PRIVATE ROOMS

Prices start around 180AS (£9; $17; DM26) p.p. and vary according to the standard of comfort and facilities available, and the location of the house.

Near the old town:

Anni Lindenthaler, St Peter-Steige 6/1 (tel. 8410257). Apartment for four available May–Sept. Line 1, 2, 5, 6, 49, 51.

Karl-Heinz Schäffl, Neutorstrasse 51 (tel. 8478073). 1 single only. Line 1, 2.

In the Lehen area (over the river from the train station):

Hildegard Wirrer, Ignaz-Harrer-Str. 20 (tel. 844310). Six apartments sleeping two to six people. Line 77 from the station.

Maria Raderbauer, Schiessstattstrasse 65 (tel. 39363). 1 single, 3 double, 1 triple. Line 49.

Hilde Radisch, Scheibenweg 5 (tel. 329932). 1 single, 2 double. Line 49.

Katharina Kücher, Scheibenweg 6 (tel. 329935). 1 double, 1 triple. Line 49.

Brigitte Lenglachner, Scheibenweg 8 (tel. 38044). 1 single, 2 double, 1 triple. Line 49.

In the suburbs (all rooms with private toilet, use of shower/ bath in the hall):

Paula Bankhammer, Moosstrasse 77 (tel. 830067). 1 single, 3 double, 1 triple. Line 60.

Josefa Fagerer, Moosstrasse 68d (tel. 843170). 2 single, 4 double. Line 60.

Lydia Gugg, Moosstrasse 97a (tel. 8428323). 2 single, 2 double. Line 60.

Johann & Theresia Nussbaumer, Moosstrasse 164 (tel. 830229). 1 single, 3 double, 1 triple. Line 60.

Anna Sommerauer, Moosstrasse 100 (tel. 845649). 3 single, 3 double. Line 60.

Maria Schwaiger, Gerhardt-Hauptmann-Str. 9 (tel. 8419785). 2 double. Line 5.

Maria Langwieder, Törringstrasse 41 (tel. 33129). 1 single, 3 double, 1 triple. Line 29.

Katharina Huber, Forellenweg 13 (tel. 347272). 1 single, 2 double. Line 29.

IYHF HOSTELS

100–130AS (£5.00–6.50; $9.50–12.25; DM14.50–18.75) for B&B.

Aigen, Aignerstrasse 34 (tel. 23248). Line 5 to Mozartsteg, then line 49 to Aignerstr.

Jugendgästehaus Salzburg-Nonntal, Josef-Preis-Allee 18 (tel. 842670). Midnight curfew. Very popular with school groups. No reservations. Arrive 7–9 a.m., or as soon as possible after 11 p.m. More expensive quads and doubles. Line 5 or 55 to just over the river.

Eduard-Heinrich-Haus, Eduard-Heinrich-Str. 2 (tel. 25976).

Open 1 July–26 Aug. 11 p.m. curfew. Line 51 from the station.

Glockengasse 8 (tel. 76241). Open 1 Apr.–15 Oct. Curfew midnight. Left leaving the station, left through the tunnel, along Gabelsbergerstr., right down Bayern-hamerstr., straight on into Glockengasse. Fifteen-minute walk. Line 29 to the town centre.

Haunspergstrasse 27 (tel. (8)75030). Open 1 July–26 Aug. Curfew 11 p.m. Left from the station, right Porschestr., left Elisabethstr., right Mertenstr., right at the end. Five-minute walk.

Plainstrasse 83 (tel. 50728). Open 8 July–31 Aug. Kaiser-schützenstr. leads away from the front of the station, on down Jahnstr. then right up Plainstr. About 5 minutes' walk. Line 6.

Schulstrasse 18, Salzburg-Walserfeld (tel. 851377). Open 1 July–25 Aug. Line 77 from the station.

HOSTELS

Institut St Sebastian, Linzergasse 41 (tel. 71386). Open May–Oct. No curfew. Dorms similarly priced to the IYHF hostels. Also more expensive doubles and triples. Breakfast costs extra. Line, 1, 2, 5, 6, 51 or 55 to the Staatsbrücke, or a 10–15 minute walk. The road runs away to your left just before the bridge.

Naturfreundhaus, Mönschberg 19 (tel. 841729). 100AS (£5; $9.50; DM14.50) without breakfast. Curfew 11 p.m. Open May–mid Oct. On top of the Mönschberg. Walk up the hill or take the elevator (20AS (£1; $1.90; DM2.90) return). Bus 1 from the station to Gstättengasse for the elevator.

International Youth Hotel, Paracelcusstrasse 9 (tel. 79649). No curfew. Dorms similar in price to IYHF hostels. Quads and doubles slightly more expensive. Left from the station, left through the tunnel. Straight on along Gabelsbergerstrasse, crossed by Paracelcusstrasse. Ten-minute walk.

CAMPING

Stadt-Camping, Bayerhamerstrasse 14a (tel. (871169).
60AS (£3; $5.75; DM8.75) (includes tent). Left from
the rear exit of the train station along Lastenstr., left
Merianstr., then right. Ten-minute walk.

Schloss Aigen, Weberbartlweg 20 (tel. 22079/272243).
Open May–Sept. 35AS (£1.75; $3.25; DM5) per tent
and p.p. Line 6 to Bürglsteinstrasse, then line 49 to
Glaserstrasse and five-minute walk. Closest train
station is Bahnhof Aigen.

Gnigl (Ost), Parscherstrasse 4 (tel. 644143/4). Open May–
Sept. 20AS (£1; $1.90; DM2.90) per tent, 30AS (£1.50;
$2.75; DM4.25) p.p. Line 27 or 29 from Mirabellplatz.

Kasern (Jägerwirt), Kasern 1 (tel. 50576). Open May–Sept.
15AS (£0.75; $1.50; DM2.25) per tent, 40AS (£2; $3.75;
DM5.75) p.p.

Stadtblick, Rauchenbichlerstrasse 21 (tel. 50652). Open
Apr.–Oct. 30AS (£1.50; $2.75; DM4.25) per tent,
around 45AS (£2.25; $4.25; DM6.50) p.p. Line 51
from the station to Itzling-Pflanzmann followed by
a five-minute walk uphill.

'Nord-Sam', Samstrasse 22a (tel. 660494). Open Apr.–Oct.
55AS (£2.75; $5.25; DM8) per tent, 33–47AS (£1.65–
2.35; $3.25–4.50; DM4.75–6.75) p.p. Line 33 from the
station to Samstrasse.

IYHF HOSTELS NEARBY

Traunerstrasse 22, Traunstein. In Germany on the line
from Munich to Salzburg. About 40 minutes from
Salzburg by local train. If you are leaving Munich in
the late afternoon during the summer you might want
to consider staying here, then getting into Salzburg
early next morning.

Vienna (Wien) (tel. code 01)

Finding a cheap bed can be a problem during the summer months. Late June is particularly bad. By this time increasingly large numbers of young travellers are arriving in town, but the extra bed space created by the conversion of student accommodation into temporary hostels is available only from July to September. In summer it is advisable to reserve accommodation in writing well in advance of your date of arrival. Failing this, try to phone ahead at least twenty-four hours in advance.

NB As the youth hostels and campsites tend to be well out from the centre, you will probably have to make use of the excellent public transport system. Only the Schnellbahn is free with railpasses, the U-Bahn and trams you have to pay for. A single trip costs about 20AS (£1; $1.90; DM2.90). If you transfer between two different types of transport you have to buy a new ticket. Fortunately, visitors can buy cheap 24-hr, 72-hr and 8-day passes, which pay for themselves after two, five and 11 journeys respectively. With one of these tickets you need not worry too much about finding central accommodation. However, the drawback is that the system shuts down just before midnight, which restricts you if you are staying in a hotel, private room, or campsite further away than walking distance (hostel curfews are normally around midnight in any case).

Offices dealing with accommodations:

Tourist Office. Various locations throughout the city. Main office at 1010 Kärtnerstrasse (tel. 513882), the street leading from the Opera House towards St Stephen's cathedral. Open daily 9 a.m.–7 p.m. Other branches at the two main stations: Westbahnhof daily 6.15 a.m.–11 p.m., Südbahnhof 6.30 a.m.–10 p.m. Also at the airport, at the ship station on the Danube near the Reichsbrücke, and on the A1 and A2 motorways.

ÖKISTA, Türkenstrasse 4–6 (tel. 3475260). Student travel office. Open Mon.–Fri. 9.30 a.m.–5.30 p.m. Another branch at Karlsgasse 3 (tel. 650128). Not as busy as the main office.

Mitwohnzentrale, Kohlengasse 6 (tel. 318666). In the Reisebuchladen. Summer only.

HOTELS

Cheapest doubles around 160AS (£8; $15.25; DM23.25) p.p. Prices include breakfast.

Zum Goldenen Stern, Breitenfurterstrasse 94 (tel. 8041382). Schnellbahn Hetzendorf or Atzgersdorf Mauer.

Cheapest doubles around 175AS (£8.75; $16.75; DM25.50) p.p.

Rosen-Hotel Europahaus, Linzerstrasse 429 (tel. 972538/ 40). ('Saisonhotel' – converted student accommodation used as a hotel from July–Sept). Schnellbahn Penzing. Trams run along nearby Linzerstrasse.

Cheapest doubles around 200AS (£10; $19; DM29) p.p.

Merlingen, Zeltgasse 13 (tel. 4219413). Near the West-bahnhof.

Goldenes Einhorn, Am Hundsturm 5 (tel. 554755). U4 Margaretengürtel, or walk from the Westbahnhof.

Auhof, Auhofstrasse 205 (tel. 825289). Far out in the west of the city.

Jägerwald, Karl Bekehrtystr. 66 (tel. 946266). Also out in the western suburbs.

Vogt, Hadersdorf Hauptstrasse 111A (tel. 972187). Schnell-bahn Hadersdorf-Weidlingau.

Kestler, Ketzergasse 356 (tel. 883212). Nearest schnell-bahn Liesing. Bus/tram 64A runs along Ketzergasse.

Cheapest doubles around 220AS (£11; $21; DM32) p.p.

Don Bosco, Hagenmüllergasse 33 (tel. 71184 or 55598).
(Saisonhotel) U3 Kardinal Nagl Platz.

Auersperg, Auerspergstrasse 9 (tel. 4325490 or 5127493).
(Saisonhotel) U2 Lerchenfelder Strasse.

Adlon, Hofenedergasse 4 (tel. 266788). Near Wien-Nord
train station. Schnellbahn Wien-Nord. U1 to Nestroy-
platz is closest.

Matauschek, Breitenseerstrasse 14 (tel. 923532). Nearest
schnellbahn Breitensee, change at Penzing.

Waldandacht, Wurzbachtalgasse 23 (tel. 971650). Far out
in the west of the city.

Cyrus, Laxenburgerstrasse 14 (tel. 6044288/622578). Schnell-
bahn/U1 Südtiroler Platz or U1 Keplerplatz are closer
than the Südbahnhof about one mile away.

Hospiz, Kenyongasse 15 (tel. 931304). Ten-minute walk
from the Westbahnhof. Diagonally left across Europa-
platz, right down Stollgasse which is crossed by
Kenyongasse.

Praterstern, Mayergasse 6 (tel. 240123). Near Wien-Nord
station. Schnellbahn/U1 Praterstern (Wien-Nord).

Cheapest doubles 230–250AS (£11.50–12.50; $21.75–23.75; DM33.50–36.25) p.p.

Strandhotel Alte Donau, Wagramerstrasse 51 (tel. 236730).
U1 Zentrum Kagran or Alte Donau.

Westend, Fügergasse 3 (tel. 5976729). Ten-minute walk
from the Westbahnhof. Fügergasse crosses Stum-
pergasse, right off Mariahilferstrasse as you walk
towards town.

Haus Neuwaldegg, Neuwaldeggerstrasse 23 (tel. 463396).
Tram 5 from the Westbahnhof to the start of Hernalser
Hauptstrasse, then tram 2 along that road.

Kagranerhof, Wagramerstrasse 141 (tel. 231187). U1 Zentrum Kagran.

Wilhelmshof, Kleine Stadtgutgasse 4 (tel. 245521 or 248365). Few minutes' walk from Wien-Nord train station. Schnellbahn/U1 Praterstern (Wien-Nord).

Kraml, Brauergasse 5 (tel. 5878588). Fifteen minutes on foot from the Westbahnhof. Walk down Mariahilferstrasse towards the centre, right Otto-Bauer-Strasse, first left, first right. U4 Pilgramgasse is at the opposite end of Otto-Bauer-Strasse. Also the two U3 stops on Mariahilferstrasse.

Madara, Alserstrasse 39 (tel. 427266/4082763). Tram 5 from the Westbahnhof to Alserstrasse.

Quisiana, Windmühlgasse 6 (tel. 5873341). Off Gumpendorferstrasse. U4 Kettenbrückengasse, or the second stop down the U3 from the Westbahnhof.

Esterhazy, Nelkengasse 3 (tel. 5875159). Off Mariahilferstrasse, to your right as you walk towards town. Fifteen-minute walk from the Westbahnhof. Second U3 stop on Mariahilferstrasse.

Wildenauer, Quellenstrasse 120 (tel. 6042153/622485). Fifteen-minute walk from the Südbahnhof. Schnellbahn Südtiroler Platz is closer, U1 Reumannplatz closer still.

Alsergrund, Alserstrasse 33 (tel. 4332317/5127493). Tram 5 from the Westbhf. to Alserstr.

Auges Gottes, Nussdorferstrasse 75 (tel. 342585). (Saisonhotel) Near the Franz-Josefs train station (Schnellbahn or U4).

PRIVATE ROOMS

Tourist Office (tel. 513882):
Rooms 150–250AS (£7.50–12.50; $14.25–23.75; DM21.75–36.25) p.p. Commission 40AS (£2; $3.75; DM5.75). Frequently in the suburbs. Three-day min. stay.

ÖKISTA (tel. 4752623): Finds cheaper rooms than the Tourist Office. No commission.

Mitwohnzentrale (tel. 318666): Summer only. Rooms

around 150AS (£7.50; $14.25; DM21.75). Price includes commission.

Irmgard Lauria, Kaiserstrasse 77, Apartment 8 (tel. 934152). Ten-minute walk from the Westbhf. Diagonally left across Europa Platz, down Stollgasse, left into Kaiserstrasse. Dorms cost 170AS (£8.50; $16.25; DM24.75). Doubles more expensive than at the hotels above. About 210AS (£10.50; $20; DM30.50) p.p. in quads.

Hedwig Gally, Arnsteingasse 25/10 (tel. 8129073/8304244). Not far from the Westbhf. Prices in doubles start around 190AS (£9.50; $18; DM27.50).

IYHF HOSTELS

Expect to pay 130–150AS (£6.50–7.50; $12.25–18.75; DM14.25–21.75) for B&B.

Jugendgästehaus Wien-Brigittenau, Friedrich-Engelsplatz 24 (tel. 3382940/331598/338294). Curfew 12.30 a.m. 24-hr reception. U1 U4 to Schwedenplatz, then tram N to Florisdorfer Brücke Friedrich-Engelsplatz.

Myrthengasse, Myrthengasse 7/Neustiftgasse 85 (tel. 936316/939429/9369055). Curfew 12.30 a.m. U6 to Burggasse, bus 48A to Neubaug. Walk back a short distance then right. Fifteen minutes on foot from the centre and the Westbahnhof. Left as you leave the station along Neubaugurtel, right down Burggasse, crossed by Myrthengasse.

Jugendgästehaus Hütteldorf, Schlossberggasse 8 (tel. 821501/820263). Curfew 11.45 p.m. Schnellbahn 50 from Westbahnhof to Hütteldorf (last train 10.15 p.m.) or U4 to the same stop. Across the footbridge, then a clearly signposted five-minute walk.

Schlossherberg am Wilhelminenberg, Savoyenstrasse 2 (tel. 458503). Curfew midnight. U6 to Thaliastrasse (or tram 5 from the Westbahnhof). Then bus 46 or 46B to the end of Thaliastrasse. Bus 46B from here to the hostel. Check these buses with the Tourist Office, or with the hostel.

Ruthensteiner, Robert Hamerlinggasse 24 (tel. 834693/ 8308265). 24-hr reception. Five-minute walk from the Westbhf. Follow Mariahilferstrasse along the side of the station, left on Palmgasse, then first right.

Turmherberge 'Don Bosco', Lechnerstrasse 12 (tel. 7131494). 11.30 p.m. curfew. Roman Catholic-run hostel in an old church bell tower. Very cheap. 60AS (£3; $5.75; DM8.75). Try not to worry about what happens in event of a fire. Open 1 Mar.–30 Nov. U4 Landstrasse, then bus 75 or a 10-minute walk.

HOSTELS

YMCA Inter Rail Point, Kenyongasse 25 (tel. 936304). Open mid July–mid Aug. Slightly cheaper than the IYHF hostels. Reluctant to take phone reservations. Ten minutes from the Westbhf. Diagonally left across Europa Platz, right down Stollgasse until it is crossed by Kenyongasse.

City-Hostel, Seilerstätte 30 (tel. 5128463/5127923). 170AS (£8.50; $16.25; DM24.75) p.p. in doubles. Open 1 July–30 Sept. From the opera walk down Kärtnerstrasse, right Krugerstr., left Seilerstätte.

Zöhrer, Skodagasse 26 (tel. 430730). Prices similar to those of the IYHF hostels. Off Alserstrasse, reached by tram 5 from the Westbhf.

Believe-It-Or-Not, Myrthengasse 10 (tel. 5264658/ 964658). Slightly more expensive than the IYHF hostels. Good location. See directions for the IYHF Hostel in Myrthengasse above.

UNIVERSITY DORMS

Porzellaneum der Wiener Universität, Porzellangasse 30 (tel. 347282). Singles and doubles around 140AS (£7; $13.25; DM20.25). About 10 per cent extra for one-

night stays. Tram D to Fürstengasse from the Südbhf.
or Franz-Josefs-Bhf (an easy walk from the latter). Tram
5 will get you from the Westbhf. to Franz-Josefs.

Katholisches Studentenhaus, Peter-Jordanstrasse 29 (tel.
349264). Singles and doubles similar prices to those
above. Tram stop Hardtgasse. Tram 38 from the
Westbhf. From the Südbhf. tram D to Schottentor
to join tram 38.

Zaunschertgasse 4 (tel. 382197). An affiliate of the dormitory above. Only doubles available.

Haus Pfeilheim, Pfeilgasse 6 (tel. 4384762). In the Hotel
Avis. B&B 180AS (£9; $17; DM26), singles 220AS
(£11; $21; DM32). Westbhf. tram 5 to Thaliastrasse/
Lerchenfelder Str. Down the latter, left Blindengasse,
first right. Südbhf. bus 13A to Strozzigasse.

CAMPING

**Expect to pay around 55AS (£2.75; $5.25; DM8)
per tent and per person.**

Wien-Sud, Breitenfurterstrasse 269 (tel. 869218). Open 26
June–16 Sept. 4½ miles from the centre. Schnellbahn
to Atzgersdorf Mauer, then an easy walk or tram/bus
66A.

Wien-West I, Hüttelbergstrasse 40 (tel. 941449). Open
15 June–15 Sept. 3¾ miles from the centre. U4 to
Hütteldorf, or Schnellbahn 50 from the Westbhf. (up
to 10.15 p.m.). Then bus 52B, or walk to the site.

Wien-West II, Hüttelbergstrasse 80 (tel. 942314). Open all
year. 4 bedded bungalows available, 100AS (£5; $9.50;
DM14.50) p.p. Just up the road from Wien-West I.

NB There have been reports that standards at Wien-West I
and II have fallen over recent years.

Schwimmbad Camping Rodaun, An der Au 2 (tel.
884154). Open 17 March–16 Nov. About 6½ miles
from the town centre. U4 to Hietzing (tram 58 from
the Westbhf.) then tram 60 to the end.

SLEEPING OUT

The Prater Park is the most obvious. Schnellbahn/U1 Praterstern (Wien-Nord) or Stadtlauer Brücke Lusthaus at the
other end of the park.

BELGIUM

Belgium poses no serious problems for the budget traveller looking for somewhere cheap to stay. The cheapest **hotels** cost around 600–750BF (£10.00–12.50; $19–24; DM29–36) in singles or doubles, but there are more attractive possibilities. There are over five hundred **campsites**, ranging in quality, and priced accordingly. Sites are heavily concentrated in the rural parts of Wallonia and along the Flemish coast, with the rest of the country more sparsely served. Though some of the major tourist centres do lack a campsite, a short rail journey will invariably find you one in a neighbouring town. A solo traveller can expect to pay around 150BF (£2.50; $4.75; DM7.25) per night, but at some of the coastal sites prices can rise to 250BF (£4.15; $8; DM12) per night.

There are two **IYHF-affiliated hostel** associations in Belgium. The Flemish Association operates around twenty hostels; its Walloon counterpart half that number. In the Walloon hostels the normal overnight charge is 200–250BF (£3.35–4.15; $6.25–8.00; DM9.75–12.00) with breakfast an optional extra. Prices at Flemish hostels are usually 285–325BF (£4.30–5.40; $8.25–10.25; DM12.50–15.75), which includes breakfast. The exceptions are the Flemish YHA-operated hostels in Bruges and Ostend, and the hostels of both associations in Brussels, where prices range from 360–600BF (£6–10; $11.50–19.00; DM17.50–29.00). Where space is available most hostels admit non-members on payment of a 100BF (£1.65; $3.25; DM4.75) supplement. Curfews are normally 11 p.m., but the hostels in the cities tend to stay open later. With the exception of Ghent, which has been devoid of hostels since the mid 1980s, the major Flemish cities offer a choice between IYHF hostels and a number of independent hostels. Generally free of both the restrictive curfews and the organized groups who head for the main IYHF hostels, the prices and standards of the independent hostels tend to be on a par with those of the official establishments. Wallonia is littered with '*gîtes d'étapes*' which can provide very cheap lodgings in places not served by hostels. An organization called 'Friends of Nature' also operates a network of hostels throughout the country. Ask the local Tourist Office for details of any such hostels in the locality.

You should only end up on the street by design, or unforeseen disaster. If you do, vagrancy charges can only be pressed if you are penniless. Late arrivals hoping to sleep in train station waiting rooms should note that only Ostend station stays open all night. The rest close for anything between two to five hours. If you are desperate, your best chance to avoid being thrown on to the street in the early hours is to try the little waiting rooms on the platforms (there are none in Antwerpen Centraal, but you can try Antwerpen-Berchem).

ADDRESSES

Flemish YHA	Vlaamse Jeugdherbergcentrale, Van Stralenstraat 40, 2060 Antwerpen (tel. 03–2327218).
Walloon YHA	Centrale Wallone des Auberges de la Jeunesse, rue van Oost 52, B–1030 Bruxelles (tel. 02–2153100).
Gîtes d'étapes	Gîte d'étape du CBTJ, rue Montoyer 31/8, 1040 Bruxelles (tel. 02–5125417). Étapes de la Route, rue Traversiere 9, 1030 Bruxelles (tel. 02–2186025).
Friends of Nature	Naturvrieden (Flanders) (tel. 03–361862). Amis de la Nature (Wallonia) (tel. 04–522875).
Camping	Map available from National Tourist Office in London or your capital city.

Antwerp (Antwerpen) (tel. code 03)

HOTELS

Cheapest doubles around 575BF (£9.60; $18.25; DM27.75) p.p.

Billard Palace, Koningin Astridplein 40 (tel. 2334455). On the left hand side of the square in front of Central Station.

Cheapest doubles around 600BF (£10; $19; DM29) p.p.

Oud Dijksterhuis, Kon. Astridplein 22 (tel. 2330800).
Rubenshof, Amerikalei 115–117 (tel. 2370789). Twenty minutes from Central Station, 10 minutes from the town centre.

Cheapest doubles around 700BF (£11.65; $22.25; DM33.75) p.p.

Florida, De Keyserlei 59 (tel. 2321443). To the left of Central Station. A few minutes' walk.

Cheapest doubles around 750BF (£12.50; $23.75; DM36.25) p.p.

Monico, Kon. Astridplein 34 (tel. 2250093).
Harmonie, Harmoniestraat 25 (tel. 2378326).
Caribou, Generaal Lemanstraat 45 (tel. 2370219).

IYHF HOSTEL

Op-Sinjoorke, Eric Sasselaan 2 (tel. 2380273). Midnight curfew. B&B in dorms around 360BF (£6; $11.50; DM17.50). From Central Station bus 27 to Camille Huysmanslaan. From there the hostel is signposted. Alternatively, tram 2 dir. Hoboken to the Bouw-centrum stop.

HOSTELS

New International Youth Home, Provinciestraat 256 (tel. 2300522). Curfew 11 p.m. B&B in dorms similarly priced to the IYHF hostel. Also one–four-bedded rooms. Singles roughly twice the cost of a dorm. Tram 11 from Central Station, or a 10-minute walk. Left along Pelikaanstraat, then the fifth turning under the railway lines.

Boomerang, Volkstraat 58 (tel. 2384782). Dorms similar in price to IYHF hostel. Breakfast included. Also two-, three- and four-bedded rooms. Small rooms are cheaper than at the hostel above. Near the Royal Art Gallery, 25-minute walk from Central Station, or bus 23 to the Museum stop. Tram 8 from Berchem station.

Square Sleep-Inn, Bolivarplaats 1 (tel. 2373748). One–four-bedded rooms. Singles are cheaper than at the New International Youth Home by about 180BF (£3; $5.75; DM8.75). Other rooms are much the same in price.

Scoutel-VVKSM, Stoomstraat 3–7 (tel. 2264606). Slightly more expensive than the hostels above. One-, two- and three-bedded rooms. Five minutes from Central Station.

International Seamen's House, Falconrui 21. Compared with the other hostels singles are cheap, doubles more expensive (tel. 2321609).

CAMPING

Both of the following sites charge the same, about 70BF (£1.15; $2.25; DM3.25) per person and per tent, and are open 1 Apr.–30 Sept.

'De Molen', Thonetlaan, St Annastrand (tel. 2196090). Across the River Schelde.

'Vogelzang', Vogelzanglaan (behind the Bouwcentrum) (tel. 2385717). Tram 2 dir. Hoboken from Central Station takes you to the Bouwcentrum.

Bruges (Brugge) (tel. code 050)

HOTELS

All within easy walking distance of both the station and the town centre.

Cheapest doubles around 480BF (£8; $15.25; DM23.25) p.p.

  't Roosterhuys, 't Zand 13 (tel. 333035). Closed 1–25 July.

Cheapest doubles around 540BF (£9; $17; DM26) p.p.
Singles around 630BF (£10.50; $20; DM30.50) as indicated.

  Merlijn, Schouwvegersstraat 11 (tel. 343958). Open July–
    Aug. Singles. Prices in triples and quads less than in
    doubles.
  't Keizerhof, Oostmeers 126 (tel. 338728). Prices p.p. fall
    in triples and quads.
  Die Roya, 't Zand 5 (tel. 343284). Cheaper prices in
    triples and quads. Singles slightly more expensive
    than quoted above.
  't Speelmanshuys, 't Zand 3 (tel. 339552). Prices fall for
    triples and quads. Singles as quoted above.

Cheapest doubles 575–625BF (£9.60–10.50; $18.25–20.00; DM27.75–30.50) p.p.

  Imperial, Dweerstraat 28 (tel. 339014).
  Leopold, 't Zand 26 (tel. 335129).
  Rembrandt-Rubens, Walplein 38 (tel. 336439).

IYHF HOSTELS

  Baron Ruzettelaan 143 (tel. 352679). Excellent for an IYHF
    hostel. Bar serves cheap beer 6 p.m.–midnight. Reserve
    in advance. Bus 2 to Steenbrugge, or a 20-minute walk

from the station or the centre. Dorms 420BF (£7;
$13.25; DM20.25). Also smaller rooms. Price includes
breakfast.

HOSTELS

All the hostels have adverts in the train station. Some will
pick you up if you give them a phone call. See the adverts
for details. Prices for dorms at all the hostels are roughly the
same as at the IYHF hostel. All the hostels include breakfast
in the overnight price.

Kilroy's Garden, Singel 12 (tel. 389382). The most recently
   opened. Only five minutes' walk from the train station,
   10 minutes from the centre. Also offers two-, three- and
   four-bedded rooms.

Bruno's Passage, Dweerstraat 26 (tel. 340232). Ten minutes from the station, five minutes from the town
   centre. Also quads.

The two hostels below were the original independent hostels
in Bruges. Both are located about 10 minutes from the town
centre, but a considerable distance from the station. When
Bruno's Passage opened it began to draw a disproportionate
share of the trade because of its proximity to the station.
Hence the development of free pick-up schemes.

Snuffel Travellers' Inn, Ezelstraat 49 (tel. 333133). Also
   double and quads.

Bauhaus International Youth Hotel, Langestraat 135–137
   (tel. 341093). With doubles, triples and quads.

CAMPING

Memling, Veltemweg 109 (tel. 355845). Open year round.
   The smaller of the two sites. Solo travellers pay 150BF
   (£2.50; $4.75; DM7.25). Supermarket located nearby.

St Michiel, Tillegemstraat 55 (tel. 380819). Open all year.
   Solo travellers pay 200BF (£3.35; $6.25; DM9.75). Bus
   7 from the station.

Brussels (Brussel/Bruxelles)

(tel. code 02)

HOTELS

Cheapest doubles 425–460BF (£7.10–7.70; $13.50–14.75; DM20.50–22.25) p.p.

Berckmans, Berckmannstraat 12 (tel. 5378948).
Ragheno, Fonsnylaan 11 (tel. 5382221).
Bosquet, Rue Bosquet 70 (tel. 5385230). Owner speaks
   English.
La Potinière, Fr. Jos. Navezstraat 165 (tel. 2166063).

Cheapest doubles around 490BF (£8.20; $15.50; DM23.75) p.p.

De France, Bd. Jamar 21 (tel. 5227935).
New Galaxy, Rue du Progres 7A (tel. 2194776/2194734).
De Paris, Bd. Poincaré 80 (tel. 5238153).
George V, 't Kintstraat 23 (tel. 5135093).

Cheapest doubles 525–575BF (£8.75–9.50; $16.50–18.25; DM25.50–27.75) p.p.

De l'Yser, Edinburgstraat 13 (tel. 5117459).
Sabina, Rue du Nord 78 (tel. 2182637).
Aux Arcades, Rue des Bouchers 38 (tel. 5112876).

Cheapest doubles around 625BF (£10.40; $19.75; DM30.25) p.p.

Du Congres, Rue du Congres 42 (tel. 2171890).
Plasky, Plaskylaan 212 (tel. 7337475/7337518).
Elysee, Bergstraat 4 (tel. 5119682/5123246).

OTHER SUGGESTIONS

Du Grand Colombier, Rue du Colombier (tel. 2179622/ 2195136).

Merlo, Avenue Fonsny, near the South Station (Zuid/ Midi).

Le Petit Coq, Av. Fonsny (tel. 5381421).

IYHF HOSTELS

'Breugel' (Flemish YHA), Helig Geeststraat 2 (tel. 5110436). Dorms, singles, doubles and quads. Dorms 400BF (£6.70; $12.75; DM19.25). Left along Keizerslaan from Central Station, then left just before the Kapellekerk. Five minutes' walk.

Centre Jacques Brel (Walloon YHA), Rue de la Sablonnière 30 (tel. 2180187). Curfew 1 a.m. Dorms, one–four-bedded rooms. Dorms 370BF (£6.20; $11.75; DM18). Metro Botanique or Madou, or walk from the North or Central stations (10 minutes and 15 minutes respectively).

'Jean Nihon' (Walloon YHA), Rue de l'Eléphant 4 (tel. 2153100). Similar prices to the other Walloon YHA hostel. Metro: Comtes de Flandres.

HOSTELS

Maison Internationale, 205 Chaussée de Wavre (tel. 6488529/ 6489787). Curfew 12.30 a.m. Three-day max. stay. Singles for the same price as dorms in the IYHF hostels. Camp in the hostel garden for 240BF (£4; $7.50; DM11.50). Five minutes' walk from the Quartier Leopold station.

CHAB, Rue Traversière 8 (tel. 2170158). Curfew 2 a.m. Large co-ed dorms 270BF (£4.50; $8.50; DM13), smaller dorms 320BF (£5.35; $10.25; DM15.50). Also one–four-bedded rooms. From the North Station a 10-minute walk, or bus 61 to Rue Traversière. From Central Station bus 65 or 66 to Rue Méridien. Metro: Botanique.

Sleep Well, Rue de la Blanchisserie 27 (tel. 2185050).
Curfew 1 a.m. Large dorms 230BF (£3.85; $7.25;
DM11.25) (July–Aug.), small dorms 300BF (£5; $9.50;
DM14.50). Also singles, doubles and rooms sleeping
four–six people. Metro: City 2. Short walk from the
North Station. Head for Place Rogier, straight on to
Rue Neuve, then first left.

Entraide Educative et Sociale, Place Loix 20 (tel. 5379642).

Foyer International Protestant 'David Livingstone', Av.
Coghen 119 (tel. 3433089).

Centre International Etudiants Tiers-Monde, Rue de
Parme 26 (tel. 5379215).

CAMPING

Beersel, Steenweg op Ukkel 75, Beersel (tel. 3762561).
Year round. Very cheap. Around 90BF (£1.50; $2.75;
DM4.25) for a solo traveller. From Nord-Bourse tram
55, then bus U.H.

Paul Rosmant, Waraneberg 52, Wezembeek-Oppem.
Open 1 Apr.–30 Sept. Around 180BF (£3; $5.75;
DM8.75) for a solo traveller. Better facilities than
Beersel (tel. 7821009).

Veldkant, Veldkantstraat 64, Grimbergen (tel. 2692597).
Open 1 Jan.–31 Oct. Slightly more expensive than the
site above. Bus G or H from the North Station.

Ghent (Gent) (tel. code 091)

HOTELS

**Cheapest singles 380BF (£6.30; $12; DM18.50),
doubles 275BF (£4.60; $8.75; DM13.25) p.p., triples 290BF
(£4.80; $9.25; DM14) p.p.**

Le Richelieu, Pr. Clementinalaan 134 (tel. 218644). Right
on leaving St Pieters station.

**Cheapest singles 480BF (£8; $15.25; DM23.25),
doubles 350BF (£5.80; $11; DM17) p.p., triples 280BF
(£4.70; $8.75; DM13.50) p.p. as indicated.**

La Paix, Pr. Clementinalaan 2 (tel. 222779). Doubles only.
Right as you leave the station.

De Ijzer, Vlaanderenstraat 117 (tel. 259873). Singles,
doubles and triples. Fifteen minutes from the centre.

**Cheapest doubles 400BF (£6.70; $12.75; DM19.25) p.p.,
triples 350BF (£5.80; $11; DM17) p.p. as indicated.**

Buitenbeentje, Charles de Kerchovelaan 191 (tel. 216806).
Doubles and triples with showers. From the station,
Kon. Elisabethlaan, Kortrijksesteenweg, then right.

Du Progrès, Korenmarkt 10 (tel. 251716). Great central
location.

**Cheapest singles 460–620BF (£7.70–10.30; $14.75–20.00;
DM22.25–30.50), doubles 475BF (£7.90; $15; DM23)
p.p., triples 400–450BF (£6.70–7.50; $12.75–14.25;
DM19.50–21.75) p.p. as indicated.**

La Lanterne, Pr. Clementinalaan 140 (tel. 201318). Singles,
doubles and triples. Turn right on leaving St Pieters
station.

De Fonteyne, Goudenleeuwplein 7 (tel. 254871). Singles
and doubles. Centre of the old town.

Royal, Heernislaan 88 (tel. 258495). Doubles and triples
with showers. From Gent-Dampoort station go along
Kasteellaan, then left as the road forks.

De Palm, G. Callierlaan 93 (tel. 259493). Doubles and
triples with shower.

**Cheapest doubles 525BF (£8.75; $16.75; DM25.50) p.p.,
triples slightly cheaper as shown.**

Ermitage, Sint-Dinijslaan 203 (tel. 224596). Doubles with/
without showers. Turn right on leaving the rear exit of
St Pieters. Five-minute walk.

Claridge, Koningin Maria Hendrikaplein 36 (tel. 222587).
Doubles with showers. The square in front of Sint-
Pieters station.

Flandria, Barrestraat 3 (tel. 230626/243880). Doubles
and triples. Five minutes' walk from the Town Hall
(Stadhuis).

**Cheapest doubles 625BF (£10.40; $19.75; DM30.25) p.p.,
triples 550BF (£9.20; $17.50; DM26.75) p.p. as indicated.**

Parkhotel, W. Wilsonplein 1 (tel. 251781). Doubles and
triples. Fifteen minutes from the centre.

Adoma, Sint-Denijslaan 19 (tel. 226550). Doubles and
triples. Left from the rear exit of St Pieters, five-minute
walk.

Trianon, Sint-Denijslaan 203 (tel. 213944). Doubles with
showers. Right from the rear exit of St Pieters.

Castel, K. Maria Hendrikaplein 8 (tel. 202354). Doubles
and triples. Square in front of St Pieters.

The Rambler, K. Maria Hendrikaplein 3 (tel. 218877).
Doubles (triples same price per person as doubles).

UNIVERSITY ACCOMMODATION

Stalhof 6 (just off Overpoortstraat) (tel. 220911). All rooms
are singles 420BF (£7; $13.25; DM20.25). Includes
breakfast and use of showers. Open 24 hrs, mid
July–Sept. Fifteen minutes' walk from St Pieters station. Kon. Astridlaan leads out the right of the square
to the Citadelpark. Cut diagonally through the park,
or follow the roads to your right around the park to
Overpoortstraat. Bus 9, 70, 71 or 90 from the station.

CAMPING

Blaarmeersen, Zuiderlaan 12 (tel. 215399). Open March–
mid Oct. 90BF (£1.50; $2.75; DM4.25) per tent, 75BF
(£1.25; $2.50; DM3.75) p.p. From St Pieters station a
20-minute walk, or bus 51, 52 or 53 to Europaburg,
then bus 38.

IYHF HOSTELS NEARBY

There are two hostels close to Ghent which may be of interest to Railpass holders who are stuck for a bed:

Kampstraat 59 (Recreatiedomein 'De Gavers', Geraardsbergen (tel. 054–416189). Geraardsbergen is roughly 20 miles from Ghent, served by frequent local trains. The hostel is five minutes' walk from Schendeleke station.

Passionistenlaan 1A, Kortrijk (tel. 056–201442). Ten minutes from the train station. Kortrijk is about 35 miles from Ghent, with frequent Intercity trains leaving from Gent–St Pieters and Gent–Dampoort.

BULGARIA

As with the other new Eastern democracies, many of the bad aspects of the state-controlled tourist industry remain in place, along with the accompanying bureaucracy, and engrained habits and attitudes of those who worked in tourism under the old regime. Be prepared to encounter obstacles and difficulties in finding and booking accommodation. How quickly all this may be altered is impossible to predict. Any statements on the accommodation scene in Eastern Europe may be swiftly rendered inaccurate. This is particularly true of the cost of accommodation. There is no guarantee that inflationary pressures (prevalent in many of the former command economies moving towards a market system) will not push prices up sharply.

There is quite a range of accommodation, with prices starting as low as £2–3 ($3.75–5.75; DM5.75–8.75) in a campsite, or in a private home (outside the main towns). However, this does not mean that the supply of cheap accommodation is plentiful. Previously, hotels had to be booked in advance during the summer. Now, with increasing numbers of tourists, it may prove impossible to book on arrival throughout much of the year.

In the past, Western visitors looking for **hotel** accommodation were more or less confined to hotels reserved through Balkantourist, or some other official agency. The hotels on offer to Westerners were those graded from two stars up to five stars. This was part of an orchestrated attempt to keep Western tourists out of the cheaper hotels intended for Bulgarian and East European holidaymakers. The policy was made almost totally effective by the practice of staff at the cheaper hotels. Only occasionally would they bend the rules and allow someone who had approached the hotel in person to stay the night. The overwhelming response in such instances was to send the person on their way, even when rooms were available. Telephoning a hotel to ask about the availability of rooms was guaranteed to meet with a 'no vacancies' response. Sadly, this seems to be the case even today. If you arrive after the tourist agencies are closed, it is better to approach the hotel in person.

Budget travellers' interest in hotels will probably be restricted to the one- and two-star categories. The only difference between the rooms in one-star and two-star hotels is that the former do not have a private bath. It is still exceptionally difficult for Western visitors to find a room in a one-star hotel. If you are lucky, you can expect to pay £9.50 ($18; DM27.50) for a single, £8.50 ($16; DM24.50) p.p. in doubles. You are more likely to be successful in finding a room in a two-star hotel. The best organization to contact regarding two-star hotels is Sofia Tourist who are the specialists in that part of the market. Prices are around £12.50 ($24; DM36) for singles, £9.50 ($18; DM27.50) in doubles.

Arranging lodgings in the home of a Bulgarian family is both a cheaper and a more interesting option than staying in hotels. Rooms in **private homes** can be booked through Balkantourist. In central Sofia rooms cost about £4.50–6.00 ($8.50–12.00; DM13.00–17.50) p.p. Prices fall for rooms located in the suburbs. As the public transport system is cheap and reasonably efficient, it is practicable to stay in the suburbs if you cannot find a room in the city centre. In the countryside, rooms cost as little as £2 ($4; DM6), but they can be difficult to find. You may also find that you are required to stay a minimum of three to five days in some private rooms. This is especially true along the Black Sea coast where you may be approached at train stations by locals offering their rooms. The standard of the rooms may be perfectly acceptable, but the problem is that you will miss an official stamp for that night on the 'carte statistique', which acts as a record of where you stay each night. You risk a fine of £150 ($285; DM435) if too many nights are unaccounted for (the border guards will decide arbitrarily on this matter).

Depending on how long you stay in the country, you might get away with saying that you spent two or three nights on the train, but any more could be pushing your luck.

The student travel organization ORBITA controls a network of hotels and **youth hostels**, as well as letting dormitory accommodation or private rooms in student flats and hostels. ORBITA is used to, and prefers, dealing with groups. Only during the summer holidays, mid July until mid September, do independent travellers have a realistic chance of finding a place in student accommodation. Charges are around £1.50 ($3; DM4.50) for a hostel bed. ORBITA youth hostels admit Westerners by prior reservation only. Whereas groups of five and upwards might be allowed to book hostels on arrival in Sofia, others will have to book months in advance. It is all but pointless turning up at hostels without a reservation. They will probably be full, but even if they have space, they are likely to turn you away regardless.

The Bulgarian Tourist Union, which is affiliated to the IYHF, also operates a chain of hostels; 56 of which are listed in the IYHF handbook. Once again these should be reserved well in advance. Facilities are little more than basic, and the hostels are often located far from the centre of town. In theory, some of these hostels are closed to Western visitors, but staff have tended to be much more accommodating than their ORBITA equivalents, so it might be worthwhile making a personal enquiry at any hostel you discover the location of.

Camping is both a cheap way to see the country, and an ideal way to meet East European travellers. Moreover. taking a tent is an insurance against having to pay out for hotels, if you cannot find a hostel bed or a private room. There are about 120 official campsites open to Western travellers, about one-third of which are located on the Black Sea coast. These sites are highly popular, and frequently crowded, so it is better to book them ahead. The same applies to sites around the main towns. All the main towns have a campsite nearby, usually on the outskirts.

Charges are around £1.50 ($3; DM4.50) per tent, with a similar fee per occupant. At most sites, comfortable chalet accommodation is available to let. A chalet sleeping two costs around £4.50 ($8; DM13) p.p. per night. The National Tourist Office in London/your capital city will provide a map of campsites, which details the facilities available and the opening periods. The camping season runs from May to mid October inclusive. Freelance camping and sleeping rough are both illegal, with the certainty of a fine for those apprehended. Even if you are not caught, either option involves missing a stamp on your *carte statistique*.

Hikers and climbers should contact the Bulgarian Tourist Union for permission to use the chain of mountain chalets (*hizha*) they operate, and to make the necessary reservations. The standard of accommodation in *hizha* varies tremendously, from those with only the bare essentials, to those which seem like hotels.

ADDRESSES

Hotels	Balkantourist, Dondukov ul. 37, Sofia (tel. 884430).
	Sofia Tourist, 18A Veslets St., Sofia (tel. 802238).
Private rooms	See Balkantourist above.
Hostels	ORBITA, Bul. Stambolijski 45a, Sofia (tel. 884801).
	ORBITA (Student Travel Office), Vitosha Boul. 4, Sofia (tel. 831659).
	Bulgarian Tourist Union, Zentralrat, Boul. Tolbuchin 18, Sofia (tel. 879405).
Mountain huts	Bulgarian Tourist Union. Address above.

Sofia (tel. code 02)

Offices dealing with accommodation:
  Balkantourist, Dondukov ul. 37 (tel. 884430). From the
    train station tram 1, 7 or 15 to Lenin Ploshtad. Go
    down the road to the left of the Sheraton Hotel, then
    left when the road splits on to Dondukov.

HOTELS

Book rooms through the Balkantourist Office on Dondukov.
One-star hotels charge around £14.75 ($28; DM42.75) for
singles, £8.25 ($15.50; DM23.75) p.p. for doubles. If Balkan-
tourist has closed by the time you arrive, go to the hotels
in person as they invariably say they are full if you phone
ahead, whether they are or not.
One-star hotels:
  Gorna Banya, Oural St. 1 (tel. 570086).
  Zdravec, Georgi Dimitrov (tel. 833949). Tram 1, 7 or 15
    from the train station or Lenin Ploshtad.
  Sredna Gora, Georgi Dimitrov 60 (tel. 835311).
  Edelvais, Georgi Dimitrov (tel. 835431).
  Hemus, Blvd. G. Traĭkov 31 (tel. 661415).
  Serdica, Blvd. V. Zaimov (tel. 443411).
  Preslav, ul. Traiditsa 3 (tel. 876586).
  Sevastopol, ul. Rakovski 116 (tel. 875941).
  Pliska, Blvd. Lenin 87 (tel. 723721).
  Bulgaria, Blvd. Ruski 4 (tel. 871977).
  Slavia, ul. Sofijski Geroi 2 (tel. 525551). Tram 13 from
    the train station. About three stops along General
    Totleben.

PRIVATE ROOMS

Available through Balkantourist on Dondukov. About £2.65
($5; DM7.75) p.p. Slightly cheaper rooms are available
through ORBITA at Bul. Stambolijski 45A (tel. 801812).

IYHF HOSTEL

Touristicheska spalnya 'Iubileyna', Komplex 'Krasma polyana'. Book through Tourist Agency 'PIRIN', 30 Al. Stambolijski Blvd. (tel. 881079).

HOSTELS

ORBITA Student Hostel, Anton Ivanov 76 (tel. 652952). ISIC/IUS required. Tram 2 or 9 to the junction of Anton Ivanov and Georgi Traĭkov.

CAMPING

The two most convenient sites are both about 6½ miles out from the centre. Both offer bungalows for hire:

Cherniya Kos. (tel. 571129). Off the road to Pernik. Tram 5 from the train station to the terminus, then bus 58 or 59. Two-person bungalows £4.25 ($8; DM12.25) p.p. Open 1 May–31 Oct.

Vrana (tel. 781213). Off the E80 to Plovdiv. Bus 313, 213 or 305 from the station, then change to bus 5 or 6. Open 1 May–31 Oct.

There are another two sites about ten miles out from the city centre:

Bankya. Open 1 May–15 Oct. Off the E80 on the way to Yugoslavia.

Lebed. Open 1 May–31 Oct. Chalets only. About £4.25 ($8; DM12.25) p.p. in two-bedded chalets. Off the road to Samokov.

CZECHOSLOVAKIA

NB As the currency finds its true value the prices quoted here may fluctuate substantially. If you find this is the case, work on the theory that at least the relative costs of the different accommodation options will remain reasonably constant.

Even before the 'Velvet Revolution' of 1989, finding cheap accommodation in Czechoslovakia was never the easiest of tasks. Due to their popularity with East European groups, hostels and the few hotels within the budget travel price range usually had to be booked months in advance. Camping also had its problems. It was not uncommon to see people turned away from the campsites in Prague and Bratislava during July and August. At the moment, the situation is far worse. In 1990 the state railway (CSD) was included in the Inter Rail scheme for the first time. This has had the expected result of drawing unprecedented numbers of young travellers to Czechoslovakia (especially to Prague, and, to a lesser extent, Bratislava). At the same time there has been a considerable growth in both the number of tour groups, and in the number of independent travellers of all ages. Many of this latter group are not necessarily budget travellers, but, with the intermediate-range hotels taken up by tour groups, they are being forced to look for lower-grade accommodation. Although there has been a sizeable growth in the numbers of private rooms available, and the establishment of a number of independent hostels, this has not been enough to stop demand far outstripping supply. (Prague is the worst affected, having seen a staggering 1000 per cent increase in the number of tourists visiting the city in 1990.) This is likely to remain the case for several years to come, until sufficient money has been invested to develop an adequate tourist infrastructure.

To make matters worse, advance booking of accommodation is difficult, and, in some cases, impossible. The CKM hostels listed in the IYHF handbook can be reserved in advance, though you will have to book three to six months before your date of arrival. There is no way of reserving campsites in advance, other than phoning ahead on arrival and hoping the staff are cooperative. Nor is there any established procedure for booking independent hostels, private rooms or cheap hotels. Čedok (London) will not book the cheaper hotels you might be interested in. You can try writing to the hotel directly, or to an agency that deals in that area of the market, such as Pragotur. Neither is guaranteed to succeed. The same is true of writing to agencies to reserve private rooms in advance, or contacting an independent hostel to reserve a bed. Nonetheless, for the little effort and cost involved, it is worth trying to arrange accommodation in Prague, Brno and Bratislava prior to your arrival. If you have no reservations, try to avoid arriving in these cities at the weekend, as crowds of Austrians and Germans on weekend breaks only exacerbate the problem of finding suitable accommodation.

Hotels are divided into five categories; A de luxe/five-star, A/four-star, B/three-star, B/two-star, and C/one-star. In Prague late cancellations and forfeited reservations might offer your best chance of success. These are reallocated from 5 p.m. by Čedok and Pragotur. Čedok says that hotels rated in the C/one-star category 'truly have no frills', but from the budget traveller's point of view they are a real bargain. In most towns the lower three grades are now within the reach of the budget traveller. Even in some popular tourist destinations there are doubles available for as little as £2.50 ($4.75; DM7.25) per person. As might be expected, prices are higher in Prague, where it is difficult to find a double room for under £8.00 ($15.25; DM23.25) per person. More likely, you will have to pay £10–15 ($19.00–28.50; DM 29.00–43.50) per person if you want a double room in the capital. *Hotel* *bills have to be settled in hard currency.* If possible, try to get written confirmation of the cost of the room from reception when you book, as it is not unknown for prices to rise mysteriously during the night.

Throughout Czechoslovakia it is possible to stay in the **homes** of private citizens. Rooms booked through an agency are inexpensive, and the standard of accommodation is quite satisfactory. Until recently prices were fixed at £5.50 ($10.50; DM16) p.p. for doubles in Prague, and elsewhere £3.50 ($6.75; DM10) for doubles, but in the wake of recent legislation on private businesses prices are expected to rise. In the cities, agencies may enforce a three-day minimum stay, although this practice may cease if it is found to be losing the old state agencies Čedok or Pragotur any business to the new agencies which have emerged in response to the obvious potential in this field. If you only want to stay for a couple of days, it might still be worth paying for the extra night, simply for the convenience of getting a room there and then. With the obvious potential for new agencies in this field there are now alternatives to dealing with Čedok or Pragotur. Nevertheless, in the country as a whole Čedok remain your best bet because of the number of rooms they control, although (as in Brno) they may insist on a three-day minimum stay. Pragotur are still the best to deal with in the capital, even though they charge a £2.20 ($4.25; DM6.25) commission, and enforce a three-day minimum stay. On the plus side, Pragotur control by far the largest stock of rooms, and also guarantee that their rooms are either centrally located, or conveniently served by public transport. Some rooms in the cities can be far from the centre, but, as public transport systems in the cities are cheap and efficient, distance should not unduly deter you, providing the room on offer is near a public transport stop. Whichever agency you are dealing with, try to hold them to the terms offered by Pragotur. Unfortunately, beggars cannot be choosers. Agencies are well aware that if you refuse a particular room, there are plenty of people who will take it. The same applies to offers made by individuals: the asking price will not be too dissimilar to that you will pay at one of the local agencies (although breakfast is usually included in private offers). Because of the sheer numbers looking for accommodation, there is little room for bargaining. You might be lucky and get a perfectly acceptable room with a reasonable location. However, the standard of such rooms varies dramatically. In Prague and Bratislava, many are situated in the centre of the vast housing schemes on the outskirts of town, and can be difficult to reach by public transport. If you are stuck, you can always stay one night, and then get into town early next morning to look for something better. If you do take up a private offer take care of your valuables.

There are roughly fifty **hostels** listed in the IYHF hand-book. These are operated by CKM (the student travel organization). Many are converted student dormitories, which open only during July and August. The permanent hostels are a great bargain. Standards are excellent as these are in fact CKM hotels which offer discounts of 70 to 80 per cent to IYHF members and students. Prices range from £2–6 ($3.75–11.50; DM5.75–17.50) – usually towards the lower end of the scale. However, a quick comparison of the hostel list with a guidebook will tell you that apart from the three main cities, the spa towns (Mariánské Lázné and Karlovy Vary), and Banská Bystrica, the places of major interest lack a hostel.

There has been a growth of **independent hostels** in Prague and Bratislava. Prices are similar to the CKM hostels. Some of the hostels that have emerged are the result of highly commendable initiatives, such as the hostel run in Bratislava by Uniatour, a travel organization founded by the Students' Union of Slovakia. A similar development in places such as České Budějovice, Tabor, Olomouc, Brno and Kosice would be welcome to increase the options open to budget travellers in these towns. The established tourist agencies (Čedok, CKM, Pragotur) may not be a fruitful source of information on independent hostels, either because they are genuinely unaware of new hostels, or because they are looking to sell you accommodation they control. Ask other travellers about hostelling possibilities, and keep your eyes open for hostels advertised at train stations. Unfortunately there is no guarantee that unscrupulous persons will not take the chance to cram large numbers of backpackers into tiny rooms, a depressing scenario for which a precedent has already been set in neighbouring Hungary.

Camping is a great way to see the country very cheaply. Apart from the sites in Prague and Bratislava (and perhaps at weekends, České Budějovice, Tabor and the spa towns), you should have little difficulty getting a space. 'Camping Czechoslovakia' (from Čedok) lists 245 sites, graded A, AB and B. Prices for a solo traveller are about £1.00–2.20 ($1.90–4.25; DM3.00–6.50) per night, but, as Čedok warns, 'don't expect luxury'. Sites are usually clean, but at the B-class sites outside showers are the norm. At the vast majority of these sites it is possible to rent comfortable two- or four-bedded chalets. You may have to pay for all the beds in the chalet, even if they are not all used. Expect to pay between £2–4 ($3.75–7.50; DM5.75–11.50) p.p. in a fully occupied chalet. Most, but not all, of the main places of interest have a convenient campsite listed in 'Camping Czechoslovakia'. However, there are a host of other sites. Previously these were aimed at East European holidaymakers, and were not advertised to Westerners. Indeed, the official agencies were loath even to admit their existence. Anyone who stumbled across one of these sites was allowed to stay, at a supplement to the advertised price (one example of the dual pricing structure previously common throughout Eastern Europe). Even then, a couple paid only what a solo traveller would pay at one of the 245 'official' sites. Prices at these sites must now be incredibly low, but facilities are spartan. The washing facilities may be the river nearby, and you may prefer using the woods nearby to using the campsite toilet facilities. Locals are the best people to ask about the existence of such campsites in the neighbourhood. Alternatively, the book *Ubytovani*

CSR lists all the hotels, hostels and campsites in the Czech Republic (in Czech, but easy to follow).

If you are stuck for a bed, but have an Inter Rail, Eurail or BIJ ticket, you can always catch a night train. One of the best ways to arrive in Brno reasonably early in the morning is to take an overnight train from Prague to Bratislava, or vice versa, and then catch the early train to Brno. Travelling overnight from Bratislava to Prague can allow you to catch early morning connections to Tabor, Olomouc, Pilsen, Cheb and the spa towns. Even leaving Prague to head out into Slovakia can show you interesting towns such as Kosice and Banská Bystrica.

ADDRESSES

Youth hostels   CKM Club of Young Travellers, Žitná 12, 121 05 Praha 2.
Secretariat: CKM, Malostranské nábřeží 1, 11 00 Praha 1–Malá Strana (tel. 02–538858).
Travel Section: CKM, Žitná 12, 121 05 Praha 2 (tel. 02–299941).

Overnight-train suggestions (check times locally, or with the Thomas Cook timetable):

Praha Hlav. Nad	23.17	Bratislava	05.35
Praha Hlav. Nad.	00.15	Bratislava	05.16 (continues to Budapest)
Praha Holešovice	22.38	Bratislava	04.55

Early morning connection to Brno:

Bratislava	05.50	Brno	07.20
Bratislava	22.50	Praha Holešovice	05.08
Bratislava	23.50	Praha Hlav. Nad.	05.45
Bratislava	00.35	Praha Hlav. Nad.	06.03

Early morning connections from Prague:

Praha Holešovice	05.57	Brno	09.19		
Praha Hlav. Nad.	06.30	Karlovy Vary	09.53		
Praha Hlav. Nad.	07.49	Tabor	10.07	ČeskéBudějovice	11.01
Praha Hlav. Nad.	07.50	Plzen	09.45	Domazlice	10.34
Praha Hlav. Nad.	08.47	Plzen	09.28	Mariánské Lázně	11.58
		Plzen	10.37	Cheb	12.32

Praha Holešovice	20.27	Kosice	05.46		
Praha Hlav. Nad.	00.00	Kosice	09.53		
Kosice	20.10	Praha Holešovice	05.32		
Kosice	20.38	Praha Hlav. Nad.	06.31		
Kosice	00.20	Olomouc	06.52	Praha Hlav. Nad.	10.05
Kosice	16.55	Karlovy Vary	07.50	Cheb	09.02
Bratislava	23.00	Kosice	05.25		
Bratislava	00.20	Kosice	07.07		
Kosice	23.10	Bratislava	05.44		
Kosice	23.55	Bratislava	06.27		

Bratislava (tel. code 07)

Offices dealing with accommodation:

CKM, Hviezdoslavovo nám. 16 (tel. 331607). In the old town, not far from the Danube. Opening hours: Mon.–Fri. 9 a.m.–5 p.m.

Uniatour, Leškova 5 (tel. 43967). Controlled by the Students' Union of Slovakia. First left off Stefánikova, the main road leading from the train station.

Čedok, Štúrová 13 (tel. 52081/52002). The only Čedok office dealing with enquiries from foreigners. Opening hours: mid May–mid Sept. Mon.–Fri. 9 a.m.–6 p.m., Sat. 9 a.m.–midday, at other times closes at 5 p.m. Mon.–Fri.

Slovakotourst, Klariska 6. On the northwestern fringe of the old town. Opening hours: Mon.–Fri. 9 a.m.– noon and 1–4 p.m.

BIPS, Leningradská 1 (tel. 334415). Do not book accommodation but give impartial advice on the hostel situation. Opening hours: Mon.–Fri. 8 a.m.–6 p.m., Sat. 8 a.m.–1 p.m. in summer. Rest of the year 8 a.m.–4.30 p.m. Mon.–Fri. only.

NB Payment in hard currency may be demanded in all forms of accommodation.

HOTELS

Agencies:
Čedok.

Palace, Poštová 1 (tel. 333656). Singles £7.50 ($14; DM21.25), doubles £6 ($11.50; DM17.50) p.p. Tram 14 from the train station to the fifth stop.

Krym (B/two-star), Satarikovo nám. 7 (tel. 554713). Singles £5.25 ($10; DM15.25), doubles £4 ($7.50; DM11.50) p.p. Off Štúrová, not far from the Danube.

Ustav vzdelávania v. stavenictve, Bárodǒsǒva 33. Tram 44 from the station to Bárodǒsǒva, the third stop.

Walk back a short distance, then uphill. Look for the three-storey building with the name of the hotel on top.

PRIVATE ROOMS

Agencies:
  Cědok.
  Slovakotourist.

HOSTELS

Expect to pay £2.50; $4.75; DM7.25.

Agencies:
  CKM. For IYHF hostels. Even if you have reservations you should go to the CKM office before going to the hostel if you arrive in town Mon.–Fri. between 9 a.m. and 5 p.m.
  Uniatour. Details of the hostels they operate during July and Aug.

IYHF HOSTELS

  Juniorhotel Sputnik, Drienová 14 (tel. 238000). Bus 24.
  Studentský domov J Hronca, Berrolákova 3 (tel. 42612). Open 1 July–31 Aug. Tram 3.

CAMPING

Two sites at Zlaté piesky, both with bungalows. Tram 2 from town centre, tram 4 from train station or tram 12 to the Zupka crossroads, then bus 32 to the third stop:
  Senecká cesta 10 (tel. 66028/214000). Grade AB site. Open year round.
  Senecká cesta 12 (tel. 65170). Grade A site, open 15 May–15 Sept.

Brno (tel. code 05)

Offices dealing with accommodation:

CKM, Ceská 11 (tel. 23641). Open Mon.–Fri. 9 a.m.–5 p.m. Fifteen minutes' walk from the train station. Cross the road and head down Masarykova (formerly Tr. Vitezstvi) into Nám Svobody. Keep going straight on along the left-hand side of the square into Ceská.

Čedok. The office serving foreign visitors is a 10-minute walk from the station. Head right until you come to the square Nám Cs. Armády. Go along the left-hand side of the square and down the road leading from the square. Tram 2, 11, 12, 15, 18 or 19.

HOTELS

Agencies: Čedok.

Singles around £5.25 ($10; DM15.25), doubles £3.50–4.50 ($6.75–8.50; DM10–13) p.p.

Společenský dům, Horova 30 (tel. 744185). From the station tram 4, 5 or 13 to Husova, then tram 10.

Europa (B/two-star), Janska 1/Masarykova (tel. 26611). Straight down the main road opposite the station. On the corner of the fourth road on the right.

Morava, Novabranska 3 (tel. 27526). Near the Čedok office. Tram 2, 11 or 18 from the station to Malinovskeho nám. Ten minutes' walk. Down Masarykova opposite the station, third right Orli, past the Menin Gate, then left.

Družba, Kounicova 90 (tel. 43545). Open July–Sept. Far out from the centre. Tram 13, 16 or 22.

Slovan, Lidická 23 (tel. 745505). More expensive than the prices quoted above.

PRIVATE ROOMS

Agencies: Čedok. Four-day min. stay.

IYHF HOSTELS

Operated by CKM in converted student dorms. All four hostels are open from 1 July–31 Aug. If you arrive in Brno Mon.–Fri. 9 a.m.–5 p.m. you should go to the CKM office before going to the hostels, even if you have a reservation.

Expect to pay around £2.50 ($4.75; DM7.25).

Kolej J E Purkyně, Husova 8.
Brno Studentská Kolej SCSP Brno, Královo Pole, Pur-
kyňova 93.
Kolej VUT, Leninova 8.
Kolej VŠZ, J.A. Komenského, Kohoutova 55.

CAMPING

Both sites are about 10 miles out of town.
Bobrava, Modrice u Brna (tel. 320110). Grade B site. Open
15 Apr.–15 Oct. Tram 2, 14 or 17 to the Modrice
terminus, then a 10-minute walk, or a local train to
Popovice, 500m from the site.
Obora, Brno-prehrada (tel. 56575). Grade B site. Open
1 Apr.–31 Oct. More difficult to reach by public
transport. A bus runs about every hour.

Karlovy Vary (tel. code 017)

Offices dealing with accommodation:
Čedok, in the Hotel Atlantic at Tržiště 23 (tel. 24378/26110/
26705).

HOTELS

Čedok recommend reserving hotels three-four months in advance. If you enquire on arrival you will probably be told that all the hotels are full. Be persistent, and try to get them to give you the names of hotels that might have space.

B/two-star hotels (all close to the main bus station (auto-busová nádraží):

Turist, Dimitrovova 18 (tel. 26837). Doubles around £2 ($3.75; DM5.75) p.p.

Národní dům, Masarykova 24 (tel. 23386). Singles £4.00 ($7.50; DM11.50), doubles £3 ($5.75; DM8.75) p.p.

Jizena, Dimitrovova 7 (tel. 25020). Singles £4.50 ($8.50; DM13), doubles £3.30 ($6.25; DM9.50) p.p.

Adria, Koněvova 1 (tel. 23765). Singles £5 ($9.50; DM14.50), doubles £3.50 ($6.75; DM10.25) p.p.

PRIVATE ROOMS

Čedok. Four-day min. stay.

IYHF HOSTEL

CKM Junior Hotel Alice, ul Pětiletky 3 (tel. 24848). Expect to pay £2.50 ($4.75; DM7.25). Set in the woods about three miles out of town. A beautiful walk. From the station bus 11 to the market place, then bus 7.

CAMPING

Březová, Slovenská č. 9 (tel. 25101). Grade A site. Open 1 May–30 Sept. Bungalows available. Close to the youth hostel.

Pilsen (Plzeň) (tel. code 019)

Offices dealing with accommodation:
Čedok. On the corner of Sedláckova and Prešková. The
latter runs out of one corner of Nám Republiky, the
centre of town. Opening hours: Mon.–Fri. 9 a.m.–noon
& 1–6 p.m., Sat. 9 a.m.–noon.
CKM, Dominikanská.

HOTELS

Enquire at the Čedok office above.
Plzeň, Žižkova 66 (tel. 272656). Doubles £3.50 ($6.75;
DM10.25) p.p. Tram 1 or 4 from the town centre.

CAMPING

Bílá Hora (tel. 35611/62850). Grade A. Open 20 Apr.–15
Sept. Also lets bungalows. Bus 20.
Ostende (tel. 520194). In Plzeň-Bolevec. Grade A, open
1 May–15 Sept. Bungalows available.

Prague (Praha) (tel. code 02)

Offices dealing with accommodation:
Čedok, Panska 5 (tel. 225657/227004). The only Čedok
office that books rooms. In a street off Na přikopě.
Opening hours: Apr.–Nov. Mon.–Fri. 9 a.m.–8 p.m.,
Sat. 8.30 a.m.–6 p.m., Sun. 8.30 a.m.–4.30 p.m.;
Dec.–Mar. Mon.–Fri. 9 a.m.–8 p.m., Sat.–Sun. 8.30 a.m.–
2 p.m.
Pragotur, U Obecního domu 2 (tel. 2317281). Opposite
the Hotel Paříž in a street off Nám Republiky. Metro:
Nám Republiky. Opening hours: Mon.–Fri. 8 a.m.–
9.30 p.m., Sat. 8 a.m.–8 p.m., Sun. 8 a.m.–3.15 p.m.

Coop Tour. Inside Hlavni nádraží station. As you come
from the platforms they are on the right, floor below.
Open daily 7 a.m.–9 p.m., but may close when they
feel like it.
AVE. Same floor as Coop Tour above.
Top Tour, Rybna 3 (tel. 2296526). Near Nám Republiky.
Open Mon.–Fri. 9 a.m.–8 p.m., weekends 11 a.m.– 7
p.m.

HOTELS

Agencies:
Pragotur. Specialize in C-class/one-star hotels.
Čedok. Deal in B/two-star hotels, but may claim to book
rooms in the expensive Interhotels only.
Both agencies reallocate late cancellations and forfeited
reservations from 5 p.m. onwards.

B/two-star hotels (central locations unless shown
otherwise):

Doubles start from £9–15 ($17–29; DM26–43) p.p.

Adria, Václavské námesti 26 (tel. 2360472).
Hvězda, Na Rovni 34 (tel. 368037/368965). (Prague 6
district).
Hybernia, Hybernská 24 (tel. 220431).
Koruna, Opatovická 15 (tel. 293933).
Erko, Kbely 723 (tel. 892105). (Prague 9).
Merkur, Těšnov 9 (tel. 231695).
Meteor, Hybernská 6 (tel. 229241/224202).
Moráň, Na Moráni 15 (tel. 294251). (Central.)
Opera, Těšnov 13 (tel. 231560).
Axa, Na poříčí 40 (tel. 2327234). In the new town, a short
walk from náměskí Republiky.
Botel Albatross, nábřeží L. Svobody (tel. 2316996). A
floating hotel moored on the Vltava near the new
town.

Kriváň, Nám I.P.Pavlova 5 (tel. 293341–44) (10 minutes from the centre.)

Praga, Plzeňská 29 (tel. 548741). Tram 4 or 9 from Anděl metro station.

Savoy, Keplerova 6 (tel. 537450).

Solidarita, Soudružská 2081 (tel. 777145). (Prague 10.)

Transit, ul. 25 února 197 (tel. 367108). (Prague 6.)

U Blaženky, U Blaženky 1 (tel. 538266). (Prague 5.)

Union, Jaromírova 1 (tel. 437858/437859).

Modrá Hvězda, Jandova 3 (tel. 830291). (Prague 9.)

C/one-star hotels:

Doubles start around £5.50–7.50 ($10.50–14.25; DM16–22) p.p.

Stará Zbrojnice, Všehrdova 16 (tel. 532815). (The only centrally located C/one-star hotel.)

Balkán, Svornosti 28 (tel. 540777). Smíchov. Metro: Anděl.

Libeň, tř. Rudé armády 2 (tel. 828227). (Prague 8.)

Moravan, U Uránie 22 (tel. 802905). Holešovice. Metro: Nádraží Holešovice.

Národní dům, Bořivojova 53 (tel. 275365). Žižkov. Tram 9, 10, 13 or 26. Also has dorms, although they are often filled with groups, and prices p.p. are slightly higher than in doubles.

Ostaš, Orebitská 8 (tel. 272860). Žižkov. A short walk from Praha-Florence bus station. Metro: Sokolovská/ Florenc.

Tichý, Seifertova 65 (tel. 273079). Žižkov. Tram 9, 10, 13 or 26.

Vltava, Žitavského 115, Zbraslav (tel. 591549). (Prague 5.)

If you want to try something a bit different there are three B/three-star hotels moored on the Vltava:

Admirál, Hořejši nábř. (tel. 548685/547445–49). (Prague 5.)

Albatros, nábř. L. Svobody (tel. 231363). (Central.)

Racek, Dvorecká louka (tel. 426051). (Prague 4.)

PRIVATE ROOMS

Agencies:
  Pragotur – three-day min. stay.
  Top Tour.

IYHF HOSTELS

  CKM Juniorhotel Žítna, Žítna 12 (tel. 292984). Expect to pay around £5 ($9.50; DM14.50) p.p. for doubles.

  Kolej Strahov, Spartakiádni 5 (tel. 3322037, or CKM at 292984). Open 1 July–31 Aug. Doubles £3.20 ($6; DM9.25) p.p. Metro to Dejvicka, then bus 217 to the sixth stop.

  Kolej VŠCHT, Praha 4–Jižni město. For details contact CKM Juniorhotel Žítna.

  Admira, Ubytovna TJ, U školsé zahrady. Year round. Book six weeks in advance through CKM Head Office (tel. 299941/538858). Tram 2 to Strelnicná, 200m from the hostel. Bus 200 stops 500m away. Metro: Fučikova.

  Internát Konstructiva, Vrbova 1233 (tel. 462641). Near Smíchov train station. Metro: B/ Smíchovské nádraží. Bus 198, 196, 197. Tram 17, 21, 3.

  Hotel Fasádostav, Jemnická 4 (tel. 431244). Bus 118, 124, 178. Metro: C/ Budějovická.

HOSTELS

Agencies:
  Coop Tour. Payment in hard currency or Koruny. No travellers' cheques.

  Top Tour.

  CKM, Žítna 12 (tel. 299941). Metro: Nám I.P.Pavlova.

  AVE. Accepts travellers' cheques, but more expensive than other agencies.

  TJ Dukla Karlin, Malého (tel. 222009). Ten bunk beds. Cots in the gym for everyone else. Dirt cheap. £0.75 ($1.50; DM2.25). Behind the Praha–Florenc bus station (autobusová nádraží). Metro: Sokolovská/Florenc.

Tourist Hotel TJ Dolní Měcholupy, Na Paloučku 223.
Open all year. Singles £1.95 ($3.70; DM5.65), doubles
£3.50 ($6.65; DM10.15) p.p. Bus 111, 228 or 229 to
Dolnomecholupska from Zelivskeho metro station.

CAMPING

Pragotur distribute the brochure 'Praha Camping' listing all
the sites. It is worth picking up a copy in case any of the
telephone numbers have changed from those given below.
Pragotur may simply say they have none left. If so, ask them
to confirm the information given here. They may also tell
you all the sites are full. Don't believe them. Call the sites
yourself (all the better if you can speak German; if not,
English should let you gather basic info).
All sites let bungalows except where indicated otherwise.

**Expect to pay around £0.60 ($1.15; DM1.74)
p.p. including tent; £2 ($3.75; DM5.75) p.p.
in a full bungalow.**

Sokol Trója, Trojská 171/82, Praha 7 (tel. 842833). Grade
    A site, open 1 June–31 Aug. Metro to Fučikova, then
    bus 112 to Kazanka or tram 5, 17 or 25 from Nádraží
    Holešovice (metro and train station).
Sokol Dolní Počernice, Dolní Počernice Nár. Hrdinů,
    Praha 9 (tel. 718034). Grade A site, open 1 May–30
    Sept. Tram 9 to the last stop, then bus 109 to the site.
    Near the Dolní Počernice train station.
Caravancamp TJ Vysoké Školy, Plzeňská, Praha 5 (tel.
    524714). Grade A, open 15 May–15 Sept. Tram 4 or 9
    from Anděl metro station.
Intercamp Kotva Braník, U ledáren 55, Praha 4 (tel.
    466085/461397). Grade A, open 1 Apr.–30 Sept. Tram
    3, 17 or 21 along the river to Braník.
Motol Sportcamp, V podhájí, Praha 5 (tel. 521632/521802).
    Grade A, open 1 Apr.–31 Oct. Up hill from the terminus
    to tram 4, 7 or 9.

Caravan, Mladboleslavská 72, Praha 9-Kbely (tel. 892532). Class B site, without bungalows. Open 1 May–15 Oct.

Slavoj Suchdol, Za sokolovnou 440, Praha 6-Suchdol (tel. 342505/342305). Grade B site. No bungalows. Open 1 July–31 Aug. (Details may well have changed after the recent reconstruction.)

Dolní Chabry, Ústecká, Praha 8-Dolní Chabry. Public camping site. No bungalows.

TJ Armita, Nad Iávkou 3 (Džbán swimming pool), Praha 6 (tel. 368551 ext. 33.) No bungalows. Tram 20 or 26 west along Benešova from Dejvická metro station.

Chalets only at the following sites:

Na Vlachovce, tř. Rudé armády 217 (note: Red Army Street will probably have been renamed), Praha 8 (tel. 841290). The bungalows are shaped like beer kegs. Tram 5, 17 or 25 from Fučíkova metro stop.

Transit, ul. 25 února 197, Praha 6 (tel. 367108).

Xaverov, Božanovská, Dolní Počernice, Praha 9 (tel. 867348).

Nedvězi, Nedvězi, Praha 10 (tel. 750312).

DENMARK

Few countries have responded as imaginatively and constructively to the growth in youth tourism as Denmark. Tourist Offices will take the time to explain the various cheap accommodation possibilities, in stark contrast to the leaflet thrown at you in some other countries. Compared to the rest of Scandinavia, accommodation prices are noticeably lower, increasing the range of your options. While you might baulk at the thought of paying £9–12 ($17–23; DM26–35) in some Norwegian hostels, the top price here is 70Dkr (£6.35; $12; DM18.50). **Hotels**, however, are still likely to be outside your budget. The cheapest doubles in Copenhagen cost 150Dkr (£13.75; $26; DM39.50) per person; elsewhere around 90–120Dkr (£8.25–11.00; $15.50–20.75; DM23.75–31.75) p.p. A room in a **private home** is more affordable at around 90Dkr (£8.25; $15.50; DM23.75), but not always easy to find. Another option, if there are a few of you, is to let a **holiday home** for a week. In high season, a simple house sleeping four costs from Dkr1000–2000 (£90–180; $173–346; DM264–528) per week. If this appeals to you, it may be wise to book ahead.

You will seldom be far from one of the hundred or so **IYHF hostels** spread throughout this small country. There is a hostel in all the main towns. Prices vary between 38–70Dkr (£3.50–6.35; $6.50–12.00; DM10.00–18.50) according to the standard of the hostel and the facilities available. Many offer a choice between dorms and small rooms. As a result of a drive by the hostel association to attract families, high standards of comfort exist. Outside the large towns and ports hostels are rarely full, but, as they may be a couple of miles out, phoning ahead is advisable in order to let you find out directions, as well as book a bed. Reservations are held until 5 p.m., unless you state that you will arrive later. Receptions close at 9 p.m., and, outside Copenhagen, an 11 p.m. curfew is normal. If advance warning is given, it is possible to arrive later than this; a service for which you may be charged 25Dkr (£2.25; $4.25; DM6.50). Bring your own bed linen as it costs around 30Dkr (£2.75; $5.25; DM8) per night to hire. It is also advisable to have an IYHF card. Otherwise you will have to pay 20Dkr (£1.80; $3.50; DM5.25) for an overnight card, or 100Dkr (£9; $17.25; DM26.50) for a membership card.

In the main towns, there are often **independent hostels** and local authority run Sleep-Ins. The latter frequently operate only for a period of a few weeks in summer (usually early August), and may be as basic as a mattress on the floor to put your sleeping bag on. Sleep-Ins differ considerably in price, from the 70Dkr (£6.50; $12; DM18.50) for B&B in Copenhagen, to the free Sleep-In in Odense run by DSB, the state railway. In theory, restrictions such as age limits and one-night maximum stays may exist, but they are seldom stringently enforced. Sleep-Ins apart, **Town Mission Hostels** can often provide the cheapest lodgings in town. Generally clean and well equipped, there is, however, a strict ban on alcohol. The local Tourist Office will inform you on whether a Sleep-In or Town Mission Hostel is in operation.

There is hardly a town of any size that does not have a **campsite**. Graded from one to three stars, the best are the three-star sites, at which one person will pay around 40Dkr (£3.75; $7; DM10.50) per night. All sites are open during the summer months; a fair number from April to September; and a few all year round. Unless you have an International Camping Carnet you will be obliged to buy either a Danish Camping Pass (valid all year, 24Dkr (£2.20; $4.25; DM6.25), or a one night pass for 6Dkr (£0.60; $1; DM1.60). Many sites let cabins or static caravans sleeping up to four people, which cost 1000–2600Dkr (£90–240; $173–450; DM264–685) per week.

Camping outside official sites is perfectly acceptable,

provided you first obtain the permission of the landowner. Do not camp on the beaches as this is against the law, and frequently results in an on-the-spot fine. It is also illegal to sleep rough, so it is asking for trouble to try sleeping in stations, parks, or on the streets.

ADDRESSES

Danish YHA   Landsforeningen Danmarks
                Vandrerhjem, Vesterbrogade 39,
                DK–1620 København V (tel. 31–313612).

Camping   Camping Club Denmark, Horsens
                Turistforening, Søndergade 26,
                DK–8700 Horsens (tel. 75–623822).
                Official guide 'Camping Denmark'
                available from Tourist Offices,
                booksellers, campsites, and by post from
                Campinggrådet, Olaf Palmesgade 10,
                DK–2100 København (tel. 31–423222).
                Not cheap. The National Tourist Office
                in London (or your capital city) has an
                abbreviated list, free on request.

Holiday homes Feriehusudlejernes Brancheforening,
                Euro Tourist, Vesterbro 89,
                DK–9100 Aalborg.
                Sammenslutningen af Feriehususlejende
                Turistforeningen, Odsherreds
                Turistbureau, Algade 52,
                DK–5400 Nykøbing S.

Bornholm

Ferries to the island arrive at Rønne. The accommodation possibilities listed below form a rough circular tour of the island, with all but the section between Dueodde and Rønne being along the coast. Distances are so small as to make this an easy walking tour.

Rønne

IYHF HOSTEL

Galløken, Sdr Alle 22 (tel. 53951340). Open 4 Apr.–31 Oct.

CAMPING

Galløken, Strandvejen 4 (tel. 53952320). Open mid May–Aug.

Nordskovens, Antoinettevej 2 (tel. 53952281). Open June–mid Sept.

Sandegårds, Haslevej 146 (tel. 53952990). Tents for hire.

Hasle

HOTELS

Svalhøj, Simblegårdsvej 28 (tel. 53964018). Open 15 May–15 Sept. B&B in singles and doubles for around 135Dkr (£12.25; $23.25; DM35.50) p.p.

IYHF HOSTEL

Fælledvej 28 (tel. 53964175). Open Easter and 1 May–15 Sept.

CAMPING

'Friheden', Fælledvej 30 (tel. 53964202). Tents for hire. Not a year round site.

Although the towns of Sandvig, Allinge, Sandkås and Tejn are listed separately there is very little distance between them. Sandvig and Allinge are actually joined to each other; Sandkås is about a mile from Allinge; with Tejn roughly another mile down the coast.

Sandvig

HOTELS

Holiday, Strandvejen 82 (tel. 53980216). Open 1 May–1 Oct. B&B in doubles for around 160Dkr (£14.50; $27.75; DM42.25) p.p.

IYHF HOSTEL

Hammershusvej 94 (tel. 53980362). Open Easter–31 Oct.

CAMPING

Lyngholt, Borrelyngvej 43 (tel. 53980574). Hires tents. Open all year.
Sandvig, v/Ostersobadet (tel. 53980447).

Allinge

HOTELS

**Expect to pay around 160Dkr (£14.50; $27.25; DM42.25)
p.p. for B&B.**

Sandboggard, Landemærket 3 (tel. 53980303). Open 1 May–
1 Oct.

Havsten, Strandvejen 45 (tel. 53981884). Open 25 June–
25 Aug.

Lis, Hammershusvej 74 (tel. 53981172). Open 1 May–
1 Oct.

Sandkås

HOTELS

**Expect to pay around 125Dkr (£11.40; $21.50; DM33)
p.p. for B&B.**

Store Lærkegard, Lærkegardsvej 5 (tel. 53980053).
Open 1 Feb.–21 Oct.

Det Hvide Hus Tejnvej 52 (tel. 53980582). Open 15
Apr.–25 Oct.

CAMPING

Sandkås, Poppelvej 2 (tel. 53980441).

Tejn

CAMPING

Tejn, Kåsevej 5 (tel. 53984171).

Gudhjem

HOTELS

Expect to pay around 100Dkr (£9.10; $17.25; DM26.50) p.p. for doubles with B&B.

Ellebæk, Melstedvej 27 (tel. 53985100). Open 1 Apr.–1 Nov.

Therns, Brøddegade 31 (tel. 53985099). Open 10 Apr.–22 Sept.

IYHF HOSTEL

Sct Jorgens Gård (tel. 53985035). Open Easter–1 Nov.

CAMPING

Bådsted, Sdr. Strandvej 91 (tel. 53984230).
Sannes, Melstedvej 39 (tel. 53985211).
'Sletten', Melsted Langgade 45 (tel. 53985256).

Melsted

CAMPING

Strandlunden, Melstedvej 33–35 (tel. 53985245).

Svaneke

IYHF HOSTEL

Reberbanevej 5 (tel. 53996242). Open 1 Apr.–1 Nov.

CAMPING

Møllebakkens, Møllebakken 8 (tel. 53996462).
Hullehavn, Reberbanevej (tel. 53996363).

Nekso

CAMPING

Nexø, Stenbrudsvej 26 (tel. 53992721).

Dueodde

IYHF HOSTEL

Skrokkegårdsvej 17 (tel. 53988119). Open 1 May–1 Oct.

CAMPING

At the Youth Hostel. See above.
Dueodde, Duegårdsvej 2 (tel. 53988149).
Bornholms Familie Camping, Krogegårdsvej 2 (tel. 53988150).

Åkirkeby

CAMPING

Aakirkeby, Haregade 23 (tel. 53975551). Tents for hire.

Copenhagen (København)

During the summer hostel beds can disappear at an alarming rate, so try to reserve ahead. Otherwise, if you do not have a tent, you will either have to sleep rough, or pay for a hotel room, neither of which is a good option. Use-It, Radhusstræde 13 (tel. 33–156518) find beds for free, as well as providing a host of useful information for young travellers.

HOTELS

Jørgensen, Rømersgade 11 (tel. 33138186). Doubles start around 100Dkr (£9; $17.25; DM26.50) p.p. In July and Aug. the hotel operates a co-ed dorm in its basement for 70 Dkr (£6.40; $12; DM18.50), similar prices to most hostels.

Turisthotellet, Reverdilsgade 5 (tel. 31229839). Doubles 160–185Dkr (£14.50–16.80; $27.50–32.00; DM42.00–48.75) p.p. Includes breakfast.

Cheapest doubles around 185Dkr (£16.80; $32; DM48.75) p.p.

Skt. Jørgen, Julius Thomsengade 22 (tel. 31371511). Breakfast included.

West, Westend 11 (tel. 31242761). Without breakfast.

Søfolkenes Mindehotel, Peder Skramsgade 19 (tel. 33134882). With breakfast.

Cheapest doubles 200–220Dkr (£18.20–20.00; $34.50–38.00; DM52.75–58.00) p.p.

Amager, Amagerbrogade 29 (tel. 31549005/31545009). Breakfast included.

Boulevard, Sønder Boulevard 53/5 (tel. 31210651). With breakfast.

Esplanaden, Bredgade 78 (tel. 33132175). With breakfast.
Cab Inn, Danasvej 32–34 (tel. 31210400).
Missionshotellet Hebron, Helgolandsgade 4
(tel. 31316906).

PRIVATE ROOMS

Prices start at 130Dkr (£11.80; $22.50; DM34.25) p.p., and
can be as high as 250Dkr (£22.75; $43.25; DM66) for singles,
175Dkr (£16; $30.25; DM46.25) for doubles, with rooms often
far from the centre. The Værelseanvining in Central Station
will make bookings for you.

IYHF HOSTELS

Expect to pay around 60Dkr (£5.50; $10.50; DM15.75).

Bellahøj, Herbergsvejen 8 (tel. 31289715). Three
miles from the town centre. From the station, or
from Rådhusplein take bus 2 or nightbus 902. Get
off at Fuglsang Allé.

Amager, Sjællandsbroen 55 (tel. 32522908). Mon.–Fri.
bus 46 from Central Station. Weekends bus 37 from
Holmens Bro. S-train B, C, H, or L to Valby station
(S-trains free with railpasses) to join bus 37 saves a bit
of time and money.

Lyngby Vandrerhjem, Rådvad 1 (tel. 42803074/42803032).
Far out, and not easy to get to. Fine if you are stuck for
a first night. S-train A, B or L to Lyngby. From there,
bus 182 or 183 to Lundtoftvej and Hjortekærsvej. The
two-mile walk to Rådvaad is marked. Bus 187 provides
a direct link between Central Station and the hostel,
but only runs four times a day. The only IYHF hostel
with a curfew, 11 p.m.

HOSTELS

City Public Hostel, Absalonsgade 8, in the Vesterbro Ungdomsgård (tel. 31312070). Open 5 May–31 Aug. More expensive than the IYHF hostels at 80Dkr (£7.25; $13.75; DM21). Without breakfast. No curfew.

YMCA Inter Rail Point, Store Kannikestræde 19 (tel. 31113031). Open 1 July–14 Aug. Check in 8 a.m.–noon, or 2.30 p.m.–12.30 a.m. 55Dkr (£5; $9.50; DM14.50). Excellent central location.

YWCA Inter Rail Point, Valdermarsgade 15 (tel. 31311574). Open 15 July–15 Aug. Similar hours and prices to the YMCA hostel above.

Active University, Olfert Fischersgade 40 (tel. 33156175/ 33119191). Cheap, but very busy during the summer.

See also the Hotel Jorgensen above.

SLEEP-IN

Per Hendriks Lings Allé 6 (tel. 31265059). Open 19 June–27 Aug. Co-ed dorms or mattresses on the floor. 75Dkr (£6.80; $13; DM19.75) with breakfast. Usually find space for last-minute arrivals. Bus 1 or nightbus 953 to Per Hendriks Alle. Alternatively bus 6 or 14, or nightbus 914 to Vedidrætsparken.

CAMPING

There are a total of seven sites around Copenhagen:

Strandmøllen, Strandmøllenweg 2 (tel. 42803883). Open mid May to Sept. Nine miles out, but only 20 minutes on S-train C dir. Klampenborg.

Absalon, Kordalsvej 132 (tel. 31410600). Open year round. 5½ miles out of town. S-train B or L to Brondbyøster, then a ¾ mile walk. Ask locals for directions.

Bellahøj, Hvidkildevej (tel. 31101150). Same buses as for the Bellahøj IYHF hostel, but get off at the stop after Hulgårdsvej.

Frederikshavn

HOTELS

Discountlogi Teglgaarden, Teglsgaardvej 3 (tel. 98420444). Open all year. Doubles without breakfast around 165Dkr (£15; $28.50; DM43.50) p.p.

IYHF HOSTEL

'Fladstrand', Buhlsvaj 6 (tel. 98421475).

CAMPING

Nordstrand, Apholmenvej 40 (tel. 98429350). Open Apr.–Sept.

Legoland

Situated in Billund, the mini-town made out of Lego is one of the main tourist attractions in Denmark. Legoland is open from May until mid September, with a number of indoor exhibitions from Easter to mid December. Hotels in Billund are expensive, so either camp at the local site, or visit Legoland on a daytrip from Vejle or Varde.

Billund

DCU-Camping Billund, Nordmarksvej 2 (tel. 75331521). Open 24 June–16 Sept. Very close to Legoland.

Vejle

Bus 912 to Billund. Most days an hourly service operates.

HOTELS

Grejsdalens Hotel and Kro, Grejsdalsvej 384 (tel. 75853004). Doubles available for about 200Dkr (£18.25; $34.50; DM52.75) p.p.

Park Hotel, Orla Lehmannsgade (tel. 75822466). Cheapest doubles around 220Dkr (£20; $38; DM58) p.p. including breakfast.

IYHF HOSTEL

Vejle Vandrerhjem, Gl. Landevej 80 (tel. 75825188).

SLEEP-IN

In the Sports Hall, Vestre Engvej. Details from the Tourist Office (tel. 75821955).

CAMPING

Nørremarksvej 18 (tel. 75823335).

Varde

HOTELS

Hojskolehjemmet, Storegade 56 (tel. 75220140). Doubles for 175Dkr (£16; $30.25; DM46.25) p.p. including breakfast.

IYHF HOSTEL

Ungdomsgården, Pramstedvej 10 (tel. 75221091). Open 15 May–1 Oct.

Odense

HOTELS

Ansgarhus Motel, Kirkegårds Alle 17–19 (tel. 66128800).
Open Jan.–Sept. Doubles without breakfast around
160Dkr (£14.50; $27.75; DM42.25) p.p.

**B&B in doubles 175–200Dkr (£16.00–18.25; $30.50–34.50;
DM46.50–52.75) p.p.**

Kahema, Dronningensgade 5 (tel. 66122821).
Fangel Kro, Fangelvej 55 (tel. 65961011). Not central,
but the bus stops about 100m from the hotel.
Staldgården, Rugårdsvej 8 (tel. 66178888).
Ydes, Hans Tausengade 11 (tel. 66121131).

IYHF HOSTEL

Kragsbjergvej 121 (tel. 65130425). Bus 6 from opposite
the town hall.

HOSTELS

The YMCA and YWCA offer accommodation at the
Inter Rail Point, Rodegårdsvej 91. Open 15 July–15
Aug. Similar prices to IYHF hostels.

SLEEP-IN

Run by the State Railway DSB. Enquire by phone
whether it is in operation either at the train station,
or at the Tourist Office (tel. 66127520).

CAMPING

'Blommenslyst', Middelfartvej 494 (tel. 65967641). Open
year round.

Odense, Odensevej 102 (tel. 66114702). Open Easter–
Sept. Bus 1 from town.

The train to Svendborg stops at Fruens Bøge, not far
from the site.

EIRE

Budget travellers should have few problems finding somewhere cheap to stay in Eire. Hostels are the best places to spend the night. The Irish YHA, An Óige, runs about 50 **hostels** throughout the country. Prices are normally IR£5.00–6.50 (£4.65–6.10; $8.75–11.50; DM13.50–17.50). There are a few exceptions, notably the Dublin hostels where prices range from IR£7.00–9.50 (£6.50–8.90; $12.50–17.00; DM18.75–25.75). Prices at all hostels vary according to the time of year. Hostels are generally very clean. There are no daytime lockouts, and the midnight curfew at all hostels is late by IYHF standards. Although you are expected to do any domestic duties required by the warden, they are more easygoing than is the norm. Indeed, a recent survey of IYHF members rated Irish (and Scottish) hostels the best for atmosphere in Europe. Wardens will happily book hostels ahead for you. Many are out in the country, ideally spaced for a day's walking, but often far from a train station. Nor are there An Óige hostels in all the main towns.

Independent hostels frequently fill these gaps, as well as offering an alternative to IYHF hostels in some towns. Unlike the IYHF hostels where membership is obligatory, these hostels have no such requirements, and they're also free of curfews. Most cost IR£5–6 (£4.65–5.60; $8.75–10.75; DM13.50–16.25), although several in Dublin charge IR£8–9 (£7.50–8.40; $14.25–16.00; DM21.75–24.25). Around 50 of these hostels have joined together to form the Independent Hostel Owners (IHO) association, while another 16, all approved by the Irish Tourist Board, are united under the name Irish Budget Hostels. Both organizations issue lists of their establishments.

Hotels are expensive, so B&B is the most likely option

left to you in towns. Expect to pay from IR£9 (£8.40; $16; DM24.50). *Watch out for single supplements* which can add IR£2–8 to the cost (£1.85–7.50; $3.50–14.25; DM5.35–21.75). In the countryside, many farmhouses offer B&B. Those which are members of the Irish Farm Holidays Association cost from IR£10 (£9.35; $17.75; DM27).

Unless you are planning on getting right out into the countryside, carrying a tent is not particularly worthwhile. On official sites, prices of IR£2–5 (£1.85–4.65; $3.50–8.85; DM5.35–13.50) mean a solo traveller can sometimes spend as much as the cost of a hostel bed. The booklet 'Caravan & Camping Parks' lists the official sites (around IR£1.50 (£1.40; $2.65; DM4) from most Tourist Offices). For IR£2.50 (£2.35; $4.50; DM7) you can camp outside some of the independent hostels, and make use of their facilities. If you ask their permission, farmers may let you camp free on their land for a short period. It is also quite legal to sleep rough, however, camping or sleeping rough leaves you open to a soaking, at any time of year. It also means missing out on meeting other travellers in the hostels.

ADDRESSES

Youth Hostels	An Óige, 39 Mountjoy Square, Dublin 1 (tel. 01–363111).
	Independent Hostel Owners (IHO), Dooey Hostel, Glencolumcille, Co. Donegal (tel. 073–30130).
	Paddy and Josephine Moloney, Irish Budget Hostels, Doolin Village, Co. Clare (tel. 065–74006).
Camping	Irish Caravan Council, 2 Offington Court, Sutton, Dublin 13 (tel. 01–323776).
B&B	Town and Country Homes Association, 'Killeadan', Bundoran Road, Ballyshannon, Co. Donegal (tel. 072–51653/51377).

The Secretary, Irish Farm Holidays
Association, Desert House, Clonakilty,
Co. Cork (tel. 023–33331).

The publication 'Guest Accommodation', from the Irish Tourist Board, London (or your capital city), lists all the registered hotels, guesthouses, town and country homes, farmhouses, hostels and campsites. The ITB can also supply the lists published by the organizations above. Some are free; others cost a small fee.

Cork (Corcaigh) (tel. code 021)

B&Bs

Expect to pay around IR£12 (£11.20; $21.25; DM32.50) p.p.

Mrs Lelia Holmes, 'Olivet', Bishopstown Road, Bishopstown (tel. 543105). City centre 1½ miles away. Bus 8.

Mrs Kay O'Donavan, 38 Westgate Road, Dunderg, Bishopstown (tel. 543078). City centre 1½ miles away. Bus 5 or 8.

Mrs Greta Murphy, 'San Antonio', 46 Maryville, Ballintemple, Blackrock (tel. 291489). Supplement for one person occupying a double IR£4 (£3.75; $7; DM10.75). City centre one mile away. Bus 2.

Mrs Mary O'Leary, 50 Maryville, Ballintemple, Blackrock (tel. 292219). Supplement for one person occupying a double IR£4 (£3.75; $7; DM10.75). City centre one mile away. Bus 2.

Mrs M. Barrett, 'Villa Ronan', Glasheen Road, Wilton/University (tel. 962459). City centre just over half a mile away. Bus 10.

Mrs Nancy Kenefick, 3 Carrig-Fern, College Road, Wilton/University (tel. 543423). Bus 5.

Mrs Rita O'Herlihy, 55 Wilton Gardens, Wilton/University (tel. 541705). Two of the rooms have private shower/bath and toilet, the other is slightly cheaper. 1¼ miles from the centre. Bus 5 or 8.

Mrs Margaret Reddy, St Anthony's, Victoria Cross, Wilton/University (tel. 541345). City centre 1¼ miles away. Bus 8 stops outside the house.

Mrs Catherine Whelan, 'Rose Villa', 1 Donscourt, Bishopstown Road, Wilton/University (tel. 545731). Supplement for one person occupying a double room IR£3.50 (£2.80; $5.25; DM8). City centre 1½ miles away. Bus 8.

IYHF HOSTEL

1–2 Redclyffe, Western Road (tel. 543289). Curfew 11.55 p.m. July and Aug. IR£6.50 (£6; $11.50; DM17.50); Mar.–June and Sept.–Oct. IR£5.50 (£5.15; $9.75; DM15). Prices fall slightly for the rest of the year. Wilton/University area. Bus 5 or 8.

HOSTELS

Cork Tourist Hotel, 10 Belgrave Place (tel. 505562). Near the bus and train stations. IR£5.50 (£5.15; $9.75; DM15). No curfew.

Cork City Hostel, 100 Lower Glanmire Road. Near the train station. IR£5.50 (£5.15; $9.75; DM15).

CAMPING

Cork City Caravan and Camping Park (tel. 961866).

Dublin (Baile Átha Cliath)

(tel. code 01)

B&Bs

Expect to pay IR£12–13 (£11.20–12.15; $21.25–23.00; DM32.50–35.25) p.p. in singles (where available) and doubles. One person occupying a double usually has to pay a supplement, with IR£4 (£3.75; $7; DM10.75) being the norm.

Mrs Oonagh Egan, 'Currow', 144 Kincora Road, Clontarf (tel. 339990). City centre 2½ miles away. Bus 30.

Mrs Moira Kavanagh, 'Springvale', 69 Kincora Drive, Clontarf (tel. 333413). Rooms with showers. City centre 2½ miles away. Bus 28, 29A, 31, 32 or 44A.

Mrs Maura J. O'Driscoll, 'Wavemount', 264 Clontarf Road, Clontarf (tel. 331744). City centre 2¾ miles away. Bus 30.

Mrs Myra O'Flaherty, 'Sea Breeze', 312 Clontarf Road, Clontarf (tel. 332787). City centre 3 miles away. Bus 30.

Mrs Erna Doherty, 16 Beechlawn Avenue, Late Coolock Avenue, Woodville Estate, Coolock (tel. 474361). City centre 2½ miles away. Bus 27A or 27B.

Mrs Roma Gibbons, Joyville, 24 St Alphonsus Road, Drumcondra (tel. 303221). Single supplement is half the norm quoted above. One mile from the city centre. Bus 3, 11, 11A, 16, 16A, or 41A.

Mrs Phil Graham, 8 Cremore Villas, Ballygall Road East, Glasnevin (tel. 341987). Single supplement a quarter of the norm. City centre 1¼ miles away. Bus 13, 19, 34 or 34A.

Mrs Rita Kenny, 'Seaview', 166 Bettyglen, Raheny (tel. 315335). City centre 3 miles. Bus 31, 31A, 32, 32B or DART.

Mrs Sheila Floyd, 22 Braemor Road, Churchtown (tel. 982105). City centre 2½ miles away. Bus 14, 14A or 16A.

Mrs Mai Bird, St Dunstans, 25A Oakley Road, Ranelagh (tel. 972286). Just under one mile from the centre. Bus 11, 11A, 11B or 13.

Mrs Monica Byrne, 'Richmon House', 59 Marian Crescent, Rathfarnham (tel. 947582). City centre 3 miles. Bus 15B.

Mrs P. McCann, 11 Prince Arthur Terrace, Rathmines (tel. 972874). City centre 2 miles. Bus 14, 14A, 15, 15A, 15B, 83 or 18.

Mrs Mary Mooney, 'Aishling House', 19/20 St Lawrence Road, Clontarf (tel. 339097/338400). Seven of the nine rooms have a private shower/bath and toilet. IR£2 (£1.85; $3.50; DM5.50) extra. Single supplement is twice the norm quoted above. Bus 30 or 44A.

Mrs McKenna, 110 Sandford Road, Ranelagh (tel. 971375).

Mrs O'Neill, 6 Whitworth Parade, Drumcondra (tel. 304733).

Mrs Ryan, 10 Distillery Road (tel. 374147).

IYHF HOSTELS

Dublin International YH, 61 Mountjoy Street (tel. 301776). Near the city centre, and a 10-minute walk from Connolly Station. Free bus from the station or North Wall if you arrive early. Relatively flexible midnight curfew. B&B July and Aug. IR£9.50 (£8.90; $16.75; DM25.75); Mar.–June and Sept.–Oct. slightly cheaper. Around IR£7.50 (£7; $13.25; DM20.25) at other times. Reserve in advance July and Aug.

69–70 Harcourt Street. Open 24 June–31 Aug. 10-minute walk from Connolly Station. Free bus. B&B same prices as the Dublin International YH.

Scoil Lorćain, Eaton Square, Monkstown (tel. 801948/ 808906). Five miles from the centre. Bus 7, 8, or DART to Monkstown/Seapoint. Open 1 July–31 Aug. IR£7.50 (£7; $13.25; DM20.50) without breakfast.

HOSTELS

ISAACS Hostel, 2–5 Frenchman's Lane (tel. 363877/ 749321). Dorms IR£5.50 (£5.15; $9.75; DM15) July and Aug. Slightly cheaper at other times. Doubles IR£8.50 (£8; $15; DM23) p.p. Singles IR£13 (£12.14; $23; DM35.25). No curfew. An Irish Budget Hostel.

Kinlay House, 2–12 Lord Edward Street (tel. 796644). Dorms IR£8.00–9.50 (£7.50–8.90; $14.25–17.00; DM21.75– 25.75), doubles IR£12 (£11.20; $21.25; DM32.50) p.p. With breakfast. Near Christ Church Cathedral. An Irish Budget Hostel.

Young Traveller, St Mary's Place (tel. 305000). Just off Dorset Street. Small dorms IR£8.50 (£8; $15; DM23) with continental breakfast. No curfew.

Goin' My Way/Cardijn House, 15 Talbot Street (tel. 788484/741720). Above Tiffany's shoe shop. Midnight curfew. B&B IR£5 (£4.65; $8.75; DM13.50). Hire of sheets/sleeping bag IR£1 (£0.90; $1.75; DM2.50).

YWCA, Radcliffe Hall, St John's Road (tel. 694521) and Lower Baggot Street.

North Strand Hostel, 49 North Strand Road (tel. 364716).

UNIVERSITY ACCOMMODATION

Enquiries to Trinity Hall, UCD, Dartry Road, Rathmines (tel. 971772).

CAMPING

Shankhill Caravan and Camping Park (tel. 820011). IR£5 (£4.65; $9; DM13.50) per tent, IR£0.50 (£0.45; $1; DM1.25) p.p. Bus 45, 45A, 84, or DART. Open from Easter to Oct.

Limerick City (Luimneach)

(tel. code 061)

B&Bs

Expect to pay around IR£12 (£11.20; $21.25; DM32.50) p.p. Supplement for one person occupying a double room is normally IR£2 (£1.85; $3.50; DM5.50).

Mrs Noreen Marsh, 'Shannon Grove House', Athlunkard, Killaloe Road (tel. 345756/343838). All rooms have private shower/bath and toilet. Just over half a mile from the city centre.

Mrs Bernadette Clancy, St Rita's, Ennis Road (tel. 55809). Five-minute walk to the centre. Buses stop outside the house.

John and Betty O'Shea, 'Lisheen', Connagh East (just off Ennis Road) (tel. 55393). Two miles from the city centre.

Mrs Mary Power, Curraghgower House, Ennis Road (tel. 54716). Just over half a mile from the city centre. Buses 2, 3, 59 and 10 stop 100m away. Supplement for one person occupying a double is twice that quoted above.

Mrs Carole O'Toole, Gleneagles, 12 Vereker Gardens, Ennis Road (tel. 55521). Supplement for one person occupying a double is twice that quoted above. Rooms with shower/bath and toilet IR£1.50 (£1.40; $2.75; DM4) p.p. extra. Within easy walking distance of the town centre.

John O'Toole, Ennis House, 2 Inagh Drive, Ennis Road (tel. 326257). Just over half a mile from the city centre. Bus stops 20m away. Two of the five rooms have shower/bath and toilet for IR£1.50 (£1.40; $2.75; DM4) p.p. extra.

IYHF HOSTEL

1 Pery Square (tel. 312107). July–Aug. IR£6.50 (£6; $11.50; DM17.50); Mar.–June and Sept.–Oct. IR£5.50 (£5.15; $9.75; DM15). Prices fall slightly at other times. Midnight curfew. Close to the bus and train stations.

FINLAND

In common with the other Scandinavian countries, simply feeding yourself in Finland costs a fair amount of money, making it all the more vital to keep the price of your accommodation down. The best way to do so is either to sleep rough, or, more advisably, to take advantage of the old law which allows you to camp anywhere as long as you have the landowner's permission. It is normal practice to camp out of sight of private homes. Despite a growing tendency to camp only on official sites you will have no trouble from the authorities, provided you leave no litter, or do anything which might cause a forest fire.

There are over 350 official **campsites**, graded with one to three stars, covering all the main tourist areas. Prices vary from 25–50FIM (£3.00–6.25; $5.75–12.00; DM8.75–18.00), according to classification. If you are not in possession of an International Camping Carnet, you will have to buy a Finnish camping pass at the first site you visit. Few sites remain open all year round. Most open for the period May/June to August/September. Many of those in and around the larger towns are very big, frequently with a tent capacity of 2000. During July and August these sites become very busy at weekends. Some sites let cottages (usually without bedding) for two to five people; well worth enquiring about if there are several people prepared to share. Cottages are available for anything between 75–400FIM (£9.50–80.00; $17.75–150.00; DM27.25–230.00) per day. In July and August it is advisable to try and reserve cottages in advance.

The 160 **IYHF hostels** are classified from one to four stars. Prices in two-star hostels range from 30–42FIM (£3.75–5.25; $7–10; DM10.75–15.25), depending on whether you stay in a dorm or a small room. Most common in the larger towns are three-star hostels which charge 40–55FIM (£5–7; $9.50–13.25; DM14.50–20.25) per night in two- to eight-bedded rooms. The largest rooms in four-star hostels are quads. Prices start at 65FIM (£8.10; $15.50; DM23.50), rising to 95FIM (£11.85; $22.50; DM34.50). Only in the most expensive hostels are IYHF cards obligatory, but at others you can expect to be charged a supplement of 10FIM (£1.25; $2.40; DM3.60) if you are a non-member. Bearing in mind that hiring bed linen can cost a similar amount, it is better to come well prepared and save your money.

All the main towns have at least one hostel. Only from June to August, and particularly from mid July to mid August, will you experience any difficulty in getting a hostel bed. At this time hostels in the large cities and in areas popular with hikers are often full, making it imperative to reserve ahead, by letter or by telephone. Reservations are held until 6 p.m., unless you make it clear you will be arriving later.

Unlike the rest of Scandinavia there has been little growth in independent hostels. Converted **student dorms**, known as 'Summerhotels', are generally clean and modern. Prices are similar to those of four-star hostels. **B&B** is available mainly in the north, especially on farms. The price of 75–150FIM (£9.50–19.00; $17.75–35.50; DM27.25–54.50) usually includes a sauna and a substantial breakfast. The cheapest **hotels** cost around 140FIM (£17.50; $33.25; DM51) in singles, 100FIM (£12.50; $23.75; DM36.25) per person in doubles, again with a large breakfast.

ADDRESSES

Finnish YHA   Suomen Retkeilymajajärjestö-SRM ry,
              Yrjönkatu 38 B 15, 00100 Helsinki
              (tel. 90–6940377).

Helsinki/Helsingfors (tel. code 90)

HOTELS

**The least expensive hotels charge 120–140FIM
(£15.00–17.50; $28.50–33.25; DM43.50–50.75) p.p.
for their cheapest doubles.**

Kongressikoti, Snellmanink 15 A 10 (tel. 174839).

Clairet, Itäinen Teatterikuja 3 (tel. 669707).

Erottajanpuista, Uudenmaankatu 9–11 (tel. 642169).

Satakuntatalo, Lapinrinne 1A (tel. 6940311). Student accommodation converted into a temporary hotel. Open 28 May–3 Sept.

Lönnrot, Lönnrotinkatu 16 (tel. 6932590).

Pilvilinna-Irmala-Terminus, Vilhonkatu 6B (tel. 630260/607072).

Mekka, Vuorikatu 8B (tel. 630265).

Tarmo, Siltasaarenk 11 B 40 (tel. 7014735/7016001).

Regina, Puistokatu 9 A 2 (tel. 656937).

Omapohja, Itäinen Teatterikuja 3 (tel. 666211).

IYHF HOSTELS

Stadionin maja, Pohj Stadiontie 3 B (tel. 496071). Curfew 2 a.m. Three-star hostel. Prices start at the bottom of the three-star price scale (see country intro, above). Twenty-five-minute walk from the train station, or tram 3T or 7A to the Olympic Stadium.

Finnhostel Academica, Hietaniemenkatu 14 (tel. 4020206/4020575). Student accommodation converted into a temporary four-star hostel. Open 1 June–1 Sept. Prices start at bottom of the four-star scale (see country intro, above).

Vantaan retkeilyhotelli, Tikkurilan Urheilupuisto, 01300 Vantaa (tel. 8393310). Three-star hostel. Ten miles from the city centre; just over half a mile from the Tikkurila train station.

HOSTELS

Kallionnretkeilymaja, Porthaninkatu 2 (tel. 70992590). Mid May–Aug. 2 a.m. curfew. 44FIM (£5.50; $10.50; DM16). Only 30 beds. Run by the city's youth organization. Fifteen-minute walk from the train station along Unionkatu, or the metro to Hakaniemi.

YWCA Interpoint, Merikasarminkatu 3 (tel. 1693699). Co-ed dorms same price as the hostel above, but non-members pay a 16FIM (£2; $3.75; DM5.75) surcharge for the first night. May let you sleep on the floor when all the other hostels are full. Open July–mid Aug. Curfew 1 a.m. Tram 4 to the Puolpäivänkatu stop in front of the hostel.

CAMPING

Rastila (tel. 316551). Open mid May–mid Sept. Cheap municipal site. 22 FIM (£2.75; $5.25; DM8) p.p. (tent included). Also lets cabins. 4½ miles from the city centre. Metro to Itäkeskus, then bus 90, 90A or 96.

Rovaniemi (tel. code (9)60)

HOTELS

Cheapest doubles 100–125FIM (£12.50–15.65; $23.75–29.75; DM36.25–45.50) p.p.

Matkakoti Matka-Kalle, Asemieskatu 1 (tel. 20130).
Rovaniemi, Koskikatu 27 (tel. 22066).
Outa, Ukkoherrantie 16 (tel. 312474).

IYHF HOSTEL

Retkeilymaja Tervashonka, Hallituskatu 16 (tel. 14644). Three-star hostel. Right from the station, up the hill, over the junction, down Hallituskatu.

CAMPING

Ounaskoski (tel. 15304). Open 1 June–31 Aug. Just over
the river from the centre of town.
Napapiirin Saari-Tuvat (tel. 60045). Year-round site.

Savonlinna (tel. code (9)57)

The closest train station to the town centre and the Tourist
Office is Savonlinna-Kauppatori, one stop before the main
station if you are coming from Helsinki.

HOTELS

Hospits, Linnankatu 20 (tel. 22443). Cheapest doubles
around 120FIM (£15; $28.50; DM43.50) p.p.

IYHF HOSTELS

Retkeilymaja Malakias, Pihlajavedenkuja 6 (tel. 23283).
Retkeilymaja Vuorilinna, Kasinosaari (tel. 24908). Open
June and 15 Aug.–30 Aug.

CAMPING

Vuohimäki (tel. 537353/716422/71223). Open 1 June–19
Aug. 4½ miles from the centre. Bus 3 runs twice
hourly.
Kyrönniemi (tel. 21507). Open during the summer. Near
Olavinlinna, in the centre of town.

Turku/Åbo (tel. code (9)21)

HOTELS

Cheapest doubles 100–120FIM (£12.50–15.00; $23.75–28.50; DM36.25–43.50) p.p.

Matkakievari, Läntinen Pitkäkatu 8 (tel. 503506).
Aura, Humalistonkatu 13 (tel. 311973).

Cheapest doubles 130–150FIM (£16.25–18.75; $31.00–35.50; DM47.00–54.50) p.p.

Domus Aboensis-SH, Piispanaktu 10 (tel. 329470). Student accommodation converted into a temporary hotel from 1 June–31 Aug.

Turisti-Aula, Käsityöläiskatu 11 (tel. 334484).

St Birgittas Convent Guesthouse, Ursininkatu 15a (tel. 501910).

Ikituuri Summer Hotel, Pispalantie 7 (tel. 376111). Converted student accommodation. Open 1 June–31 Aug.

IYHF HOSTELS

Turun kaupungin retkeilymaja, Linnankatu 39 (tel. 316578). Three-star hostel. From the ferry terminal a 20-minute walk along Linnankatu. Bus 1.

Finnhostel Kåren, Hämeenkatu 22 (tel. 320421). Student accommodation serving as a temporary four-star hostel. Open 1 June–31 Aug.

CAMPING

Ruissalo (tel. 589249). Open 1 June–2 Sept. About 6½ miles out of town. Bus 8 runs twice hourly from the Market Square.

FRANCE

Budget travellers should have little difficulty in finding suitable accommodation in France, as there is a wide range of options available. Even in Paris, there are plenty of cheap places to stay, although you may have to make a number of phone calls before you find somewhere with space. Try to avoid staying in Montmartre or Pigalle because many of the hotels there are used by prostitutes, and these areas can be dangerous at night. A better alternative than looking for a room on your own, is to use the room-finding service of the Tourist Offices. The 15FF commission (£1.50, $3; DM4.50) charged for finding a one-star hotel room (5FF; £0.50; $1; DM1.50 for a hostel bed) is likely to be money well spent. Elsewhere, you should manage quite easily on your own. In Marseilles, avoid the area around the Porte D'Aix, as it is not particularly safe.

The French Ministry of Tourism categorizes most **hotels** from one star up to four stars, then the deluxe 'four stars L'. Only a relatively small number of hotels remain unclassified. Prices at classified hotels are regulated by the Ministry of Tourism. By law, the maximum price for a room must be clearly displayed at the reception, and on the door of the room. Singles, where they are available, usually cost at least two-thirds the price of doubles. It is always advisable to ask if breakfast is compulsory, as what will invariably be only a meagre continental breakfast, can nonetheless add 20–30FF (£2–3; $3.75–5.75; DM5.75–8.75) to the price of a room. You may also have to pay 10–22FF (£1.00–2.20; $2.00–4.25; DM3.00–6.50) for showers.

The cheapest hotels charge around 55FF (£5.50; $10.50; DM16) in singles, 30FF (£3; $5.75; DM8.75) p.p. in doubles, except in Paris where 80FF (£8; $15.25; DM23.25) in singles,

60FF (£6; $11.50; DM17.50) each in doubles, are about the lowest prices you can hope for. Facilities in these establishments are likely to be basic. There may be no hot water in the room, and you will certainly have to share a toilet (occasionally still the hole-in-the-floor type). A few one-star hotels, especially in the larger cities, can be dirty and cockroach infested, so make a point of checking the room before agreeing to take it. Conversely, many unclassified hotels, especially in rural areas, offer perfectly adequate standards of accommodation. It is possible to find the odd two-star hotel which charges around 60FF (£6; $11.50; DM17.50) p.p. in doubles, but more normally you will pay upwards of 80FF (£8; $15.25; DM23.25) each in doubles, and from 100FF (£10; $19; DM29) in singles. If you can afford these prices, you can expect a room with a private bathroom. Throughout the provincial towns, there are some 4000 hotels and inns operated by the Logis et Auberges de France. These functional establishments are government sponsored, providing one- and two-star accommodation, with guaranteed standards of comfort and service. Also included in the network are a number of smaller 'auberges'. Although these are unclassified, the standard of accommodation provided is perfectly satisfactory. To make a reservation at any hotel, you only need to write or phone in advance. To make the process easier for all concerned, you can obtain bilingual booking forms from the French National Tourist Office, in London or your capital city.

There are two **youth hostel** associations in France; the IYHF-affiliated Fédération Unie des Auberges de la Jeunesse (FUAJ), and the Ligue Française pour les Auberges de la Jeunesse (LFAJ). Relations between the two are strained, to say the least. The IYHF handbook lists the FUAJ hostels, but only a few of the LFAJ establishments. It is worthwhile finding out about the LFAJ hostels, as they fill in many of the gaps in the FUAJ network, so that there are not many places of major interest that lack a hostel.

Most hostels stay open all year round, except perhaps

for a few weeks in winter. Hostelling can certainly be a cheap way to see the country, at virtually any time of year, provided you take the trouble to reserve well ahead for hostels in the more popular tourist towns. The drawbacks are the poor quality of some of the hostels, and the curfews. Even the top-rated hostels vary enormously in quality. While some are well maintained and efficiently run, at the other extreme are those in dilapidated buildings, where the warden only appears at certain times, and is not on the premises at night. In the very worst of this latter type, you may well have reason to worry about your personal safety. Curfews are normally 11 p.m. at the latest, except in a very small number of hostels.

Generally hostel prices vary according to the grade of establishment. Prices at both FUAJ and LFAJ hostels can be as low as 25FF (£2.50; $4.75; DM7.25), but are normally around 40–50FF (£4–5; $7.50–9.50; DM11.50–14.50). However, in popular tourist destinations such as Paris, Strasbourg, Avignon and Bayeux even low-grade hostels may charge well above the normal hostel price. In these towns expect to pay around 85FF (£8.50; $16.25; DM24.75) in the hostels of either association. The IYHF card permits entry to both FUAJ and LFAJ hostels. Technically, the IYHF card is obligatory at FUAJ hostels, but non-members are normally allowed to stay on the payment of a 10–20FF (£1–2; $1.90–3.75; DM2.90–5.75) supplement per night, or are restricted to a one-night stay.

In some of the larger towns, a further possibility available to IYHF members and students are the 'Foyers des Jeunes Travailleurs/Travailleuses'. These are residential hostels, whose main function is to provide cheap living accommodation for young workers and students. As such, they tend to offer a higher standard of accommodation than hostels (mainly singles and doubles). Prices are usually on a par with local hostels, but you are getting better value for money. It is worth enquiring about 'foyers' at any time of year, but your chances of finding a place are obviously better during the student vacations.

Camping is very popular in France. Practically every town of any size has a campsite. There are over 7000 in all, rated with from one to four stars. The overnight fee varies from 5–20FF (£0.50–2.00; $1.00–3.75; DM1.50–5.75) p.p., depending on the classification of the site. Usually, the cheapest you will find is a site run by the local authority (*camping municipal*). Charges are normally under 10FF (£1; $1.90; DM2.90) p.p. per night. Outside the main season there may not even be an attendant to collect the fees, so you can camp for free. At other times these sites are clean and well maintained, and lack only the shopping and leisure facilities of higher-graded sites.

With a few exceptions, camping is a cheap, convenient, and pleasant way to see France. There is no centrally located site in Lyon, so you will have to travel to one of the sites on the outskirts. The only site in Nice is pitifully small, and far from the centre. Along the Mediterranean, many sites become ridiculously overcrowded during the summer months; so much so that 11 regional information posts, 21 telephone information centres, and 59 local reception centres have been established to deal with the problem. The addresses and telephone numbers of these centres are listed in the brochure 'Mémento du Campeur Averti', available from Tourist Offices. Try to reserve coastal sites in advance.

In rural areas many farms are part of a scheme which allows you to camp on the farm (*Camping à la ferme*). These are listed in 'Accueil à la Campagne', a useful publication for anyone wanting to explore rural France. Facilities are very basic, yet prices are similar to those of other campsites. Many farmers will allow you to camp on their land free of charge, provided you ask their permission first. If you pitch your tent without their consent, expect a hostile confrontation.

Gîtes d'étapes are widespread in rural areas, particularly those popular with hikers and cyclists. They offer basic, cheap accommodation; usually bunk-bedded dorms, and simple cooking and washing facilities. The LFAJ maintains

11 gîtes d'étapes in the Aveyron-Le Lot area, and another 27 in Corsica. These are ideal for cycling or walking tours in two of the most beautiful parts of the country. Overnight fees range from about 20–40FF (£2–4; $3.75–7.50; DM5.75–11.50).

These are not to be confused with 'Gîtes de France', which are self-catering accommodations let by an association of French families. Sleeping between four and six people, they can normally be rented for 900–1500FF (£90–150; $170–285; DM260–435) per week. They are usually located in and around small villages, and may be village houses, rural or farm cottages, or flats in private homes. Another option in the countryside are 'chambres d'hôtes' (B&B in private homes). Prices are similar to those of cheap hotels, but 'chambres d'hôtes' probably offer better value for money.

Both gîtes d'étapes and chambres d'hôtes are listed in 'Accueil à la Campagne'. Also listed is a selection of the **mountain huts** that are plentiful in mountain areas. Most of these are operated by the Club Alpin Français (CAF). Huts are open to non-members, but members of the CAF and associated clubs receive a reduction on the normal overnight fee of 40FF (£4; $7.50; DM11.50).

Sleeping rough is legal, and the weather will seldom cause you any problems, except in the north outside the summer months. However, sleeping rough is not advisable, especially in the cities, or along the beaches of the Mediterranean. Petty criminals realized the easy pickings to be had from those sleeping in and around stations a long time ago (Paris and Marseilles are particularly unsafe). The beaches are 'worked' by French and North African gangs who steal for a living. If you are stuck for a place to stay, some stations have emergency lodgings. Ask for the 'Accueil en Gare'. Failing this, you would be better to take an overnight train. If you are going to sleep rough, leave your pack at the station, and try to bed down beside other travellers. If you are attacked, hand over your money. Thieves have been known to become violent if their victims try to resist. If you have been sensible and taken out travel

insurance you will incur only a small loss, which is preferable
to risking serious injury.

ADDRESSES

Youth hostels	Fédération Unie des Auberges de la Jeunesse, 27 rue Pajol, 75018 Paris (tel. 01–46070001).
	Ligue Français pour les Auberges de la Jeunesse, 38 Bd. Raspail, 75007 Paris (tel. 01–45486984).
Mountain huts	Club Alpin Français, rue de la Boëtie, 75008 Paris (tel. 01–47423846).
Hotels	Logis de France, 83 av. d'Italie, 75013 Paris (tel. 01–45848384).
Gîtes de France	Gîtes de France Ltd, 178 Piccadilly, London W1V 9DB (tel. 071–4933480). (or via your local French Tourist Office).
Camping	Michelin's 'Camping and Caravanning in France' lists some of the best sites. 'The Camping Traveller to France' is available from the National Tourist Office in London, or your local French Tourist Office.
Rural accommodation	'Accueil à la Campagne' is available from the National Tourist Office in London. Contact them for the current price. Expect to pay around £5 ($8.50; DM14.50). (Alternately contact French Tourist Office in your capital city.)

Aix-en-Provence (tel. code (0)42)

HOTELS

**Cheapest doubles around 50–75FF (£5.00 7.50;
$9.50–14.25; DM14.50–21.75) p.p.**

Pax, 29 rue Espariat (tel. 262479).
Vendome, 10 cours des Minimes (tel. 644501).
Bellegarde, 2 pl. Bellegarde (tel. 234337) (closed Aug.).
Paul, 10 av. Pasteur (tel. 232389).

**Cheapest doubles around 75–100FF (£7.50–10.00;
$14.25–19.00; DM21.75–29.00) p.p.**

Des Arts (sully), 69 bd. Carnot (tel. 381177).
Splendid, 69 cours Marabeau (tel. 381953).
Vigouroux, 27 rue Cardinale (tel. 382642).
Casino (1), 38 rue Victor-Leydet (tel. 260688).
Concorde, 68 bd. du Roi Rene (tel. 260395).
De France, 63 rue Espariat (tel. 279015).
Le Moulin, 1 av. Robert Schumann (tel. 594168).

YOUTH HOSTEL

3 av. Marcel Pagnol (FUAJ), Quartier Jas de Bouffan (tel.
201599). 1½ miles from the station. Bus 8 or 12 dir.
Jas de Bouffan to the Etienne d'Orves Vasarely stop.
Watch for the Vasarely building.

FOYERS

Club des Jeunes Travailleurs, Les Milles, av. Albert
Einstein (Zone Industrielle) (tel. 244138). Four miles
from the centre.
St Eloi, 9 av. Jules Isaac (tel. 234499).
Foyer Hotel Sonacotra, 16 av. du petit Bartélémy (tel.
642087).
Foyer pour les Filles, 15 rue du Bon Pasteur (tel. 233398
(females only).
Sed Abeilles, av. Maréchal Leclerc (tel. 592575).

CAMPING

Airotel Chantecler, Val St-André (tel. 261298).

Avignon (tel. code (0)90)

HOTELS

Cheapest doubles 50–75FF (£5.00–7.50; $9.50–14.25; DM14.50–21.75) p.p.

Near the station:
Monclar, 13 av. du Monclar (tel. 862014).
Near the station and the town centre:
Du Parc, 18 rue Agricol-Perdiguier (tel. 827155).
Pacific, 7 rue Agricol-Perdiguier (tel. 824336).
Centrally located:
Innova, 100 rue Joseph Vernet (tel. 825410).
Des Arts, 9 rue de l'Aigarden (tel. 866387).
Central, 31 rue de la République (tel. 860781).
Across the river:
Hostellerie de l'Ile, Ile de la Barthelasse (tel. 866162).
Bagatelle-Pavillon Bleu, Ile de la Barthelasse (tel. 863039).

Cheapest doubles around 75–100FF (£7.50–10.00; $14.25–19.00; DM21.75–29.00) p.p.

Near the station:
St Roch, 9 impasse Mérindol (tel. 821863).
De la Bourse, 6 rue Portail Boquier (tel. 823443).
Near the station and the centre:
Splendid, 17 rue Agricol-Perdiguier (tel. 861446).
Central:
Mignon, 12 rue Joseph Vernet (tel. 821730).
Provencal, 13 rue Joseph Vernet (tel. 852524).
Medieval (studio), 15 rue Petite Saunerie (tel. 861106).
Paris Nice, 38 cours Jean Jaurès (tel. 820321).

GUESTHOUSES

Ferme Etienne Jamet, Ile de la Barthelasse (tel. 861674).

B&Bs

Mme Salaun, 34 rue de la Masse (tel. 861905).
Les Logis St Eloi, 14 pl. de l'Oratoire (tel. 254036).

HOSTELS/FOYERS

Centre de Rencontres International (LFAJ), 7 rue Porte-Eveque (tel. 851324).
The Squash Club, 32 bd. Limbert (tel. 852778).
Foyer Hameau de Champfleury, 33 av. Eisenhower (tel. 853502).
Residence Pierre Louis Loisil, av. Pierre Sémard (tel. 250792).
Foyer Bagatelle, Ile de la Barthelasse (tel. 863039).
La Bastide de Bonpas, route de Cavaillon, Montfavet (tel. 230457).
Foyer YMCA, 7bis bd. de la Justice (tel. 254620).

CAMPING

There are four sites grouped closely together on the Ile de la Barthelasse, just across the river. Within walking distance of the station, or take the infrequent bus 10 from the station or from the Post Office.

Bagatelle (tel. 863039). Open all year.
Camping Municipal Pont St Benézet (tel. 826350). Open 1 Mar.–31 Oct.
Camping Parc des Libertés (tel. 851773). Open for a few weeks around Easter, then from 15 June–15 Sept.
Les Deux Rhônes, Chemin de Bellegarde (tel. 854970). Open 1 June–15 Sept.

Bordeaux (tel. code (0)56)

HOTELS

Centrally located, one-star:

Cheapest doubles around 60FF (£6; $11.50; DM17.50) p.p.

La Boëtie, 4 rue de la Boëtie (tel. 817668). One star hotel.

D'Amboise, 22 rue de la Vieille Tour (tel. 816267). Slightly cheaper than above.

Abadie, 127 rue Dubordieu (tel. 916085).

De Biarritz, 21 rue de Loup (tel. 443851).

Le Blayais, 17 rue Mautrec (tel. 481787).

Le Bourgogne, 16 cours Victor Hugo (tel. 928227).

Dauphin, 82 rue du Palais-Gallien (tel. 522462).

De Dax, 7 rue Mautrec (tel. 482842).

De Famille, 76 cours Georges-Clemenceau (tel. 521128).

D'Italie, 4 rue des Ayres (tel. 814992).

De l'Opera, 35 rue Esprit-de-Lois (tel. 814127).

Du Parc, 10 rue de la Verrerie (tel. 527820).

Du Parlement, 38 rue des Piliers-de-Tutelle (tel. 445818).

Saint-François, 22 rue de Mirail (tel. 915641).

Saint-Rémi, 34 rue Saint-Rémi (tel. 485548).

Unclassified, but with a large capacity:

Unotel, 37 cours Maréchal-Juin (tel. 901000).

Near St Jean train station:

Cheapest doubles around 55FF (£5.50; $10.50; DM16) p.p.

Hotel-Bar-Club Les 2 Mondes, 10 rue St-Vincent-de-Paul (tel. 916303). Turn left on leaving the station, then right.

One-star hotels:

Noel, 8 rue St-Vincent-de-Paul (tel. 916248) (directions as above).

San Michel, 32 rue Charles-Domercq (tel. 919640). As you leave the station you are on rue Charles Domercq.

De Poissy, 210 cours de la Marne (tel. 915591). Turn left on leaving the station. Cours de la Marne is the main road off to the left.

Du Lion d'Or, 38 pl. André-Meunier (tel. 917162). As you head up cours de la Marne (see immediatcly above) pl. André-Meunier is on your right.

HOSTELS

22 cours Barbey (FUAJ) (tel. 915951). Turn left on leaving the station, left up cours de la Marne, then fourth on the left. 11 p.m. curfew.

Maison des Etudiants, 50 rue Ligier (tel. 964830). Oct–June women only, open to men July–Sept. Half-hour walk from the station. Up cours de la Marne, straight across pl. de la Victoire to cours Aristide-Briand which runs into cours de la Libération. Rue Ligier is on the right. Alternatively, bus 7 or 8 from the station to the Bourse du Travail stop on cours de la Libération. Keep on going the same way, then right on rue Ligier.

CAMPING

No really convenient site.

Lorréjean. From the bus station on Quai Richelieu by the river take bus B to the end of the line (30-minute trip), then a couple of minutes' walk.

Les Gravières, Pont-de-la-Maye, Villeneuve d'Ornon (tel. 870036).

Chamonix (tel. code (0)50)

As it can be difficult to find accommodation, try to reserve ahead. If you write to the Tourist Office they will make reservations for you. Letters with only the name of the hotel will get there.

HOTELS

Cheapest doubles under 60FF (£6; $11.50; DM17.50) p.p.

Valaisanne (tel. 531798).

Cheapest doubles around 75FF (£7.50; $14.25; DM21.75) p.p.

Les Lacs (tel. 530208).

Cheapest doubles under 100FF (£10; $19; DM29) p.p.

Aiguille Verte (tel. 530173).
Nantillons (tel. 530871).
Lion d'Or (tel. 531509).
Stade (tel. 530544).
Bon Coin (tel. 531567).

Cheapest doubles around 100–120FF (£10–12; $19.00–22.75; DM29.00–34.75) p.p.

Planards (tel. 534686).
  Touring (tel. 535918).
  Roma (tel. 530062).
  Maronniers (tel. 530573).

YOUTH HOSTEL

103 Montée J. Balmat (FUAJ), Les Pélerins (tel. 531452). A 15-minute walk from Chamonix. Nearest train station Les Pélerins. The hostel is about half a mile uphill from the station. Alternatively, take the bus dir. Les Houches from pl. de l'Eglise in Chamonix to the school (école) in Les Pélerins.

CHALETS

Cheap dormitory accommodation is provided in several chalets in and around Chamonix.

Expect to pay around 45FF (£4.50; $8.50; DM13) per night.

In Chamonix:
>   Ski Station, 6 route des Moussoux (tel. 532025). Up the
>   hill from the Tourist Office.
>   Le Chamoniard Volant, 45 route de la Frasse (tel. 531409).

In Les Bossons:
>   La Crèmerie du Glacier, 333 route des Rives (tel. 559010).

CAMPING

Three sites are located about 10–15 minutes' walk from the
centre of town, just off the road to Les Pélerins.
>   Les Arolles, 281 Chemin du Cry-Chamonix (tel. 531430).
>   Open 25 June–30 Sept. 100 places.
>   L'Ile des Barrats (tel. 535144). Open 1 June–30 Sept. 150
>   places.
>   Les Tissourds (tel. 559497). Open 1 July–31 Aug. 20
>   places. Cold water only.
>   Les Moliasses (tel. 531861). Fifteen-minute walk from the
>   town centre.

Dieppe (tel. code (0)35)

HOTELS

Centrally located:

**Cheapest doubles 35–50FF (£3.50–5.00; $6.75–9.50;
DM10.25–14.50) p.p.**

>   Les Arcades, 1 et 3 Arcades de la Bourse (tel. 841412).
>   L'Hibiscus, 2 et 4 pl. Louis-Vitet (tel. 841390).
>   Du Havre, 13 rue Thiers (tel. 841502).
>   De la Jetée, 5 rue de l'Asile-Thomas (tel. 848998).
>   La Pêcherie, 3 rue Mortier-d'Or (tel. 820462).
>   Du Rocher de Cancale, 47 rue de l'Epée (tel. 841791).

Cheapest doubles 55–75FF (£5.50–7.50; $10.50–14.25; DM16.00–21.75) p.p.

Pontoise, 10 rue Thiers (tel. 841457).
Select, 1 rue Toustain (tel. 841466).
Tourist, 16 rue de la Halle-au-Blé (tel. 061010).

YOUTH HOSTEL

48 rue Louis Fromager (FUAJ), Quartier Janval, Chemin des Vertus (tel. 848573). Twenty-five minutes' walk from the station. Bus 2 dir. Val Druel to Château Michel, or bus 1 to Javie.

CAMPING

No really convenient site.
Camping du Pré St-Nicolas (tel. 841139). Two-star site Open all year. Located just off the road to Pourville.
Camping Vitamin, Dieppe-Les Vertus (tel. 821111). Four-star site. Open 1 Apr.–31 Oct.

Lyon (tel. code (0)78)

HOTELS

One-star hotels unless stated. Names in brackets refer to the area of the city:

Cheapest doubles 55–70FF (£5.50–7.00; $10.50–13.25; DM16.00–20.25) p.p.

Pension Baudelaire N H, 6 rue d'Auvergne (Perrache. The area around the station of that name) (tel. 378534).
Vaubecour, 28 rue Vaubecour (Perrache) (tel. 374491).
De Geneve, 10 quai Perrache (Perrache) (tel. 371159).
D'Ainay, 14 rue des Remparts d'Ainay (Perrache) (tel. 424342).

De La Marne, 78 rue de la Charité (Perrache) (tel. 370746). Two-star hotel. Closes for three weeks in August.

Saint-Etienne, 39 rue Victor Hugo/entrance rue Jarente (Perrache) (tel. 370192).

Chez-Soi, 4 place Carnot (Perrache) (tel. 371830). Closes for three weeks in August.

Alexandra, 49 rue Victor Hugo (Perrache) (tel. 377579).

Des Savoies, 80 rue de la Charité (Perrache) (tel. 376694). Closes for 10 weeks at the end of the year. Two-star hotel.

Normandie, 3 rue de Bélier (Perrache) (tel. 373136). Two-star.

Du Mont-Blanc, 26 cours de Verdun (Perrache) (tel. 373536). Two-star.

La Maison d'Hôtes N H, 2 rue d'Amboise (Bellecour) (tel. 373640).

Des Marronniers, 5 rue des Marronniers (Bellecour) (tel. 370482).

Des Celestins, 4 rue des Archers (Bellecour) (tel. 376332).

Croix-Pâquet, 11 place Croix-Pâquet (Terreaux) (tel. 285149).

Saint-Vincent, 9 rue Pareille (Terreaux) (tel. 286797).

Cheapest doubles around 70–85FF (£7.00–8.50; $13.25–16.25; DM20.25–24.75) p.p.

All two-star hotels around Perrache:
Dauphine, 3 rue Duhamel (tel. 372419).
De La Loire, 19 cours de Verdun (tel. 374429).
Du Simplon, 11 rue Duhamel (tel. 374100).
Touring, 37 cours de Verdun (tel. 373903).
Victoria, 3 rue Delandine (tel. 375761).

HOSTELS

Lyon-Venissieux (FUAJ), 51 rue Roger Salengro (tel. 763923). Three miles from the city centre. From Perrache station take bus 53 to Etats-Unis/Viviani;

from Part-Dieu station bus 36 to Viviani/Joliot Curie, or the métro to place Bellecour, then bus 35 to Georges Levy (until 9 p.m.).

Résidence Benjamin Delessert, 145 avenue Jean Jaures (tel. 614141). From Part-Dieu métro to Marce, then a 10-minute walk. From Perrache, take any of the frequent trains to Part-Dieu, then the métro.

CAMPING

All the sites are about six miles out of the city.

Dardilly, Terrain de Ville de Lyon (tel. 698007/356455). Four-star site. Open 1 Mar.–31 Oct. Bus 19 from the Town Hall (métro: Hôtel de Ville) dir. Ecully-Dardilly to the Parc d'Affaires stop.

'Les Barolles', Saint Genis Laval (tel. 560556). One-star site to the south-west of the city. Open 1 Mar.–31 Dec.

There are another three sites at the Parc de Loisirs de Miribil-Jonage, north-east of the city.

If for any reason you cannot get a room, head for the 'Accueil en Gare', located in the covered walkway linking Lyon-Perrache train station to the Centre Perrache.

Marseilles (Marseille) (tel. code (0)91)

HOTELS

Cheapest doubles in the one-star hotels below cost 55–75FF (£5.50–7.50; $10.50–14.25; DM16.00–21.75) p.p. Most are within easy walking distance of the station.

Guillemain, 357 av. du Prado (tel. 778853). Metro: RD–PT du Prado.

Lutia, 31 av. du Prado (tel. 792263). Métro: Perier or Castellane.

Salvator, 6 bd. Louis Salvator (tel. 487825). Estrangin or N.D. du Mont.

Pretty, 34 bd. Louis Salvator (tel. 486727). Estrangin or N.D. du Mont.

Nady, 157 Cours Liautaud (tel. 487021). Castellane.

Ariana, 12 rue du Théâtre Français (tel. 479164). Noailles or Reformes.

Caravelle, 5 rue Guy-Moquet (tel. 484499). Noailles.

Dijon, 33 Allées Léon Gambetta (tel. 626222). Reformes or Noailles.

Gambetta, 49 Allées Léon Gambetta (tel. 620788). Reformes or Noailles.

Moderne, 11 bd. de la Libération (tel. 622866). Reformes.

Pavillon, 27 rue Pavillon (tel. 337690). Vieux-Port.

Provençal, 32 rue Paradis (tel. 331115). Vieux-Port.

Quillici, 13 place des Marseillaises (tel. 901448). St-Charles. Main station.

Sphinx, 16 rue Sénac (tel. 487059). Reformes or Noailles.

Titanic, 27 rue Sénac (tel. 480156). Reformes or Noailles.

Athénée, 63 rue de la Palud (tel. 543674). Estrangin or N.D. du Mont.

Bearn, 63 rue Sylvabelle (tel. 377583). Estrangin.

Edmond Rostand, 31 rue Dragon (tel. 377495). Estrangin.

Impéria, 36 bd. Louis Salvator (tel. 486701). Estrangin or N.D. du Mont.

Montgrand, 50 rue Montgrand (tel. 333381). Pierre Puget.

If you are prepared to pay a bit more, the cheapest doubles at the two-star hotels below cost around 75–100FF (£7.50–10.00; $14.25–19.00; DM21.75–29.00) p.p.

Bellevue, 34 quai du Port (tel. 911164). By the Old Port. Vieux-Port.

Estérel, 124 rue Paradis (tel. 371390). Estrangin or Castellane.

Monthyon, 60 rue Montgrand (tel. 338555). Pierre Puget.

La Préfecture, 9 bd. Louis Salvator (tel. 543160). Estrangin or N.D. du Mont.

Ste-Anne, 23 rue Bretueil (tel. 331321). Vieux-Port.
Du Velay, 18 rue Berlioz (tel. 483137). Castellane.
Pharo, 71 bd. Charles Livon (tel. 310871).
Peron, 119 corniche Kennedy (tel. 310141).

YOUTH HOSTELS

Both the hostels are about four miles out from the city centre.

Marseille-Bois Luzy (FUAJ), Château de Bois Luzy, Allée des Primivères (tel. 490618). The smaller of the two hostels, with 90 beds in summer. Also has space for tents. Bus 8 from Bourse, near La Canabière.

Marseille-Bonneveine (FUAJ), 47 av. Joseph Vidal (Impasse de Bonfils), Bonneveine (tel. 732181). 185 beds. From St-Charles train station take the métro to RD-PT du Prado, then bus 44 dir. Roy d'Espagne to pl. Bonnefons.

CAMPING

Camping de Bonneveine, 187 av. Clot-Bey (tel. 732699). About four miles from the city centre. Metro and bus as for the Bonneveine hostel (see above). Ask the driver for the stop near the campsite.

Camping Municipal des Mazargues, 5 av. de-Lattre-de-Tassigny (tel. 400988).

Les Vagues (tel. 730488). A long way out of town.

See also the Bois Luzy hostel above.

Nice (tel. code (0)93)

HOTELS

Near to the station or the town centre:

Cheapest doubles 50–70FF (£5–7; $9.50–13.25; DM14.50–20.25) p.p.

Chauvain, 8 rue chauvain (tel. 853401).

Les Orangers, 10 bis av. Durante (tel. 875141). Closed
Nov.

Astrid, 26 rue Pertinax (tel. 621464). Closed Nov.

La Belle Meuniere, 21 av. Durante (tel. 886615). Closed
Jan.

Mme Garstandt, 55B rue Gambetta.

Ann Margaret, 1 av. St-Joseph (tel. 961570).

De Calais, 2 rue Chauvain (tel. 622244).

Commodore, 10 rue Barbéris (tel. 89084).

Les Mimosas, 26 rue de la Buffa (tel. 880559).

Lorrain, 6 rue Gubernatis (tel. 854290).

Mignon, 26 rue de la Buffa (tel. 880743).

Little Massena, 22 rue Massena (tel. 877234).

Interlaken, 26 av. Durante (tel. 883015).

Darcy, 28 rue d'Angleterre (tel. 886706).

Family, 34 bd Gambetta (tel. 885892).

De France, 24 bd Raimbaldi (tel. 851804).

Ideal Bristol, 22 rue Paganini (tel. 886072).

Ostend, 3 rue Alsace-Lorraine (tel. 887248).

Des Nations, 25 av. Durante (tel. 883058).

Normandie, 18 rue Paganini (tel. 884883).

Miron, 4 rue Miron (tel. 621660).

Du Centre, 2 rue de Suisse (tel. 888385).

Notre-Dame, 22 rue de Russie (tel. 887044).

Pastoral, 27 rue Assalit (tel. 851722).

Au Picardy, 10 bd Jean-Jaurès (tel. 857551).

Saint-François, 3 rue Saint-François (tel. 858869).

Regency, 2 rue Saint-Siagre (tel. 621744).

Place du Pin, 10 rue Bonaparte (tel. 564219).

Rex, 3 rue Massena (tel. 878738).

Rialto, 55 rue de la Buffa (tel. 881504).

Mono, 47 av. Thiers (tel. 887584).

Similar prices, less conveniently located:

Pension Scoffier, 256 bd. de la Madelaine (tel. 441471).

Astoria, 6 bd François Grosso (tel. 447410).

Lavalliere, 57 bd René Cassin (tel. 831869).

Porte-Bonheur, 146 av. St-Lambert (tel. 846610).
Reseda, 19 av. Audiffret (tel. 847915).
De la Victoire, 43 av. Jean Médecin (tel. 880205).
Soleil d'Or, 16 av. des Orangers (tel. 965594).

HOSTELS

Route Forestière du Mont Alban (FUAJ) (tel. 892364). On top of a hill about three miles from the station. Bus 14 from Alban Fort costs 8FF (£0.80; $1.50; DM2.25) per trip.

Cité Universitaire, Résidence 'Les Collinettes' (FUAJ), 3 avenue Robert Schumann (tel. 892364). Open from 3 July–29 Aug. Bus 17 dir. Parc Imperial.

Let's Go Meublés, 22 rue Pertinax 3rd floor and 26 bd. Raimbaldi (tel. 809800). Both hostels are near the station. Raimbaldi has a midnight curfew. Bring your own sheets or sleeping bag.

Meublé Abadie, 22 rue Pertinax 2nd floor (tel. 858121). Midnight curfew.

HOSTELS NEARBY

Plateau St Michel, Menton (tel. 93–359314). A short trip by train.

FOYERS

Bale des Anges, 55 chemin de St-Antoine (tel. 867674).
Jean Médecin, 25 Ancien Chemin de Lanterne (tel. 833461).
Montebello, 96 av. Valrose (tel. 841981).
Saint-Antoine, 69 chemin de St-Antoine (tel. 863719).
Forum Nice-Nord, 10 bd Comte de Falicon (tel. 842437).
Espace Magnan, 31 rue Louis de Coppet (tel. 862875).
De la Plaine (tel. 299004) and Des Bluets (tel. 299005). Both at 273 Route de Grenoble. (Men aged 18 and over only.)
'Les Sagnes', 59 bis Route de Grenoble (tel. 837628). (Men aged 18 and over.)

Riquier, 248 bd du Mont-Boron (tel. 554428). (Men 18 and over.)

Sonacotra, Quartier due Château a St Andre de Nice (tel. 548570).

UNIVERSITY ACCOMMODATION

Often available in summer. Details from CROUS, 18 av. de Fleurs (tel. 967373). At any time of year women can try calling 'Les Collinettes', 3 av. de Robert Schumann (tel. 970664).

CAMPING

No really convenient site in Nice. Camping Terry, 768 route de Grenoble St-Isidore (tel. 081158) is located four miles north of the airport, but has only 30 places. Those with a railcard would be better heading for one of the many sites in Villeneuve-Loubet, only five miles along the coast on the line to Cannes. The Tourist Information Centre at Nice station can give you a map of these sites, some of which are listed below. Open all year unless shown.

L'Orée de Vaugrenier, bd des Groules (tel. 335730). Open 15 Mar.–31 Oct.

La Vielle Ferme, bd des Groules (tel. 334144). Two sites: four star and one star.

De l'Hippodrome, 2 av. des Rives (tel. 200200).

L'Ensoleillado, 49 av. de l'Eglise Christophe (tel. 209004). Open 15 Feb.–15 Oct.

Neptune, av. des Baumettes (tel. 739381). Open 15 Mar.–15 Oct.

La Tour de la Madone, Route de Grasse (tel. 209611). Open 15 Mar.–31 Oct.

Paris (tel. code (0)1)

Your first consideration should be a room-finding service as this can save you time and money. The best rooms go early in the day, so get there early if you can.

Accueil des Jeunes en France (AJF). A tourist agency especially for young travellers, with no charge for booking hotel rooms or beds in hostels/foyers as AJF is run on a non-profit-making basis. Payment on booking is the norm. Various locations in the city. Normal office hours are Mon.–Fri. 9.30 a.m.–6.30/7.00 p.m.

Gare du Nord (tel. 42858619). In the arrival hall beside the Agences de Voyages SNCF. June–Sept. open Mon.–Sat. 8 a.m.–10 p.m. Métro: Gare du Nord.

119 rue St-Martin (tel. 42778780). Opposite the Pompidou Centre. Métro: Les Halles or Rambateau.

16 rue du Pont Louis Philippe (tel. 42780482). Métro: Hôtel-de-Ville or Pont Marie.

139 bd. St-Michel (tel. 43549586). Normal office hours. Open June and July only. Métro: Port Royal.

Accueil de France. Commission for one-star hotel rooms 15FF (£1.50; $2.75; DM4.25), for beds in hostels/ foyers 5FF (£0.50; $1; DM1.50).

Main office 127 av. des Champs-Elysées (tel. 47236172). Open daily 9 a.m.–8 p.m. Métro: Etoile.

Other offices at:

Gare du Nord (tel. 42858619).

Gare de l'Est (tel. 46071773).

Gare d'Austerlitz (tel. 45849170).

Gare de Lyon (tel. 43433324).

Eiffel Tower (open May–Sept. only) (tel. 45512215).

HOSTELS/FOYERS

Expect to pay 90–110FF (£9–11; $17–21; DM26–32) in most of these establishments.

Association des Etudiants Protestants de Paris (AEPP), 46 rue de Vaugirard (tel. 46332330/43543149). Cheaper singles, doubles and dorms than normal. Métro: Odéon. RER: Luxembourg.

Association des Foyers de Jeunes Filles, 234 rue de Tolbiac (tel. 45890642). Women only. Slightly cheaper than normal. Accept written reservations. Short stays allowed during July and August, at other times one-month minimum stay. Métro: Tolbiac.

Foyer Franco-Libannais, 15 rue d'Ulm (tel. 43294760). Cheaper than normal. Métro: Cardinal Lemoine. RER: Luxembourg.

Y & H Hostel, 80 rue Mouffetard (tel. 45350953). 1 a.m. curfew. Métro: Monge.

3 Ducks Hostel, 6 pl. E. Pernet (tel. 48420405). 1 a.m. curfew. Métro: Commerce.

Maison des Clubs UNESCO, 43 rue de Glacière (tel. 43360063). 1 a.m. curfew. Only groups can make reservations. Métro: Glacière.

Foyer International des Etudiantes, 93 bd. St-Michel (tel. 43544963). Women only Oct.–June, both sexes July–Sept. Best reserved in writing two months in advance. Métro: Luxembourg.

Hôtels de Jeunes (AJF), five locations in the city. No reservations:

Résidence Bastille, 151 av. Lédri Rollin (tel. 43795386). Slightly dearer than the other AJF foyers. Métro: Voltaire.

Le Fauconnier, 11 rue de Fauconnier (tel. 42742345). Métro: St-Paul or Pont Marie.

Le Fourcy, 6 rue de Fourcy (tel. 42742345). Métro: St-Paul.

Maubisson, 12 rue des Barres (tel. 42727209). Métro: Pont Marie.

Ask AJF for details of the Residence Luxembourg, open from July–Sept.

Centre International de Séjour de Paris (CISP). Two locations. Try to reserve at least two days in advance:

Kellerman, 17 bd Kellerman (tel. 45807076). Métro: Porte d'Italie.

Ravel, 6 av. Maurice Ravel (tel. 43431901). Métro: Porte de Vincennes.

Centre International de Paris (BVJ). Four locations. No reservations, so get there by 9 a.m. Three-day maximum stay at all but one of these foyers.

Quartier Latin, 44 rue des Bernardins (tel. 43293480). Most singles, no maximum stay. Métro: Maubert.

Louvre, 20 rue Jean-Jacques Rousseau (tel. 42368818). Métro: Louvre.

Les Halles, 5 rue du Pélican (tel. 40269245). Métro: Palais Royal.

Opéra, 11 rue Thérèse (tel. 42607723). Métro: Pyramides or Opéra.

CIS Léo Lagrange, 107 rue Martre Clichy (tel. 42700322). Métro: Mairie de Clichy.

Foyer International d'Accueil de Paris, 30 rue Cabanis (tel. 45898915). Métro: Glacière.

Reserve ahead for the following two FUAJ hostels, or arrive early. Bookings for a temporary FUAJ hostel in the university (open 1 July–19 Sept.) should be made through the 'Jules Ferry' hostel.

'Jules Ferry' (FUAJ), 8 bd Jules Ferry (tel. 43575560). 2 a.m. curfew. Métro: République.

'Le d'Artagnan' (FUAJ), 80 rue Vitruve (tel. 43610875). No curfew. Métro: Porte de Montreuil or Porte de Bagnolet.

The booking office for the six LFAJ hostels in the city is at 119 rue St-Martin (tel. 42727209). LFAJ also let space in *peniches* (houseboats) along the Seine.

In the suburbs are two hostels charging around 40FF (£4; $7.50; DM11.50) per night:

3 rue Marcel Duhamel (FUAJ), Arpajon (tel. 64902855). From Paris Austerlitz take the RER-C4 dir. Dourdan to Arpajon (free with railpasses). The hostel is 400m from the station. Also space for camping.

C.A.I. (LFAJ), 25 rue de 8 mai 1945, Acheres (tel. 39111497). RER from Paris St Lazare dir. Cergy-St Christophe to Acheres. The hostel is about half a mile from the station.

UNIVERSITY ACCOMMODATION

15 bd. Jourdain (tel. 45893579). Prices similar to foyers. Rooms available in summer, 7–10-day min. stay. Ask

in person at the secretariat, or reserve ahead by writing to: M. le Délégue Général de Cité Universitaire de Paris, 19 bd Jourdain, 75690 Paris, Cedex 14. Métro: Cité Universitaire.

CAMPING

Camping du Bois de Boulogne, allee du Bord de l'Eau (tel. 45243000). Fills fast in summer. Solo travellers around 60FF (£6; $11.50; DM17.50) per night. Métro: Port Maillot. Then bus 244, followed by a short walk.

B&Bs

Usually you have to write well in advance.

Cheapest singles 120–160FF (£12–16; $22.75–30.50; DM34.75–46.50), doubles 75–110FF (£7.50–11.00; $14.25–21.00; DM21.75–32.00).

Résidence St-Germain, 16 rue du Pour (tel. 43546061). Métro: St-Germain-des-Prés.

Paris Reveries Bed & Breakfast, 179 bd Voltaire. Accommodation available in houseboats and apartments.

B&B 1, 73 rue Notre Dame des Champs (tel. 43254397). Book in advance, or arrive early in the morning.

HOTELS

Cheapest doubles from 50–90FF (£5–9; $9.50–17.00; DM14.50–26.00) p.p.

Right Bank:

Chancelier Boucherat, 110 rue de Turenne (tel. 42728683). Métro: Filles-du-Calvaire.

Grand Hôtel Malher, 5 rue Malher (tel. 42726092). Métro: St Paul.

Moderne, 3 rue Caron (tel. 48879705). Métro: St-Paul.

Grand Hôtel des Arts-et-Métiers, 4 rue Borda (tel. 48877389). Métro: Arts-et-Métiers.

Loiret, 8 rue des Mauvais-Garcons (tel. 48877700). Métro: Hôtel de Ville.

Tiquetonne, 6 rue Tiquetonne (tel. 42369458). Métro: Etienne Marcel.

Rivoli, 2 rue des Mauvais-Garcons (tel. 42720841). Métro: Hôtel de Ville.

De Nice, 42 bis rue de Rivoli (tel. 42785529). Métro: Hôtel de Ville.

Ile de la Cité:

Henri IV, 25 pl. Dauphine (tel. 43544453). Métro: Pont-Neuf or Cité.

Left Bank:

Sorbonne, 6 rue Victor Cousin (tel. 43545808).

Notre Dame, 1 Quai St-Michel Métro: St-Michel.

Avenir, 52 rue Gay-Lussac (tel. 43547660). Métro/RER: Luxembourg.

Henri IV, 9 rue St-Jacques (tel. 43545143). Métro/RER: Luxembourg.

Dacia, 41 bd St-Michel (tel. 43543453). Métro: Odeon.

Du Commerce, 14 rue de la Montagne-Ste-Geneviève (tel. 43541466). Métro: Maubert.

Des Alliés, 20 rue Berthollet (tel. 43314752). Métro: Censier-Daubenton.

De Medicis, 214 rue St-Jacques (tel. 43295364/43541466). Métro/RER: Luxembourg.

Montparnasse:

Ouest, 27 rue Gergovie (tel. 45426499). Métro: Pernety or Place.

Plaisance, 53 rue Gergovie (tel. 45421139). Métro: Pernety.

Grand Hôtel Pasteur, 155 av. du Maine (tel. 45407068/ 45408636). Métro: Alésia.

St-Germain-Des-Pres:

Nesle, 7 rue de Nesle (tel. 43546241). Métro: Odéon.

Around Gare du Nord and Gare de l'Est

Kuntz, 2 rue des Deux Gares (tel. 40357726/40377529). Métro: Gare du Nord or Gare de l'Est.

De Nevers, 53 rue de Malte (tel. 47005618). Métro: République.

De l'Industrie, 2 rue Gustave Goublier (tel. 42085179). Métro: Strasbourg-St-Denis or Château d'Eau.

Marclau, 78 rue de Faubourg Poissonière (tel. 47707350). Métro: Poissonière.

Palace, 9 rue Bouchardon (tel. 40400945/40400946). Métro: Strasbourg-St-Denis.

Metropole Lafayette, 204 rue Lafayette (tel. 46077269). Métro: Louis Blanc.

Lafayette, 198 rue Lafayette (tel. 40357607). Métro: Louis Blanc.

Du Progrès, 7 rue Pierre Chausson (tel. 42081655). Métro: Jacques-Bonsergent.

Cheapest doubles around 90–120FF (£9–12; $17.00–22.75; DM26.00–34.75) p.p.

Left Bank:

Plaisant, 50 rue des Bernardins (tel. 43547457). Métro: Maubert.

Gay-Lussac, 29 rue Gay-Lussac (tel. 43542396). Métro/RER: Luxembourg.

Marignan, 13 rue de Sommerard (tel. 43546381). Métro: Maubert.

Oriental, 2 rue d'Arras (tel. 43543812). Métro: Cardinal Lemoine.

Le Home Latin, 15–17 rue Sommerard (tel. 43262521). Métro: St-Michel or Maubert.

De Nevers, 3 rue de l'Abbé-de-l'Epée (tel. 43268183). Métro/RER: Luxembourg.

Le Centrale, 6 rue Descartes (tel. 46335793). Métro: Maubert or Cardinal Lemoine.

Des Carmes, 5 rue des Carmes (tel. 43297840). Métro: Maubert.

St-Germain-des-Pres:

Stella, 41 rue Monsieur-le-Prince (tel. 43264349). Métro: Odeon.

St-Michel, 17 rue de Git-le-Coeur (tel. 43269870). Métro:
St-Michel.

Rheims (Reims) (tel. code (0)26)

HOTELS

Centrally located:

Cheapest doubles under 50FF (£5; $9.50; DM14.50) p.p.

Thillois, 17 rue de Thillois (tel. 406565).
Saint-André, 46 av. Jean Jaurès (tel. 472416).
Le Parisien, 3 rue Périn (tel. 473289). Closed Aug. and
Sun. 9 a.m.–8 p.m.
Linguet, 14 rue Linguet (tel. 473189). Closed Sun. 10 a.m.–
8 p.m.
Au Bon Accueil, 31 rue de Thillois (tel. 885574).

Cheapest doubles around 50–60FF (£5–6; $9.50–11.50; DM14.50–17.50) p.p.

Le Bourgeois, 5 pl. Léon Gambetta (tel. 474272). Closed
Aug. and Sun.
Saint-Maurice, 90 rue Gambetta (tel. 850910).
Porte-Paris, 39 rue de Colonel Fabien (tel. 087350).
Monopole, 28 pl. Drouet d'Erlon (tel. 471033).
Central, 16 rue des Telliers (tel. 473008). Closed Sun.
Arcades, 16 passage Subé (tel. 474239).
Alsace, 6 rue du Général Sarrail (tel. 474408).
Cecyl, 24 rue Buirette (tel. 475747).
Les Consuls, 7 rue de Général Sarrail (tel. 884610).
Victoria, 35 pl. Drouet d'Erlon (tel. 472179).
D'Anvers, 2 pl. de la République (tel. 402835).
Ardenn'Hotel, 6 rue Caqué (tel. 474238).
Azur, 9 rue des Ecrevées (tel. 474339).

Cheapest doubles 70–100FF (£7–10; $13.25–19.00; DM25–29.00) p.p.

Touring, 17ter bd du Général Leclerc (tel. 473815).
Gambetta, 13 rue Gambetta (tel. 474164).
Le Baron, 85 rue de Vesle (tel. 474624).

UNIVERSITY ACCOMMODATION

Available July and August.
> Contact CROUS, 34 bd Henri Vasnier (tel. 855016). Rooms
> are quite far from the centre.

YOUTH HOSTELS

> Centre International de Séjour et de Rencontres (FUAJ),
> 1 chaussée Bocquaine. Opposite parc Léo Lagrange
> (tel. 405260). Fifteen minutes' walk from the station.
> ALEJT, 66 rue de Courcelles (tel. 474652).
> Méridienne, 36 rue de la Cerisaie (tel. 856517). Closed
> Aug.

CAMPING

> Airotel de Campagne, avenue Hoche (Route de Châlons)
> (tel. 854122). Open 23 Mar.–30 Oct.

St Malo (tel. code (0)99)

Accommodation can be very difficult to find in July and
August, so reserve ahead if you can.

HOTELS

Near the station or the old town:

**Cheapest doubles 50–75FF (£5.00–7.50; $9.50–14.25;
DM14.50–21.75) p.p.**

> Le Tivoli, 61 chaussée du Sillon (tel. 561198).
> Hôtel de la Mer, 3 rue Dauphine (tel. 816105).

L'Auberge au Gai Bec, 4 rue des Lauriers (tel. 408216).
Le Vauban, 7 Boulevard de la République (tel. 560939).
Les Voyageurs, 2 Boulevard des Talards (tel. 563035).
Le Britannic, 1 av Louis Martin (tel. 563036).
L'Europe, 44 bd de la République (tel. 561342).
La Petite Vitesse, 42 bd de la République (tel. 563176).
Paris, 3 rue Alphonse Thébault (tel. 563144).
Suffren, 4 bd des Talards (tel. 563171).
L'Avenir, 31 bd de la Tour d'Auvergne (tel. 561333).
Le Neptune, 21 rue de l'Industrie (tel. 568215).

Cheapest doubles 75–100FF (£7.50–10.00; $14.25–19.00; DM21.75–29.00) p.p.

Le Terminus, 6 bd des Talards (faces the station) (tel. 561438).
Auberge de l'Hermine, 4 Place de l'Hermine (tel. 563132).
Armeric, 5 bd de la Tour d'Auvergne (tel. 405200).
L'Arrivée, 52 bd de la République (tel. 563078).
Le Bois Joli, 10 av de Marville (tel. 407700).

YOUTH HOSTEL

37 Avenue du Reverend-Pere-Umbricht (FUAJ) (tel. 402980). Fills quickly in summer.
Avenue de Moka (FUAJ) (tel. 563155). Open mid July to Aug. The annex of the main FUAJ hostel above. Roughly half the price.
L'Hermitage (LFAJ), 13 rue des Ecoles (tel. 562200).

CAMPING

La Cité d'Aleth (Municipal site), Cité d'Aleth (tel. 816091).
Les Nielles (Municipal), av. John Kennedy (tel. 402635).
Le Nicet (Municipal), av. de la Varde (tel. 402632).
Les Ilôts (Municipal), av. de la Guimorais (tel. 569872).
Camping de la Fontaine, rue de la Fontaine aux Pélerins (tel. 816262). Open 15 June–15 Sept. On the road to Mont St Michel.

Strasbourg (tel. code 088)

HOTELS

Cheapest doubles 50–70FF (£5–7; $9.50–13.25; DM14.50–20.25) p.p.

La Cruche d'Or, 6 rue des Tonneliers (tel. 321123).
Michelet, 48 rue du Vieux-Marché-aux-Poissons (tel. 324738).
Patricia, 1A rue des Puits (tel. 321460).
Weber, 22 bd de Nancy (tel. 323647). Turn left on leaving the station, along bd de Metz, to bd de Nancy.
Du Jura, 5 rue du Marché (tel. 321272).
De l'Ill, 8 rue des Bateliers (tel. 362001).

Cheapest doubles 70–100FF (£7–10; $13.25–19.00; DM20.25–29.00) p.p.

De l'Europe, 38 rue du Fossé des Tanneurs (tel. 321788).
Auberge du Grand Duc, 33 route de l'Hôpital (tel. 343176).
Couvent du Franciscain, 18 rue Faubourg de Pierre (tel. 329393).
Eden, 16 rue d'Obernai (tel. 324199).
Pax, 24–26 rue du Faubourg National (tel. 321454).
Kleber, 29 pl. Kleber (tel. 320953).
Carlton, 15 pl. de la Gare (tel. 326239).
In the suburb of Wolfisheim:
Hotel Henriette, 69 rue Leclerc (tel. 780384) charges around 80FF (£8; $15.25; DM23.25) for singles, 55FF (£5.50; $10.50; DM16) p.p. for doubles.

YOUTH HOSTELS

'René Cassin' (FUAJ), 9 rue de l'Auberge de Jeunesse (tel. 302646). Space for 60 tents. 1 a.m. curfew. Bus 3, 13, or 23 from Marché Ste-Marguerite. On foot 1½ miles. Leave the station, turn right. Along bd de Metz, de

Nancy, de Lyon. Right off de Lyon down rue de la Broque. Straight on under the motorway, along the cycle path through the park to the bridge. Up and over the bridge to the hostel.

Centre International de Rencontres du Parc du Rhin (FUAJ), rue des Cavaliers (tel. 601020). Bus 1, 11 or 21 from the station to Pont-du-Rhin. Nearest train station half a mile away is Kehl/Rhein in Germany.

Amitel Galaxie (LFAJ), 8 rue de Soleure (tel. 255891). 1½ miles from the train station. Bus 10 to place de Lattre, or bus 1, 11 or 21 to pl. Corbeau.

CIARUS, 7 rue Finkmatt (tel. 321212). Fifteen-minute walk from the station. Across pl. de la Gare, up rue du Maire Kuss. Do not cross the bridge. Follow the I11 to your left. Keep going until you see rue Finkmatt on your left.

Altrheinweg 11, Kehl/Rhein (tel. 19 49 7851–2330). An international call. Kehl is in Germany, although it is virtually a suburb of Strasbourg, frequently served by buses, and less frequently by trains (10-minute trip). Fine if you are stuck.

FOYERS

Du Jeune Travailleur, rue du Maçon (tel. 396901).
Du Jeune Ouvrier Chrétien, 6 rue de Bitche (tel. 351275).
De l'Ingenieur, 54 bd d'Anvers (tel. 615989).
De l'Etudiant Catholique, 17 pl. St-Etienne (tel. 353620).
De la Jeune Fille, 8 rue de Soleure (tel. 361528). Women only.

CAMPING

7 rue l'Auberge de Jeunesse (tel. 302646). Next to the 'Rene Cassin' hostel. For directions see above.

GERMANY

From the point of view of the budget traveller wanting to see the eastern part of the country, German reunification could not come quickly enough. Previously only those budget travellers who could supply an itinerary months in advance could hope to make a decent tour of the DDR. Even then they were paying handsomely for the privilege, with the cost of hostels and campsites vastly outstripping those of the bankrupt state's western neighbour. Some determined, relatively well-off travellers did travel to the DDR without advance bookings, merely taking whatever was available on arrival. This invariably meant spending several nights in the exorbitantly priced Interhotels (prices in 1989 started around DM120 (£40; $80) per person in singles or doubles). In the wake of reunification the bureaucratic and politically inspired restrictions on travel in the east of Germany have gone, and accommodation prices have fallen to below western levels. The two Youth Hostel Associations were amalgamated in 1991. Superficially, these developments imply a unity between the two parts of Germany as regards accommodation, but in truth, for several years at least, Germany will still be like two separate countries. Happily, the money available to be ploughed into tourism in the eastern part of Germany will ensure that the old DDR will have a tourist infrastructure comparable to Western Europe long before any of its former Soviet bloc partners.

At a first glance the impressive network of over 750 **IYHF hostels** created in 1991 by the fusion of West Germany's Deutsches Jugendherbergswerk (DJH) and the Jugendherbergsverband der DDR seems to suggest that the budget traveller need look no further for a cheap bed. It is certainly possible to see the country cheaply if you hostel, as there is one in virtually every town you would be likely to visit, even in a four-month trip. And as in other countries, hostelling is a good way to meet other travellers. One thing that should not deter you from hostelling in Germany is the image of German hostels as highly institutional and impersonal establishments, run by dour and officious staff. This is no more true than in most countries. Generally the staff are approachable, and happy to provide you with any information to help you enjoy your stay in town. However, there are some real drawbacks to hostelling as a means of visiting Germany.

German hostels are open to IYHF members only. In Bavaria there is a maximum age restriction of 26; elsewhere hostels are open to people of all ages. Curfews, which are rigorously enforced, are normally 10 p.m., except in the larger cities where hostels may stay open until midnight or 1 a.m. In either case, small town or large city, the curfew coincides with the time that the local nightlife starts to get going. The Association recommends that hostels should be reserved in advance at all times, but particularly between 15 June and 15 September (good advice, but not always possible to adhere to). Unless your reservation is for a longer period, you will be limited to a three-night stay, except where there is plenty of space at a hostel. If you have a reservation be sure to arrive before 6 p.m. unless you have notified the hostel that you will arrive later, otherwise your reservation will not be held, and your bed may be given to someone else. If you turn up without a reservation, priority is given to visitors aged up to 27 until 6 p.m. where beds are available. In theory this means anyone older is not assigned a bed until after 6 p.m. in case younger guests arrive. In practice this rule is often ignored. The association handbook states that no beds are let after 10 p.m., even in the city hostels which are open late. Again this is a rule that many wardens choose to ignore, so if you are stuck there is nothing to be lost by approaching city hostels after 10 p.m.

There are six types of hostel, at which prices vary

according to the standard of comfort, facilities available, location, and the time of the curfew. However, the main divide as regards price is between *jugendherberge* (youth hostel) and *jugendgästehaus* (youth guest house). Juniors (age 24 and under) normally pay between DM12–18 (£4.15–6.20; $7.75–11.75) in a jugendherberge, but in a jugendgästehaus prices range from DM22–28 (£7.60–9.65; $14.50–27.75). Seniors pay a surcharge of around DM4.50 (£1.50; $3) at all hostels. The overnight fee includes breakfast, but not bed linen, which you must hire if you do not have your own sheets or sleeping bag. The charge for sheets varies between the 15 regional hostel associations, but expect to pay at least DM4.50 (£1.50; $3) for the duration of your stay.

Jugendgästehäuser are expensive because they have been modernized in an effort to attract groups. This means that individual travellers are obliged to pay extra for leisure and recreation facilities that will rarely be available for their use. Groups can be a great source of annoyance to individual travellers. Hostels are frequently full of school and youth groups. This is especially true of hostels in the cities, along the Rhine and in the Black Forest, and in the more picturesque small towns; in short, all the places you are most likely to visit. The worst times are weekdays during the summer months, and weekends throughout the rest of the year. Space for individual travellers in hostels is often at a premium, and even by 9.30 a.m. you may be turned away. Even if you do squeeze into a hostel packed with groups it may be none too pleasant. As groups bring in a lot of money wardens tend to turn a blind eye to poorly controlled or noisy groups, no matter what the rules say. While the various problems discussed above relating to groups are by no means peculiar to Germany, the sheer number of groups you encounter here causes greater irritation than in most other countries.

As well as the IYHF hostels the western part of Germany has a network of hostels run by the 'Naturfreundhaus' organization (Friends of Nature Hostels). Most are located in the countryside just outside the towns. Accommodation is in singles, doubles, or small dorms, and prices are on a par with those of jugendgästehauser. Again you may have problems finding a bed because of groups; not of schoolchildren this time, but of middle-aged guests, with whom the hostels are very popular. Possibly the best advice is neither to avoid the hostels, nor to try and stay in them all of the time. Certainly in the east of Germany they are the cheapest widely available accommodation option. However, given that you may struggle to find a hostel bed, anyone travelling extensively in Germany would be well advised to take a tent, unless you can afford to pay upwards of DM25–30 (£8.60–10.35; $16.25–19.75) per person for a room in a hotel or pension. A tent will also stand you in good stead if you are unfortunate enough to arrive in town during one of the many trade fairs that take place in German cities throughout the year. At these times the cheaper hotels and pensions, and the youth hostels, fill rapidly, so unless you can camp you will most likely have to pay for an expensive hotel, sleep rough, or leave town. Like the hostels, Germany's campsites are great places to meet other travellers. They have always been cosmopolitan affairs, and this is likely to be even more the case as East Europeans begin to head west for holidays.

Camping is an excellent way to see the west of the country cheaply, without having to bother about restrictive curfews. Apart from a few towns (for example Heidelberg, where sites are inconveniently located), you will have little trouble getting back late by public transport, or on foot. The only problem is likely to be the occasional site that keeps your passport at the reception, so preventing you leaving before the office opens in the morning (usually 7.30–8.30 a.m.), but this applies to most hostels in any case. In the west of Germany there are around 2000 sites, covering all the main places of interest, and most towns and villages, even those with a minimal tourist trade. In any large city where there is a choice of sites with similar prices, railpass holders may save on transportation costs if there is a site located near a train station or a S-Bahn stop, as railpasses are often valid on city S-Bahn (but not U-Bahn) systems. Municipal sites are usually cheaper than those run by the Deutscher Camping-Club (DCC), but standards of amenities and cleanliness are normally very high, irrespective of who operates the site. Some DCC sites are quite exceptional. Charges are around DM3–5 (£1.00–1.75; $2.00–3.25) for a tent, DM4.50–7.00 (£1.50–2.40; $2.75–4.50) per person, which, considering the standard of the sites, represents excellent value for money.

While it is still worth taking a tent to the east of Germany, at present there is nowhere near the same density of sites as in the west. Even some of the major places of interest lack a campsite (for instance, Weimar, Erfurt and Stralsund), as do many of the more interesting small towns. Hopefully this will have changed significantly by 1993 as new sites are being opened. Prices are similar to those in the west, but standards tend to be lower. Sites in the east are also likely to be very crowded, a problem you will rarely encounter in the west. In part this is due to the shortage of sites, but it is also a result of the general shortage of rooms in the east.

Cheap hotels, *pensionen* and *gasthäuser* are widely available in the west of the country. There is also a fair supply of private rooms, found mainly in the smaller towns. During the summer many farms also let rooms. Prices in all these various types of accommodation start at around DM25–30 (£8.60–10.35; $16.25–19.75) p.p. In the east, cheap hotels, pensionen and gasthaüser are few and far between when compared to the west. Instead, **private rooms** are your main option in the east. The growth in the letting of private rooms since the practice was legalized in the DDR in 1990 has gone some way to easing the shortage of accommodation in the east. Expect to pay DM15–30 (£5.15–10.35; $9.75–19.75) per person for singles or doubles. Tourist Office accommodation services throughout Germany are usually more than willing to help you find a room in any of these categories. In the smaller towns it is feasible to look for rooms on your own. Simply make enquiries at hotels, or wherever you see a '*gasthof*' or '*zimmer*' sign.

With the possible exception of staunchly Roman Catholic rural Bavaria, unmarried couples are unlikely to face any difficulties as regards sharing a room.

In an effort to safeguard the environment **camping outside official sites** has been made illegal, but it is still possible to sleep rough, providing you obtain the permission of the landowner and/or the police. There is little point trying to sleep out in parks or town centres. Apart from this being dangerous in some cities, the police will send you on your way if they find you. Police attitudes to **sleeping in stations** vary from place to place. In some of the smaller towns and cities they will wake you to check if you have a valid rail ticket, and if you have they will then let you lie until around 6 a.m., but when they come back at that time be prepared to move sharpish. If you do not have a ticket you will be ejected from the station, and arrested if you return later. In Munich tolerance is shown (especially during the Oktoberfest) but do not expect a peaceful night before you are asked to move on in the morning. The stations of the northern ports and the central cities around Frankfurt are rough, and potentially dangerous at night. Do not consider sleeping in Leipzig Hauptbahnhof as the station has literally been taken over by gangs of young neo-fascists whom the Bahnpolizei (transport police) are powerless to confront due to lack of numbers.

Railpass holders can always take a **night train** if they are stuck for somewhere to sleep. Trains leave the main stations for a multitude of destinations, internal and international. In the central area around Mainz-Heidelberg-Mannheim-Würzburg-Nuremberg there are trains leaving at virtually all hours through the night. Alternatively there is the 'Bahnhofsmission', a church-run organization which operates in the stations of all reasonably sized towns in the west of the country (shelters will no doubt be opened in the east as well). They are meant for travellers who have no place to stay, or who are leaving early in the morning. If you approach the Bahnhofsmission during the day it is likely that you will be told to return before 8 p.m. This highly restrictive curfew helps prevent abuses of the system by those who are simply looking to fix themselves up with a cheap bed. You cannot stay more than one night in the shelter. B&B and use of the showers costs DM5–12 (£2.70–4.15; $5.25–7.75).

ADDRESSES

German YHA	Deutsches Jugendherbergswerk (DJH), Hauptverband, Bismarckstrasse 8, Postfach 1455, D–4930 Detmold (tel. 05231–7401, fax 05231–7401/7466).
Friends of Nature Hostels	Naturfreundejugend, Grossglockner Strasse 28, 7000 Stuttgart 60 (tel. 0711–481076).
Camping	Deutscher Camping-Club (DCC), Mandlestrasse 28, 8000 München 23 (tel. 089–334021). The DCC sell the official, comprehensive guide to Germany's campsites. Expect to pay around DM25 (£8.60; $16.50) for the guide. A considerably abridged list is available from the National Tourist Office, in London or your capital city.

Berlin (tel. code 030)

Finding a place to stay can be a problem, so it is advisable to reserve in advance. If possible, write at least one month before your date of arrival, making clear how much you are prepared to spend.

IYHF hostel reservations to:
   DJH Landesverband Berlin, Tempelhofer Ufer 32, 1000 Berlin 61 (tel. 2623024 fax 2629529).
   Other accommodation:
Verkehrsamt Berlin, Europa Center, D-1000 Berlin 30 (tel. 21234 fax 21232520).

Railpasses are not valid on the S-bahn. Consider buying one of the reasonably priced tickets valid on the whole transport system for a varying number of days.

HOTELS

Prices may vary according to season, and during trade fairs.

Cheapest doubles around DM27.50 (£9.50; $18) p.p.
Slightly cheaper prices in larger rooms where indicated.
Singles around DM35 (£12; $23) also indicated.

   Alcron, Lietzenburgerstrasse 76 (tel. 8834806). Singles and larger rooms. U-Bahn: Uhlandstrasse.
   Von Oertzen, address as above (tel. 8833964). Singles and larger rooms.
   Molthan, address as above (tel. 8814717). Singles and larger rooms.
   Iris, Uhlandstrasse 33 (tel. 8815770). Larger rooms. U-Bahn as above.
   Elton, Pariserstrasse 9 (tel. 8836155–56). Singles. With breakfast. U-Bahn: Spichernstrasse.
   Fischer, Nürnbergerstrasse (tel. 246808). Singles. U-Bahn: Nürnbergerstrasse. 20 minutes' walk from Bahnhof Zoologischer Garten. Main station and S-Bahn.

Am Lehniner Platz, Damaschkestrasse 4 (tel. 3234282).
Singles and larger rooms. With breakfast. S-Bahn:
Charlottenburg. U–Bahn: Adenauer Platz.
Centrumpension Berlin, Kantstrasse 31 (tel. 316153). Sin-
gles and larger rooms. S-Bahn: Savigny Platz.
Domino, Neue Kantstrasse 14 (tel. 3216906). Singles.
Prices apply Nov.-Mar. and July-Aug. only. S-Bahn:
Charlottenburg.

Out in the suburbs:
Pension Vera Steinert, Machnowerstrasse 13 (tel. 8156097).
Pension Haus Schliebner, Dannenwalder Weg 95&99 (tel.
4167997).

**Cheapest doubles around DM30–35 (£10.35–12.00;
$19.75–23.00) p.p. Cheaper prices in larger rooms
indicated, as are singles at the prices quoted above.**

Near the Charlottenburg S-Bahn stop:
Charlottenburger Hof, Stuttgarterplatz 14 (tel. 3244819).
Larger rooms.
Cortina, Kantstrasse 140 (tel. 3139059). Larger rooms.
Near Charlottenburg and Savigny Platz S-Bahn stops:
Niebuhr, Niebuhrstrasse 74 (tel. 3249595). Larger rooms.
Majesty, Mommsenstrasse 55 (tel. 3232061). Larger rooms.

Around the Savigny Platz S-Bahn stop:
Pariser Eck, Pariserstrasse 19 (tel. 8812145). With breakfast.
Astor, Grolmanstrasse 40 (tel. 8817087–88). Single. With
breakfast. Opposite the Uhlandstrasse U-Bahn stop.
De Luxe, Lietzenburgerstrasse 76 (tel. 8821828). Larger
rooms. U-Bahn Uhlandstrasse is closer.
München, Güntzelstrasse 62 (tel. 8542226).
Ten minutes' walk from Zoolögischer Garten and Savigny
Platz S-Bahn stops:
Bialas, Carmerstrasse 16 (tel. 3125025). With breakfast.
Alexis, Carmerstrasse 15 (tel. 3125144). With breakfast.

Fifteen minutes' walk from Zoolögischer Garten:
   Trautenau, Nürnbergerstrasse 14/15 (tel. 8613514). Singles.
      With breakfast. U-Bahn: Nürnbergerstrasse.
   Pension Zimmer des Westens, Tauentzienstrasse 5 (tel.
      2141130). U-Bahn: Nürnbergstrasse or Wittenbergplatz.

In the Kreuzberg area:
   Kreuzberg, Grossbeerenstrasse 64 (tel. 2511362). Singles
      and larger rooms. With breakfast.
   Sudwest, Yorckstrasse 80 (tel. 7858033). Singles.

In the suburbs:
   Wendenhof, Spreewaldplatz 8 (tel. 6127046).
   Wilhelmshöhe, Brandensteinweg 6 (tel. 3619094/3625711).
      With breakfast.
   Pension 22, Schambachweg 22 (tel. 3655230).

Cheapest doubles around DM38 (£13; $25) p.p.

Near Charlottenburg S-Bahn stop:
   Zumpe, Sybelstrasse 35 (tel. 3232067).
   Ursula, Sybelstrasse 63 (tel. 8826204).
Near Uhlandstrasse U–Bahn stop:
   Elfert, Knesebeckstrasse 13/14 (tel. 3121236).
   Knesebeck, Knesebeckstrasse 86 (tel. 317255).
   Zeinert, Meinekestrasse 5 (tel. 8813319).
   Witzleben, Meinekestrasse 6 (tel. 8816395).

B&B

Ask at the Tourist Office about B&Bs in East Berlin, where
a growth in this type of accommodation is making up for
the lack of cheap hotels and pensions in the eastern part of
the city.

STUDENT ROOMS

   Student Village Schlachtensee, Wasgenstrasse 75 (tel.
      801071). Students only. Outside term time there is a
      three-day max. stay. U2 to Krumme Lanke, then bus

3 dir. Potsdammer Chausee to Wasgenstrasse. First night DM18 (£9.50; $18), then DM12 (£4.20; $7.80). Good value, as all rooms are single.

Student Home Hubertusallee, Hubertusallee 61, at the corner of Delbruckstrasse (tel. 8919718). Bus 10 or 29. Open 1 Apr.–30 Sept.

B&B in singles DM54 (£18.60; $35.50), Students DM38 (£13.10; $25).

In doubles p.p. DM32 (£11; $21) Students DM22 (£7.60; $14.50)

In triples p.p. DM27 (£9.30; $17.75) Students DM20 (£6.90; $13)

IYHF HOSTELS

Members only; cards available from DJH, Tempelhofer Ufer 32. All the hostels charge Jugendgästehaus-type prices; juniors around DM23 (£8; $15), seniors DM27 (£9.30; $17.75).

'Ernst Reuter', Hermsdorfer Damm 48–50 (tel. 4041610). U6 to Tegel, then bus 15 dir. Frohnau to the fourth stop.

Jugendgästehaus, Kluckstrasse 3 (tel. 2611097). From Kurfurstendamm, bus 29. Oranienplatz or Hermannplatz to the hostel.

Jugendgästehaus Wannsee, Badeweg 1, at the corner of Kronprinzessinnenweg (tel. 8032034). S-3 to Nikolassee, then a 10-minute walk towards the beach.

The two hostels previously operated by the Jugendherbergsverband der DDR were both closed in 1991. Check with the IYHF handbook or the local Tourist Office to see if they have re-opened in 1992. The former Jugendtouristhotel 'Egon Schultz' was located at Franz-Mett-Strasse 7, near the Tierpark; it's a well-signposted 150m walk from the Tierpark U-Bahn stop. Given the shortage of beds in the city, the availability of its huge capacity (747 beds) would be most welcome. If this hostel has re-opened, expect it to be operating under another name. The smaller Grünau hostel (130 beds) was located at Dahmestrasse 6, in the Grünau district of the city.

HOSTELS

Jugendgästehaus am Zoo, Hardenbergerstrasse 9a (tel. 3129410). U-Bahn Ernst-Reuter-Platz, or a 20-minute walk from Zoolögischer Garten (main station and S-Bahn). Singles DM38 (£13.10; $25); doubles DM32.50 (£11.20; $21.25) p.p.; quads DM27 (£9.30; $17.75) p.p.

Studenthotel, Meiningerstrasse 10 (tel. 7846720). U-Bahn Rathaus Schoneberg or Bus 73 from Zoolögischer Garten to the same stop. B&B in doubles DM32 (£11; $21) p.p.; in quads DM30 (£10.35; $19.75) p.p.

INTERNATIONAL YOUTH CAMP

Waidmannsluster Damm, Ziekowstrasse (tel. 4338640). A similar idea to 'The Tent' in Munich; a large covered area, with mattresses and sheets provided. Three-day max. stay. About DM9 (£3.10; $6). U6 to Tegel, then bus 20.

CAMPING

Kladow I & II, Krampnitzer Weg 111/117 (tel. 3652797). Bus 35, then bus 35E. Open all year.

Haselhorst, Pulvermühlenweg (tel. 3345955). U-Bahn to Haselhorst, then along Daumster to Pulvermühlenweg. Open year round.

Dreilinden, Albrechts-Teerofen (tel. 8051201). Bus 18, then a 20-minute walk along Kremnitzufer to Albrechts-Teerofen. Open all year.

Kohlhasenbeück, Neue Kreise-Ecke Stuberrauchstrasse (tel. 8051737). Open Apr.-Sept.

Krossinsee (the former Intercamping site of East Berlin), Wernsdorfer Landstrasse (tel. 6858687). Tram 86 to the end of the line, then across the bridge and the third turning on the right. 1½-mile walk.

SLEEPING ROUGH

The Grünewald is the most obvious, but there are lots of places at the end of the S-Bahn lines, or along the shores of the Krossinsee.

If you are stuck for a bed, but do not want to sleep out, go to the Bahnhofsmission in Zoolögischer Garten station, where you will be given a bed for DM10 (£3.50; $6.50). One night only.

Cologne (Köln) (tel. code 0221)

HOTELS

Cheapest doubles around DM30 (£10.35; $15.75) p.p.

Schmidt, Elisenstrasse 16 (tel. 211706). Central.
Henn, Norbertstrasse 6 (tel. 134445). About five minutes' walk from the centre.
Friedrich, Domstrasse 23 (tel. 123303). Good location. Near the main train station and the centre.
Stern am Dom, Andreaskloster 10 (tel. 135462). Also located near both the train station and the town centre.
Strunder Hof, Sürther Hauptstrasse 59 (tel. 02236–62056). Far out in Sürth. Whether it is worth the journey depends on what else is available.
Rheinhotel St Martin, Frankenwerft 31–33 (tel. 234031–32). With shower/bath. Central.
Lindenhof, Lintgasse 7 (tel. 231242). Central.

Cheapest doubles DM32–35 (£11–12; $21.00–22.75) p.p.

Berg, Brandenburger Strasse 6 (tel. 121124). Central.
Flintsch, Moselstrasse 16–20 (tel. 232142). Just outside the Sudbahnhof (South station).

En Blomekörvge, Josephstrasse 15 (tel. 323660). Ten minutes' walk from the Sudbahnhof and the town centre.

Göbbels, Stammstrasse 2a (tel. 523414). With shower/bath. Ten minutes' walk from Ehrenfeld station.

Kirchner, Richard-Wagner-Strasse 18 (tel. 252977).

Hubertushof, Mühlenbach 30 (tel. 217386). Central.

Rossner, Jakordenstrasse 19 (tel. 122703). Central.

Jansen, Richard-Wagner-Strasse 18 (tel. 251875). Central.

Cheapest doubles around DM38 (£13; $25) p.p. Central unless indicated.

Dom, Domstrasse 28 (tel. 123742). Near the main train station and the centre.

Schmitze-Lang, Severinstrasse 62 (tel. 318129). Ten minutes from the centre in the southern part of the old town.

Einig, Johannisstrasse 71 (tel 122128/137158).

Brandenburger Hof, Brandenburger Strasse 2–4 (tel. 122889).

Stapelhäuschen, Fischmarkt 1–3 (tel. 212193/213043).

An der Oper, Auf der Ruhr 3 (tel. 245065).

Drei Könige, Marzellenstrasse 58–60 (tel. 132088).

Thielen & Tourist, Brandenburger Strasse 1–7 (tel. 123333/121492).

IYHF HOSTELS

Siegestrasse 5a (tel. 814711). Curfew 12.30 a.m. DM20 (£7; $13). Fills quickly. Reception opens 12.30 p.m. 150m from Köln-Deutz station. Well signposted. Frequent connections from the main train station by local train or S-Bahn (free with railpasses). Twenty minutes from town centre across the Deutzer Brücke.

Jugendegästehaus Köln-Riehl, An der Schanze 14 (tel. 767081). Phoning ahead will let you find out the situation as regards rooms, but no reservations are accepted. Reception opens at 11 a.m. Rooms go fast, so get there as soon as possible. DM28 (£9.65; $18.25). Two miles from the main train station. Down to the river, left, on under the Zoobrücke, along Niederlander Ufer into An der Schanze.

CAMPING

All the sites are quite a distance from the centre. If you take tram 16 to Marienburg there are two sites on the opposite side of the Rhine, about 15 minutes' walk over the Rodenkirchener Brücke in Köln-Poll.

Campingplatz der Stadt Köln, Weidenweg (tel. 831966). Open 1 May–10 Oct. Intended mainly for families, but you will not be turned away.

Alfred-Schütte-Allee (tel. 835989). Open 1 July–15 Sept. Site for young people.

Campingplatz Berger, Uferstrasse 53a is in Köln-Roden-kirchen (tel. 392421). Open year round.

Campingplatz Waldbad, Peter-Baum-Weg is in Köln-Dünnwald (tel. 603315). Open all year.

IYHF HOSTELS NEARBY

'Jugendhof', Macherscheiderstrasse 113 Neuss-Uedesheim (tel. 02101–39273). There are frequent connections between Cologne and Neuss by train and S-Bahn.

Dresden (tel. code 051)

HOTELS

Cheapest doubles around DM14 (£4.80; $9.25) p.p.

Pension Preusche, Wilhelm-Müller-Str. 19 (tel. 4328115). B&B.

Cheapest doubles around DM17 (£5.85; $11.25) p.p.

Pension Bück, Wachwitzer Höhenweg 28 (tel. 36336).

Cheapest singles and doubles around DM18 (£6.20; $11.75) p.p.

Fremdenheim Lössnitzer Hof, Wilhelm-Pieck-Str. 202, Radebeul (tel. 75353). On the outskirts of the city. Train to Radebeul. 5–10-minute trip.

Cheapest doubles around DM22 (£7.60; $14.50) p.p.

Pension Eggert, Wurgwitzer Str. 1b (tel. 4325241). Singles same price.
Pension Bellmann, Kretschmerstrasse 16 (tel. 38150).
Pension Magvas, Gondelweg 3 (tel. 2236084).
Pension Glück im Winkel, Hietzigstrasse 4 (tel. 37339). Singles are cheaper.
Pension Jarosch, Wilhelm-Müller-Str. 3 (tel. 4326790).

Cheapest singles and doubles around DM24 (£8.25; $15.75) p.p.

Hotel Stadt Rendsburg, Kamenzer Str. 1 (tel. 51551).

Cheapest doubles around DM28 (£9.65; $18.25) p.p.

Waldparkhotel, Prellerstrasse 16 (tel. 34441). B&B.
Parkhotel, Bautzner Landstrasse 17 (tel. 36851/36852). B&B.
Pension Deckwer, Rädestrasse 26 (tel. 4327192). Same price in singles. B&B.
Pension Eichlepp, Dr.-Rudolph-Friedrichs-Str. 15, Radebeul (tel. 78742). On the outskirts. Short train trip to Radebeul.

PRIVATE ROOMS

Dresden-Information, Prager Strasse 10/11 (tel. 4955025). A five-minute walk from Dresden Hauptbahnhof.

Singles DM15–30 (£5.20–10.35; $10.00–19.75). Doubles
DM15–35 (£5.20–12.00; $10–23) p.p. Larger rooms
DM20 (£6.90; $13) p.p.

IYHF HOSTELS

'Rudi Arndt', Hübnerstrasse 11 (tel. 470667). Tram line 3
to Sudvorstadt, the last stop. Walk down Juri-Gargarin-
Strasse from the station, right on to Reichenbach which
runs into Altenzellerstrasse, then on until you join
Hübnerstrasse. Not far to walk.
Oberloschwitz, Sierksstrasse 33 (tel. 36672). Tram 5 to
Nürnburger Platz, then bus 61 or 93 to the second
stop over the Elbe bridge, then a short walk.

IYHF HOSTELS NEARBY

'Wilhelm Dieckmann', Weintraubenstrasse 12, Radebeul
(tel. 74786). On the edge of the city. Short train trip to
Radebeul, then a 10-minute walk to the hostel.
Pirna-Copitz, Birkwitzer Strasse 51, Pirna (tel. 04–2388).
About 15 minutes' walk from the train station, bus L
dir. Sportplatz. Pirna is about 10 miles from Dresden.

CAMPING

Mockritz, Boderitzer Strasse 8 (tel. 478226). Also lets
two- to six-bedded bungalows. DM20 (£6.90; $13) p.p.
Am Bad Sonnenland, Reichenberg (tel. 75070).
There are several sites located in the woods to the north of
the city. About 15 minutes' walk from the last stop on bus
line 81.

Frankfurt-am-Main (tel. code 069)

HOTELS

Cheapest doubles around DM24 (£8.25; $15.75) p.p.

Backer, Mendelssohnstrasse 92 (tel. 747992). Fifteen minutes from the main train station (Hbf)

Cheapest doubles around DM28 (£9.65; $18.25) p.p.

Haussecker, Frankenallee 3 (tel. 235408). Five minutes from the Hbf.

Cheapest doubles around DM32.50 (£11.20; $21.25) p.p.

Goldener Stern, Karlsruher Strasse 8 (tel. 233309). Five minutes from Hbf.

Lohmann, Stuttgarter Strasse 31 (tel. 232534). Five minutes from Hbf.

Am Schloss, Bolongarostrasse 168 (tel. 301849). Further out, in the area between the Nied and Höchst S-Bahn stops (S-Bahn free with railpasses).

Cheapest doubles DM35.00–37.50 (£12–13; $22.75–24.75) p.p.

Atlas, Zimmerweg 1 (tel. 723946). S-Bahn: Taunusanlage. Within walking distance of the Hbf. and the town centre.

Bruns, Mendelssohnstrasse 42 (tel. 748896). Fifteen minutes from the Hbf.

Ilona, Mainzer Landstrasse 123 (tel. 236204). Five–ten minutes from the Hbf.

Doubles around DM40 (£13.75; $26.25) p.p.

Brukner, Stuttgarter Strasse 9 (tel. 253545). Five minutes from the Hbf.

Am Anlagenring, Escenheimer Anlage 23 (tel. 590768).
Five minutes from the town centre. S-Bahn: Kon-
stablerwache.

Vera, Mainzer Landstrasse 118 (tel. 745023). Five–ten
minutes from the Hbf.

Tourist, Baseler Strasse 23–25 (tel. 233095). Follow the
main road in front of the Hbf. to the right. Five
minutes' walk.

IYHF HOSTEL

'Haus der Jugend', Deutscherrnufer 12 (tel. 619058). Midnight curfew. During the morning and evening rush
hours bus 46 from the station is your best bet. The
Frankensteinerplatz stop is only 50m from the hostel.
After 7.30 p.m. take tram 16 to Textorstrasse, again
leaving you a short walk.

IYHF HOSTELS NEARBY

Beckerstrasse 47, Aschaffenburg (tel. 06021–92763). Trains
hourly (at least), 45-minute journey.

Schützengraben 5, Gelnhausen (tel. 06051–4424). Hourly
trains, 40-minute trip.

Blücherstrasse 66, Wiesbaden (tel. 06121–48657/449081).
Forty-five-minute trip by S–14 or regular train, every
20–30 minutes.

CAMPING

Niederrad, Niederräder Ufer 20 (tel. 673846). Tram 15 or
a 20-minute walk from the station.

An der Sandelmühle 35 (tel. 570332).

Freiburg-im-Breisgau (tel. code 0761)

Many of the cheapest places to stay are a fair distance from the centre, including the hostel and the campsites. To cut transport costs ask at the Tourist Office about their 24-, 48- and 72-hour tickets. The 24-hour ticket costs only slightly more than the cost of two journeys.

HOTELS

Near the station or the town centre:

Cheapest doubles around DM33 (£11.40; $21.75) p.p.

Roseneck, Urachstrasse 1 (tel. 72954). Ten minutes from the old town.

Schemmer, Eschholzstrasse 63 (tel. 272424). Five minutes from the station.

Cheapest doubles around DM36 (£12.40; $23.50) p.p.

Stadt Wien, Habsburgerstrasse 48, (tel. 36560/39898). Fifteen minutes from the old town.

Alleehaus, Marienstrasse 7 (tel. 34892/33652). Five–ten minutes from the centre of the old town.

Gihring, Eggstrasse 10 (tel. 74963). Ten minutes from the centre.

PRIVATE ROOMS

Cheapest doubles around DM18.50 (£6.40; $12.25) p.p. Singles DM25 (£8.60; $16.50)

Ehret, Mozartstrasse 48 (tel. 33387). Near the station.

Cheapest doubles around DM21 (£7.25; $13.75) p.p.

Tritschler, Ziegelhofstrasse 40 (tel. 86077). Singles half the price of doubles. Two miles from the station.

Burger, Waldallee 14 (tel. 84357). Singles half the price of doubles. Non-smokers only. About two miles from the station.

Sumser, Neuhäuser Strasse 2 (tel. 63623). With showers. Far out from the centre.

Cheapest doubles around DM23.50 (£8.10; $15.50) p.p.

Brüstle, Kleintal Strasse 62 (tel. 63021). With showers. Far out from the centre.

Faubert, Häherweg 25 (tel. 131651). With showers. About two miles from the station.

Idhe, Marchstrasse 5 (tel. 273421). With showers. Non-smokers only. Ten–fifteen minutes from the centre.

Cheapest doubles around DM26 (£9; $17) p.p.

Busse, Waldseestrasse 77 (tel. 72938). Non-smokers only. Fifteen–twenty minutes from the centre.

Cheapest doubles around DM27.50 (£9.50; $18) p.p.

Bernard, Erlenweg 7 (tel. 494862). Near the station and the town centre.

IYHF HOSTEL

Kartäuserstrasse 151 (tel. 67656). Curfew 11.30 p.m. Far from the centre. Tram 1 dir. Littenweiler from the station to Römerhof. Along Fritz-Geiges-Strasse, over the water, then right.

UNIVERSITY ACCOMMODATION

Enquiries regarding the availability of rooms during the university vacation to Studentenhaus 'Alte Universität', Wohrraumabteilung, Bertoldstrasse 12, 7800 Freiburg (tel. 2101272).

CAMPING

Hirzberg, Kartäuserstrasse 99 (tel. 35054). Open 1 Apr.–
15 Oct. Tram 1 from the station dir. Littenweiler to
Messeplatz. Twenty minutes' walk from the centre
of the old town. Cheapest site in town, and the best
location.

Mösle-Park (tel. 72938). Open 20 Mar.–31 Oct. Near
the FFC stadium. Tram 1 dir. Littenweiler. Twenty
minutes' walk from the town centre.

St Georg, Basler Landstrasse 62 (tel. 43183). Open year
round.

Breisgau, Freiburg-Hochdorf (tel. 07665–2346). Open all
year.

Tunisee, Freiburg–Hochdorf (tel. 07665–2249/1249). Open
1 Apr.–31 Oct.

IYHF HOSTELS NEARBY

Rheinuferstrasse 12, Breisach-am-Rhein (tel. 07667–7665).
Opened in 1990. Breisach is a beautiful small town
about 12½ miles from Freiburg. Trains and German
railway buses hourly.

Hamburg (tel. code 040)

HOTELS

Prices are high: expect to pay from DM35–40 (£12.00–13.80;
$22.75–26.25) p.p. for doubles. The Tourist Office sell the
guide 'Hotelführer' (DMO.50; £0.20; $0.35) which has details
of the city's hostels and pensions. Some of the cheapest
places in town are near Hamburg Hauptbahnhof, along
Bremer Weg, Bremer Reihe and Steindamm (although some
are used by prostitutes).

Cheapest doubles around DM35 (£12; $22.75) p.p.

Hotel-Pension Terminus, Steindamm 5 (tel. 2803144). Slightly cheaper in triples and quads.

Hotel-Pension Nord, Bremer Reihe 22 (tel. 244693). Triples slightly cheaper. Breakfast included.

Cheapest doubles DM40–45 (£13.80–15.50; $26.25–29.50) p.p.

Bei der Esplanade, Colonnaden 45 (2nd storey) (tel. 342961).

Alameda, Colonnaden 45 (tel. 344290).

Steen's Hotel, Holzdamm 43 (tel. 244642). Near Hamburg Hauptbahnhof.

IYHF HOSTELS

'Auf dem Stintfang', Alfred-Wegener-Weg 5 (tel. 313488). Curfew 1 a.m. From the Hauptbahnhof take S1, S2, S3 (S-Bahn free with railpasses) or the U3 to Landungsbrücke. The hostel is on top of the hill.

Jugendgästehaus 'Horner-Rennbahn', Rennbahnstrasse 100 (tel. 6511671). Open Mar.–Dec. Curfew 1 a.m. Quite far out. U3 to Horner-Rennbahn, then a 10-minute walk. Alternatively take the Wandsbek bus from the centre.

HOSTELS

Kolpinghaus St Georg, Schmilinskystrasse 78 (tel. 246609). Reception open round the clock. Singles around DM38 (£13; $25), doubles DM27.50–35.00 (£9.50–12.00; $18.00–22.75) p.p., triples DM30 (£10.35; $19.75) p.p.

Jugendhotel MUI, Budapester Strasse 45 (tel. 431169). Singles around DM45 (£15.50; $29.50), doubles from DM32–45 (£11.00–15.50; $21.00–29.50) p.p., larger rooms around DM27 (£9.30; $17.75).

CAMPING

Buchholz, Kielerstrasse 374 (tel. 5404532). S3 dir. Pinneberg, or S21 dir. Elbgaustrasse to the Stellingren station. The best of the city's campsites. Phone ahead to see if they have space.

IYHF HOSTELS NEARBY

Soltauerstrasse 133, Luneberg (tel. 04131–41864). The beautiful town of Luneberg is about 30 miles from Hamburg. Frequent trains. About 45 minutes from Hamburg Hbf.

Konrad-Adenauer-Ring 2, Bad Oldesloe (tel. 04531–504294). Trains at least twice hourly, 25–45-minute trip depending on classification of train.

Hannover (tel. code 0511)

An expensive city to stay in as accommodation prices are inflated by the large number of trade fairs the city plays host to. If possible, try not to arrive during a fair, as finding rooms becomes very difficult. Dates of the fairs are available from the National Tourist Office, in London or your capital city, or Tourist Offices in Germany.

HOTELS

The hotels listed below are all within two miles of the station (except where noted). Prices for the cheapest singles in these hotels are only slightly above the cost per person in the cheapest doubles, while the cost per person in the cheapest triples is about 15–20 per cent lower.

Cheapest doubles around DM37 (£12.75; $24.25) p.p.

Haus Tanneneck, Brehmstrasse 80 (tel. 818650).

Cheapest doubles around DM42.50 (£14.75; $27.75) p.p.

Flora, Heinrichstrasse 36 (tel. 342334). Triples also.

Cheapest doubles around DM45–50 (£15.50–17.25; $29.50–32.75) p.p.

Hospiz am Bahnhof, Joachimstr. 2 (tel. 324297).
Nordstadter Hof, Gustav-Adolf-Str. 6 (tel. 327585).
  Triples.
Eden, Waldhausenstr. 30 (tel. 830430). Triples.
Gildehof, Joachimstrasse 6 (tel. 363680/363691–92). Triples.
Elisabetha, Hindenburgstr. 16 (tel. 816096–97). Triples.
Schwab, Sedanstr. 20 (tel. 345569). Triples.
Westfalia, Eichstr. 35 (tel. 342692).
Similarly priced to the hotels immediately above, but another
mile or so further out:
Lindenhof, An der Feldmark 5 (tel. 462691).
Eilenriede, Guerickstr. 32 (tel. 5476652). Triples.

IYHF HOSTEL

Ferdinand-Wilhelm-Fricke-Weg 1 (tel. 322941). Twenty
  minutes' walk from the station, or Stadtbahn U3 or
  U7 direction Mühlenberg to Fischerhof. Normal hostel
  prices. A more expensive Jugendgästehaus operates at
  the same location.

HOSTELS

Naturfreundhaus in der Eilenriede, Hermann-Bahlsen-
  Allee 8 (tel. 691493). Listed in the IYHF handbook,
  but a Naturfreundhaus establishment, with discounts
  for Naturfreundhaus members. Normal prices similar
  to those of a Jugendgästehaus. Stadtbahn U3 dir. Lahe
  or U7 dir. Fasanenkrug to Spannhagengarten, or a
  30-minute walk from the station.

IYHF HOSTELS NEARBY

Weghausstrasse 2, Celle (tel. 05141–53208). At least two trains each hour, 20 minutes by express train, 30–45 minutes by local train.

Fischbeckerstrasse 33, Hameln (of Pied Piper fame) (tel. 05151–3425). Hourly trains, 45–minute trip.

Schirrmannweg 4, Hildesheim (tel. 05121–42717). Trains at least once an hour, 25-minute trip by local train.

CAMPING

Birkensee, Hannover-Laatzen (tel. 529962). Laatzen is a 10-minute journey from Hannover Hbf. Frequent local trains.

Heidelberg (tel. code 06221)

Finding suitable accommodation can be difficult in this city because it is especially popular with older, more affluent tourists. Consequently hotel prices are relatively high as the hotels are guaranteed a steady trade. Heidelberg is also very popular with young travellers, so you cannot always count on getting a room in the hostel, even with its 451 beds. Even camping is not without its problems: the two sites are about five miles out of town, and although there is a train station nearby, the service is so infrequent that you will almost certainly have to travel by bus, adding to the cost of an overnight stay at either of the sites.

HOTELS

Jeske, Mittelbadgasse 2 (tel. 23733). Two- to five-bedded rooms, DM21 (£7.25; $13.75) p.p. Centre of the old town. From the station bus 33 to Kornmarkt.

Cheapest doubles DM23 (£8; $15) p.p. with breakfast.

Sonne, Schmitthennerstrasse 1 (tel. 72162). Bus 42 to
Fritz-Albert-Strasse from the town centre. About 15–20-
minute trip.

**Cheapest doubles DM27–30 (£9.30–10.35; $17.75–19.75)
p.p.**

Zum Weinberg, Heiliggeiststrasse 1 (tel. 21792). Right in
the heart of the old town, near the town hall and the
Church of the Holy Ghost. Bus 33 to Kornmarkt from
the train station.

**Cheapest doubles DM35–40 (£12.00–13.75; $22.75–26.25)
p.p.**

Auerstein, Dossenheimer Landstrasse 82 (tel. 480798).
Quite a distance from the town centre.

Brandstätter, Friedrich-Ebert-Anlage 60 (tel. 23944). Ten
minutes from the old town.

Goldenes Lamm, Pfarrgasse 3 (tel. 480834). Far from the
centre.

Elite, Bunsenstrasse 15 (tel. 25734). Ten minutes from the
station.

Deuser-Cop, Zähringer Strasse 32 (tel. 22694). Five–ten
minutes from the station.

Deutscher Kaiser, Mühltalstrasse 41 (tel. 401537). Far out
from the centre.

IYHF HOSTEL

Tiergartenstrasse 5 (tel. 412066). 2½ miles from the train
station. Bus 11 from the station, or Bismarckplatz
(between the station and the old town). Also bus 12,
33 or 330. After 8 p.m. tram 1 to Chirugische Klinik,
then the bus to the first stop after the zoo.

DORMS

Hotel Krokodil, Kleinschmidtstrasse 12 (tel. 24059). The hotel rooms are more expensive than those listed above, but there are dorms available for DM20 (£6.90; $13). About 5–10 minutes from the station.

IYHF HOSTELS NEARBY

'Lindenhof', Rheinpromenade 21, Mannheim (tel. 0621–822718). In many ways the best hostel option for anyone with a railpass. Set on the banks of the Rhine, the Mannheim hostel is both cheaper and more pleasant to stay in than the Heidelberg hostel. Midnight curfew. Ten–fifteen minutes' walk from Mannheim Hbf (main station). Train journey from Heidelberg around 12–20 minutes.

CAMPING

Haide (tel. 06223–2111). Located between Ziegelhausen and Kleingemünd. Bus 35 to the Orthopedic Clinic in Schlierbach-Ziegelhausen, about five miles out of town. The site is across the Neckar. Popular with groups on camping holidays.

Neckartal (tel. 06221–802506). Same bus as above. The site is near the clinic. More basic than the site across the river, but perfectly adequate. Tends to be free of the groups. Passports held at reception, which means you cannot leave before the office opens at 8 a.m.

CAMPING NEARBY

'Strandbad', Karin Ebner, Mannheim-Neckarau (tel. 0621–856240). Probably the best site if you have a railpass. The site is close to Mannheim-Neckarau station. Frequent trains from Mannheim Hbf. Last train around 11.45 p.m. except Sat. and Sun. night. Also local buses. About two miles from Mannheim

Hbf, so you will pay less travelling by bus to this site than those above. If you stay late in Heidelberg there are trains to Mannheim Hbf at 11.49 p.m., 1.20 a.m. and various trains between 2–3 a.m. (check times locally).

Kiel (tel. code 0431)

HOTELS

Cheapest singles and doubles around DM20 (£7; $13.25) p.p.

Friesenhof, Kaiserstrasse 63a (tel. 731789). In Kiel-Gaarden, about 20 minutes' walk from the train station.

Cheapest doubles around DM29 (£10; $19) p.p.

Krauthammer, Grabastrasse 73 (tel. 722810). In Kiel-Ellerbek, about two miles from the train station.

Cheapest doubles around DM33–38; £11.40–13.10; $21.75–25.00. All within two miles of the station.

Hotel Runge, Elisabethstr. 16 (tel. 731992). In Kiel-Gaarden.

Holsteiner Hof, Johannesstr. 38 (tel. 731923). In Kiel-Gaarden.

Motel Karlstal, Karlstal 18–20 (tel. 731690). In Kiel-Gaarden.

Hotel Schweriner Hof, Königsweg 13 (tel. 61416/62678). About 250m from the station.

Hotel Angler-Hof, Knooper Weg 96 (tel. 554839).

Hagemann, Hasseer Strasse 52–54 (tel. 681525). In Kiel-Hassee.

Similarly priced but further out:

Rendsburger Hof, Rendsburger Landstrasse 363 (tel. 69131). In Kiel-Russee.

Central Hotel Wick, Preetzer Ch. 123–125 (tel. 783246). In Kiel-Elmschenhagen.

Hotel-Pension Petra, Gravensteiner Strasse 4 (tel. 362100). In Kiel-Holtenau.

Margaretenhöh, Kirchberg 14 (Strohredder) (tel. 202725). In Kiel-Dietrichsdorf.

Dietrichsdorfer Hof, Heikendorfer Weg 54 (tel. 26108). In Kiel-Dietrichsdorf.

IYHF HOSTEL

Johannesstrasse 1 (tel. 731488). About 1½ miles from the station in Kiel-Gaarden.

IYHF HOSTEL NEARBY

'Haus der Jugend', Franz-Rohwer-Strasse 10, Neumünster (tel. 04321–403416). Hourly trains, 20-minute journey.

CAMPING

Kiel-Falkenstein/Ostsee, Palisadenweg 171 (tel. 392078).

Leipzig (tel. code 041)

While not wishing to be alarmist, it must be pointed out that Leipzig station, at least in 1991, was a dangerous place. The station serves as a meeting point for gangs of neo-Nazi youths, who make money from pickpocketing and petty theft. However, they have been involved in more violent incidents; notably throwing Molotov cocktails at some of the city's squatters, and the riot after a football match which ended with the police firing on the hooligans. If anything untoward happens you cannot rely on the transport police to intervene, as they are far too short of manpower to risk a confrontation with the gangs, and consequently tend simply to look the other way.

HOTELS

Haus Ingeborg Hotel, Nordstrasse 58 (tel. 294816). DM30 (£10.35; $19.75) p.p. Close to the Interhotel Merkur. From the train station head right; Nordstrasse is to the right off Tröndlin-Ring. Five-minute walk.

Pension am Zoo, Dr.-Kurt-Fischer-Strasse 23 (tel. 291838). DM25 (£8.60; $16.50) p.p. Tram 20 from the station or a 10-minute walk. Right along Trönglin-Ring, then right. Near Leipzig Zoo.

Oehmigen, Kreuzstrasse 3B (tel. 281218). About 5–10 minutes' walk from the station. Left out of the square in front of the station along Wintergartenstrasse, first right, then on down Querstrasse, left along Dörrienstrasse to its end. Kreuzstrasse is opposite, just to the left.

Dymke, Gellertstrasse 9 (tel. 200939). Same directions as Oehmigen, but turn right off Querstrasse. Ten-minute walk.

Hillemann, Rosa-Luxemburg-Strasse 2 (tel. 282482). From the square in front of the station go left along Wintergartenstrasse until it joins Rosa-Luxemburg-Strasse. Ten-minute walk from the train station, or tram 2, 27 or 57.

Heidenreich, Hainstrasse 10 (tel. 298839).

PRIVATE ROOMS

Zimmernachweis des Reisebüros Hauptbahnhof Ostseite, Platz der Republik (tel. 7921297). On the eastern side of the main train station.

Zimmernachweis Leipzig-Information, Sachsenplatz 1 (tel. 79590). Five minutes' walk from the station.

IYHF HOSTELS

Käthe-Kollwitz-Strasse 62–66 (tel. 475888/470530). Tram 2 from right in front of the Hauptbahnhof, tram 1 stops at the far right-hand side of the station as you leave. A

10–15-minute walk. Left along Tröndlin-Ring. Follow the road round to the left at Engels Platz, then right on down Kollwitz-Strasse at the next main junction.

Am Anensee, Gustav-Esche-Strasse 4 (tel. 57189). Five miles from the town centre, but only about 10 minutes' walk from the Wahren station (S-Bahn). Tram 10, 11 or 28 from the Hauptbahnhof.

IYHF HOSTELS NEARBY

'Halle', August-Bebel-Strasse 48a, Halle (tel. 046–24716). Halle is an interesting city about 22 miles from Leipzig. The two cities are linked by frequent trains.

CAMPING

Am Anensee, Gustav-Esche-Strasse. Same directions as the IYHF hostel of the same name. A little further on down the street.

Lübeck (tel. code 0451)

HOTELS

Cheapest doubles around DM30–35 (£10.30–12.00; $19.75–23.00) p.p.

Banhofs-Hotel, Am Bahnhof 21 (tel. 83883). Opposite the station.

Pension am Park, Hüxtertorallee 57 (tel. 797598). Just outside the old town.

Hotel Stadtpark, Roeckstrasse 9 (tel. 34555). Just outside the old town.

Marienburg Hotel Garni, Katharinenstr. 41 (tel. 42512). Ten minutes from the station and the old town.

Gästehaus Lentz, An der Untertrave (tel. 71045). Good location on the harbour of the old town.

Pension Koglin, Kottwitzstr. 39 (tel. 622432/823733). Twenty minutes' walk from the old town.

Cheapest doubles DM35–40 (£12.00–13.75; $23.00–26.25) p.p.

Hotel Victoria, Am Bahnhof 17/19 (tel. 81144–46). Opposite the station.

Hotel Wakenitzblick, Augustenstrasse 30, An der Moltke-brücke (tel. 791792/791796). Ten minutes' walk from the old town.

Hotel Hanseatic, Hansestrasse 19 (tel. 83328–30). A few minutes' walk from the station.

'Zur Bergtreppe', Hinter der Burg 15 (corner of Kl. Burgstrasse) (tel. 73479). Close to the centre of the old town.

Hotel Petersen, Hansestrasse 11a (tel. 84519). A couple of minutes from the station.

Hotel Lübscher Adler, Koberg 4 (tel. 74274). In the centre of the old town.

PRIVATE ROOMS

Cheapest doubles DM27.50–32.50 (£9.50–11.25; $18.00–21.25) p.p.

Frau Schräger, Ginsterweg 5 (tel. 891407).
Familie Nickel, Kahlhorststr. 1a (tel. 593139).
Frau Reimer, Vermehrenring 11e (tel. 65596).

IYHF HOSTEL

'Folke-Bernadotte-Haus, Am Gertrudenkirchhof 4 (tel. 33433). Roughly two miles from the station. Bus 1, 3 or 12 to Burgfeld.

HOSTELS

Sleep-In (YMCA), Gross Petersgrube 11 (tel. 78982). In an 800-year-old house in one of the most beautiful streets in the town. Cheaper than the IYHF hostel, and a later curfew (midnight). Open to men and women.

CAMPING

Steinrader Damm 12, Lübeck-Schönböcken (tel. 893090/ 892287). Open 1 Apr.–31 Oct. From the centre of town only a 10-minute trip on bus 7 or 8 dir. Dornbreite. Both stop near the entrance to the site.

Meissen (tel. code 053)

As Meissen is only about 15 miles from Dresden, it is possible to visit the town while staying in Dresden.

HOTELS

Hamburger Hof, Dresdner Strasse 9 (tel. 2118). Singles DM27–37 (£9.30–12.75; $17.75–24.25); doubles DM23–30 (£8.00–10.35; $15.00–19.75) p.p.; triples DM27–30 (£9.30– 10.35; $17.75–19.75) p.p.

Goldener Löwe, Heinrichsplatz 6 (tel. 3304). Singles DM42 (£14.50; $27.50); doubles DM35–50 (£12.00–17.25; $23.00– 32.75) p.p.; quads DM35 (£12; $23) p.p. Overnight price includes breakfast.

Mitropa, Grossenhaimer Strasse 2 (tel. 3320). Singles around DM45 (£15.50; $29.50); doubles around DM37 (£12.75; $24.25) p.p.; triples around DM35 (£12; $23) p.p.

PRIVATE ROOMS

Book through Meissen Information, An der Frauenkirche 3 (tel. 4470). B&B from DM15–30 (£5.15–10.35; $9.75–19.50) p.p. Also let apartments DM60–90 (£20.70–31.00; $39.25– 59.00) per night.

IYHF HOSTEL

The 'John Scherr' YH at Wilsdruffer Strasse 28 was closed in 1991. Check with Meissen Information or the IYHF handbook to see if it has re-opened in 1992.

IYHF HOSTEL NEARBY

'Coswig', Elbstrasse 16, Coswig (tel. 2390). A 20-minute walk from Coswig train station. The town is about five miles from Meissen on the line to Dresden.

CAMPING

Campingplatz Scharfenberg (tel. 2680). By the Elbe, in the direction of Dresden. For further information contact Dietmar Sieber, Siebeneichen 6b, Meissen, 08250.

Munich (München) (tel. code 089)

The city is busy all year round, with beds becoming especially hard to find during the Oktoberfest. To reach accommodation out from the centre use the S-Bahn (free with railpasses) or the U-Bahn (cheap multi-ride tickets).

HOTELS

Maisinger, Pippingerstrasse 105 (tel. 8112920). Very cheap. Singles around DM33 (£11.40; $21.60), doubles around DM25 (£8.60; $16.40) p.p. S2 to Obermenzing; then Bus 75 or a 20-minute walk along Dorfstrasse to Pippingerstrasse.

Cheapest doubles DM30–35 (£10.25–12.00; $19.75–23.00) p.p.

Schiller, Schillerstr. 11 (tel. 592435). Ten minutes' walk from the station.

Bergbauer, Schillerstr. 32 (tel. 591005). As above.

Josefine, Nordenstr. 13 (tel. 2710043). U3 U6 to Universität.

Obermenzing Gästehaus, Verdistrasse 80 (tel. 8112763). S1 S2 to Obermenzing.

Gastof Fischergartl, Rothenbühlerstr. 2, corner of Limes-strasse (tel. 876021). S3 S4 S5 S6 to Pasing.

Würmtalhof, Eversbuschstr. 91 (tel. 8122185). S2 to Allach. Far out, but cheap.

Theresia, Luisenstr. 51 (tel. 521250/5233081–2). Twenty minutes' walk from the station, U2 to Theresienstrasse.

Geiger, Steinheilstr. 1 (tel. 521556). As above.

Härtl, Verdistrasse 135 (tel. 8111632). S1 S2 to Ober-menzing.

Isabella, Isabellastrasse 35 (tel. 2713503). U2 to Hohen-zollernplatz.

Cheapest doubles DM35–40 (£12.00–13.75; $23.00–26.25) p.p.

Agnes, Agnesstrasse 58 (tel. 1293061). U2 to Hohen-zollernplatz.

Wilhelmy, Amalienstrasse 71 (tel. 283971). U3 U6 to Universität.

Westfalia, Mozartstrasse 23 (tel. 530377–78). Twenty min-utes' walk from the station, U3 U6 Goetheplatz.

Zöllner, Sonnenstrasse 10/1V and VV (tel. 554035). Near the station and the town centre.

Gebhardt, Goethestrasse 38 (tel. 539446). Ten minutes' walk from the station.

Augsburg, Schillerstrasse 18 (tel. 597673). As above.

Am Knie, Strindbergstr. 33 (tel. 886450). S3 S4 S5 S6 to Pasing, 10-minute walk.

Baumann, Emanuelstrasse 26 (tel. 303400). U2 to Hohen-zollernplatz.

Am Kaiserplatz, Kaiserplatz 12 (tel. 349190). U3 U6 to Munchener Freiheit.

Beck, Thierschstrasse 36 (tel. 225768). S1–S7 to Isartor then a 15-minute walk along Thierschstrasse.

Gästehaus Drexl, Aidenbachstr. 122 (tel. 783680). U3 to Aidenbachstrasse, S7 S27 to Siemenswerke leaves you a slightly longer walk.

Beim Haus der Kunst, Bruderstr. 4/I (tel. 222127). U4 U5 St Anna Klosterkirche. Just outside the centre.

Erika, Landwehrstrasse 8 (tel. 554327). Ten minutes' walk from the station and the centre.

Karl-Friedrich, Mozartstr. 13 (tel. 534078). Twenty minutes' walk from the station, U3 U6 Goetheplatz.

Haydn, Haydnstr. 9 (tel. 531119). As above.

Herzog-Heinrich, Herzog-Heinrich-Str. 3 (tel. 532575). Fifteen minutes from the station.

Hungaria, Briennerstr. 42/II (tel. 521558). U2 Konigsplatz, 15 minutes from the station and the centre.

Frauenhofer, Frauenhoferstrasse 10 (tel. 2607238). U1 U2 Frauenhoferstrasse.

Frank, Schellingstr. 24 (tel. 281451). U3 U6 Universität.

Flora, Karlstr. 49 (tel. 597067). U1 to Stigmaierplatz.

Schubert, Schubertstrasse 1/I (tel. 535087). Fifteen minutes from the station, U3 U6 Goetheplatz.

Süzer, Mittererstr. 1/III (tel. 533521/536642). Five minutes from the station.

Scheel, Isabellastr. 31/II (tel. 2713611). U2 to Hohen-zollernplatz.

Marion, Luisenstr. 25 (tel. 592554). U2 Konigsplatz 15 minutes from the station and the town centre.

Mainburg, Mainburgerstr. 62 (tel. 7148318). S7 S27 Mittersendling U6 Partnachplatz, 15 minutes' walk from both stations.

Lucia, Linprunstrasse 12 (tel. 5234016). U1 Maillinger-strasse.

Marie-Luise, Landwehrstr. 37/IV (tel. 554230). Ten minutes' walk from the station.

Luna, Landwehrstr. 5 (tel. 597833). As above.

IYHF HOSTELS

Jugendgästehaus Thalkirchen, Miesingerstrasse 4 (tel. 7236550). 1 a.m. curfew. U1 or U2 from the main train

station to Sendlingertor, then U3 dir. Forstenrieder
Allee to Thalkirchen (Tierpark). Walk down Frauen-
bergstrasse, left on Kirchweg, then right on Miesingerstrasse.

Wendl-Dietrich-Strasse 20 (tel. 131156). 1 a.m. curfew.
U1 from the main train station to Rotkreuzplatz, then
a short walk along the Wendl-Dietrich-Strasse. The
entrance is on Winthirplatz, second road on the right.
Slightly above normal hostel prices.

Burg Schwaneck, Burgweg 4–6, Pullach (tel. 7930643/4).
1 a.m. curfew. About 7½ miles from the town centre,
but the trip on the S7 from the main train station to
Pullach only takes about 25 minutes. From the station,
follow the signs to the hostel (about eight minutes'
walk). Normal hostel prices.

HOSTELS

Jugendhotel Marienberge, Goethestrasse 9 (tel. 555891).
Midnight curfew. Girls only, aged 25 and under.
Five minutes from the main station. Leave by the
Bayerstrasse exit, turn right, then left on to Goethe-
strasse. Prices similar to a Jugendgästehaus. Breakfast
included.

CVJM, Landwehrstrasse 13 (tel. 555941). 12.30 a.m.
curfew. YMCA hostel, but open to girls as well.
Ten minutes' walk from the main station. Leave
by the front of the station, turn right and keep
going down Schillerstrasse, which is cut across by
Landwehrstrasse. Prices for B&B start around DM35
(£12; $23) p.p. in triples. Prices fall after two nights.
Those aged 27 and over pay an extra 14 per cent.

Haus International/Youth Hotel, Elisabethstrasse 87 (tel.
12006). U2 to Hohenzollernplatz, then bus 33 or tram
12 to Barbarastrasse, the second stop. Prices for B&B
start around DM35 (£12; $23) p.p. in five-bedded
rooms; cheapest singles around DM43 (£14.75; $28).
Prices fall slightly from mid Nov.–late Feb.

IYHF HOSTELS NEARBY

Beim Pfaffenkeller 3, Augsburg (tel. 0821–33909). Trains to Augsburg every 20–30 minutes, 30–40-minute trip.

'THE TENT'

Jugendlage Kapuzinerhölzl, Franz-Schrank-Strasse 8 (tel. 1414300). Actually two circus tents, with mattresses and blankets provided. Open 5 p.m.–9 a.m., late June–early September. DM8 (£2.75; $5.25). Three-night max. stay. Max. age 24, not rigorously enforced. Leave your pack at the station. U1 to Rotkreuzplatz, then tram 12 dir. Amalienburgstrasse to the Botanischer Garten stop on Miesingerstrasse. Along Franz-Schrank-Str. and left at the top on to In den Kirschen. 'The Tent' is on the right.

CAMPING

Munich-Thalkirchen, Zentralländstrasse 49 (tel. 7231707). Cheap, municipal site. From the train station, S1–S7 to Marienplatz, then U3 dir. Forstenrieder Allee to Thalkirchen (Tierplatz), followed by bus 57 to Thalkirchen (last stop). Site open mid March–late October. Crowded, especially during the Oktoberfest.

Munich-Obermenzing, Lochhausenerstrasse 59 (tel. 8112235). S2 to Obermenzing, then bus 75 to Lochhausenerstrasse. Open 15 Mar.–31 Oct.

Nuremberg (Nürnberg) (tel. code 0911)

HOTELS

Centrally located hotels, gasthäuser and pensions:

Cheapest doubles for DM30–40 (£10.35–13.80; $19.75–26.25) p.p.

Roland, Hastverststrasse 33 (tel. 355836/359133).

Brendel, Blumenstr. 1 (tel. 225618).

Vater Jahn, Jahnstr. 13 (tel. 444507).

Fischer, Brunnengasse 11 (tel. 226189).

Sonne, Königstr. 45 (entrance on Theatergasse) (tel. 227166).

Kronfleischküche, Kaiserstrasse 22 (tel. 227845).

Zum Schwänlein, Hintere Sterngasse 11 (tel. 225162).

Keim, Peuntgasse 10 (tel. 225940).

Peter Henlein, Peter-Henlein-Str. 15 (tel. 412912).

Royal, Theodorstrasse 9 (tel. 533209).

Am Ring, Am Pfärrer 2 (tel. 265771).

Altstadt, Hintere Ledergasse 2 (tel. 226102).

Goldener Adler, Klaragasse 21 (tel. 208500/221360).

Alt-Nürnberg, Breite Gasse 40 (tel. 224129).

Noris, Prinzregentenufer 3 (tel. 552818).

Maar, Breite Gasse 31 (tel. 224535).

Melanchton, Melanchtonplatz 1 (tel. 412626).

Berndt, Wölckernstr. 80 (tel. 448066) (from 5 p.m.)

There are plenty of similarly priced accommodations further out from the centre. If you are stuck, rooms are a bit cheaper in nearby Fürth and Erlangen, both about 15–30 minutes away by frequent local trains.

IYHF HOSTEL

Jugendgästehaus 'Kaiserstallung', Burg 2 (tel. 221024/241352). Age limit 27. 1 a.m. curfew. Formerly the castle stables. A 20-minute walk from the station, through the town centre. You will see the castle on the horizon. Tram 9 dir. Thon to Krelingstrasse. From Krelingstrasse the castle is on the left. Through the grounds to the hostel.

HOSTELS

Jugendhotel Nürnberg, Rathsbergerstrasse 300 (tel. 529092).
Around DM26 (£9; $17). More expensive than the IYHF
Jugengästehaus. Thirty minutes' walk from the centre.
Tram 3 to terminus, then bus 41 to Felsenkeller.

IYHF HOSTEL NEARBY

'Frankenhof', Sudlicher Stadtmauerstrasse 35, Amt fur
Freizeit, Erlangen (tel. 09131–862555/862274). Thirty
minutes by frequent local train.

CAMPING

Haus-Kalb-Strasse 56 (tel. 225618). Open May–Sept.
Behind the football stadium (IFCN, one of Germany's
all-time greats). U-Bahn to Messenzentrum. If you
have a railpass one of the local trains stops nearby.
Ask for a train towards the Dutzendteich/Zeppelin
Stadium.

Potsdam (tel. code 033)

In contrast to most German cities, do not get off at the
Hauptbahnhof if you are arriving by train as it is far from
the centre. Potsdam-Stadt is closest to the town centre and
the Tourist Office. If all you want to see is the Sanssouci
Palace and the New Palace then Potsdam-West is the closest
station.

HOTELS

'Lindenpension', Kopernikusstrasse 39 (tel. 75283). Singles DM30 (£10.35; $19.75), triples DM26 (£9; $17)
p.p.
'Babelsberg', Stahnsdorferstrasse 68 (tel. 78889). Doubles
DM30 (£10.35; $19.75) p.p., triples DM27 (£9; $17)
p.p.

PRIVATE ROOMS

Potsdam-Information, Friedrich-Ebert-Strasse 5 (tel. 23385). A short walk from Potsdam-Stadt station over the Lange Brücke. DM15–35 (£5.20–12.00; $9.75–22.75) per night.

IYHF HOSTELS

'Am Neuen Garten', Eisenhartstrasse 5 (tel. 22515). Bus F from the Hauptbahnhof to Neuen Garten, or tram 1, 4 or 6 Platz der Einheit, tram 2 or 5 Johannes-Dieckmann-Strasse.

'Karl Liebknecht', Pirschheide (tel. 94988). Closed in 1991, as were a fair number of the East German hostels. Enquire at the Tourist Office if it has re-opened (most likely under another name).

IYHF HOSTELS NEARBY

'Havelland', Berliner Strasse 113a, Werder (tel. 2440). Buses run to Werder from Potsdam-Hauptbahnhof. Nearest train station 2½ miles away.

'Werder', Am Schwielowsee 110, Werder (tel. 2850). Also closed in 1991. The Tourist Information in Potsdam will tell you if it has re-opened. Previously a Youth Tourist Hotel operated by the East German hostel association (more expensive than a normal Youth Hostel).

CAMPING

Potsdam-Gaisberg. On the Templiner See. Ask the Tourist Office for directions to the site.

Werder-Riegelspitze. On the Glindower See. Three miles outside Werder. Bus D–31 runs to the site from Potsdam-Hauptbahnhof.

If you are stuck for a room you can hire camping equipment from An der Windmühlen, 21 in the Babelsberg area of town. Open Mon.–Fri. 8 a.m.–4 p.m.

Weimar (tel. code 0621)

HOTELS

Pension Liszt, Lisztstrasse 3. Doubles start around DM35
(£12; $23) p.p.

PRIVATE ROOMS

Weimar-Information, Marktstrasse 4 (tel. 5384). Mar.–
Oct. open 1.30–7.30 p.m. Mon.–Fri., 9 a.m.–2 p.m.
Sat. Weekday mornings you can make enquiries at
their office at Marktstr. 4 (tel. 2173).

IYHF HOSTELS

'Am Poseckschen Garten', Humboldstrasse 17 (tel. 4021).
About 1¼ miles from the train station.
'Ernst Thälmann', Windmühlenstrasse 16 (tel. 2076). 1¾
miles from the train station.
Touristhotel am Wilden Graben, Zum Wilden Graben 12
(tel. 3471). (Formerly known as the 'Maxim Gorki'
hostel.) Two miles from the train station.
'Germania', Leninstrasse 13 (tel. 2076). A 100m walk
downhill from the train station.

HOSTELS

Jugendgästehaus der Stadt Weimar, Erich-Weinert-Strasse
11 (tel. 3383). Around the same price as the IYHF
hostels.

CAMPING

Unless a new site opens in 1992 the closest site will be
in Bad Kosen, about 30–40 minutes by local train in the
direction of Naumburg. Ask at the Tourist Office about the
latest situation.

GREECE

As far as accommodation goes, Greece is an excellent place for the budget traveller. By European standards accommodation is a bargain, the range of cheap possibilities is probably unsurpassed, and, at most times of the year, there is an ample supply of cheap beds. Except in July and August, you are unlikely to encounter any trouble in finding a place to stay, even if you arrive late in the day. However, during the months of July and August, the supply of accommodation on the islands fails miserably to satisfy the huge demand.

Hotels are graded into six categories; de luxe, and then downwards from A to E. A fixed minimum rate is set for each category, and this should be displayed at the reception. D- and E-class hotels are well within the range of the budget traveller. A double without a shower or bath should cost around 1000dr (£3.50; $6.75; DM10) per person. For approximately double that amount you can get a similar room in a C-class hotel. Even in Athens a decent double with a shower in a D- or E-class hotel should only cost around 1500dr (£5; $8.50; DM14.50) per person. During the peak season, hotels may levy a 10 per cent surcharge if you stay for less than three nights. In the off-season, hotels cut their prices by up to 40 per cent. At this time hoteliers are prepared to negotiate about room prices, as they know you can easily take your custom elsewhere. Pensions are cheaper than hotels. You may not notice much of a difference between the prices of pensions and cheap hotels in Athens, but in rural areas prices are as low as 500dr (£1.70; $3.25; DM5) per person. Again, you may have some success in attempting to bargain owners down from the stated price.

Rooms in **private homes** (*dhomatia*) are normally a fair amount cheaper than hotels. These are also officially classified, from A to C. Top prices are around 1000dr (£3.50; $6.75; DM10) per person. Dhomatia are most common on the islands, and in the coastal resorts. Rooms are often advertised in several languages in an effort to attract tourists' attention (typically Greek, German, English, French and Italian). If you spot such a sign, you can try to fix yourself up with a room there and then. Alternatively, rooms are often touted at train and bus stations, or ferry terminals. Failing this, the Tourist Police can book private rooms for you. In some places they control all the private rooms. Occasionally they operate an annoying policy whereby rooms are only let out when the local hotels are filled to capacity. Also few private rooms remain open during the period from November to April. This is the direct result of an official policy intended to maintain a steady trade for the hotels. Few owners of rooms flout this system, and there is little point searching for those who do. The miscreants will tout their rooms when they have vacancies. For any small group looking to stay put for a week or so, renting a house or a flat can be a useful option, particularly on the islands. Unfortunately you will have to make enquiries locally as to what possibilities exist.

The **youth hostel** network is not extensive, numbering around 30 hostels in total. Generally they are a bit ramshackle, but the atmosphere is usually quite relaxed. Only rarely are IYHF membership cards asked for. Even then you can buy a card at the hostel, or will be allowed to stay on the payment of a small surcharge. The overnight fee ranges from £2.35–4.00 ($4.50–7.50; DM6.75–11.50). Between June and September curfews are usually 1 a.m.; at other times of the year, midnight. However, there are some hostels which close as early as 10 p.m. With the warden's agreement you can stay longer than the normal three-day maximum. In Athens there are a number of **Student Houses**. These are non-official hostels which offer cheap dormitory accommodation. As the train from

Belgrade finally nears Athens, young people from various Student Houses often board the train to hand out leaflets advertising their establishment. The leaflets are always flattering, of course, but some of these accommodations are fine. Others, however, are of very poor quality. By and large, the cheapest of these hostels are also the least secure for your belongings. The average price for dorms is 1000dr (£3.35; $6.25; DM9.75).

Student houses frequently offer sleeping accommodation on their roof, as do some hotels and IYHF hostels. In the countryside, and on the islands, the best bet for **renting roof space** are the local 'tavernas'. To find out about the availability you will have to ask in person, question the hostel touts, or rely on word of mouth. The Tourist Office are unlikely to be very expansive regarding the availability of roof space, as the practice was made illegal in 1987, ostensibly because the government was concerned about hoteliers overcharging. At present, the law is flouted on a wide scale, and renting a spot on a roof to throw down a mat and a sleeping bag remains a cheap and pleasant way to spend the summer nights. In Athens you can expect to pay about 750dr (£2.50; $4.75; DM7.25), but elsewhere you will pay much less than this.

Camping and **sleeping rough** was made illegal as long ago as 1977, although many travellers are completely unaware of this. In part this is because many people still camp and sleep rough without encountering any difficulties with the authorities. Certainly, the law is not always stringently enforced. In the rural parts of the mainland there is virtually no chance of you having any problems, provided you ask permission before you pitch a tent, and do not litter the area. Even on the islands the police are tolerant of transgressions of the law, within certain limits. You will usually be all right if you show some discretion in your choice of site. This is important because in July and August your chances of finding a room or hostel bed are slim, so at some point you are likely to have to camp or sleep rough. *Avoid the main tourist beaches as the local police patrol them regularly*. Raids are also likely if the police hear that large numbers are beginning to congregate in one spot. The police are increasingly prone to using force to clear people away.

There are 90 or so official **campsites,** of which 13 are run by the National Tourist Organization, with the rest being privately operated. The Tourist Organization's sites are usually large, regimented establishments. Some of the private sites, especially those on the islands, are little more than fenced off patches of land (or sand). While private sites may be prepared to drop their prices a little, there is no chance of this at state-run sites. Typical prices are 600dr (£2; $3.75; DM5.75) per tent, and 250dr (£0.85; $1.60; DM2.50) per occupant, which means that solos and doubles can pay as much as the cost of a cheap room.

In most of the mountainous regions of the country the Hellenic Alpine Club (HAC) maintains **refuge huts** for the use of climbers and hikers. Some of these are unmanned, so you have to visit the local HAC office in advance to pick up a set of keys. Unless you are a member of the HAC, or one of its foreign associates, you will have to pay a surcharge on the normal overnight fee.

ADDRESSES

Hotels	Advance reservations. Greek Chamber of Hotels, 6 Aristidou Street, Athens (tel. 01–3236962).
Greek YHA	Greek Youth Hostel Association, 4 Dragatsaniou Street, Athens 105–59 (tel. 01–3234107/3237590).
Camping	List of sites and facilities from the National Tourist Organization, London, or your local NTOG.
Mountain Refuges	Hellenic Alpine Club (HAC), 7 Karageorgi Street, Athens (tel. 01–3234555).

Athens (Athina) (tel. code 01)

Unless you arrive late in the day during August you should find a reasonably cheap place to stay quite easily.

Expect to pay 1800–2400dr (£6–8; $11.50–15.25; DM17.50–23.25) in singles, 1200–2000dr (£4.00–6.75; $7.75–12.75; DM11.50–19.50) p.p. in doubles, around 1100dr (£3.65; $7; DM19.25) in dorms, 700dr (£2.35; $4.50; DM6.75) for roof space in a pension or Student Hostel.

PENSIONS/STUDENT HOSTELS

The Plaka, beneath the Acropolis, is both centrally located, and a cheap area to stay in:

Dioscouri, Pitakou 6 (tel. 3248165).
Student Inn, Kidathineon 16 (tel. 3244808).
Kouros, Kodrou 11 (tel. 3227431).
Adonis, Kodrou 3 & Voulis (tel. 3249737/3249741).
Acropolis House, Kodrou 6–8 (tel. 3222344/3226241).

Accommodations around Sindagma Square are slightly more expensive than in the Plaka, but are conveniently located, near the centre and the places of interest. As you look across Sindagma with the Parliament to your rear, Ermou is the road leading out the centre of the square. Kar. Servias (which becomes Perikleous) runs from the far right-hand corner, Mitropoleos from the far left. Filelinon runs from the left-hand side of the square.

Pella Inn, Ermou 104 (tel. 3250598).
Theseus, Thissios 10 (tel. 3245960). Off Perikleous.
Festos, Filelinon 18 (tel. 3232455).
George, Nikis 46 (tel. 3226474). Nikis crosses Ermou and
    Mitropoleos, one block along from Sindagma.
Peter's, Nikis 32 (tel. 3222697).
Myrto, Nikis 40 (tel. 3227237/3234560).
Christ, Apolonos 11 (tel. 3220177/3234581). Left down
    Nikis from Mitropoleos, then first right.

Aphrodite, Apolonos 21 (tel. 3234357/3226047).

Amazon, Pentelis 7 & Mitropoleos (tel. 3234002/3234004).
Pentelis is off Mitropoleos, three blocks from Sindagma.

John's Place, Patroou 5 (tel. 3229719). A block further on
from Pentelis.

In the area stretching from the train station towards the
Areos Park and Omonia Square. The road running from
the station is Filadelfias, which becomes Ioulianou.

Olympos (tel. 5223433). Opposite the train station.

Athens Connection, Ioulianou 20 (tel. 8213940).

Lydia, Liossion 121 (tel. 8219980). The major road crossing
Filadelfias/Ioulianou a short distance from the station.

Diethnes, Peoniou 52 (tel. 8832878). Short walk left from
the station, then right.

Aphrodite, Einardou 12 (tel. 8832878). Left from the station,
right up the second or third streets on the right,
diagonally left across Liossion, then right.

San Remo, Nissirou 8 (tel. 5222404). Right from the
station along Theodorou Diligiani, then left just before
Diligiani bends away to the left.

Santa Mavra, Mezonos 74 (tel. 5223138/5225149). Off Theodorou Diligiani just as it bends to the left.

Argo, Viktoros Ougo 25 (tel. 5225939). Crosses Theodorou
Diligiani a few blocks after it bends to the left.

Athens Inn, Viktoros Ougo 13 (tel. 5246906).

Annabel, Kommoundourou 28 (tel. 5245834). Off Veran-
zerou, the continuation of Viktoros Ougo in the
direction of Omonia Square.

Pergamos, Aharnon 14 (tel. 5231991). Vathi district. Going
right down Liossion from Filadelfias will take you to Pl.
Anexartissias. Aharnon is the next round the square on
your left.

Angela, Stournara 38 (tel. 5233262/5233263/5234263). Off
Aharnon, a block up from Pl. Anexartissias.

Feron, Feron 43 (tel. 8232083). Along Ioulianou, left up
Mihail Voda, then second right.

Hara, Feron 38 (tel. 8231012).

Elli, Heiden 29 (tel. 8815876). Along Ioulianou, left up Aharnon, then right.

Sun Light, Filis 68 (tel. 8811956). Crosses Ioulianou one block after Aharnon.

Athens House, Aristotelous 4 (tel. 5240539). Crosses Ioulianou one block after Filis. On the right-hand side runs towards the Vathi district.

Iokastis House, Aristotelous 65 (tel. 8226647).

Zorbas, Giifordou 10 (tel. 8232543). Off Tritis Septemvriou. Go left from Ioulianou.

Patissia, Patission 221 (tel. 8627511/8657512). The main road leading from near Omonia Square towards the Areos Park. Also known as 28 Oktovriou, it crosses Ioulianou after Tritis Septemvriou.

Athens City, Patission 232 (tel. 8629115–6).

Diana, Patission 70 (tel. 8223179).

Milton, Kotsika 4 (tel. 8216806). Off Patission at the Areos Park.

Veikou district. On the other side of the Acropolis from the Plaka.

Art Gallery, Erehthiou 5 (tel. 9238376/9231933). More expensive than most. Trolleybus 1 or 5 from Sindagma to Veikou.

Koukaki district. A little further out than Veikou.

Marble House, An. Zini 35 (tel. 9234058). Trolleybus 1 or 5 from Sindagma to Zini.

Tony's, Zaharitsa 36 (tel. 9236370).

Arditos district. Near the Panathenian Stadium.

Joseph House, Markou Moussouro 13 (tel. 9231204).

Pangrati district. Further out than Arditos.

Youth Hostel No. 5, Damareos 75 (tel. 7519530). Trolleybus 2, 11 or 12 to Pl. Pangratiou. Down Frinis, crossed by Damareos.

Kolonaki district. Near the National Garden and Sindagma.

Athenian Inn, Haritos 22 (tel. 7238097/7239552).

IYHF HOSTEL

Kypselis 57 (tel. 8225860). Kipseli district. Trolleybus 2, 4 or 9 from Sindagma to Zakinthou.

YWCA HOSTEL

Amerikis 11 (tel. 3626180). Looking at the parliament from Sindagma go left along the main road Amalias, which turns left and becomes Venizelou. Amerikis is off to the right.

HOTELS

Eva, Viktoros Ougo 31 (tel. 5223079). From the train station head right along Theodorou Diligiani, which is crossed by Viktoros Ougo a few blocks after it bends to the left.

Acropole, 7 Gounari (tel. 4173313). About 200m from the ferry terminal in Piraeus.

CAMPING

190 Athinon Avenue, Peresteri (tel. 5814114). Bus 822 or 823 from Eleftherias Square. Metro: Thission.

Voula, 2 Alkyonidon (tel. 8952712). Bus 118, 122 or 153 from Vass. Olgas Avenue.

Dafni Camping. Eight miles out in Dafni (tel. 5811562–3). Bus 853 or 870.

SLEEPING OUT

Definitely not to be advised. It is illegal and the police make regular checks on the city's parks, especially those located close to the train station. The police, however, are likely to be the least of your worries given the considerable numbers of travellers who are robbed or assaulted while sleeping rough.

Corfu Town (Kerkira) (tel. code 0661)

If you are arriving in Corfu from Patras or Italy you will most
likely be approached by hoteliers at the ferry terminal. As
the island is quite large, be sure to find out the location of
rooms on offer, otherwise you could end up far from town.
Also be sure to find out precisely how much the hotelier
is charging for the room. If you go looking for rooms on
your own, the streets between the Igoumenítsa Dock and
N. Theotóki are your best bet, especially if it is singles you
are after.

HOTELS

Europa (tel. 39304). Not far from the ferry terminal. 1700dr
(£5.65; $10.75; DM16.50) p.p. in doubles.

Cyprus, 13 Agion Pateron (tel. 30032). Close to the National
Bank on Voulgareos. 1900dr (£6.35; $12; DM18.50) p.p.
in doubles. Slightly cheaper p.p. in triples.

Elpis, 4,5H Parados N. Theotóki (tel. 30289). In an alley
across from 128 N. Theotóki, near the Old Port. Singles
1500dr (£5; $9.50; DM14.50); doubles 1200dr (£4; $7.50;
DM11.50) p.p.; triples 950dr (£3.15; $6; DM9.25) p.p.

Constantinoupolis (tel. 39826). At the end of N. Theotóki.
Doubles 1600dr (£5.35; $10.25; DM15.50) p.p.; triples
1300dr (£4.35; $8.25; DM12.50) p.p.

Atlantis (Neo Lamani) (tel. 35560–62).

Bretannia (tel. 30724).

Hermes (tel. 39321).

Dalia (tel. 32341).

Calypso (tel. 30723).

Splendid (tel. 30034).

Ionion (tel. 39915).

IYHF HOSTEL

Kontokali Beach (tel. 91202). Three miles north of town, a
20-minute trip on bus 7 from Platia San Rocco, every
30 minutes.

CAMPING

Kontokali Beach International (tel. 91170). Same bus as the hostel.

Crete (Kriti) – Agios Nikalaos

(tel. code 0841)

In mid-season it is exceptionally difficult to find rooms. The best places to look are the streets up the hill from the hostel, and the side streets off the roads leading out of town.

HOTELS

C Class:
  Atlantis (tel. 28964). Situated close to the bus station.
  New York, 21 Kondoyanni St (tel. 28557). Also close to the bus station.
  Lato, 12 Iossif Kountourioutou St (tel. 23319).
  Perla (tel. 23323).

B Class:
  Amalthia, 13 Pring. Georgiou St. (tel. 28914–5).
  Athina, 34a Pringipos Armostou St. (tel. 28225).
  Cri-Cri, Ag. Paraskevi (tel. 23720).
  Diana, 28 Ethn. Antistaseos St. (tel. 22694).
  Eva, 20 Stratigou Koraka St. (tel. 22587).
  Ikaros, 11 Alexomanoli St. (tel. 28901–2–3).
  Iris, K. Loukareos-Minoos St. (tel. 22407/23902).
  Lida, 3 Salaminos St. (tel. 22130).
  Magda, 13 Gournon St. (tel. 23925).
  Marigo, Paleologou-Katehaki St. (tel. 28439).
  Niki, 16 Idomeneos St. (tel. 22095).
  Odysseas (tel. 23934).
  Polydoros (tel. 22623/28792). On the beach.

Sun Rise, 1 Idomeneos St. (tel. 23564/24564).
Victoria, 34 Akti Kountouriotou St. (tel. 22731/22266).

IYHF HOSTEL

3 Odos Stratigou Koraka (tel. 22823). Walk up the concrete
steps from the bridge at the harbour.

CAMPING

Although some people camp on the beach in front of the
bus station, this is not to be recommended. It is better to
head out of town to some of the beaches along the coast.
The cove at Kalo Horio, about eight miles out, is one of the
best places to pitch a tent.

Ios (tel. code 0286)

There are plenty of cheap places to stay, except in July
and August when rooms become difficult to find. During
these two months try to look for rooms as early in the day
as you can. At other times you should have little trouble
finding a double for 1000–1500dr (£3.35–5.00; $6.25–9.50;
DM9.75–14.50) p.p. Sleeping on the beach is no longer to
be recommended, despite its past popularity. Not only is
there a considerable risk of theft but police patrols are
becoming increasingly regular, as is their readiness to clear
the beach forcibly. However, you should have few problems
with the authorities if you stick to the quieter beaches such
as Koumbara or Manganari.

HOTELS

Draco Pension. Immediately to the right of the bus
stop.
Francesco's (tel. 91223). Up the hill from the bank.

The Wind (tel. 91139). Below the George Irene Hotel.
Marko's Pension (tel. 91060). Doubles around 1750dr (£5.85; $11; DM17) p.p. Just to the left of The Wind.

C-class hotels in the Old Town
  Corali (tel. 91272).
  Filippou (tel. 91290).
  Flisvos (tel. 91315).
  Fragakis (tel. 91231).
  Homer's Inn (tel. 91365).

CAMPING

Camping Ios (tel. 91329). About 700dr (£2.35; $4.50; DM6.75) p.p. Tent included.
There are two sites in Milopotamos, about 1¼ miles away.
Both charge much the same price as Camping Ios:
  Stars (tel. 91302, or 01–4821083) (Athens number of the company who run the site).
  Souli (tel. 91554 or 01–8940657).

Mykonos (tel. code 0289)

In the high season (May–Oct.) cheap rooms can be very difficult to find, especially if you do not start looking until after midday. At this time of year, unless you are prepared to camp, or sleep rough, it makes sense to accept any offer of a room which seems reasonable, bearing in mind the inflated price of accommodation on the island. Otherwise your options may be restricted to spending a night in an expensive C-class hotel (doubles 2750dr (£9.20; $17.50; DM26.50) p.p.).

HOTELS

For reasonably priced rooms:
   Hotel Phillipi (tel. 22294).
   Hotel Apollon (tel. 23271).
   Hotel Karbonis (tel. 22475).
   Angela's Rooms, Taxi Square (tel. 22967). Also roof space
      800dr (£2.70; $5; DM7.75).
   13 Mitropoleos. This old white house offers doubles at
      1250dr (£4.15; $8; DM12) p.p.; triples 1050dr (£3.50;
      $6.75; DM10.25) p.p.

C-class hotels in the Old Town:
   Adonis (tel. 22434).
   Marianna (tel. 22072).
   Pelekan (tel. 23454).
   Vencia (tel. 23665).
   Aeolos (tel. 23535).
   Marios (tel. 22704).
   Zannis (tel. 22481).
   Mykonos Beach (tel. 22572).
   Bellou (tel. 22589).
   Matogianni (tel. 22217).
   Thomas (tel. 23148).
   Zorzis (tel. 22167).
   Manto (tel. 22330).
   Mykonos (tel. 22434).
   To Horio (tel. 23148).

CAMPING

Freelance camping is illegal, but is widely practised on
the Paradise, Super Paradise and Elia beaches. There is
an official site on Paradise beach. Paradise Beach (tel.
22129/22852/22937).

Naxos (tel. code 0285)

Finding cheap accommodation in Naxos town is not as easy as it used to be. As the island has become more popular with package-tour operators, so there has been a fall in the number of cheap rooms available. However, unless you arrive during July or August, you should still be able to find a double for 1000–1650dr (£3.35–5.50; $6.25–14.25; DM9.75–16.00) p.p. The best area to search for rooms is up the hill from the ETO office where there is a concentration of pensions.

HOTELS

Hotel Annixis, 330 Amfitritis (tel. 22112).
Hotel Okeanis (tel. 22436). Directly opposite the docks. Doubles around 1200dr (£4; $7.50; DM11.50) p.p.
Hotel Pantheon, Old Market Street (tel. 22379). Doubles 1000dr (£3.35; $6.25; DM9.75) p.p., with shower 1500dr (£5; $9.50; DM14.50) p.p.
Hotel Dionyssos (tel. 22331). In the Old Market quarter, straight up the hill from the docks. Singles 1300dr (£4.35; $8.25; DM12.50); doubles 900dr (£3; $5.75; DM8.75) p.p.; triples 750dr (£2.50; $4.75; DM7.25) p.p. Basement dorms 600dr (£2; $3.75; DM5.75). Roof 450dr (£1.50; $2.75; DM4.25).

C-class hotels in the Old Town:
Aegeon (tel. 22852).
Aeolis (tel. 22321).
Hermes (tel. 22220).
Panorama (tel. 22330).
Sergis (tel. 23195).
Apollon (tel. 22468).
Grotta (tel. 22215).
Koronis (tel. 22626).
Renetta (tel. 22952).
Sfinx (tel. 23811).

CAMPING

Naxos (tel. 41291/23500). Located by the Agios Giorgios beach.

Rhodes (Rodos) (tel. code 0241)

There are plenty of cheap pensions, virtually all of which are conveniently situated in the area bounded by Sokrátous on the north, Perikléos on the east, Odhós Omírou on the south, and Ippodhamou on the west.

HOTELS

Hotel Faliron, Faliriki (tel. 85483).
Steve Kefalas's Pension, 60 Omírou (tel. 24357). Dorms 1050dr (£3.50; $6.75; DM10.25); 600dr (£2; $3.75; DM5.75) in cots on the roof.
Pension Apollon, 28c Omírou (tel. 32003). Rooms for 1000dr (£3.35; $6.25; DM9.75) p.p. Also roof space.
Pension Dionisos, 75 Platonos (tel. 22035). Rooms similar in price to Apollon. Roof space.

Santorini (tel. code 0286)

During the summer beds can be very hard to find in the capital Thira (Fira). The small village of Karteradhos, a 20-minute walk south of Thira, is the best place to look if you are having no luck in the capital.

HOTELS/PENSIONS

Delfini (tel. 71272). Near the IYHF hostel. Doubles 1650dr (£5.50; $10.50; DM16) p.p.

C-class hotels:
  Antonia (tel. 22879).
  Kavalari (tel. 22455).
  Roussos (tel. 22752).
  Theoxenia (tel. 22455).
  Kallisti Thira (tel. 22317).
  Panorama (tel. 22481).
  Pelikan (tel. 23113).

IYHF HOSTEL

Kontohori, Agios Eleftherios (tel. 22722/22577). About a quarter of a mile north of town.

CAMPING

Perissa (tel. 81343). On the beach.

Thessolonika (Thessoloniki)

(tel. code 031)

The bulk of the cheapest accommodation is concentrated at the west end of Egnatia, not far from the train station.

HOTELS

E class:
  Argo, Egnatia 11 (tel. 519770).
  Atlantis, Egnatia 14 (tel. 540131).

D class:
  Augoustos, Elénis Svoronoú 4 (tel. 522550).
  Ilios, Egnatia 27 (tel. 512620).
  Atlas, Egnatia 40 (tel. 537046).
  Alexandria, Egnatia 18 (tel. 536185).
  Lido, Egnatia 60 (tel. 223805).
  Tourist, Mitropóleos 21 (tel. 270501).

C class:

ABC, Angelaki 41 (tel. 265421).
Continental, Komninon 5 (tel. 277553).
Grande Bretagne, Egnatia 46 (tel. 530735).
Delta, Egnatia 13 (tel. 516321).
Mandrino, Antigonidon 2 & Egnatia (tel. 526321).
Thessalonikon, Egnatia 60 (tel. 223805).
Vergina, Monastiriou 19 (tel. 527400).
Rex, Monastiriou 39 (tel. 517051).
Park, Ionos Dragoumi 81 (tel. 524121).
Pella, Ionos Dragoumi 61 (tel. 524221–4) (five lines).

IYHF HOSTEL

Alex. Svolou 44 (tel. 225946).

YWCA HOSTEL

Agias Sofia 11 (tel. 276144). Women only. Prices similar to those of IYHF hostels.

YMCA HOSTEL

Hanth Square (tel. 27400). Men only. Prices on a par with IYHF hostels. Ring ahead to check the hostel is open.

CAMPING

There are no really convenient sites. Ask at the Tourist Office about the easiest site to get to. There are sites on the beaches of Perea and Agia Trias, but both are about 13 miles outside the city.

HUNGARY

In the past Hungary was the Soviet bloc country which presented the fewest problems to the budget traveller, with cheap accommodation being no more difficult to find than in many West European countries. Now the situation is vastly different, with the supply of accommodation being swamped by the unprecedented volume of tourists visiting the country. In the first five months of 1991 alone, that is, before the peak season rush, there was an 85 per cent increase in numbers visiting Hungary. Over the year the country received 36 million visitors, and two-thirds of these stayed in the capital Budapest. This represented a huge increase on previous levels, and not surprisingly chaos was the result. It will be several years before Hungary has an adequate supply of accommodation to cope with the demand. In the meantime, trips to Hungary will inevitably involve a certain amount of frustration as regards finding suitable sleeping facilities. The problem for the budget traveller is two-fold: firstly, finding somewhere cheap to stay (which is difficult enough); secondly, avoiding establishments which are grossly exploiting the predicament of travellers struggling to find cheap accommodation.

One blessing is that unlike their counterparts elsewhere in the former Soviet bloc, neither the local offices of the state tourist agency IBUSZ, nor the regional or local Tourist Offices, will attempt to pressure you into staying in expensive hotels. On the contrary, they will generally do their best to book you into whatever type of accommodation you want. For a fee of just over £1 ($2; DM3) IBUSZ will make reservations at your next destination. IBUSZ offices outside Budapest are normally open on Saturday mornings only, so it makes sense to book for the whole weekend on Fridays.

One useful publication you can pick up free from IBUSZ or the regional Tourist Offices is 'Hotel Camping' which lists many of the hotels and campsites in Hungary, and can be an invaluable aid to the budget traveller.

Hotels (*szalladok*) are rated from 1 up to 5 stars. There is a shortage of singles in all grades of hotels, so unless solo travellers can find someone to share with, they may have to pay for a double. Rooms in one-star hotels are normally perfectly acceptable, unless you are looking for a private bathroom. Outside Budapest and the Lake Balaton area, where prices are generally about 30 per cent higher, doubles in a one-star hotel average around £4 ($7.50; DM11.50) per person. Pensions are cheaper than hotels, and more likely to have singles. In a Budapest pension (*penzio*) you can pay anything from £2 to 6 ($3.75–11.50; DM5.75–17.50) for a single. In the off-season prices at some of the higher-rated hotels fall to affordable levels; for instance, to around £10 ($19; DM29) p.p. in doubles in some of the three-star hotels in Budapest. Enquire locally about the availability of such rooms. Breakfast is included in the overnight price at all hotels and pensions. This may be only an uninspiring continental breakfast, but on other occasions you may be treated to a substantial buffet of cold meats. As the cheaper hotels in Budapest are often filled with groups it makes sense to book ahead, although this is easier said than done. A phone call, or even a letter, may not result in a reservation being made and held, so try to get written confirmation of your booking from the hotel concerned (if you can write in German as well as English all the better). If you arrive without a reservation hotel staff usually speak enough English to make telephone enquiries about the availability of rooms worthwhile.

In an attempt to earn some extra money increasing numbers of Hungarians are letting rooms in their homes. This growth in rooms available in **private homes** is acting as a palliative to the shortage of accommodation. Outside Budapest it is feasible to look for rooms on your own. Look out for houses displaying a 'szobe kiado' or 'zimmer' sign, then simply approach the owner to view the rooms on offer. However, for those who do not intend to camp, it may be wise to use an agency to help find your accommodation. The vast majority of rooms are controlled by state tourist organizations such as IBUSZ or EXPRESS (the student travel organization), or by more specialized local and regional tourist agencies such as Szegedtourist or Egertourist (in the towns of those names), or Balatontourist (around Lake Balaton). Some new agencies have been established, and, with such a potentially lucrative market to be tapped, further growth seems inevitable.

You should have little complaint about the standard of rooms booked through an agency, but try to make sure the location is acceptable. It might be hoping for a bit much to get a centrally located room in the centre of the cities, but make a point of asking for one that is well served by public transport. There is a shortage of singles, so again solo travellers might want to find someone to share with. Expect to pay anything between £2.75 and 5.50 ($5.25–10.50; DM8–16) in singles, £2.25–6.00 ($4.25–11.50; DM6.50–17.50) p.p. in doubles. A surcharge is added to the price of the room if you stay less than four days; for example, another 30 per cent for one-night stays. It is standard practice to pay the agency rather than the householder. As rooms at one agency may cost double those offered by another office in town, try to find out in advance from other travellers which is the best to deal with. In the more popular towns where long queues can act as a deterrent to shopping around try asking people who have just been served. As a rough guide, IBUSZ offers the best service in Budapest as they control the major share of the market and have a good supply of very cheap rooms, although they may enforce a three-day minimum stay. If you are arriving in Budapest from another Hungarian town it is well worth getting the local IBUSZ to reserve one of these cheap rooms for you. Outside the capital IBUSZ generally cannot compete with the more localized agencies in terms of price, or the numbers of rooms they control. However, if for any reason you think you might have trouble getting fixed up at your next destination it is probably worth paying a little extra to reserve a room through IBUSZ and save yourself the bother of looking when you arrive.

You may be approached by locals offering rooms; most likely in and around the train stations, and in the IBUSZ offices (some touts even try to pass themselves off as IBUSZ staff). Outside Budapest these rooms are likely to be fine, but you should be more wary of offers made in Budapest. The rooms on offer in the capital are generally of an inferior standard to rooms booked through an agency, and, most likely, poorly located as well, although the asking price will be similar. However, if you arrive late in the afternoon such offers may well be worth considering for the first night. If you do accept a private offer keep an eye on your valuables, or, better still, leave them at the station.

EXPRESS operates a chain of 32 **hostels** and **youth hostels,** a number of which are listed in the IYHF handbook. They also control the letting of the non-EXPRESS hostels listed in the IYHF handbook, and of the temporary hostels set up in college dormitories during the summer vacation (late June to end of August). The locations of these temporary dorm hostels change annually, but you can find out the latest locations from the comprehensive list of Hungarian hostels that EXPRESS publishes each July. Expect to pay £2–4 ($3.75–7.50; DM8.75–11.50) for a bed in a dormitory, and up to £6.30 ($12; DM10.50) p.p. in doubles or quads in one of the EXPRESS youth hotels. Any individual occupying a small room on their own must pay for all the bed space, so if you are prepared to share you should make that perfectly clear. Couples wishing to share a double will encounter no difficulties. There are no curfews, but you are expected to remain quiet after midnight.

During the summer months EXPRESS accommodations are frequently filled to capacity by school groups and youth organizations, making advance booking essential, although this can be difficult. The IYHF handbook advises the use of Advance Booking Vouchers which should effect a reservation, and put a deposit against it. Unfortunately this is not certain to succeed as EXPRESS make a habit of sending vouchers back, explaining that their value was less than that of the accommodation requested. EXPRESS student vouchers, which you must purchase at least 10 days in advance, give you priority at EXPRESS hostels and youth hotels until 6 p.m. The problem is getting the vouchers. In 1991 Danube Travel informed us that they had no information on EXPRESS vouchers, so you will either have to contact EXPRESS in Budapest, or OKISTA in Vienna (see Vienna section). In the end you may have no choice but to try and book these hostels at an EXPRESS office on arrival in Hungary.

There are also a number of local hostels, which are known by different names according to their location. In provincial towns enquiries should be made regarding the availability of 'turistaszalle', but in highland areas they are referred to as 'turistahaz'. Expect to pay £1.50-4.00 ($2.75–7.50; DM4.25–11.50) for an overnight stay.

In 1990 there was a growth in **independent hostels** in Budapest. These were illegal, and so could not be advertised publicly by the owners. The locations of these hostels were passed amongst travellers by word of mouth, or by owners approaching backpackers. While some of these hostels are reasonable, there are a large number which simply squeeze as many people as possible into small rooms. The latter type are simply ripping people off. It is easy to say avoid these hostels at all costs, but the current accommodation situation tends to dictate otherwise.

Hungary's **campsites** are unlikely to give you any cause for complaint. Camping is very popular with Hungarians, and the Magyar Camping and Caravanning Club (MCCC) is very active. The MCCC is exceptionally helpful to foreign visitors. Both the MCCC and an organization called Tourinform produce excellent, easy-to-follow lists of the sites, complete with opening times, facilities available, and a map showing their locations. Sites are graded from one to three stars. The three-star sites usually have a supermarket and leisure facilities, whereas the one-star sites are more or less restricted to the basic necessities. Apart from July and August there is usually no need to make reservations, or to check about the availability of space before heading out to the site, except perhaps in Budapest and the Lake Balaton area. There are about 140 sites in total, with quite a concentration along the shores of Lake Balaton. The season runs from May to October inclusive, but many sites only open for the peak months of July and August. In peak season prices range from £1 ($2; DM3) per tent, £0.40 ($0.75; DM1.25) per person at a one-star site, to £2.20 ($4.25; DM6.50) per tent, £0.80 ($1.50; DM2.25) p.p. at a three-star site. Members of the International Camping and Caravanning Club (FICC) and holders of student ID cards are given generous discounts on peak-season prices. Either side of the high season sites reduce their prices by 25–30 per cent, but your choice of sites is more limited at these times. At the larger sites it is possible to rent bungalows. To hire a typical bungalow sleeping four people generally costs around £10 ($19; DM29), but you pay for all the bed space whether you fill the bungalow to capacity or not. The camping maps available from Tourist Information Offices show where bungalows are available for rent, as does 'Hotel Camping'.

Freelance camping is illegal but is practised by many young people (Hungarians especially); most likely because offenders are rarely heavily punished. Favourite locations are the forests of the Danube Bend, and the highland regions where rain shelters (esöház) are common. Camping is seldom permitted in youth-hostel grounds (Hotel Aranypart in Gyor is one notable exception). In an effort to prevent young visitors sleeping in the train stations of Budapest the authorities showed admirable initiative in establishing a free campsite in the 1980s. The site is closed during the day, and you should avoid leaving anything at the site as the risk of theft is high.

In the countryside it is possible to stay in **farm cottages** and **B&Bs.** Details of these establishments are contained in the brochure 'Holidays in the Countryside' available from IBUSZ, although in the vast majority of cases it is the regional Tourist Offices rather than IBUSZ with whom you must make reservations.

ADDRESSES

Youth hostels and youth hotels	Magyar Ifjúsági Házak-EXPRESS, Szabadság tér 16, 1395 Budapest V (tel. 1129887/1530660).
Camping	Magyar Camping & Caravanning Club (MCCC), Üllői útja 6, 1085 Budapest (tel. 336536). TOURINFORM, Sütő u.2, 1052 Budapest (tel. 1179800).

Lists available from Danube Travel, London or from IBUSZ/ Hungarian National Tourist Office in your capital city.

Budapest (tel. code 01)

Offices dealing with accommodation:

IBUSZ, Main office Tanács Krt 3c (tel. 1186866). Open
  Mon.–Fri. 8.30 a.m.–5 p.m., Sat. 8 a.m.–1 p.m. Metro:
  Deák tér. Tanács Krt exit. Branch offices in all the train
  stations. Open daily 8 a.m.–8 p.m. Felszabadulás tér
  5 (tel. 186866). Open Mon.–Fri. 8 a.m.–7.45 p.m., Sat.
  8 a.m.–4.45 p.m. Petöfi tér 3. Open round the clock.

EXPRESS, Szabadság tér 16 (tel. 1317777/1129887). Open
  Mon.–Fri. 8 a.m.–8 p.m., Sat. 9.30 a.m.–8.30 p.m., Sun.
  10.30 a.m.–5.30 p.m. Located between the Arany János
  (blue line) and Kossuth Lajos (red line) metro stops.
  Branch office in Keleti train station (tel. 142772). Open
  daily 8 a.m.–9 p.m.

Budapest Tourist, Roosevelt tér 5–6 (tel. 1186600). Open
  Mon.–Sat. 8 a.m.–8 p.m., Sun. 9 a.m.–3 p.m. Near the
  Széchenyi bridge. Metro: Deák tér, then a 10-minute
  walk.

Coopturist, Bajcsy-Zsilinszkyút 17 (tel. 1310992).

Student Accommodation Office, Irinyi József u. 9. Open
  June–Aug.

HOTELS

Of the agencies listed above,

IBUSZ book the more expensive hotels in Budapest, from
  £10.50 ($20; DM30.50) p.p., while EXPRESS book their
  own youth hotels and the non–EXPRESS youth hotels
  listed in the IYHF handbook.

From mid April to mid October, plus a few days at New
  Year, the two-star hotels Park, Wien and Metropol
  have doubles for £10.50–11.50 ($20–22; DM30.50–33.25)
  p.p. At other times prices fall to around £7.75 ($14.50;
  DM22.25) p.p. Rooms in these hotels can be booked
  through Danube Travel in London or your capital city,
  or through IBUSZ in Budapest.

Cheapest doubles from £3.50–5.50 ($6.75–10.50; DM10.25–16.00) p.p.

Citadella, Gellérthegy (tel. 1665794). In the citadel on Gellért Hill. Also offers cheap dorms £1 ($2; DM3). Advance reservation essential. Recommended.

Lidó (IYHF), Nánási u. 67 (tel. 1886865/805576). North of the city, in the suburbs of Buda. Bus 134 from Flórián tér stops outside. HÉV stop Római-Fürdő is a 10-minute walk away.

Kandó, Bécsi út 104–108 (tel. 1682032). Triples and quads available. Bus 60 from Battyani tér.

Strand penzió, Pusztakúti út 3 (tel. 1671999). Next to the Árpád baths. HÉV to Csillaghegy. Roughly one mile from the centre.

Sport penzió, Szép juhászné út 9. Located in the Buda Hills. From Moszkva tér take bus 22.

Trio penzió, Ördögorom u. 10 (tel. 865742). Open 15 May–15 Oct. No singles. Sasad district of Buda. Bus 8 to the terminus, then a 10-minute walk.

Duna-Party Pansió (IYHF), Kossuth Lajos üdülöpart. 43–44 (tel. 687029). Far out from the centre. Bus 34 stops 50m from the door.

Depo fogadó, Törökbálint Pf. 3 (tel. 263388). Doubles only. Out in the suburb of Újpest.

Saturnus, Pillangó u. 10 (tel. 421789). In the east of Pest, close to the Nepstadion (the national stadium). Metro line 3.

Hotel Express, Beethoven u. 7–9 (tel. 1753082). IYHF EXPRESS youth hotel.

Ifjúság, Zivitar u. 1–3 (tel. 353331/154260). EXPRESS youth hotel.

Diàk Hotel, Dózsa György ut 152 (tel. 1408585). IYHF.

Épitök, Nagy Lajos Király útja 15–17 (tel. 1840677).

Hala dás Motel, Váci út 102 (tel. 1891114). Tram 104.

Unikum penzió, Bod Péter u. 13. No singles available. From Felszabadulás tér bus 8 or 8A to Zolyomi út on the Buda side of the river. Keeping Sas-Hegy (Eagle

Hill) on your right walk along Zolyomi until you see
Bod Péter on the right.

PRIVATE ROOMS

Agencies:
IBUSZ: Singles from £4 ($7.50; DM11.50), doubles £3–6
($5.75–11.50; DM8.75–17.50) p.p.
Budapest Tourist: Singles £5 ($9.50; DM14.50), doubles
£4.00–7.50 ($7.50–14.25; DM11.50–21.75) p.p.
Cooptourist: Singles and doubles £5 ($9.50; DM14.50)
p.p.

TEMPORARY HOSTELS

The locations of these temporary hostels, converted from
student residences, change frequently, so some of the
hostels listed below may not be in operation in 1992.
Agencies EXPRESS:
Csúcshegy, Menedékház u. 122 (tel. 686015).
Strand. Same address and tel. no. as the Strand penzió.
See above.
Elte Hostel Kollégium, Budaörsi út 101 (tel. 1667788).
Open 15 July–20 Aug. IYHF hostel.
Student Hostel PSZF, Antos Istvan út 6–10 (tel. 631681).
Open 2 July–25 Aug. IYHF hostel.
Sote Balassa Kollégium, Tömö u 39/43 (tel. 1168932). Open
7 July–21 Aug. IYHF hostel. Book through Hungary
Holiday, Seepvölgyl 1/6, Budapest 1036.
Student Hostel 'KEK', Szüret u. 2–18 (tel. 1852369). Open
7 July–20 Aug. IYHF hostel.
Hostel Donàti, Donàti u. 4/6 (tel. 1168932). Open 22 June–
24 Aug. IYHF hostel.
Hostel Felvinci, Felvinci u. 8 (tel. 1168932). Open
22 June–24 Aug. IYHF hostel.
Econotour Hostel, Kinizsi u. 2–6. Near the university.

CAMPING

Agencies: Budapest Tourist. Book two- and four-bedded bungalows at the city's campsites. Around £2.60 ($5; DM7.50) p.p., assuming all the bed space is taken.

Hárs-hegyi, Hárshegyi ut 5–7 (tel. 1151482/1761921). Open 13 May–20 Oct. Bungalows available. Bus 22 from Moszkva tér.

Római, Szentendrei út 189 (tel. 1686260). Open year round. Bungalows. From Batthyany tér take the HÉV tram to Rómaifürdő.

Zugligeti 'NICHE', Zugligeti út 101. Open 15 Mar.–15 Oct. Bungalows. Bus 158 from Moszkva tér.

Tündérhegyi 'Feeberg', Szilágyi út 8. Open year round. Bungalows. Close to the Istenhegy stop on the cog railway.

Rosengarten, Pilisi út 7. Open 15 June–15 Sept. Bungalows.

Metró-Tenis, Csömöri út 158 (tel. 1638505). Open 1 June–31 Oct. In the Pest suburb of Rákosszentmihály.

Római Mini Camping, Rozgonyi Piroska u 19. Open 1 May–31 Oct.

Mini Camping, Vöröshadsereg útja 307. Open 1 May–30 Sept.

Caraván Camping, Konkoly Thege u. 18/b. Open 1 June–15 Oct.

EXPO-AUTOCAMP, Dobi I. út 10 (tel. 1470990). Open 1 June–31 Aug.

FREE CAMPSITE

Situated close to the Jászberényi út bridge in the Budapest X district. To get there take metro line 2 as far as Őrs vezer tere, then change to bus 61 to the Jászberényi út bridge. Do not leave anything here during the day.

Eger   (tel. code 36)

Offices dealing with accommodation:
   Egertourist, Bajcsy-Zsilinszky u (tel. 11724). Open Mon.–
      Sat. 8 a.m.–7.30 p.m. Well-informed staff speaking
      excellent English.
   IBUSZ. Behind Egertourist (tel. 11451). Open Mon.–Fri.
      7.30 a.m.–4 p.m., Sat. 7.30 a.m.–noon.
   Cooptourist, Dobó tér 3. Open Mon.–Fri. 9 a.m.– 4.30 p.m.,
      Sat. 9 a.m.–noon.
   EXPRESS, Széchenyi István u. 28 (tel. 10727/11865). Open
      Mon.–Fri. 8 a.m.–4 p.m.

HOTELS

Enquire about these hotels at IBUSZ. For advance booking
try Danube Travel, London or your capital city.
   Eger (two star). Doubles without bath, B&B £7.35 ($14;
      DM21.25) p.p. in the off-season (Oct.–May).
   Senator (two star). B&B in doubles £9 ($17; DM26) p.p.
      during the off-season.

PENSIONS

Book these pensions through Egertourist:
   Kapasi u. 35a.
   Lenin út 11.
   Mekchey u. 2.

PRIVATE ROOMS

Agencies:
   Egertourist: singles £3.50 ($6.75; DM10.25); doubles
      £3.50–5.00 ($6.75–9.50; DM10.25–14.50) p.p.
   Cooptourist: doubles from £2 ($3.75; DM5.75) p.p.
   IBUSZ: doubles from £4 ($7.50; DM11.50) p.p.

HOSTELS

Agencies:
  EXPRESS arrange university accommodation throughout the year. Usually located far from the town centre Also information on temporary hostels set up during the summer.
  Egertourist. Late June–end Aug. Rooms in student dorms around £1.30 ($2.50; DM3.75).

  Buttler-Ház, Kossuth Lajos út 26 (tel. 22866). Dorm beds £1.30 ($2.50; DM3.75). Also at Szarváster 1. Book through Egertourist or EXPRESS.
  Hotel Unicornis, Hibay Karolu u 22 (tel. 12886). EXPRESS hostel. Around £3 ($5.75; DM8.75).
  Student Hostel 'Ho Shi Minh', Leányka u 2 (tel. 12066). EXPRESS hostel, open 10 July–20 Aug. Same price as the Hotel Unicornis.

CAMPING

  Autós Camping, Rákóczi út 79 (tel. 10558). Open 1 May–31 Oct. A 10-minute walk from the town centre. Bus 5. Bungalows can be hired at the site.

Esztergom (tel. code 27)

Offices dealing with accommodation:
  IBUSZ, Martirok u 1 (tel. 12552). Open Mon.–Fri. 8 a.m.–11.50 a.m. and 12.30 p.m.–4 p.m., Sat. 8–11 a.m.
  Komtourist, Maritok u 6 (tel. 12082). Open Mon.–Fri. 9 a.m.–5 p.m., Sat. 9 a.m.–noon.
  EXPRESS, Szechenyi tér 7 (tel. 13133/13712).

HOTELS

Esztergom (three star). £10 ($19; DM29) p.p. for B&B
in doubles with showers Oct.–May. Enquire about
vacancies at IBUSZ. For advance booking try Danube
Travel, London or your capital city.

Volan, Jozsef Attila 2 (tel. 12714). Doubles around £3.50
($6.75; DM10.25) p.p. By the Danube.

Furdo, Bajcsy-Zsilinszky ut. Cheaper than the Volan.

PRIVATE ROOMS

Agencies:

Komtourist: doubles from £2.20 ($4.25; DM6.50) p.p.

IBUSZ: More expensive than Komtourist, but the IBUSZ
staff speak much better English if you have any special
requirements.

HOSTELS

Agencies: Komtourist. Enquire about 'turistaszalle'.

Tourist Hostel, Dobó u. 8, near Béke tér (tel. 12714).
Cheap.

CAMPING

Vadvirág, Bánomi-dűlő (tel. 174). Open 15 Apr.–15 Oct.
Bungalows available. Two miles from the train station.
A 10-minute bus trip. From the station or the town
centre take the Visegrad bus (departs the station at 55
minutes past the hour). A few minutes' walk from the
stop nearest the site.

GRAN Camp. és üdültőlep, Primás-sziget, Nagyduna-
sétány. Open 1 May–30 Sept. Bungalows available. 1¼
miles from the train station. Ten minutes' walk from
the nearest bus stop.

Siófok (tel. code 84)

Offices dealing with accommodation:
Siótour, Szabadság tér 6 (tel. 10800). Off Fő utca. Open
Mon.–Sat. 8 a.m.–8 p.m., Sun. 9 a.m.–1 p.m. and
2–6 p.m.
IBUSZ, Fő utca 174 (tel. 11066).

HOTELS

Two-star and three-star hotels become affordable during the
short off-season periods from the opening of the hotel until
11 May and from 28 Sept. until the hotel closes. To book in
advance try Danube Travel, London or your capital city.
Enquire about vacancies on arrival at IBUSZ.

Three-star hotels:

**Expect to pay around £8.40 ($16; DM24.50)
p.p. for doubles.**

Balaton, Europa, Hungária and Lidó.

Two-star hotels:

**Expect to pay around £7.10 ($13.50; DM20.50)
p.p. for doubles.**

Napfény, Vènusz and Sżantòd Touring. Rooms in the
Sżantòd Touring have showers.

PRIVATE ROOMS

Some rooms can be a considerable distance from the beach.
Try to coax the agencies into giving you a room near the
lake.

Agencies:

Siótour. Doubles £3.50–6.00 ($6.75–11.50; DM10.25–17.50) p.p.

IBUSZ. Doubles £4.00–4.50 ($7.50–8.50; DM11.50–13.00) p.p.

Doubles at around £4.50 ($8.50; DM13) p.p. are available in a number of the elegant houses which line Balthyány Lajos u. Excellent value, and close to the beach. Look for the 'zimmer' or 'szobe kiado' signs and then approach the owner to book a room.

HOSTELS

Altálános School, Fő tér. Open 1 July–20 Aug.

CAMPING

Kék Balaton (tel. 10851). Open 15 June–31 Aug. One of several sites near Aranypart (the so-called 'Golden Beach'). Close to Siófok, but sandwiched between the train lines and the road.

Aranypart Nyaralótelep (tel. 11801). Open 1 May–30 Sept. Bungalows available.

Ifjúság, Pusztatorony tér (tel. 11471). Open 15 May– 25 Sept. With bungalows. Close to the lakeside, as is Gamasza campsite, open July and Aug.

Fűfza, Szőlő-hegy, Fő u. 7/a. Open July and Aug. Bungalows available.

Strand, Szent László u. 183, Fürdőtelep (tel. 11804). Open 15 May–15 Sept. By the lake.

Bus 2 runs from Siófok train station 2½ miles away. Nearest train station is 100m from the site.

Mini Camping, Szent László út 74. Open 1 May–15 Sept.

TOT, Viola u. 19–21, Fürdőtelep. Open 1 June–31 Aug. 500m from the nearest train station.

Szentendre (tel. code 26)

Offices dealing with accommodation:
IBUSZ, Bogdányi u. 11 (tel. 2610333). Open Mon.–Fri.
10 a.m.–4 p.m.
Dunatour, Bogdányi u. 1 (tel. 2611311). Open June–Aug.
Mon.–Fri. 8 a.m.–4 p.m., Sat. 7 a.m.–7 p.m., Sun.
10 a.m.–4 p.m.

HOTELS

**Expect to pay £5.50 ($10.50; DM16) for singles,
and £7 ($13.35; DM20.40) p.p. for doubles.**

Party, Ady utca (tel. 12491).
Danubius, Ady utca (tel. 12511).

PENSIONS

Slightly cheaper than the hotels above.
Coca Cola, Dunakanyar körút 50 (tel. 10410).
Hubertus, Tyukosdűlő 10 (tel. 10616).

PRIVATE ROOMS

Agencies
IBUSZ: Singles £6 ($11.50; DM17.50), doubles £4 ($7.50;
DM11.50) p.p.
Dunatour. Usually they can find you a room when IBUSZ
have filled the rooms they control.

HOSTELS

ET Hostel 'Duna-Parti Diaakhotel', Szentendre Somogyi
Basco Part 12. Open mid July to mid Aug. About £1.20
($2.25; DM3.50). Ask Dunatours about the availability
of space at this hostel (or at any others).

CAMPING

Pap-sziget (tel. 10697). On Pap Island. Open 1 May–
30 Sept. Bungalows available. About a quarter of a
mile from the town centre. There is also a smaller
site on Szentendrei Island. This site lacks many of the
facilities of the three-star Pap-sziget campground, but
is much less crowded. Take the ferry from the northern
landing stage.

ITALY

Anyone who thinks of Italy as a place where accommodation prices are low is likely to be disappointed. Compared to Greece, Portugal and Spain, accommodation is no bargain, and, in some ways, this is also true when comparisons are made with Northern Europe. In the major Italian cities, hostels are around the same price as those in the Netherlands and Denmark, but rarely approach the quality of hostels in those countries. Similarly, cheap Italian hotels cost roughly the same as their German counterparts, but the latter offer much higher standards of comfort and cleanliness.

In the main places of interest, accommodation options for solo travellers can be restricted to hostelling or camping, unless they can find someone to share a room with, or can afford to pay upwards of 25,000–30,000L (£11.75–14.00; $22.25–26.50; DM34–41) for one of the limited supply of singles. For two or more people travelling together, hostelling or staying in cheap hotels are the best, easily available options. Rooms in private homes (*camere libre*) can be much cheaper than hotels, but are not easy to find. Ask the Tourist Office for details regarding their availability.

Hotels are rated from one up to five stars. Charges, which are fixed by the Provincial Tourist Board, should be clearly displayed in the room. It should also be stated whether overnight price is inclusive of breakfast, showers and IVA (service tax), as these are often charged separately. If there is no notice in the room, ask the management for written confirmation of the relevant details. At the lower end of the hotel market IVA is charged at 10 per cent. Showers normally cost 1000–3000L (£0.50–1.50; $1–3; DM1.50–4.50). Breakfast can add anything from 3000–10,000L (£1.40–4.75;

$2.75–9.00; DM4.00–13.75) to the overnight price per person, but, legally, breakfast is optional for those staying only a few days. Hoteliers can insist, however, that you take half-board if you stay for a lengthy period.

In most of the main towns you can consider yourself fortunate if you find a double in the region of 20,000L (£9.50; $17.75; DM27.25) per person. More likely you are going to pay around 25,000L (£11.75; $22.25; DM34) p.p. For triples, you will rarely pay more than another third on top of the price of doubles. Florence, Milan, Bologna and Venice are the places most likely to cause you problems in your search for one of the cheaper rooms, due to a combination of higher than average prices and demand exceeding supply. If you are beginning to despair in Venice, consider staying in nearby Mestre, or Padua (regular trains leave right up to midnight; 10- and 30-minute trips respectively). In the off-season, hotels often reduce their prices. If they have not already done so, you can expect some success if you try to bargain them down.

The **Italian YHA** operates about 50 hostels, split into three grades. Even the top-rated hostels can vary dramatically in quality. Prices start at 8500L (£4; $7.50; DM11.50), but normally you will pay around 10,000–12,500L (£4.65–5.80; $8.75–11.00; DM13.50–16.75). In some of the main cities, such as Rome, Venice, Florence, Milan and Naples, prices range from 15,000–17,500L (£7–8; $13.25–15.25; DM20.25–23.25). At hostels charging 11,000L (£5.10; $9.75; DM15) and over, breakfast is included in the price. Non-members are usually admitted on the payment of a small surcharge (2000L (£0.90; $1.75; DM2.75) per night). In Venice non-members are only admitted if they buy a membership card, costing 24,000L (£11.25; $21.50; DM32.75). In summer, hostel curfews are normally 11.30 p.m. Hostels are seldom conveniently located in the centre of town, and many of the smaller towns of particular interest have no hostel.

In the cities there are also a number of independent and local authority-run youth hostels. Prices and curfews are similar to those of IYHF hostels. In most of the larger cities women have the option of staying in one of the dormitories run by the various religious orders. These establishments, known as 'Protezione della Giovane', offer high standards of accommodation and security to female travellers. Prices are normally around 15,000L (£7; $13.50; DM20.50) in singles, 10,000L (£4.75; $9; DM13.75) in doubles, but can reach 27,500L (£13; $24.50; DM37.50) p.p. in some institutions in Venice. Curfews are usually between 10.00 and 11.30 p.m. During university vacations it is possible to stay in vacant **student accommodations**. Applications should be made to the local 'Casa dello Studento'. Ask the local Tourist Office for the location and the telephone number.

There are over 2000 registered **campsites**. Strictly speaking, you are not supposed to camp outside these sites, but the authorities are unlikely to trouble you if you are camping on privately owned land with the permission of the owner. Unless you are planning to do a considerable amount of touring outside the main cities there is not much to commend taking a tent, other than as an insurance should all else fail. Sites serving the cities are usually large, crowded, noisy and located far from the centre; by and large, they are more suited to those travelling by car than those relying on public transport. Camping is also quite expensive. Normally, charges are around 3000L (£1.40; $2.75; DM4) per tent, and 5500L (£2.50; $5; DM7.50) per occupant, but can rise well above this in city sites. It is not unusual to be charged 6000L (£2.75; $5.25; DM8.25) per tent and per person. Some of the sites near Venice charge a ridiculous 15,000L (£7; $13.25; DM20.25) per tent, 5000L (£2.35; $4.50; DM6.75) per person, and above, in the peak season. Security is also a problem, so you can add to the cost of camping and public transport the cost of storing your pack at the station (at 1500L (£0.70; $1.25; DM2) per day, or each time you want access to it within that period).

Sleeping in train stations has recently been made illegal, and the police are not too well disposed to those sleeping rough elsewhere. If you are **sleeping rough**, however, the police are likely to be the least of your problems. Places which seem well suited to sleeping out also tend to be the places where naïve and foolish travellers are stripped of their cash and belongings (and, where the thieves have a sense of humour, their clothes too). The Borghese Gardens in Rome is one prime example. Naples is especially dangerous, but you should avoid sleeping rough in Italy as a whole.

Anyone who would like to spend some time in the countryside might consider **renting a cottage or a farmhouse**. These can be rented for as little as 3500–8000L (£1.65–3.75; $3.15–7.15; DM4.75–10.85) per night, which represents excellent value for money. Hikers and climbers should contact the Italian Alpine Club for details of the 465 refuge huts in the Italian Alps. The overnight fee is normally around 6000L (£2.75; $5.25; DM8.25), but this rises by 20 per cent in winter.

ADDRESSES

Italian YHA	Associazone Italiana Alberghi per la Gioventù, Via Cavour 44 (terzo piano), 00184 Roma (tel. 06-4746755/4871152).
Student accommodation	'Guide for Foreign Students' booklet is available through the Ministry of Education, Viale Trastevere, Roma.
Camping	Federcampeggio, Casella Postale 23, 50041 Calenzalo (Firenze) supplies lists and maps, as does the State Tourist Office, London or your capital city. If you want to buy a guide while in Italy, the 'Euro Camping' guide is easy to pick up and one of the best available, for around 10,000L (£4.75; $9; DM13.75)

Farmhouses and cottages	Agriturist, Corso V Emanuele 101, Roma (tel. 06-6512342).
Mountain Refuges (Rifugi Alpini)	Club Alpino Italiano, Via Ugli Foscolo 3, Milano (tel. 02–72022555).

Assisi   (tel. code 075)

The train stops in Assisi-Santa Maria degli Angeli, three
miles from the old town of Assisi (a bus to the old town
leaves from the station). Accommodation is cheaper in Santa
Maria degli Angeli than in the old town.

HOTELS

In the old town

**Cheapest doubles around 18,000L
(£8; $15.25; DM23.25) p.p.**

  Ancajani, Via Ancajani 16 (tel. 812472).
  Anfiteatro Romano, Via Anfiteatro Romano (tel. 813025).
  Italia, Vicolo della Fortezza (tel. 812625).
  La Rocca, Via Porta Perlici 27 (tel. 812284).

**Cheapest doubles around 20,000L
(£8.75; $16.75; DM25.75) p.p.**

  Sole-Rist. Ceppo Della Catena, Corso Mazzini 35 (tel.
    812373).
  Sole (dipendenza), Corso Mazzini 35 (tel. 812922).

Cheapest doubles around 22,500L (£10; $19; DM29) p.p.

  Viole, S.S. 147h Viole d'Assisi (tel. 814109).
  Belvedere, Via Borgo Aretino 13 (tel. 812460).
  Da Angelo, Località S. Potente 35c (tel. 812821).
  Da Rina, Piaggia S. Pietro 20 (tel. 812817).
  Europa, Via Metastasio. 2b (tel. 812412).
  Lieto Soggiorno, Via A. Fortini (tel. 816191).

If you can afford to pay around 28,000L (£12.50; $23.75;
    DM36) p.p. you can get a double with a private
    shower/bath at the four hotels below, or at the first
    four hotels listed above:

Bellavista, S. Pietro Campagna 140 (tel. 8041636).
Cavalluci, S. Pietro Campagna (tel. 813279).
Grotta Antica, Via Macelli Vecchi 1 (tel. 813467).
Properzio, Via S. Francesco 38 (tel. 813188).

HOSTEL

In the small village of Fontemaggio, just over a mile
outside the old town (tel. 813636). Around 12,000L
(£5.30; $10.25; DM15.50).

CAMPING

Also in Fontemaggio. Same tel. no. as the hostel.

In Santa Maria degli Angeli:

**Cheapest doubles around 15,000L
(£6.75; $12.75; DM19.25) p.p.**

Donnini, Via Los Angeles 47 (tel. 8040260).

**Cheapest doubles around 18,000L
(£8; $15.25; DM23.25) p.p.**

Dal Moro, Via Bechetti 11 (tel. 8041666).
Marconi, Piazza Dante Alighieri 3 (tel. 8040277).
Patrono d'Italia, Via Patrono d'Italia (tel. 8040221).

**Cheapest doubles around 20,000L
(£8.75; $16.75; DM25.75) p.p.**

Porziuncola, Piazza Garibaldi 10 (tel. 8041020).
Moderno, Via G. Carducci 33 (tel. 8040410).

Bologna (tel. code 051)

Although there are some inexpensive hostels, it can be difficult to find one with rooms available. Fortunately the Tourist Office (IAT) in the main train station books rooms for free. When they are closed they put up a list of hotels with vacancies. Surprisingly, the cheapest singles are in two- and three-star hotels, at 20,000–26,000L (£8.75–11.50; $16.75–22.00; DM25.75–33.50), but these are in short supply, and the other singles in these hotels are expensive. For singles in this price range try Due Torri (two star), Via degli Usberti 4 (tel. 269826) (expensive doubles) and the hotels indicated below.

HOTELS

One star unless shown:

Cheapest doubles around 13,500L (£6; $11.50; DM17.50) p.p. – one star unless indicated.

Minerva, Via De Monari 3 (tel. 239652).

Cheapest doubles around 15,000–16,750L (£6.75–7.50; $12.75–14.25; DM19.50–21.75) p.p.

Gianna, Via Belle Arti 8 (tel. 270653). All rooms in this price range.

Rossini (two star), Via Bibbiena 11 (tel. 237716). Cheap singles.

Orologio (two star), Via IV Novembre 10 (tel. 231253). Singles.

Touring (two star), Via Mattuiani 1/2 (tel. 584305). Cheap singles.

Nuovo (two star), Via del Porto 6 (tel. 247926). Singles.

**Cheapest doubles around 19,000L
(£8.50; $16.25; DM24.75) p.p.**

Metropolitan (three star), Via dell'Orso 4 (tel. 272801).
  Singles.
Roveri, Via Mattei 72 (tel. 532118).

**Cheapest doubles around 22,500–25,000L
(£10–11; $19–21; DM29–32) p.p.**

Pedrini, Strada Maggiore 79 (tel. 346912).
Tre Poeti, Via Caldarese 7 (tel. 228605).
Apollo, Via Drapperie 5 (tel. 223955).
Il Guercino, Via 1. Serra 7 (tel. 369893). English spoken.
Tuscalano (two star), Via Tuscalano 29 (tel. 324024). Some
  rooms with a bath/shower at the prices above.
Farini, Via Farini 13 (tel. 271969).

**Cheapest doubles around 27,000L
(£12; $22.75; DM34.75) p.p.**

Paderno (two star), Via di Paderno 1 (tel. 589080).
Centrale (two star), Via della Zecca 2 (tel. 223899).
Garisenda, Galleria del Leone 1 (tel. 272902).

**Cheapest doubles around 28,500L
(£12.75; $24; DM36.75) p.p.**

Borsa, Via Goito 4 (tel. 222978).
Ferraresi, Via Livraghi 1 (tel. 221802).
Giardinetto, Via Massarenti 76 (tel. 342793/309826).
San Vitale, Via San Vitale 94 (tel. 225966).
Sterlino, Via Murri 71 (tel. 342751).
Villa Azurra, Via Felsina 49 (tel. 535460).
Marconi, Via Marconi 22 (tel. 262832).
Ideale, Via Sirani 5 (tel. 358270).
Perla, Via San Vitale 77/2 (tel. 224579).
San Mamolo, Via Falcone 8 (tel. 583056).

Try also:

    Neva, Via Serra 7 (tel. 369893). Behind the station.
    Fiorita, Via San Felice 6 (tel. 229560).
    Testoni, Via Testoni 3 (tel. 23968).

IYHF HOSTEL

'San Sisto', Via Viadagola 14 (tel. 519202). About four
    miles from the main train station. From Via Irnerio
    (near the main station, off Via dell'Indipendenza) take
    bus 93 heading east. Mon–Sat. Last bus 8.15 p.m.
    Sundays and during 1–24 August bus 301.

CITY HOSTEL

Ask at the Tourist Office if the 'Dormitorio Comunale' is in
operation.

CAMPING

No convenient site. Piccolo Paradiso is in Marzabotto, some
distance away (tel. 842680). Open Mar.–Dec. Ask the Tourist
Office how to get to the site.

Brindisi (tel. code 0831)

HOTELS

**Cheapest singles around 8500L (£3.75; $7.25; DM11),
doubles around 6750L (£3; $5.75; DM8.75) p.p.**

Locanda Doria, Via Fulvia 38 (tel. 26453). Cheapest in
    town, but best avoided by women travelling alone.

**Cheapest doubles around 18,000L (£8; $15.25; DM23.25)
p.p., singles slightly more expensive.**

Roial, Piazza Cairoli (tel. 28547).
Venezia, Via Pisanelli 6 (tel. 25411).
Villa Blanca, Via Armengol 23 (tel. 25438).

Cheapest doubles around 22,500L (£10; $19; DM29) p.p.

Bologna, Via Cavour 41 (tel. 222883).
Altair, Via Tunisi 2 (tel. 24911).

Few people stay in Brindisi for any other reason than the fact
it is the ferry port to/from Greece. This is hardly surprising
as it is basically a dirty, unattractive place. If you are going
to spend a night in the area you would be better heading
for Bari, only 75 miles away on the train line to Rome and a
1½-hour journey. Not only is Bari an interesting city in itself,
but there is also an area where you can **camp** or **sleep out**
for free. There are toilet and washing facilities on site, and
free luggage storage.

Pineta San Francesco (tel. 080-441186) (24 hours). Bus 5
from the train station. The site is run by an organization
called Stop-Over, who also offer two-night stays in **private
flats** for 26,000L (£11.50; $22; DM33.50); great value if you
want to stay a couple of days. Any of the four Stop-Over
offices will give you details of the other offers open to
under 30s for one day, such as free bus travel, free bike
hire. Stop-Over Offices:

OTE, Via Dante 111 (tel. 080-5214538).
Piazza Moro. By the main train station.
At the Maritime Station, c/o the Adriatica Office.
Registration desk at Pineta San Francesco.

There is also an **IYHF hostel** in Bari-Palese, about five
miles from the town centre: 'del Levante', Via Nicola
Massaro 33 (tel. 080-320282).

Florence (Firenze) (tel. code 055)

Prices in Florentine hotels have now surpassed those of their Venetian equivalents. Expect to pay in the region of 20,000–27,000L (£9–12; $16.75–23.25; DM25.75–35.50) per person for a double in a one-star hotel, with around 23,000L (£10.25; $19.50; DM29.75) p.p. being the norm. There are plenty of hotels around the station, but these tend to fill up fast during the summer, and around Easter. If you are having trouble finding a room, use the Informazioni Turistiche Alberghiere service at the station (tel. 283500), but remember to state what price range you can afford, as otherwise they will offer you expensive rooms.

HOTELS

Near the station, all one star:

Ausonia e Rimini, Via Nazionale 24 (tel. 496547).

Cely, Piazza Santa Maria Novella 24 (tel. 218755).

Delle Rose, Canto de Nelli 2 (tel. 296373).

Erina, Via Fiume 17 (tel. 284343).

Ester, Largo F.11i Alinari 15 (tel. 212741).

Giacobazzi, Piazza Santa Maria Novella 24 (tel. 294679).

Fiorentina, Via dei Fossi 12 (tel. 219530).

Giovanna, Via Faenza 69 (tel. 261353).

Iris, Piazza Santa Maria Novella 22 (tel. 296735).

La Mia Casa, Piazza Santa Maria Novella 23 (tel. 213061).

La Romagnola, Via della Scala 40 (tel. 211597).

La Scala, Via della Scala 21 (tel. 212629).

Margareth, Via della Scala 25 (tel. 210138).

Mariella, Via Fiume 11 (tel. 212302).

Montreal, Via della Scala 43 (tel. 262331).

Nettuno, Piazza Santa Maria Novella (tel. 294449).

Palmer, Via degli Avelli 2 (tel. 262391).

Pina, Via Faenza 69 (tel. 212231).

Tamerici, Via Fiume 5 (tel. 214156).

Universo, Piazza Santa Maria Novella 20 (tel. 211484).

Azzi, Via Faenza 56 (tel. 213806).
Enza, Via S. Zanobi 45 (tel. 490990).
La Rosa Thea, Piazza Indipendenza 24 (tel. 474316).
Lombardi, Via Fiume 8 (tel. 283151).
Fiorentino, Via degli Avelli 8 (tel. 212692).
Mary, Piazza Indipendenza 5 (tel. 496310).

The cathedral is about 15 minutes' walk from the station.
The hotels below are located about midway, again all one
star:
Il Perseo, Via Cerretani 1 (tel. 212504).
Parodi, Piazza Madonna degli Aldobrandini 8 (tel. 211866).
San Giovanni, Via Cerretani 2 (tel. 213580).
Giappone, Via dei Banchi 1 (tel. 210090).
Stazione, Via dei Banchi 3 (tel. 283133).
Varsavia, Via Panzani 5 (tel. 215615).

In the area around San Marco and the university:
Sampaoli, Via San Gallo 14 (tel. 284834).
San Marco, Via Cavour 50 (tel. 284235).
Colomba, Via Cavour 21 (tel. 263139).
Colorado, Via Cavour 66 (tel. 217310).

Around the cathedral and Palazzo Vecchio:
Brunori, Via del Proconsolo 5 (tel. 263648).
Colore, Via Calzaiuoli 13 (tel. 210301).
Cristina, Via Condotta 4 (tel. 214484).
Davanzati, Via Porta Rossa 15 (tel. 283414).
Esperanza, Via dell'Inferno 3 (tel. 213773).
Esplanade, Via Tornabuoni 13 (tel. 287078).
Firenze, Piazza Donati 4 (tel. 214203).
Maria Luisa de Medici, Via del Corso 1 (tel. 280048).
Maxim, Via de Medici 4 (tel. 217474).
Orchidea, Borgo degli Albizi 11 (tel. 2480346).
Por Santa Maria, Via Calimaruzza 3 (tel. 216370).
Te-Ti e Prestige, Via Porta Rossa 5 (tel. 298248).
Aldini, Via Calzaiuoli 13 (tel. 214752).

Near the Ponte Vecchio:
  Cestelli, Borgo SS Apostoli 25 (tel. 214213).

Across the river, near Santo Spirito (the best area for good
cheap food):
  Bandini, Piazza Santo Spirito 9 (tel. 215308).

IYHF HOSTEL

  Viale Augusto Righi 2–4 (tel. 601451). 16,000L (£7; $13.50;
  DM20.50) per night. About 3½ miles from the town
  centre. Bus 17B from the station.

HOSTELS

  Ostello Santa Monaca, Via Santa Monaca 6 (tel. 268338).
  Midnight curfew. Price similar to that of the IYHF hostel.
  No reservations, so arrive anytime after 9.30 a.m. to sign
  the list and put some form of ID in the box. Go back
  to check in from 4.00–4.30 p.m. Bus 36 or 37 from the
  station to the first stop over the river, or 20 minutes
  on foot.
  Pensionato Pio X-Artigianelli, Via de Serragli 106 (tel.
  225044). Two-day min. stay. Midnight curfew. No
  reservations, arrive really early. Slightly more than
  the nearby Santa Monaca hostel at around 17,500L
  (£7.65; $14.50; DM22.20). Same buses, to the second
  stop across the river.
  Istituto Gould, Via de Serragli 49 (tel. 212576). About
  30 per cent more expensive than the Santa Monaca
  hostel, but all rooms are doubles. Oct.–June usually
  full of local students. At other times requires pre-paid
  reservations. Write 3–4 months before your date of
  arrival for details. Same directions as the Santa Monaca
  hostel.

CAMPING

Parco Communale. Viale Michelangelo 80 (tel. 6811977). Open April to October. Frequently crowded. Tend to say they are full if you phone during the peak season, but usually find space if you turn up. Bus 13 from the station.

Villa di Camerata, Viale Augusto Righi 2–4 (next to the youth hostel) (tel. 610300). Open Apr.–Oct. Slightly cheaper than the Parco Communale site. Bus 17b from the station.

'AREA DE SOSTA'

A covered area where you can put down a mat and a sleeping bag. Run by the city authorities in Villa Favard, about four miles from the town centre. Washing and toilet facilities are available at the site. No charge. Max. stay one week. Open from 7 p.m.–10 a.m. Bus 14a, 14b or 14c from the station. Leave your pack at the station.

Milan (Milano) (tel. code 02)

Milanese hotel prices are amongst the highest in Italy. In recent years prices seem to have risen faster than in other cities. Expect to pay around 20,000–27,500L (£9–12; $16.75–23.25; DM25.75–35.50) per person for a double in a one-star hotel. Some hotels have a few cheap rooms, but these tend to fill up quickly. The best place to find cheap (by Milanese standards) rooms is around Centrale Station.

HOTELS

All located near Central Station:

Ambrosiana, Via Plinio 22 (tel. 279670).

Arno, Via Lazzaretto 17 (tel. 652782).

Arthur, Via Lazzaretto 14 (tel. 2046294).

Bussentina, Via Settala 3 (tel. 288517).

Canna, Viale Tunisia 6 (tel. 224133).

Charly, Via Settala 78 (tel. 278190).

Due Giardini, Via Settala 46 (tel. 220093).

Valley, Via Soperga 19 (tel. 6692777).

Villa Victoria, Via Vitruvio 18 (tel. 2046870).

Manzoni, Via Senato 45 (tel. 791002).

Principe, Corso Buenos Aires 75 (tel. 6694377).

Rivoli, Via G. Lulli 11 (tel. 2046815).

Soperga, Via Soperga 19 (tel. 278228) (not the three-star
hotel at Via Soperga 24).

Trentina, Via F. Lippi 50 (tel. 2361208).

Eva, Via Lazzaretto 17 (tel. 6592898).

Internazionale, Via Dante 15 (tel. 873697).

Italia, Via Vitruvio 44 (tel. 6693826).

Merano, Via Lazzaretto 10 (tel. 279378).

Nazionale, Via Vitruvio 46 (tel. 6693059).

Plinius, Via Plinio 2 (tel. 276827).

Ugoletti, Via Settala 56 (tel. 222366).

Vitruvio, Via B. Marcello 65 (tel. 2711807).

Ballarin, Via Soncino 3 (tel. 800822).

Brera, Via Pontaccio 9 (tel. 873509).

Dante, Via Dante 14 (tel. 866471).

Paganini, Via Paganini 6 (tel. 278443).

IYHF HOSTEL

Ostello Piero Rotta, Via Martino Bassi 2/Viale Salmoiraghi
2 (tel. 367095). Curfew 11.30 p.m. (Not far from the
San Siro/Guiseppe Meazza stadium. Football every
Sunday. Milan or Internazionale.) From Central Station
metro line 2 to Cadorna, then line 1 heading for S.
Leonardo to QT8/San Siro. Line 1 splits, so make sure
you don't get on a train to Inganni.

DORMITORIES

Casa Famiglia ACISJF, Corso Garibaldi 121a–123 (tel. 6595206). Women only. Around 23,000L (£10.25; $19.50, DM29.75) per night. Very safe, but a 10.30 p m curfew. Near Garibaldi station. Take a train from Centrale, walk down Corso Como which leads into Garibaldi.

CAMPING

The three closest sites are all a considerable distance away:
Il Barregino, Via Corbettina, Bareggio (tel. 9014417). Open all year.
Autodromo, Parco di Monza, Monza (tel. 387771). Open Apr.–Sept.
Agip Metanopoli, Via Emilia, San Donato Milanese (tel. 5272159). Open all year.
Ask at the Tourist Office for directions to the sites.

Naples (Napoli) (tel. code 081)

Accommodation prices are lower here than in the other major cities, and there are plenty of one-star hotels where you can get a double for 20,000L (£8.90; $16.75; DM25.50) per person. Unfortunately the standard of accommodation in these Neapolitan one-star hotels does not compare favourably with their more northern counterparts, especially as regards cleanliness and security. You might want to leave your pack at the station. There are a few two-star hotels which are reasonably cheap, and which are safer for your belongings. Expect to pay around 25,000L (£11; $21; DM32.25) p.p. in those listed. Do not allow hotel owners to cheat you (this is second nature to many of them). The price for rooms must be clearly displayed on the door of the room.

Finding a hotel with a decent location can be difficult.

The area around the Central train station is hardly choice, but is more intimidating than really dangerous (unless you are stupid enough to wander through it with your pack at night). Two areas which are dangerous at night are the university quarter (around Via Roma and Piazza Dante) and the Santa Lucia district. The area around the Mergellina station is one of the best, but hotel options here are limited. The IYHF hostel is in this part of town. Even those who are usually none too keen on hostels might want to consider staying here. The hostel itself is fine, and you will have no problems as regards personal security (although you should still leave your pack at the station).

HOTELS

Near the Campi Flegrei station – one star unless indicated:
  Cesare Augusto (two star), Viale Augusto 42 (tel. 615981). Walk round the right-hand side of the square on leaving the station until you see Viale Augusto on the right.
Near Mergellina station:
  The Tourist Information Office in the station opens irregularly. If it is open ask them to show you the locations of the following hotels on a map. All are within easy walking distance of the station.
  Muller (two star), Piazza Mergellina 7 (tel. 669056). Down towards the sea from the metro stop.
  Bella Napoli (two star), Via Carraciolo 10 (tel. 680234). If you get no response the Tourist Office (tel. 7644871 or 268779) will give you the new tel. no. Via Carraciolo lines the waterfront, so just go down to the sea from the station.
  Colibri, Via Carraciolo 10 (tel. 681486).
  Ausonia, Via Carraciolo 11 (tel. 682278). Prices similar to those of a cheap two-star hotel.
  Crispi, Via Francesco Giordani 2 (tel. 664804). Walk away from the sea, then right along Via A. d'Isernia, left on to Via Giordani. From Piazza Garibaldi outside Central

Station you can take bus 4 to Via M. Schipa which is crossed by Via Giordani.

Santa Lucia district:
Teresita, Via Santa Lucia 90 (tel. 412105). Safe hotel, but an unsafe surroundings.

University quarter:
Imperia, Piazza Miraglia 386 (tel. 459347). Another good hotel in a bad area. Bus 185, CD or CS from Piazza Garibaldi.

Around Central Station:
Sayonara (two star), Piazza Garibaldi 59 (tel. 220313). The square in front of Central Station.
Aurora, Piazza Garibaldi 60 (tel. 201920).
Dalia, P. Garibaldi 49 (tel. 224058).
Ginestra, P. Garibaldi 60 (tel. 221053).
Potenza, P. Garbaldi 120 (tel. 286330).
Regina, P. Garbaldi 42 (tel. 336165).
Caterino, Via Firenze 61 (tel. 220603). Turn right on leaving the station. This leads you into Via Firenze.
Marconi, Via Firenze 32 (tel. 223764).
Zara, Via Firenze 81 (tel. 287125).
Giglio, Via Firenze 16 (tel. 287500).
Atlas, Corso Meridionale 39 (tel. 285718). Turn right on leaving the station, right on to Via Firenze, which leads into Corso Meridionale.
Casanova (two star), Via Venezia 2 (tel. 268287). Just off Via Milan. One of the best in the area.
Elisa, Via Mancini 11 (tel. 269494). Straight across P. Garibaldi as you look out from the station.
Washington (two star), Corso Umberto I 311 (tel. 286729). Corso Umberto I runs from the far left corner of P. Garibaldi as you look out from the station.
Orchidea, Corso Umberto I 7 (tel. 283412).
Alberto Trentino, Corso Umberto I 31 (tel. 5540397). One of the best hotels in the area.

IYHF HOSTEL

'Mergellina', Salita della Grotta a Piedigrotta 23 (tel. 7612346). Only 300m from the Mergellina station.

CAMPING

Camping Solfatara (tel. 8673413). On the edge of a volcano crater. Bus 152 from Piazza Garibaldi to the site. Alternatively catch a local train from beneath Central Station to Pozzuoli, the last stop. Train free with Inter Rail. From the station the site is a half-mile walk, mostly uphill.

Pisa (tel. code 050)

HOTELS

Expect to pay around 20,000L (£8.90; $17; DM25.75) p.p. in doubles at the hotels listed, though some of the hotels below have a number of rooms at considerably lower prices. Where this is the case a rough idea is given as to the cost of these rooms.

Rinascente, Via del Castelletto 28 (tel. 502436). 50–60% of price above.

Serena, Via D. Cavalca 45 (tel. 24491). 50–60% of price above.

Galileo, Via Santa Maria 12 (tel. 40621).

Villino Aurora, Via Pietro da Pisa 4 (tel. 44109). 50–60% of price above.

Clio, Via San Lorenzo 3 (tel. 28446). Rooms with a shower/bath only slightly more expensive than price above.

Di Stefano, Via Sant'Apollonia 35 (tel. 26359).

Giardino, Via C. Cammeo (tel. 562101).

Helvetia, Via Don G. Boschi 31 (tel. 41232). 75% of price above. Small number of rooms with shower/bath only slightly above price quoted.

Graziella, Via La Nunziatina 24 (tel. 42152).
San Rocco, Via Contessa Matilde (tel. 42380).
Gronchi, Piazza Arcivescovado 1 (tel. 561823).
Maggiore, Via Colombo 51 (tel. 501459).
Milano, Via Mascagni 14 (tel. 23162).
Modena, Piazza Toniolo 20 (tel. 501076).

DORMITORIES

Casa della Giovane, Via Corridoni 31 (tel. 22732). Women
only. Around 19,000L (£8.50; $16; DM24.50) per night,
including breakfast. Reception open until midnight. A
short distance from the station. Turn right on leaving
the station.

CAMPING

Torre Pendente, Viale delle Cascine 86 (tel. 560665). Open
mid Mar. to Oct. About five minutes' walk from the
Leaning Tower, past the cathedral and baptistry, out
through the old walls, turn right, then left.

Rome (Roma) (tel. code 06)

Rome has a vast stock of hotel rooms, so even in July
and August when hordes of visitors flock into the city,
there are still enough beds to go round. Prices for one-star
hotels vary considerably, from 19,500–32,500L (£8.75–14.25;
$16.50–27.50; DM25.25–42.00) per person in doubles. Prices
are cheapest around the Termini station, where on average you
can expect to pay about 23,500L (£10.25; $19.50; DM29.75) p.p.
for doubles. Understandably, this is the area most popular with
budget travellers. The large concentration of rooms means you
can make personal enquiries at a lot of hotels without having to
walk very far, but consider leaving your pack at the station as

many establishments are on the upper floors. The city centre is within walking distance of this area. Public transport links between the station and the centre are good (by bus or metro). Rooms tend to be more expensive in the city centre.

One problem you may encounter if you phone ahead is that hoteliers invariably speak Italian only. While they may be able to tell you that rooms are available in several languages, any further communication is unlikely. If this is the case, consider getting the Tourist Office (EPT) or Student Tourist Centre (CTS) to phone for you, but insist on them phoning the hotels you suggest, because the rooms they will find you otherwise will be well outside your price range. In July and August EPT are none too keen on looking for rooms.

Agencies

> EPT: Office in Termini station, between platforms 1 and 2 (tel. 4750078). Open daily 8.15 a.m.–7.00 p.m. Long queues are the norm. Head Office, Via Parigi 5 (tel. 463748). Open Mon.–Sat. 8.15 a.m.–7.00 p.m. About half a mile from Termini, yet much shorter queues. On leaving the station head for the far left-hand corner of the square, up Viale L. Einaudi, across Piazza della Repubblica. Go round the right-hand side of the roundabout, up Via G. Romita, then right to Via Parigi.

> CTS: Via Genova 16 (tel. 46791). Open Mon.–Fri. 9 a.m.–1 p.m. and 4–7 p.m., Sat. 9 a.m.–1 p.m. only.

HOTELS

Near the station – all one star:

> Ascot, Via Montebello 22 (tel. 4741675).
> Bianca, Via Volturno 48 (tel. 4040672).
> Bolognese, Via Palestro 15 (tel. 490045).
> Capri, Via Magenta 13 (tel. 491367).
> Castelfidardo, Via Castelfidardo 31 (tel. 4742894).
> Cina, Via Montebello 114 (tel. 4041379).

Corallo, Via Palestro 44 (tel. 4456340).
Cressy, Via Volturno 27 (tel. 486956).
Danubio, Via Palestro 34 (tel. 4041305).
Dell'Urbe, Via del Mille 27a (tel. 4455767).
Elide, Via Firenze 50 (tel. 4741367).
Esedra, Piazza della Repubblica 47 (tel. 463912).
Ethel, Via Palestro 34 (tel. 4958134).
Eureka, Piazza della Repubblica 47 (tel. 4755806).
Iride, Via M. D'Azeglio 24 (tel. 465270).
Jose, Via Palestro 55 (tel. 490895).
Katty, Via Palestro 35 (tel. 4751385).
Lachea, Via San Martino della Battaglia 11 (tel. 4957256).
Lella, Via Palestro 9 (tel. 484940).
Magic, Via Milazzo 20 (tel. 4959880).
Marini, Via Palestro 35 (tel. 4040058).
Palestro, Via Palestro 88 (tel. 4953218).
Petrucci, Via Palestro 87 (tel. 491803).
Piemonte, Via Vicenza 34 (tel. 4452240).
Rubino, Via Milazzo 3 (tel. 4452323).
Sileo, Via Magenta 39 (tel. 4450246).
Simonetta, Via Palestro 34 (tel. 4742784).
Stefanella, Via Magenta 39 (tel. 4451646).
Tre Stelle, Via San Martino della Battaglia 11 (tel. 493095).
Ventura, Via Palestro 88 (tel. 4451951).
Wetzler, Piazza della Repubblica 47 (tel. 4827994).
Dolomiti, Via San Martino della Battaglia 11 (tel. 491058).
Cortorillo, Via Principe Amedeo 79a (tel. 7316064).
Contilia, Via Principe Amedeo 79 (tel. 730074).
Govoni, Via Principe Amedeo 76 (tel. 4814970).
Papà Germano, Via Calatafimi 14a (tel. 486919).
Di Rienzo, Via Principe Amedeo 79a (tel. 736956).
Pezzotti, Via Principe Amedeo 79a (tel. 734633).
Tony, Via Principe Amedeo 79d (tel. 736994).
Tortoriello, Via Principe Amedeo 76 (tel. 4743575).
Tommasini, Via Principe Amedeo 76 (tel. 4824222).

Between the station and the city centre:
Fiorella, Via del Babuino 196 (tel. 3610597).

Galatea, Via Genova 24 (tel. 4743070).
Giardino, Via XXIV Maggio 51 (tel. 6794584).
Irene, Via del Lavatore 37 (tel. 6791131).
Jonella, Via della Croce 41 (tel. 6797966).
Lina, Via Rassella 44 (tel. 4755066).
Panda, Via della Croce 35 (tel. 6780179).
Perugia, Via del Colosseo 7 (tel. 6797200).

Centrally located:
Sud America, Via Cavour 116 (tel. 4745521).
Chic, Via Cavour 266 (tel. 4758614).
Arenula, Via S. Maria del Calderari 47 (tel. 6879454).
Della Lunetta, Piazza del Paradiso 68 (tel. 6861080).
Ida, Via Germanico 198 (tel. 386717).
Lady, Via Germanico 198 (tel. 314938).
Manara, Via Luciano Manara 25 (tel. 5890713).
Nautilus, Via Germanico 198 (tel. 315549).
Navona, Via del Sediari 8 (tel. 6543802).
Ottaviano, Via Ottaviano 6 (tel. 383956).
Primavera, Piazza San Pantaleo 3 (tel. 6543109).
Schiavo, Viale G. Cesare 47 (tel. 380021).
Sole, Via del Biscione 76 (tel. 6540873).
Ticino, Via del Gracchi 161 (tel. 388122).
Zurigo, Via Germanico 198 (tel. 350139).

IYHF HOSTEL

'Foro Italico-A.F. Pessina', Viale delle Olimpiadi 61 (tel.
3964709). By the Olympic stadium (football every
Sunday during the season, Roma or Lazio). Metro
A to Ottaviano, then bus 32. Well out from the
centre. 11 p.m. curfew. About 22,000L (£9.75; $18.50;
DM28.50) for B&B.
The Italian YHA also let rooms in three university halls from
about 20 July to 20 Sept.
Via Cesare de Lollis 20. About a mile from Termini. Bus
492 from the station.
Viale del Ministerio degli Affari Esteri 6. Near the IYHF

hostel. The hostel is the check-in point for this residence.

Via Domenico de Dominicis 13. Just over two miles from Termini. Metro A to Colli Albani, then bus 409.

Price for B&B at the three residences is similar to that of the IYHF hostel. Enquiries for all three residences tel. 385943 or 3599295. Advance reservation: AIG, Via Carlo Poma 2, 00195 Roma.

HOSTELS

Centro dei Giovane, Via degli Apuli 40 (tel. 4953151). Near the station. Fills fast. Locando del Conservatorio, Via del Conservatorio 62 (tel. 659612). Singles for the price you will pay for dorms at the IYHF hostel, doubles slightly cheaper. Central location. Understandably popular, so write in advance.

YWCA, Piazza Indipendenza 23c (tel. 462520). Near the station. Safe, if not cheap. Around 35,000L (£15.50; $29.50; DM45) for singles. Midnight curfew. Reports differ as to whether men are admitted.

CAMPING

No central site.

Flaminio, Via Flaminia Nuova (tel. 3279006). Open Mar.–Oct. Quite expensive. One of the closest to the centre (five miles out). Metro A to Flaminio, then bus 202, 203, 204 or 205.

Roma, Via Aureli 831 (tel. 6223018). Open all year. Bus 38 from Termini station to Piazza Fiume, then bus 490 to the last stop. Change to bus 246.

Nomentana, Via Nomentana (corner of Via della Cesarina) (tel. 6100296). Open Mar.–Oct. Bus 36 from Termini to Piazza Sempione, then bus 336 to Via Nomentana.

Salaria, Via Salaria 2141 (tel. 17642). Open June to Oct. About 10 miles from the centre.

Capitol, Via Castelfusano 195, Ostia Antica (tel. 5662720). Open all year. Two miles from the ruins. Metro to Piramide, train to Lido Centro then bus 5 to the campsite. The train from Piramide to Ostia Antica leaves you a two-mile walk to the site.

Venice (Venezia) (tel. code 041)

If you arrive in Venice during the summer it is safe to say you will never have seen a city so packed with tourists. This is especially true of August, when the Italians are on holiday. Many visitors only stay in the city a few hours, but sufficient numbers stay overnight to make finding a room difficult. You can try phoning ahead (at least a day before you plan to arrive), but many hoteliers are loath to reserve one of their cheap rooms. They will probably try to make you accept a room with a private shower/bath, and breakfast, thus adding a further 7500L (£3.30; $6.25; DM9.75) p.p. to what you would pay in a basic double. Writing in advance (Italian or English) enclosing a deposit for the first night is more likely to secure the type of room you want. Agree a time to arrive, and get there early to be on the safe side.

In the last few years accommodation prices have not risen as fast as in other Italian cities. While Venetian hotels are by no means cheap, they are now roughly on a par with those in Rome, whereas a few years ago they were considerably more expensive. Singles are still exorbitantly priced, so solo travellers would be advised to find a room-mate. For a basic double in a one-star hotel expect to pay from 15,000–28,500L (£6.75–12.75; $12.75–24.25; DM19.50–37.00) p.p., with 25,000L (£11; $21; DM32.25) being about average.

The Tourist Office (tel. 715016) in the train station will find rooms for you, as will another branch at the bus station in Piazzale Roma (tel. 27402, summer only) and the Student

Tourist Office (CTGS), Dorsoduro 3252 (tel. 705660). Stress the price range you are interested in, otherwise they will offer you expensive rooms. The office at the train station opens at 8 a.m. Queue earlier if you can (it could save you money, and is a good place for solo travellers to team up). If you decide to look for a room on your own, the Cannaregio area to the left of the train station is a good place to start, especially around Lista da Spagna, home to many of the cheapest pensions. Another good area is Santa Croce, across the bridge in front of the station.

The Tourist Office hands out 'Dormire Giovane', a publication listing all the youth accommodations and their respective prices. If you want to stay in the IYHF hostel reservation is recommended at all times. In the summer you have to spend about three hours in a queue to have a hope of getting in without a reservation. Reservations for the city-run hostels are best made in writing one month in advance. Girls can stay at one of the dorms run by the religious orders: curfews can be restrictive, but they are safe, and are more likely to have rooms than cheap hotels. Prices vary: some cost the same as hostels, others as much as hotels.

If you are having trouble finding suitably priced accommodation, prices are lower in nearby Mestre and Padua. Both are linked to Venice by frequent trains, right up to midnight (Mestre is a 10-minute trip, Padua is 30 minutes).

HOTELS

Cannaregio area:
  Archie's House, Cannaregio 1814 San Leonardo (tel. 5220884).
  Villa Rosa, Calle della Misericordia 389. Off Lista da Spagna (tel. 5216569/716569).
  Smeraldo, Canneregio 1333. On Rio Terrà San Leonardo, across the Guglie bridge (tel. 717838).
  Nives Ottolenghi, Calle del Forno. Just off Lista da Spagna by the Hotel Continental (tel. 715206).

Adua, Lista da Spagna 233/A (tel. 716184).

Al Gobbo, Campo S. Geremia 312 (tel. 715001).

Alle Guglie, San Leonardo 1523 (tel. 717351). Near the Guglie bridge.

Bernardi Semenzato, SS Apostoli 4366 (tel. 5227257). English spoken.

Casa Boccassini, Calle del Fumo 5295 (tel. 5229892).

Casa Carrettoni, Lista da Spagna 130 (tel. 716231).

Eden, Rio Terrà Maddalena 2357 (tel. 720228).

Marte, Pont della Guglie 338 (tel. 716351). Near the Guglie bridge.

Minerva, Lista da Spagna 230 (tel. 715968).

Moderno, Lista da Spagna 154/B (tel. 716679).

Rossi, Calle del Procuratie 262 (tel. 715164).

San Geremia, Campo San Geremia 290/A (tel. 716245).

Santa Lucia, Calle Misericordia 358 (tel. 715180). Off Lista da Spagna.

Tintoretto, San Fosca 2316 & 2317 (tel. 721522).

Vagon, Campiello Selvatico 5619 (tel. 5285626).

Santa Croce district:

Antiche Figure, S. Simeon Piccolo 686/A (tel. 718290).

Basilea (Dipendenza), Rio Manin 804 (tel. 718667) (not the two-star hotel at no. 817).

Casa Peron, Salizzada S. Pantalon 85 (tel. 5286038).

Da Bepi, Fondamenta Minotto 160 (tel. 5226735).

Dalla Mora, Salizzada San Pantalon 42/A–44 (tel. 5235703).

Marin, Ramo dei Traghetto 670/B (tel. 718022).

Stefania, Fondamenta Tolentino 181/A (tel. 5203757). Across the bridge from the station, left at the first canal. Watch out for the small lantern.

San Polo district:

Sturion, Calle del Sturion 679 (tel. 5236243).

Alex, Rio Terrà Frari 2606 (tel. 5231341).

Guerrato, Calle dietro la Scimmia. 240/A (tel. 5227131).

San Marco area:

Apollo, at the corner of Campo S. Angelo and Calle della Madonna (tel. 5204909).

Casa Petrarca, Calle delle Colonne 4394 (tel. 5200430). English spoken.

Al Gambero, Calle del Fabbri 4687 (tel. 5224384).

Al Gazzetino, Calle delle Acque 4971 (tel. 5286523).

Budapest, Corte Barozzi 2143 (tel. 5220514).

Fiorita, Campiello Nuovo 3457/A (tel. 5234754).

Orion, Spadaria 700/A (tel. 5223053).

San Salvador, Calle Galiazza 5264 (tel. 5289147).

San Samuele, Piscina S. Samuele 3358 (tel. 5228045).

Dorsuduro district:

Ca'Foscari, Calle della Frescada 3888 (tel. 5225817).

Montin, Fondamenta di Borgo 1147 (tel. 5227151).

Alla Salute-Da Cici, Fondamenta Ca'Balà 222 (tel. 5222271).

Galleria, Accademia 878/A (tel. 5204172).

Casa de Stefani, Calle Traghetto S. Barnaba 2786 (tel. 5223337).

Casa Messner, Salute 216 & 237 (tel. 5227443).

Da Pino, Crossera S. Pantalon 3942 (tel. 5223646).

Antico Capon, Campo S. Margherita 3004/B (tel. 5285292).

Castello – probably the district least visited by tourists:

Al Piave-Da Mario, Ruga Giuffa 4840 (tel. 5285174).

Casa Verardo, Ruga Giuffa 4765 (tel. 5286127).

Sant'Anna, Sant'Anna 269 (tel. 5286466).

Toscana-Tofanelli, Via Garibaldi 1650 (tel. 5235722).

Tiepolo, SS. Filipo e Giacomo 4510 (tel. 5231315).

Silva, Fondamenta Remedio 4423 (tel. 5227643).

Belvedere, Via Garibaldi 1636 (tel. 5285148).

Bridge, SS Filipe e Giacomo 4498 (tel. 5205287).

Canal, Fondamenta Remedio 4422/C (tel. 5234538).

Caneva, Ramo della Favia 5515 (tel. 5228118).

Corona, Calle Corona 4464 (tel. 5229174).

Doni, S. Zaccaria 4656 (tel. 5224267).

Rio, SS Filipo e Giacomo 4356 (tel. 5234810).

Riva, Ponte dell'Anzolo 5310 (tel. 5227034).

IYHF HOSTEL

'Venezia', Fondamenta di Zitelle 86, Isola della Giudecca (tel. 5238211 Fax 041–5235689). On Giudecca island. 11 p.m. curfew. Waterbus 5 from the train station, or 8 from S. Zaccaria (left along the canal as you leave St Mark's Square) to Zitelle, then walk right. Hostel opens 6 p.m. Queue from 3 p.m. if you have not reserved in advance.

CITY HOSTELS

Run by the city authorities during the summer (mid July to mid Sept.) Advance reservation recommended. Reservations handled by the IYHF hostel (address above). Write at least one month before your date of arrival. Prices and curfews similar to those of the IYHF hostel, but more convenient locations.

S. Caboto, Cannaregio 1105f (tel. 716629). Ten minutes from the station. Various accommodation options. Cheapest of all is throwing down a mat and a sleeping bag in the grounds; then camping in your tent in the grounds; followed by a night in the tents they hire out; and, lastly, dorm beds.

R. Michiel, Dorsoduro 1184 (tel. 5227227). Close to the Accademia (waterbus 1, 2 or 34).

S. Fosca, Cannaregio 2372 (tel. 715775). A short walk from Campo S. Fosca. Phone ahead to check the hostel is open.

DORMITORIES

Run by various religious orders. Women only.

Instituto Canossiane, Fondamente del Ponte Piccolo 428, Isola della Giudecca (tel. 5222157). Curfew 10.30 p.m. Dorms. Slightly cheaper than the IYHF hostel on the island. Same waterbuses (see above) but get off at the Sant'Eufemia stop. Short walk to your left.

Foresteria Valdese, Castello 5170 (tel. 5286897). No

curfew. Small dorms. Slightly more expensive than the IYHF hostel. Nearest waterbus stop: S. Zaccaria, near St Mark's Square.

Domus Civica, Calle Chiovere & Calle Campazzo, San Polo 3082. Near the Frari church (tel. 5227139). Open June–July and Sept–mid Oct. Singles around 27,000L (£12; $22.72; DM34.75); doubles 21,000L (£9.30; $17.75; DM27) p.p.

Istituto Ciliota, Calle delle Muneghe 2976, San Marco (tel. 5204888). 11 p.m. curfew. Singles start around 37,000L (£16.50; $31.25; DM47.75); doubles from 31,500L (£14; $26.50; DM40.50) p.p. Waterbus 2 to S. Samuele.

Suore Mantellate, Calle Buccari 10 (tel. 5220829). Open Sept–July. Reserve ahead. B&B in doubles or triples around 31,000L (£13.75; $26.25; DM40) p.p. Waterbus 1 or 2 to Sant'Elena, then across the park.

Domus Covanis, Rio Foscarini 899, Dorsoduro (tel. 5287374).

CAMPING

Waterbus 15 will take you to the Littorale del Cavallino, a peninsula with a string of campsites along its beach. Some charge ridiculously high prices.

Marina da Venezia, Via Hermada (tel. 966146). Open all year. 9,000–20,000L (£4–9; $7.50–17.00; DM11.50–26.00) per tent; 3,500–7,000L (£1.50–3.00; $3.00–5.75; DM4.25–8.75) p.p. depending on the time of year.

Ca' Pasqualli, Via Fausta (tel. 966110). Only slightly cheaper than the site above.

Camping Fusina, Via Moranzani, Fusina (tel. 5470055). From Mestre bus 13 from opposite the Pam super-market to the last stop. Last bus at 10 p.m., a one-hour trip. Waterbus 5 to Zattere, then 16 to Fusina takes about 30 minutes. Prices similar to those above. Mosquito repellent is essential.

San Nicolo, on the island of Lido (tel. 767415). Ferry to Lido, then bus A.

See also the city hostels section above.

SLEEPING ROUGH

Thieves patrol the beaches of the Lido island looking for easy targets. If you choose to sleep here, bed down beside other travellers. Even then ants and mosquitoes can make for an unpleasant night. Sleeping on the train station forecourt is illegal, and the police occasionally use water hoses to clear people away.

Accommodation nearby:

Mestre

PENSIONS/ONE-STAR HOTELS

Maria Luisa, Via Parini 2 (tel. 931968). Near the train station.

Dina, Via Parini 4 (tel. 926565).

Cortina, Via Piave 153 (tel. 929206). The main road facing you as you leave the station.

Giovannina, Via Dante 113 (tel. 926396). Right on leaving the station, then left.

Adria, Via Cappuccina 34 (tel. 989755). Right on leaving the station. Turning on the left after Via Dante.

Al Veronese, Via Capuccina 94/A (tel. 926275).

Da Tito, Via Capuccina 69 (tel. 932390).

Padua (Padova)

CITY HOSTEL

Ostello Citta di Padovà, Via Aleardi 30 (tel. 8752219). Curfew 11 p.m. Around 15,000L (£6.75; $12.50; DM19.25) for B&B. Bus 3, 8 or 18 from the station.

Verona (tel. code 045)

HOTELS

**Cheapest doubles around 15,250L
(£6.75; $12.75; DM19.75) p.p.**

Alla Cancellata, Via Col. Fincato 4/6 (tel. 532820).
Catullo, Via V. Catullo 1 (tel. 8002786). Singles start
around 20,000L (£8.75; $17; DM25.75).
Da Luigi, Via Rodigina 92 (tel. 548737).

**Cheapest doubles around 18,000L
(£8; $15.25; DM23.25) p.p.**

Ciopeta, Vicolo Teatro Filarmonico 2 (tel. 8006843).
Da Andrea, Vicoletto Cieco Disciplina 2 (tel. 32291).
Da Armando, Via Dietro Pallone 1 (tel. 8004824).
Bianca, Via Valverde 66 (tel. 8006791).
Castello, Corso Cavour 43 (tel. 8004403).
Al Cigno, Corso Milano 26 (tel. 567716).
Romano, Via Tombetta 38 (tel. 505228).
Rosa, Vicolo Raggiri 9 (tel. 8005693).
Serenissima, Viale del Lavoro 24 (tel. 501858).
Santa Teresa, Via Scuderlando 87 (tel. 501508).
Usignolo, Stradone S. Lucia 36 (tel. 954344).
Volto Citadella, Vicolo Volto Citadella 8 (tel. 8000077).

**More expensive, with doubles about 24,000L
(£10.75; $20.25; DM31) p.p.**

Marina, Via Ponte Nuovo 5 (tel. 25968).

IYHF HOSTEL

Salita Fontana del Ferro 15 (tel. 590360). Curfew 11 p.m.,
extended for opera goers. Camping permitted. Two
miles from the station, but only 10 minutes' walk from
the town centre. Bus 2 from the station, over the Ponte
Nuovo to Piazza Isolo, then a few minutes' walk.

DORMITORIES

Both are open to women only. Prices start around the same
level as the IYHF hostel, although Casa della Giovane offers
more expensive rooms. Both extend their normal curfew if
you are going to the opera.

Casa della Giovane, Via Pagni 7 (tel. 596880). Curfew
10.30 p.m.

Casa della Studentessa, Via G. Trezza 16 (tel. 8005278).

CAMPING

Romeo e Giulietta, Via Bresciana 54 (tel. 989243). Open all
year. Via Castel San Pietro (tel. 590360). Phone ahead
to check if the site is open. Bus 3. Also at the IYHF
hostel (see above).

LUXEMBOURG

Due to the small size of Luxembourg it is possible to visit all the places of interest on daytrips from the capital. However, accommodation prices are generally higher in the city, and can be more difficult to find. Not only do many people choose to make the city a base for touring about, but it is also the arrival/departure point for Americans travelling on cheap Icelandair tickets looking for a place to spend their first or last night in Europe. If you do head out into the country it is quite feasible to make several daytrips from one of the smaller towns.

If you choose to stay in different places as you travel around, come prepared to camp in summer, or book hostels in advance, because finding cheap accommodation can be quite tricky and **hotels and pensions** are none too cheap. Expect to pay from 550LF (£9.25; $17.25; DM26.50) per person in doubles, while singles start around 650LF (£10.75; $20.50; DM31.25). In the more popular tourist towns the Tourist Office might be able to find you a room in a **private home** for 350–600LF (£5.85–10.00; $11–19; DM17–29). These tend to fill up quickly, so it is best to make enquiries early in the day.

To stay at one of the 11 **IYHF hostels** a valid membership card is essential. The cost of B&B varies between 260 and 300LF (£4.35–5.00; $8.25–9.50; DM12.50–14.50), except in Luxembourg where prices range from 300–340LF (£5.00–5.65; $9.50–10.75; DM14.50–16.50). Duvet covers are supplied, but you must have a linen sheet sleeping bag – either your own, or one hired from the hostel costing 100LF (£1.65; $3.25; DM4.75) – for the duration of your stay. This could be shorter than you might hope, as the length of stay is limited to three days at any hostel, and only one day at peak periods

(July and August). These rules are only enforced when the hostel is full, but it is as well to be aware of them. Curfews are normally 11 p.m. (midnight in Luxembourg). All the hostels are open from mid April to September, but at other times different hostels are closed for anything between two days to six weeks.

Most of the main places of interest have a hostel. One notable exception is Clervaux, but here there is the choice of two of the small network of **gîtes d'étapes**, of which nationwide there are between six and eight in operation at any one time. Most are open all year and prices range from 100 to 130LF (£1.70–2.15; $3.25–4.25; DM5.00–6.25).

Of the 120 or so **campsites**, only around 30 are open for the whole year. However, the vast majority are open March/April to September. The pamphlet 'Camping Grand-Duché de Luxembourg' clearly lists both opening periods and amenities. Standards do vary, but even the more basic sites are perfectly acceptable. Two people can expect to pay roughly 275LF (£4.60; $8.75; DM13.25) per night. All the main places of interest are covered, often with several sites. During the peak season the 'Camping Guidage' service of the National Tourist Office is available to those having difficulty finding sites with vacancies (tel. 481199 from 11 a.m. to 7.30 p.m.). Those with a small tent are unlikely to have to struggle to find space at one of the sites in town, even during the peak season.

ADDRESSES

Luxembourgeois YHA	Centrale des Auberges de Jeunesse Luxembourgeoises, 18 Place d'Armes, BP 374, L–2013 Luxembourg (tel. 25588).
Camping	List available from the National Tourist Office in London or your capital city, or from local offices.

Gîtes d'Étapes   Gîtes d'Étapes de Grand-Duche de
                        Luxembourg, Bd. Prince Henri 23,
                        L–1724 Luxembourg
                        (tel. 23698/472172).

Luxembourg

HOTELS

All about 5–10 minutes' walk from the train station.

Cheapest doubles around 600LF (£10; $19; DM29) p.p.

Zurich, 36 rue Joseph Junck (tel. 491350). All rooms have baths/showers, but some are more expensive than the price quoted.
Pax, 121 route de Thionville (tel. 482563).

Cheapest doubles around 650LF (£10.80; $20.50; DM31.50) p.p.

Red Lion, 50 rue Zithe (tel. 481789).
Paradiso, 23 rue de Strasbourg (tel. 484801/403691).
Carlton, 9 rue de Strasbourg (tel. 484802).

Cheapest doubles around 730LF (£12.20; $23.25; DM35.25) p.p.

Axe, 34 rue Joseph Junck (tel. 490953).
Mertens, 16 rue de Hollerich (tel. 482638).
Sporting, 15 rue de Strasbourg (tel. 484332).

IYHF HOSTEL

2 rue de Fort Olisy (tel. 26889). 1 a.m. curfew, reasonably flexible. About 1½ miles from the station. Bus 9 from the station (or the airport) to the Vallee d'Alzette.

CAMPING

Luxembourg-Kockelscheur (tel. 471815). Open Easter/mid Apr. to Oct. 2½ miles from the train station. Bus 2 from the station.

MOROCCO

The good news is that the price of accommodation in Morocco is so low that a decent hotel room should be well within your budget. **Hotels** are divided into two main categories, classé and non-classé. The former are regulated by the National Tourist Authority, which both grades them on a scale rising from one star to five-star luxury, and fixes their prices. The one- to four-star grades are further subdivided A and B. At the lower end of the scale there is only a small variation in prices, and in the facilities offered. Even the one-star establishments offer a level of comfort and cleanliness you are unlikely to find in a non-classé hotel. As a rule, classé hotels are situated in the ville nouvelle – the new town or administrative quarters built during the French colonial period. All classé hotels are listed in the publication 'Royaume de Maroc Guide des Hôtels'.

Non-classé hotels enjoy two advantages over classé hotels: location, and, outside peak periods, price. In peak season (August, Christmas and Easter) it is not uncommon for non-classé hotels to raise their prices sharply, so that they actually exceed the price of one-star B and one-star A establishments. Non-classé hotels, which are neither listed nor regulated by the National Tourist Authority, are generally located in the medina, the old, Arab-built part of the town. Staying here, you will be close to the markets, historic buildings and the bewildering array of street performers. However, the medina, with its twisting, narrow streets, can be an intimidating place. The quality of hotels varies greatly: while some offer spotless, whitewashed rooms looking out on to a central patio, there are also a considerable number that are filthy and flea ridden. You are also far more likely to encounter problems with a poor water supply and primitive toilet facilities in the medina.

A room in the medina should cost in the region of 20–30 dh (£1.25–1.90; $2.40–3.75; DM3.75–5.50). A spacious, more comfortable room in a classé hotel in the ville nouvelle might cost about 50–60 dh (£3.25–3.80; $6.00–7.25; DM9.25–11.00), possibly with a small extra charge for showers. At this lower end of the price scale hot water may only be available at certain times of the day. Only during the peak season are you likely to have any problem finding a room, although any difficulties will probably be restricted to Tangier, Fez, Agadir, Rabat (in July) and, occasionally, Tetouan.

For those reaching the end of their funds, even cheaper possibilities exist. Prices at Morocco's 46 **campsites** are extremely cheap, at around 7dh (£0.45; $0.85; DM1.25) per tent, and 5dh (£0.30; $0.60; DM0.90) per person. On no account should you leave any valuables unattended. All the major towns have a campsite, and most also have an **IYHF hostel**. The 11 hostels differ tremendously in quality. Prices range from 10–30 dh (£0.65–1.90; $1.25–3.50; DM1.75–5.50). Anyone without a membership card is usually permitted to stay on the payment of a small supplement. All but one of the hostels are situated in the larger towns. The other, at Asni, is well worth considering as a base by those interested in hiking in the Atlas Mountains. The French Alpine Club (CAF) have a network of **refuge huts** for the use of those hiking in the Atlas.

ADDRESSES

Hotels	'Royaume de Maroc Guide des Hôtels' Free from National Tourist Office in London or your capital city, or from any local office.
Moroccan YHA	Fédération Royale Marocaine des Auberges de Jeunes, Boulevard Okba Ben Nafii, Meknès (tel. 05–524698).
Refuge huts	Club Alpin Français, rue de la Boëtie, 75008 Paris (tel. 01–47423846).

Fez (Fès) (tel. code 06)

The best of the cheap rooms in the new town are located just to the west of bd Mohammed V, between av. Hassan II (close to the Post Office) and av. Slaoui (near the CTM bus station. Rooms in the old town are concentrated around Bab Boujeloud.

UNCLASSIFIED HOTELS

Du Commerce, place des Alouites, Fes el-Jdid. Singles and doubles 35dh (£2.20; $4.25; DM6.50) p.p. Singles with a terrace 55dh (£3.50; $6.75; DM10).

Du Jardin Public, Kasbah Boujeloud 153 (tel. 33086). Prices similar to above in singles and doubles. In an alleyway near Bab Boujeloud.

Also situated around Bab Boujeloud are the hotels National, Erreha, Kaskade, Mauritania and Lamtani.

Renaissance, rue Abdekrim el-Khattabi (tel. 22193). Singles 30dh (£1.90; $3.50; DM5.50); doubles 23dh (£1.50; $2.75; DM4.25) p.p. Near place Mohammed V.

CLASSIFIED HOTELS

Two star A:
Olympic, bd Mohammed V (tel. 24529/22403).
Two star B:
Amor, rue du Pakistan 31 (tel. 23304/22724).
Royal, rue d'Espagne 36 (tel. 24656).
Lamdaghri, Kabbour El Mangad 10 (tel. 20310).
One star A:
Kairouan, rue du Soudan 84 (tel. 23590).
Central, rue du Nador 50 (tel. 22333). Singles 55–100dh (£3.50–6.35; $6.50–12.00; DM10.25–18.50); doubles 38–55dh (£2.40–3.50; $4.50–6.50; DM7.00–10.25) p.p. There are baths in the most expensive rooms.

One star B:

CTM, bd Mohammed V (tel. 22811).

Excelsior, rue Larbi el-Kaghat (tel. 25602). Right off bd Mohammed V, three blocks up from the main Post Office. Slightly cheaper than Hotel Central above.

IYHF HOSTEL

rue Abdeslam Seghrini (tel. 24085).

CAMPING

Camping Moulay Slimane, rue Moulay Slimane (tel. 22438).

Marrakech (tel. code 04)

UNCLASSIFIED HOTELS

Café de France, Djemaâ El Fna (tel. 43901). The centre of the medina. Double room for 45dh (£2.90; $5.50; DM8.50) p.p.

Oukaimedon, Djemaâ El Fna.

Near Djemaâ El Fna Hôtel des Amis and Hôtel Cecil charge around 25dh (£1.60; $3.00; DM4.50) p.p. in doubles.

Ali, rue Moulay Ismail (tel. 44979). Singles with shower 118dh (£7.50; $14.25; DM21.75); doubles with shower 70dh (£4.50; $8.50; DM13) p.p. Near Djemaa El Fna.

De la Jeunesse, Derb Sidi Bouloukate 56. tel. 43631 Singles 35dh (£2.25; $4.25; DM6.50); doubles 23dh (£1.50; $2.75; DM4.25) p.p.; triples 19dh (£1.25; $2.50; DM3.75) p.p. Facing Hotel CTM on Djemaa El Fna go through the first arch to your right, then down the little street.

De France, Riad Zitoune el-Kedim 197 (tel. 43067). Singles similarly priced to Hotel de la Jeunesse, doubles slightly more expensive. Further on down the street from de la Jeunesse.

CLASSIFIED HOTELS

Cheapest single around 120dh (£7.60; $14.50; DM22), doubles 150dh (£9.50; $18; DM27.75) p.p.

Two star A:
  Al Mouatmid, av. Mohammed V 94 (tel. 48854–5).
  Koutoubia, bd Mansour 51 Eddahbi (tel. 30921).
  Les Ambassadeurs, av. Mohammed V 2 (tel. 47159).
Two star B:
  De Foucauld, av El Mouahidine (tel. 45499).
  Gallia, rue de la Recette 90 (tel. 45913).
  Grand Hôtel Tazi, at the corner of av. El Mouahidine &
    Bab Agnaou (tel. 42152/42787). Single for around 115dh
    (£7.30; $14; DM21.50), doubles 135dh (£8.55; $16.25;
    DM25) p.p.
One star A:
  CTM, Djemaa El Fna (tel. 42325). Singles 50dh (£3.15;
    $6; DM9.25); with shower 66dh (£4.20; $8; DM12.25),
    doubles 32dh (£2; $3.75; DM5.75) p.p., with shower
    46dh (£2.90; $5.50; DM8.50) p.p.
  Oasis, av. Mohammed V 50 (tel. 47179).
One star B:
  Des Voyageurs, av. Zerktouni 40 (tel. 47218).
  Franco Belge, bd Zerktouni 62 (tel. 48472).

IYHF HOSTEL

  rue El Jahid, Quartier Industriel (tel. 44713/32831). 700m
    from the train station. Lockout between 9 a.m.–noon,
    2–6 p.m. 15dh (£0.95; $1.75; DM2.70) per night.

CAMPING

  Camping Municipal, rue El Jahid (tel. 31707). Down the
    road from the IYHF hostel, about 10 minutes' walk
    from the railway station. 10dh (£0.60; $1.20; DM1.80)
    p.p.

Rabat (tel. code 07)

UNCLASSIFIED HOTELS

Marrakesh, rue Sebbahi 10 (tel. 27703). Singles 38dh
(£2.40; $4.50; DM7); doubles 28dh (£1.75; $3.50; DM5.25)
p.p. Turn right three blocks after entering the medina
from av. Mohammed V.

Also in the medina: Hôtel el Alam and Hôtel Regina.
Both in rue Gebbali.

CLASSIFIED HOTELS

Two star A:

Royal, rue Amman 1 (tel. 21171/21172).

Splendid, rue de Ghazzah 24 (tel. 23283).

Two star B:

Velleda, av. Allal Ben Abdellah 106 (tel. 69531). Off av.
Mohammed V.

One star A:

Capitol, av. Allal Ben Abdellah 34 (tel. 31236). Singles
58dh (£3.65; $7; DM 10.75); with shower 78dh (£5;
$9.50; DM14.50); doubles 35dh (£2.25; $4.25; DM6.50)
p.p.; with shower 50dh (£3.15; $6; DM9.25) p.p.

Central, rue Al Basra 2 (tel. 67356). Prices for rooms
without showers are similar to those of Hotel Capitol,
but rooms with showers are cheaper. Off av. Mohammed
V between the train station and the medina.

Majestic, av. Hassan II 121 (tel. 22997).

Dahir, av. Hassan II 429 (tel. 33026/22096).

Dakar, rue Dakar (tel. 21671).

Gaulois, rue Hims 1 (tel. 23022/30573).

IYHF HOSTEL

rue Marassa, Bab El Had (tel. 25769). Just outside the
medina.

CAMPING

Camping de la Plage. In Salé, across the River Bou Regreg.
Bus 6 leaves av. Hassan II for Salé. Also bus 24. Get off
at Bab Bou Haja, then follow the signs to the site on
the beach.

Tangier (Tanger) (tel. code 09)

If you are looking for accommodation near the station there
are a number of hotels in rue Salah Eddine el-Ayoubi
(previously rue de la Plage). From the train station walk
down avenue d'Espagne and take the first turning on your
right. If you would prefer to stay in the medina, one of
the best places to look for a room is rue Mokhtar Ahardan
(formerly rue de la Poste), just off the Petit Socco.

PENSIONS/UNCLASSIFIED HOTELS

In the medina:
Pension Palace, rue Mokhtar Ahardan 2 (tel. 39248).
Around 35dh (£2.20; $4.25; DM6.50) p.p.
Hôtel Grand Socco (tel. 33126). On Grand Socco.
Hôtel Fuentes (tel. 34669), Hôtel Mauretania (tel. 34677)
and Pension Becerra (tel. 32369). On Petit Socco.
Pensions in the new town:
Miami, rue Salah Eddine el-Ayoubi 126 (tel. 32900).
Singles 35dh (£2.20; $4.25; DM6.50); 28dh (£1.75; $3.50;
DM5.25).

CLASSIFIED HOTELS

Three star A:
Villa de France, rue de Hollande 143 (tel. 31475/37135). Far
from being the cheapest in town, but the hotel offers

a superb view over the city and immaculate rooms. Doubles 100dh (£6.35; $12; DM18.50) p.p.

Two star A:

Anjou, rue Ibn El Banna 3 (tel. 34344/34244).

Mamora, rue Mokhtar Ahardan 19 (tel. 34105). In the medina. Singles 100dh (£6.35; $12; DM18.50); doubles 60dh (£3.80; $7.25; DM11) p.p. Prices are for rooms with showers. Rooms with baths are about 25 per cent more expensive.

Valencia, av. d'Espagne 72 (tel. 31714).

Marco Polo, av. d'Espagne (tel. 38213/36087).

Miramar, av. des F.A.R. (tel. 38948).

Two star B:

Astoria, rue Ahmed Chaouki 10 (tel. 37202).

Djenina, rue Grotins 8 (tel. 34759/36075).

Lutetia, av. My Abdellah 3 (tel. 31866).

One star A:

De Paris, bd Pasteur 42 (tel. 38126/31877). Singles 50dh (£3.15; $6; DM9.25); with shower 75dh (£4.75; $9; DM13.75); doubles 33dh (£2.10; $4; DM6) p.p., with shower 45dh (£2.85; $5.50; DM8.25) p.p.

Panoramic Massilia, rue Marco Polo 3 (tel. 35009).

Hotel Residence Ritz, rue Soraya 1 (tel. 38074-5).

Al Farabi, Zankat Essadia 10 (tel. 34566).

Andalucia, rue Vermeer 14 (tel. 41334).

Biaritz, av. d'Espagne 102 (tel. 32473).

Continental, rue Dar el Baroud (tel. 31024/31143).

One star B:

Ibn Batouta, rue Magellan 8 (tel. 37170).

Olid, rue Mokhtar Ahardan 12 (tel. 31310).

IYHF HOSTEL

Tanger Youth Hostel, rue El Antaki 8, av. d'Espagne (tel. 46127). 20dh (£1.25; $2.40; DM3.60) per night.

CAMPING

Miramonte (tel. 37138). Bus 1, 2 or 21 from Grand Socco.
7dh (£0.45; $0.85; DM1.25) per tent, 5dh (£0.30; $0.60;
DM0.90) p.p.
Tingis (tel. 40191). Bus 15 from Grand Socco.
Camping Sahara. One mile north of train station, on
beach.

THE NETHERLANDS

It is a pleasure to travel in Holland, not least because the Dutch are responding particularly well to the growth in budget tourism. The Tourist Offices (VVV) are generally very helpful, and understand what you mean when you request cheap lodgings. They will also book ahead for you for a small fee, which is a service you might wish to use if you know you will be arriving late at your destination. The local VVV can advise you on the availability of rooms in **private homes**. Prices range from 20–50 Dfl (£5.75–14.25; $11.00–27.25; DM16.75–41.75) per person, with around 28 Dfl being the norm (£8.60; $16.50; DM25), making them a cheaper option than pensions or hotels. If you are very fortunate you might find a **pension** or **hotel** with singles and doubles available for around 30 Dfl (£9.25; $17.50; DM26.75) p.p., but these are few and far between. More likely you will pay 40–50 Dfl (£12.25–15.50; $23.25–29.50; DM35.50–45.00) p.p. and upwards for singles and doubles. Do not assume that a bed in a private hostel will necessarily be cheaper: although prices may start as low as 15 Dfl (£4.60; $8.75; DM13.50), they can be as high as 35 Dfl (£10.75; $20.50; DM31.25). It is worth asking the VVV about whether a **Sleep-In** operates in the town. Several places have followed Amsterdam and set up dorm hostels which charge about 20 Dfl (£6.25; $11.75; DM17.75) for B&B. Some Sleep-Ins are open in summer only.

In the 44 **IYHF hostels**, B&B will cost you 20–23 Dfl (£6.25–7.00; $11.75–13.50; DM17.75–20.50) depending on the location and the time of year. Full board is available with reasonable prices and meals that are excellent value for money. The IYHF hostels are good value all round; usually spotlessly clean, equipped with a bar and games room, and serving more substantial breakfasts and staying open later than is the norm for official hostels. Unfortunately, not all the main places of interest have a hostel in town, but those with a railpass will invariably find one in a town not too far away. Hostels in the major towns stay open all year. Most of the others are open from Easter to late September, but a few are open for the summer only. IYHF cards are compulsory.

There are some 2000 **campsites** around the country and so no matter where you choose to visit there is always a campsite close by. Generally clean and well equipped, prices for a solo traveller will normally be in the 10–15 Dfl range (£3.10–4.60; $5.75–8.75; DM9.00–13.50). Camping outside official sites is illegal, but **sleeping rough** is not, though that is not to say the latter is safe, particularly in Amsterdam and Rotterdam. If you are sleeping in any public place the police are likely to wake you up: they will only press vagrancy charges if you have no money on you, so, ironically, in order to remain within the law you make yourself an attractive target for muggers. If you do decide to sleep out in Amsterdam and Rotterdam try to bed down close to other travellers rather than in some quiet area on your own. Do not even think about staying in the stations in these cities, as they are not just noisy, but also quite violent.

ADDRESSES

Dutch YHA	Stichting Nederlandse Jeugdherberg Centrale NJHC, Prof Tulplein 4, 1018 GX Amsterdam (tel. 020–5513155).
Sleep-Ins	MAIC, Hartenstroaat 16–18, Amsterdam (tel. 020–240977).

Camping

A list is available from the Netherlands Board of Tourism in London or your capital city, complete with a form for reserving sites, which you can photocopy if you want to reserve several sites. Campsites can be reserved free of charge through the National Reservations Centre, P O Box 404, 2260 AK Leidschendam (tel. 070–202500).

Hotels, Pensions and B&Bs

Lists for some of the main towns are available from the Netherlands Board of Tourism in London or your local one. Free reservations can be made through the National Reservations Centre in Leidschendam (see above). A deposit of 25 per cent may be requested, which you lose if you make a late cancellation.

Amsterdam (tel. code 020)

HOTELS

**Cheapest doubles around 27.50 Dfl
(£8.50; $16; DM24.50) p.p.**

Beurstraat, Beurstraat 9 (tel. 263701).

Cheapest doubles around 32.50 Dfl (£10; $19; DM29) p.p.

Van Ostade, Van Ostadestraat 123 (tel. 793452).
Pax, Radhuisstraat 37 (tel. 249735).
Ronnie, Radhuisstraat 41 (tel. 242821).
Schröder, Haarlemerdijk 48b (tel. 266272).

**Cheapest doubles around 37 Dfl
(£11.40; $21.75; DM33) p.p.**

La Bohème, Marnixstraat 415 (tel. 242828).
Brian, Singel 69 (tel. 244661).
De Westertoren, Radhuisstraat 35b (tel. 244639).
Sphinx, Weteringschans 82 (tel. 273680).
Impala, Leidsekade 77 (tel. 234706).
Clemens, Radhuisstraat 39 (tel. 246089).
Beirvliet, Nassaukade 368 (tel. 188404).
Aroza, Nieuwendijk 23 (tel. 209123).
Casa Cara, Emmastraat 24 (tel. 6623135). Good value, a
    two-star hotel.
San Luchesio, Waldeck Pyrmontlaan 9 (tel. 716861).

**Cheapest doubles around 40 Dfl
(£12.30; $23.50; DM35.75) p.p.**

De Leydsche Hof, Leidsegracht 14 (tel. 232148).
Oosterpark, Oosterpark 72 (tel. 930049).
Weber, Marnixstraat 397 (tel. 270574).
Galerij, Radhuisstraat 43 (tel. 248851).
Bema, Concertgebouwplein 19 (tel. 791396).
Arcade, Radhuisstraat 31 (tel. 266714).

Adolesce, Nieuwe Keizersgracht 26 (tel. 6263959).
Kap, Den Texstraat 5b (tel. 6245908).
King, Leidsekade 85–86 (tel. 6249603).
Kitty, Plantage Middenlaan 40 (tel. 6226819).
Rokin, Rokin 73 (tel. 6267456).
Stadhouder, Stadhouderskade 76 (tel. 6718428).
The Village, Kerkstraat 25 (tel. 6269746).

**Cheapest doubles around 47.50 Dfl
(£14.60; $27.75; DM42.25) p.p.**

Van Onna, Bloemgracht 102 (tel. 6265801).
Fantasia, Nieuwe Keizersgracht 16 (tel. 6248858).
Other suggestions:
De Beurs, Beursstraat 7 (tel. 6222308/6220741).

PRIVATE ROOMS

Enquire at the VVV. Expect to pay around 45 Dfl (£13.85; $26; DM40) p.p.

IYHF HOSTELS

'Vondelpark', Zandpad 5 (tel. 6831744). Curfew 2 a.m. No phone reservations accepted. Best arrive early. Tram 1, 2 or 5 from the station to Leidseplein. Zandpad is off Stadhouderskade, the main road across the Singelgracht.

'Stadsdoelen', Kloveniersburgwal 97 (tel. 6246832). Open 1 Mar.–4 Nov. and 27 Dec.–2 Jan. Curfew 1.30 a.m. Between Nieuwmarkt and Muntplein. From the station tram 4, 9, 16, 24 or 25 will take you to Muntplein. There is a metro stop at the Nieuwmarkt but the area is best avoided as many of the casualties of the hard drug scene hang around here.

CHRISTIAN HOSTELS

Both are safe, cheap, and not as rule-bound as you might imagine. 1 a.m. curfew Fri. and Sat., midnight the rest of the week. Around 15 Dfl (£4.60; $8.75; DM13.50) for B&B.

Eben Haëzer, Bloemstrasse 179 (tel. 6244717). Tram 13 or 17 to Marnixstraat.

'The Shelter', Barndesteeg 21–25 (tel. 6253230). In the red light area. Approach the hostel from the Damrak side rather than from the Nieuwmarkt.

HOSTELS

Prices for dorms start around the price charged by the IYHF hostels: 23 Dfl (£7; $13.50; DM20.50). Where doubles are available you will normally pay 35–40 Dfl (£10.75–12.30; $20.50–23.50; DM31.25–35.75) p.p., which is poor value when compared with the hotels listed above.

Frisco Inn, Beursstraat 5 (tel. 6201610). Doubles start at around 30 Dfl (£9.25; $17.75; DM27.25) p.p.; triples from 26 Dfl (£8; $15.25; DM23.25) p.p. On the fringe of the red light district, near Central Station. No curfew.

International Budget Hotel, Leidsegracht 76 (tel. 6242784). Dorms have four beds only. No curfew. Tram 1, 2 or 5 to Prinsengracht. Doubles available.

Hotel Kabul, Warmoesstraat 38–42 (tel. 6237158). No curfew. In the red light area, five minutes' walk from Central Station. Doubles available.

Euphemia Budget Hotel, Fokke Simonszstraat 1–9 (tel. 6229045). Price includes breakfast. Tram 16, 24 or 25 to Weteringschans. Go back over the Lijnbaansgracht, then turn right. Doubles available.

Bill's 'Happy Hours' Youth Hostel, Binnen Wieringerstraat 8 (tel. 6255259). Dorms are amongst the cheapest available. Same price charged in the hostel's one double. Small breakfast included. Off Haarlemerstraat, near the end of Herengracht.

Bob's Youth Hostel, Nieuwezijds Voorburgwal 92 (tel. 6230063). Dorms at the bottom of the price range above. Mattresses on the floor slightly cheaper. Breakfast included. Not far from Dam Square. A short walk from the station, or tram 1, 2, 5, 13 or 17.

't Ancker, De Ruijterkade 100 (tel. 6229560). Dorms 35 Dfl (£10.75; $20.50; DM31.25). Includes breakfast, where you can eat as much as you like. Doubles available. About 100m to the right from the rear exit of Central Station.

SLEEP-IN

s'-Gravesandestraat 51–53 (tel. 6947444). Large dorms with mattresses on the floor, 14 Dfl (£4.30; $8.25; DM12.50). Hire of sheets 3 Dfl (£0.90; $1.75; DM2.75) with 25 Dfl (£7.75; $14.50; DM22.25) deposit. Open late June–early Sept. Also one week at Easter, and at New Year. Trams 3, 6, 9, 10 or 14 to Mauritskade, then back along Sarphatisstraat. Night bus 76 or 77.

HOUSEBOATS

Unless you have been informed of a good houseboat by a reliable source they are best avoided. Cleanliness is not a strong point, and many seriously breach fire regulations.

CAMPING

Zeeburg, Zuider-Ijdijk 44 (tel. 6944430). Open mid Apr.–Oct. Aimed at young travellers. Live music regularly. Direct ferry from Central Station, or tram 10, bus 22 or 37. Night bus 71 or 76.

Gaasper, Loosdrechtdreef 7 (tel. 6967326). Metro to Gaasperplas or night bus 72. Twenty-minute trip from Central Station.

Vligenbos, Meeuwenlaan 138 (tel. 6368855). From Central Station tram 1, 2 or 5 to Leidseplein, then bus 172.

Delft (tel. code 015)

PENSIONS

**Cheapest singles and doubles around 34 Dfl
(£10.50; $20; DM30.25) p.p.**

Van Leeuwen, Achterom 143 (tel. 123716).
Rust, Oranje Plantage 38 (tel. 126874).

STUDENT FLATS

Krakeelhof, Jacoba Van Beierlaan 9 (tel. 135953/146235).
Open June–Aug. Singles 18 Dfl (£5.50; $10.50; DM16)
(price falls by about 25 per cent if you stay more than
seven days); doubles 15 Dfl (£4.60; $8.75; DM13.50)
p.p. As you leave the station turn right along Van
Leeuwenhoeksingel, right at the end of the road,
through the underpass, right at the first set of traffic
lights, left on to Van Beierlaan, and left again over the
bridge.

CAMPING

Delftse Hout, Hoflaan (tel. 570515, 602323). In a wood
about 20 minutes' walk from the town centre. Bus
133 to Hoflaan. Expensive. About 12 Dfl (£3.70; $7;
DM10.75) to pitch a tent, 5 Dfl (£1.50; $3; DM4.50)
p.p. Anyone with a railpass might be better staying
at the site in Rijswijk, only about six minutes from
Delft on the line to Den Haag. See the section on The
Hague.

HOSTELS

There is no hostel in Delft. Again railpass holders might
want to travel to Rijswijk. See hostels in the section on The
Hague.

The Hague (Den Haag) (tel. code 070)

Cheap accommodation in The Hague is in limited supply.
Most of the cheaper hotels are in Scheveningen, on the coast
to the north-west of the city. The various hostels are also
outside the central area, in Scheveningen or Rijswijk. There
is a train station in Rijswijk, but you will have to take a tram
to get to Scheveningen.

HOTELS

Cheapest doubles around 20 Dfl
(£6.15; $11.75; DM17.75) p.p.

Mont Blanc, Stevinstraat 66, Scheveningen (tel. 3559785).

Cheapest doubles around 27.50 Dfl
(£8.50; $16; DM24.50) p.p.

De Uitkomst, Fultonstraat 12 (tel. 3608193). Out from the
centre of the city.
Huize Rosa, Badhuisweg 41, Scheveningen (tel. 3557796).
Meyer, Stevinstraat 64, Scheveningen (tel. 3558138).

Cheapest doubles around 32.50 Dfl (£10; $19; DM29) p.p.

Minstreel, Badhuiskade 5, Scheveningen (tel. 3520024).
Duinroos, Alkmaarsestraat 27, Scheveningen (tel. 3546079).
Neuf, Rijswijkseweg 119 (tel. 3900748). Out from the
centre. Walk down Rijswijksweg from the Hollandse
Spoor train station (Den Haag HS).
Jodi, Van Aerssenstraat 194–196 (tel. 3559208). Far from
the centre of The Hague, near Scheveningen.
Aristo, Stationsweg 164–166 (tel. 3890847). In front of
Den Haag HS train station (Hollandse Spoor, not CS
Centraal Station).
Enak, Keizerstraat 53, Scheveningen (tel. 3556169).
Huize Clavan, Badhuiskade 8, Scheveningen (tel. 3552844).

Cheapest doubles around 37 Dfl (£11.40; $21.75; DM33) p.p. All in Scheveningen.

Berkhout, Badhuisweg 37 (tel. 3546631).
Danny, Leuvensestraat 56 (tel. 3552118).
Lansink, Badhuisweg 7 (tel. 3559967).
Lunamare, Badhuisweg 9 (tel. 3546075).
Schuur, Badhuiskade 2 (tel. 3556583).
Van Zanen, Leuvensestraat 39 (tel. 3554636).
El Cid, Badhuisweg 51 (tel. 3546667).
Pension Central, Haagsestraat 61 (tel. 541653).

Cheapest doubles around 40 Dfl (£12.30; $23.50; DM35.75) p.p.

Astoria, Stationsweg 139 (tel. 3840401). The road in front of Hollandse Spoor train station.

PRIVATE ROOMS

Expect to pay around 30 Dfl (£9.25; $17.50; DM26.75)

These are arranged through VVV; occasionally they will not let private rooms until the hotels are full.

IYHF HOSTEL

Ockenburgh, Monsterseweg 4 (tel. 3970011). Five miles from the city centre in Kijkduin. Bus 122, 123 or 124 to Central Station. Ask the driver for the nearest stop. Ten-minute walk, follow the signs. Midnight curfew. B&B in dorms 25 Dfl (£7.70; $14.50; DM22.25).

HOSTELS

Herberg Vlietzigt, Jaagpad 7, Rijswijk (tel. 015–131004). 15 Dfl (£4.60; $8.75; DM13.50) without breakfast.
Marion, Havenkade 3/3a, Scheveningen (tel. 3543501). Around 30 Dfl (£9.25; $17.50; DM26.75) with breakfast.

Scheveningen, Gevers Deynootweg 2, Scheveningen (tel.
3547003). Prices start at around 30 Dfl (£9.25; $17.50;
DM26.75).

Minstreel, Badhuiskade 5, Scheveningen (tel. 3520024)
Similar price to the latter two hostels above.

CAMPING

Ockenburgh, Wijndaelerweg 25 (tel. 3252364). Open Apr.–
mid Oct. Tram 3 from Central Station. Expensive for solo
travellers. 12 Dfl (£3.75; $7; DM10.75) per tent; 4 Dfl
(£1.25; $2.25; DM3.50) p.p.

Duinrell, Duinrell 5, Wassenaar (tel. 01751–19212/19314).
10 Dfl (£3; $5.75; DM8.75) p.p. (tent included). Open
all year.

Duinhorst, Buurtweg 135, Wassenaar (tel. 3242270). 5.50
Dfl (£1.70; $3.25; DM5) p.p. and per tent.

Vlietzigt, Jaagpad 7, Rijswijk (tel. 015–131004). Open
1 Apr.–1 Oct. Beside the hostel. 3 Dfl (£0.90; $1.75;
DM2.75) per tent, 5.50 Dfl (£1.70; $3.25; DM5) p.p.

Rotterdam (tel. code 010)

HOTELS

**Cheapest doubles around 27.50 Dfl
(£8.50; $16; DM24.50) p.p.**

Bagatelle, Provenierssingel 26 (tel. 4676348). At the rear
of the train station.

Cheapest doubles around 32.50 Dfl (£10; $19; DM29) p.p.

Heemraad, Heemraadssingel 90 (tel. 4775461). Tram 1, 7
or 9.

Simone, Nieuwe Binnenweg 162a (tel. 4362585). Tram
4, 5 or metro to Eendrachtsplein. Or walk across

Stationsplein. Keep on going, then right off Wester-
singel at Eendrachtsplein.

India, Mathenesserlaan 399 (tel. 4776921). Out from the
centre. Tram 4.

**Cheapest doubles around 37 Dfl
(£11.40; $21.75; DM33) p.p.**

Metropole, Nieuwe Binnenweg 13a (tel. 4360319). Directions see Simone above.

Rox-Inn, s'-Gravendijkwal 14 (tel. 4366109). Tram 1, 7 or
9.

De Gunst, Brielselaan 190–192 (tel. 4850940). Outside the
centre. Metro Maashaven, then tram 2.

**Cheapest doubles around 40 Dfl
(£12.30; $23.50; DM35.75) p.p.**

Breitner, Breitnerstraat 23c (tel. 4360262). Off Neiuwe
Binnenweg. See directions for Simone above.

Bienvenue, Spoorsingel 24 (tel. 4669394). At the rear of
the train station.

Het Wapen van Charlois, Doklaan 59 (tel. 4296921). Outside the centre. Metro Maashaven, then tram 2.

IYHF HOSTEL

Rochussenstraat 107–109 (tel. 4365763). Curfew 2 a.m.
Metro or tram 4 to Dijkzigt. B&B 24 Dfl (£7.50; $14;
DM21.50) July–Aug.; 20 Dfl (£6.15; $11.75; DM18) at
other times.

SLEEP-IN

Mauritsweg 29 (tel. 121420/143256). Open mid June to mid
Aug. Age 27 and under only. B&B 12 Dfl (£3.70; $7;
DM10.75).

CAMPING

Kanaalweg 84 (tel. 4159772).

NORWAY

Not surprisingly, cheap accommodation options are severely limited in Norway, reputedly the most expensive country in mainland Europe. Even if the prices below seem affordable to you, remember that you are also going to spend a considerable amount simply feeding yourself. A room in a small **boarding house**, known as a *pensjonat* or *hospit*, will cost you at least 140kr (£12.75; $24.25; DM37) for a single, 125kr (£11.40; $21.50; DM33) per person for a double, without breakfast. These are usually available in the more popular tourist towns.

As the Norwegian Tourist Board admit, 'Hotel accommodation in Norway is not cheap'. This is a bit of an understatement, as, even in summer when **hotels** reduce their prices, it is rare to find prices lower than 250kr (£22.75; $43.25; DM66) for singles, 200kr (£18.25; $34.50; DM52.75) each for doubles, with the only consolation being the chance of gorging yourself on the buffet breakfast.

More affordable is a room in a private home, at 80–150kr (£7.25–13.75; $13.75–26.00; DM21.00–39.50) for singles and 80–110kr (£7.25–10.00; $13.75–19.00; DM21–29) p.p. for doubles, without breakfast. These have to be booked through the local Tourist Office, which charges a fee of 15kr (£1.40; $2.50; DM4). Unfortunately, private rooms may be difficult to find outside the larger towns, and may also have a specified minimum stay.

There are around 90 **IYHF hostels** around the country, with convenient clusters in the western fjords, the popular hiking areas of the centre, and in the vicinity of Oslo. Standards are unquestionably excellent, but prices are high. Overnight fees start at around 70kr (£6.35; $12; DM18.50), but are normally around 90–120kr (£8.20–10.90;

$15.50–20.75; DM23.75–31.75). However, prices can be as high as 140kr (£12.75; $24.25; DM37) in some hostels. One slight consolation is that a substantial buffet breakfast is included in the overnight price at most hostels charging over 120kr (£10.90; $20.75; DM31.75). It is advisable to have an IYHF card, otherwise you will have to pay an extra 20kr (£1.80; $3.50; DM5.25), assuming you are admitted to the hostel. Only a few hostels operate throughout the year. Most open from June to September only; some for even shorter periods.

Groups of three to seven travellers planning to stay in the same area for a while might consider hiring a chalet. **Chalets** (*hytte*) are let by the week only and prices vary from 50 to 140kr (£4.50–12.75; $8.75–24.25; DM13.25–37.00) per person per night. In the peak period of late June to mid August expect to pay about 90kr (£8.25; $15.50; DM23.75) p.p. per night. At other times prices fall, so that in May, or September to December, chalets are let out for perhaps two-thirds of the peak-season price. Most chalets are located in rural areas, ideal for hiking and fishing, but if you can find one with a train station nearby, it can make a good base for touring about. Just occasionally, a chalet can be found in the suburbs of the main towns.

There are some 1300 **campsites**, rated with from one to three stars according to the facilities available. High standards are assured, but there are no fixed prices, and charges can vary considerably. Most charge 45–55kr (£4.10–5.00; $7.75–9.50; DM11.75–14.50) for a tent, with a fee of 5–10kr (£0.45–0.90; $0.85–1.70; DM1.30–2.60) per occupant. Sites do not accept reservations, but these are not necessary in any case, and while the FICC camping carnet is valid, it is not essential. An increasing number of sites offer self-catering chalets for rent, with one-night stays possible. Sleeping between four and six people, these chalets have fully equipped kitchens and prices range from 250 to 350kr (£22.75–31.75; $43.25–60.50; DM66.00–92.25) per night. All the sites, complete with addresses, telephone numbers, facilities and opening times are listed in the brochure 'Camping in Norway', published annually by the Norwegian Tourist Board. Prices are not listed because they are set later in the year.

As in neighbouring Sweden and Finland, the right to **camp rough** is written into the law, with certain restrictions. You are allowed to camp for two days on any uncultivated land or open area without asking permission, provided you pitch your tent at least 150 metres away from the nearest habitations. Between 15 April and 15 September avoid setting fires in open fields or woodland areas. Do not leave litter lying around. Wherever you may be camping or sleeping rough, it is likely to get very cold at night, even during the summer, so a good sleeping bag and tent with a flysheet is recommended. Nor is there any time of the year that is particularly free of rain (Bergen especially is renowned for its wet weather). It is also advisable to have a good mosquito repellant.

Anyone heading out into the countryside who would prefer a roof over their head should contact the Norwegian Mountain Touring Association for a list of the simple **mountain huts** they operate throughout the country. Open at Easter, and from late June to early September, these huts cost 50–120kr (£3.75–11.00; $7.00–20.75; DM10.50–31.75) per night. Non-members pay an additional 50kr (£4.50; $8.75; DM13.25) surcharge. Mountain huts can provide an alternative to hostelling, or act as a supplement in areas where there are no hostels. In the Lofoten Islands it is possible to rent old fishermen's cabins (*rorbuer*). These were once the temporary homes of fishermen from other parts of the country who needed a base during the winter. Most have been modernized; some come equipped with a shower and toilet, while others still lack running water. One-night stays are possible in some cabins. Advance booking of 'rorbuer' is essential.

ADDRESSES

Norwegian YHA   Norske Vandrerhjem, Dronningensgate 26, N–0154 Oslo 1 (tel. 02–421410).

'Hytte' (Chalets)	Den Norske Hytteformidling, Kierschowsgate 7, Boks 3207 Sagene, N–0405 Oslo 4 (tel. 02–356710).
	Fjordhytter, Jan Smørgsgate 11, 5011 Bergen (tel. 05–232080).
'Rorbuer'	Lofoten Reiselivslag, Boks 210, N–8301 Svolvaer (tel. (0)88–71053).
Mountain huts	Den Norske Turistforening, Stortinsgate 28, Oslo 1.
Camping	Norges Campingplassforbund, Dronningensgate 10–12, N–0152 Oslo 1 (tel. 02–421203).

Bergen (tel. code 05)

HOTELS

Fagerheim Pensjonat, Kalvedalsveien 49A (tel. 310172). Singles around 185kr (£16.80; $32; DM48.75); doubles 135–160kr (£12.25–14.50; $23.25–27.50; DM35.50–42.00) p.p.

Myklebust Pensjonat, Rosenbergsgt. 19 (tel. 311328). Singles around 165kr (£15; $28.50; DM43.50); doubles 160–175 kr (£14.50–15.90; $27.50–30.25; DM42–46) p.p.

PRIVATE ROOMS

Book through the Tourist Office (tel. 321480). From the train station, a 10-minute walk up Kaigaten, then look for the pavilion on Torgalmenning. Singles 140–160kr (£12.75–14.50; $24.25–27.50; DM37–42); doubles 100–125kr (£9.10–11.35; $17.25–21.50; DM26.50–33.00 p.p.

Vågenes, J.L. Mowinckelsvei (tel. 161101). 100kr (£9.10; $17.25; DM26.50) p.p. for doubles with kitchens. Bus 19. Ten-minute trip. Phone ahead.

IYHF HOSTEL

Montana YH, Johan Blyttsveien 30 (tel. 292900). Open 10 May–30 Sept. 100kr (£9.10; $17.25; DM26.50). Best reserved ahead. You can enquire about the availability of beds at the IYHF Information Office at Strandgaten 4 (tel. 326880). Not far from Torget. 2½ miles from town, roughly halfway up Mt Ulriken. Bus 4 to Lægdene.

HOSTELS

KFUM (YMCA), Kalfarveien 77 (tel. 320746). Open 1 July–10 Aug. Mattresses on the floor. 70kr (£6.35; $12; DM18.50). Along Kong Oscars Gate from the town centre, 10-minute walk.

Intermission, Kalfarveien 8 (tel. 313275). Open mid June–
Sept. Coed dorm 80kr (£7.25; $13.75; DM21). Along
Kong Oscars Gate from the centre.

CAMPING

Bergenshallen, Vilhelm Bjerknesveien 24 (tel. 282840).
Open 24 July–10 Aug. 45kr (£4.10; $7.75; DM11.75)
per tent and all occupants. From Strandgaten yellow
bus 3.
Lone (tel. 240820). Not cheap. Far from the centre.

FREELANCE CAMPING

At the top of Mt Fløyen. One hour on foot by
a well-maintained path, or accessible by funicular
costing about 30kr (£2.75; $5.25; DM8) (half price for
students).

Oslo (tel. code 02)

HOTELS

Bella Vista, Årrundveien 11B (tel. 654588). Around 220kr
(£20; $38; DM58) for singles, 210kr (£19; $36.25;
DM55.50) p.p. for doubles with bath/shower. Some
cheaper doubles are available.
Holtekilen Sommerhotell, Micheletsveien 55 (tel. 533853).
Singles around 220kr (£20; $38; DM58), doubles 160kr
(£14.50; $27.75; DM42.25) p.p.
Ellingsens Pensjonat, Holtegt. 25 (tel. 600359). Singles
160kr (£14.50; $27.75; DM42.25); doubles 125kr (£11.35;
$21.50; DM33) p.p. Not many rooms.
Oslo Sjømannshjemmet, Fred Olsengate 2 (tel. 412005).
Near the harbour. Singles 220kr (£20; $38; DM58);
doubles 150kr (£13.65; $26; DM39.50) p.p.

St Katarinahjemmet, Majorstuveien 21b (tel. 601370).
Open mid June–mid Aug. Run by nuns. Singles and
doubles similar in price to the Sjømannshjemmet.

PRIVATE ROOMS

Innkvartering in the Central Station book rooms with
a two-day min. stay Singles are in short supply 140kr
(£12.75; $24.25; DM37); doubles 110kr (£10; $19; DM29)
p.p. Commission 15kr (£1.35; $2.50; DM4).

IYHF HOSTELS

Haraldsheim, Haraldsheimveien 4 (tel. 222965). No
curfew. B&B 135kr (£12.25; $23.25; DM35.50) May–
Sept. Price increases slightly at other times. Tram 1 or 7
to the Sinsen terminus, or the local train to Grefsen.
Pan, Sognsveien 218 (tel. 222965). Open 1 June–20 Aug.
B&B 145kr (£13.20; $25; DM38.25). Tram 13 to the
Kringsja station from Nationaltheatret, then over the
lines and downhill for about 500m. No curfew.

HOSTELS

KFUM (YMCA), Møllergata (tel. 421066). Open mid July
–mid Aug. 75kr (£6.80; $13; DM19.75).
Holtekilen Summer Hotel, Micheletsvej 55 (tel. 533853).
Classrooms converted into 10-bedded dorms.

CAMPING

Ekeberg, Ekebergveien 65 (tel. 198568). Open 20 June–
20 Aug. About 55kr (£5; $9.50; DM14.50) for tent
space. Two miles from the centre. Bus 24 runs from
the Central Station. Beautiful view from the site.
Bogstad, Ankerveien 117 (tel. 247619). Similar in price to
Ekeberg. Bus 41.

FREELANCE CAMPING

You can pitch a tent in the woods to the north of Oslo, provided you stay clear of public areas. Take the metro to Sognsvann.

Stavanger (tel. code 04)

HOTELS

Stavanger Sommerhotell, Madlamarkveien 6, Hafrsfjord (tel. 554800). Doubles start at around 160kr (£14.50; $27.75; DM42.25) p.p. Open 1 June–31 Aug.

IYHF HOSTEL

Stavanger YH, Mosvangen, H. Ibsensgt. 21 (tel. 870977).

HOSTELS

KFUM (YMCA) Inter Rail Point, Rektor Bernstensgate 7 (tel. 532888). Open July and first week of August.

CAMPING

One site is adjacent to the KFUM hostel above. The other is Camping Ølberg (tel. 654375). Both sites are open during the summer only.

POLAND

In common with the other countries of the former Soviet bloc, Poland has recently been receiving unprecedented numbers of tourists, with the inevitable result that the supply of accommodation is falling far short of demand. The situation in 1990 was not quite as drastic as in Czechoslovakia or Hungary because the country was spared an onslaught of budget travellers by virtue of its non-participation in the Inter Rail scheme. With the inclusion of the Polish State Railway (PKP) in the scheme in 1991, however, the brief respite was over.

Finding a cheap bed is now extremely difficult in Poland. While there is quite a range of cheap accommodation possibilities, most of them have to be booked well in advance. Even if you do not camp it might be a good idea to take a tent if you are travelling between May and September, and especially so in July and August. At least this will ensure that you have somewhere to stay that you can afford if all else fails.

It is difficult to say anything specific about Polish hotels, other than that standards of cleanliness and comfort are fine. Previously ORBIS, like most other East European state tourist organizations, tried to push Westerners into the most expensive hotels and were loath to admit even the existence of the cheapest hotels, which were not meant to admit Western guests in any case. Now that these **hotels** can open their doors freely there are some great bargains to be found. Although you will struggle to find doubles for less than £9 ($17; DM26) per person in Warsaw and Cracow, elsewhere there are some excellent hotels which offer doubles for as little as £4 ($7.50; DM11.50) p.p. However, it is very difficult to find a room in one of the cheaper hotels, so try to reserve ahead, preferably in writing a month or so in advance. Even without prior reservation there is no reason to rule out hotels as an accommodation option. Ask around about the availability of cheap hotels (other travellers may be a more fruitful source of information than ORBIS).

'**Domy Turysty**' is a network of cheap hotels run by PTTK. The local Tourist Office will inform you as to the whereabouts of any such hotels operating in town, the prices of which vary quite substantially across the country. Whereas in Lublin you can get a single for £4 ($7.50; DM11.50), a bed in an eight-bedded room in Warsaw will cost you the same amount. Usually the dormitories fill quickly, leaving the rather cramped triples, doubles and singles as the only option available to you. In the more expensive Domy Turysty these probably represent poor value for money, especially as Domy Turysty are frequently very noisy. You would probably be better off spending a similar amount of money on a private room.

In most towns **private rooms** can be arranged through the Biuro Zakwaterowania (and occasionally by other organizations). You can expect to pay £6.50 ($12.25; DM18.75), except in Warsaw (and Cracow in July) where you will pay around £9 ($17; DM26). Payment is made at the Biuro rather than to your host. It is not uncommon to be approached by locals offering **rooms,** particularly in the vicinity of the train stations and Tourist Offices. These rooms are normally clean, and safe for you and your belongings. As a rule, prices are a bit lower than rooms fixed up through the local Biuro. The one problem you might have with such offers is the location of the rooms. Try to find out if they are centrally located, or, at the very least, well served by public transport. If you are not specifically asked to pay in hard currency you can often obtain a reduction on the asking price by offering to do so (Deutschmarks are especially welcome).

During the university/college summer holidays (July to Aug./mid Sept.) the student travel organization ALMATUR runs 'International Student Hostels' in **vacant student flats.** Accommodation is usually in two- or four-bedded rooms.

While rooms are supposedly only available to holders of the ISIC/IUS card who are aged under 35, this rule is rarely enforced if there is space. There is very little chance of simply turning up and finding a bed in the hostels in Cracow, Danzig or Warsaw, and this is likely to become the case in other cities as well. Possibly your only chance of getting a bed on arrival is to head for the local ALMATUR office early in the morning and enquire if there are any beds available (the office is invariably much easier to reach than the hostel as the latter tends to be situated out from the centre). **International Student Hostels** can be reserved in advance using ALMATUR vouchers, and with these reservations you can reserve a bed until 2 p.m., but thereafter reservations are invalid. It is probably worth making the effort to reserve International Student Hostels in this manner, at least in the main cities, because although initially you pay a bit more this way, you are still getting reasonable value for money as the hostels are by and large very comfortable, and a good place to meet other travellers. Moreover, you will save yourself time and aggravation looking for accommodation on arrival, and perhaps save yourself money as well.

The Polish affiliate of the IYHF, the **Polish Federation of Youth Hostels** (PTSM), runs a network of 1500 hostels covering all the main places of interest. A comprehensive list of Polish hostels is available from PTSM, but the abbreviated list in the IYHF handbook covers the towns that you are most likely to visit. Again, hostels in the main towns should be reserved in advance, preferably by means of a reservation card. At all hostels priority is given to school children and students, but there is no maximum age limit. All hostels have a 10 p.m. curfew, but you must arrive before 9 p.m. Prices are very low, and, for example, in the top-rated hostels overnight fees for dormitory accommodation vary between £0.80–1.35 ($1.50–2.50; DM2.25–4.00). Unfortunately, standards are also low, hostels tend to be very crowded, and facilities are rudimentary, while standards of cleanliness at many hostels leave a lot to be desired.

There are **campgrounds** in all the places you are likely

to visit. They are certainly cheap, though facilities can be very basic. At one of the more expensive sites (in Cracow) a solo traveller will pay around £1.20 ($2.25; DM3.50) to stay the night; elsewhere overnight prices can be as low as £0.30 ($0.50; DM0.80), even in some of the more popular towns, such as Danzig. At many sites it is possible to hire bungalows sleeping two to four people. Average prices work out at around £3.25 ($6.25; DM9.50) p.p., assuming all the beds are taken. Otherwise you can usually expect to be charged extra to cover the empty bed space. The first-class publication 'Polska Mapa Camingów' lists details of all the sites, and shows their locations on a map. Copies are available from the main bookstores, or from the National Automobile Club. ALMATUR also operates a chain of sites in summer. Any of their local offices will supply you with a list. A few of the IYHF hostels will allow you to camp in their grounds, but this is not usually permitted.

ADDRESSES

Hostels   ALMATUR, ul Ordynacka 9, 00364 Warszawa
                 (tel. 262356).
              Polskie Towarzystwo Schronisk
                 Mlodziezowych, ul Chocimska 28, 00791
                 Warszawa (tel. 498354/498128).
Camping Polska Federacja Camingów, ul Królewska 27a,
                 Warszawa.

Cracow (Kraków) (tel. code 012)

HOTELS

Wawel Tourist, ul. Pawia 6 (inside the Hotel Warszawski)
books hotels. Tel. 229370 for same-day bookings, tel. 221509
to reserve in advance. A short walk from the main train and
bus stations.

Cheapest doubles around £7.50 ($14.25; DM21.75) p.p.

PTTK Domy Turysty, Westerplatte 15–16 (tel. 229566).
Central location, near the main post office.
Juventur, ul. Sławkowska 3 (tel. 214222). Central.
Korona, ul. Pstrowskiego 9/15 (tel. 666511). On the fringe
of the wartime Jewish ghetto.
Wisła, ul. Reymonta 22 (tel. 334922). By the main football
stadium. Bus 144 stops nearby.

Cheapest doubles £10–12 ($19.00–22.75; DM29.00–34.75) p.p.

Polera, ul. Szpitalna 30 (tel. 221044). Central, highly
recommended.

Near the main bus and train stations are three hotels
charging the prices quoted above. All three are noisy and
a bit on the rough side:
Warszawski, ul. Pawia 6 (tel. 220622).
Polonia, ul. Basztowa 25 (tel. 221661).
Europeijski, ul. Lubicz 5 (tel. 220911).

PRIVATE ROOMS

Biuro Zakwaterowańia, ul. Pawia 8 (tel. 221921). Open
Mon.–Fri. 7 a.m.–9 p.m.; Sat. 1–6 p.m. Doubles £6.50
($12.25; DM18.75). In July prices rise by 50 per cent.

IYHF HOSTELS

ul Oleandry 4 (tel. 338822/338920). Doubles, three- to six-bedded rooms and 16-bedded dorms. £0.60–3.00 ($1.25–5.75; DM1.75–8.75). A 15-minute walk from the centre, or tram 15 or 18.

ul Kościuszki 88 (tel. 221951). Tram 1, 2 or 6.

ul Złotej Kielni 1 (tel. 372441). Open 1 July–26 Aug.

INTERNATIONAL STUDENT HOSTEL

ALMATUR, Rynek Główny 7–8 (tel. 215130). ALMATUR will inform you of the current location, as it changes almost annually. Open July–mid Sept.

HOSTELS

Student Hotel Zaczka, ul. Karasia (tel. 331914). Cheap singles and larger rooms.

CAMPING

Krak, ul. Radzikowskiego 99 (tel. 372122). Open May–Sept. Far from town centre. Tram 8 or 12 to Fizyków, or bus 208.

Danzig (Gdańsk) (tel. code 058)

The beaches of Danzig and nearby Sopot are the most popular in Poland, which ensures that the towns are full during the summer, so it is advisable to reserve ahead if you are arriving in July or August.

HOTELS

Cheapest doubles around £7.50 ($14.25; DM21.75) p.p. Both central.

Jantar, Długi Targ 19 (tel. 316241). Also triples.
Mesa, ul. Waly Jagelliońskie 36 (tel. 318052).

PRIVATE ROOMS

Biuro Zakwaterowańia, ul. Elżbietańska 10–11 (tel.
319444/338840). Opposite Dworzec Główny train
station. Open daily 7.30 a.m.–7 p.m. (5 p.m. in
winter).

IYHF HOSTELS

ul. Smoluchowskiego 11 (tel. 323820). About one mile
from Dworzec Główny. Tram 12 or 13.
ul. Dzierżyńskiego 11 (tel. 414108). 10 p.m. curfew.
Ten-minute walk from Gdańsk-Wrzeszcz train station.
Tram 2, 4, 7, 8 or 14.
ul. Walowa 21 (tel. 312313). Ten-minute walk from
Dworzec Główny station.
Grunwaldzka 238/240 (tel. 411660). Open 1 July–25 Aug.
Closest to Gdańsk-Zaspa station, or tram 2, 4, 7, 8 or
14.
ul. Karpia 1 (tel. 318219). Open 1 July–30 Aug.
There is another IYHF hostel in Gydnia, which with Danzig
and Sopot makes up the conurbation often referred to as the
'tri-city'.
ul. Czerwonych Kosynierow 108C (tel. 270005). Local
train to Gdynia-Grabowek. Tram 22, 25, 26 or 30.

INTERNATIONAL STUDENT HOSTEL

ALMATUR, Długi Targ 11, third floor (round the back)
will tell you where the hostel is in 1992. Open Mon.–
Fri. 9 a.m.–3 p.m. (tel. 312403).

CAMPING

Gdańsk-Jelitkowo, ul. Jelitkowska (tel. 532731). Open
June–mid Sept. Two-bedded bungalows for hire. Tram
5 or 8 from the Oliwa train station to the last stop, then
a short walk.

Gdańsk-Brzeźno, ul. Marska 234 (tel. 566531). Open mid
May–Oct. Tram 7, 13 or 15.

Warsaw (Warszawa) (tel. code 02 or 022)

HOTELS

Centrum Informacji Turystycnej, pl. Zamkowy 1–13 (tel.
270000). Open Mon.–Fri. 10 a.m.–6 p.m., Sat. and Sun.
10 a.m.–4 p.m. Does not book accommodation but distributes a very useful guide to the city listing all the hotels.

**Cheapest doubles £6–9 ($11.50–17.00;
DM17.50–26.00) p.p.**

ZNP (Teachers' Hotel), Wybrzeże Kościuszki 33 (tel.
262600). By the river. Admits non-teachers when space
permits.

PTTK Dom Turysty, Krakowskie Przedmieście 4/6 (tel.
263011). Near the university campus, a short walk
from the train station and the Old Town. The main
PTTK office is at Marszalkowska 124.

Pensjonat Stegny, ul. Idzikowskiego 4 (tel. 422768). Far
out, on the road to Wilanow Palace.

Skra, ul. Wawelska 5 (tel. 225100). In the Ochota suburb.
Bus 167, 187 or 188.

Orzel, ul. Podskarbińska 11/15 (tel. 105060). In the Praga
suburb. Bus 102 or 115.

Druh, ul. Niemcewicza 17 (tel. 6590011). Trams 7, 8, 9 or
25.

Dom Chłopa, pl. Postańców (tel. 279251). Located between Nowy Świat and the Palc Kultury. Slightly more expensive than the prices quoted.

PRIVATE ROOMS

Syrena, ul. Krucza 17 (tel. 287540/257201). Around £9 ($17; DM26) p.p. in doubles. Left from the station at ul. Jerozolimskie, which runs into Krucza.

Romeo and Juliet, Emilii Plater 30 (third floor) (tel. 292993). Left of Jerozolimskie. Centrally located rooms £7 ($13.25; 20.25). Payment in US dollars only.

IYHF HOSTELS

ul. Karolkowa 53a (tel. 328829). 11 p.m. curfew. Clean, but not central. Tram 24 from the train station.

ul. Smolna 30 (tel. 278952). 10 p.m. curfew. Central location, opposite the National Museum. Bus 158 or 175, or tram 8, 22 or 24. No showers.

INTERNATIONAL STUDENT HOSTEL

ALMATUR, ul. Kopernika 23 (tel. 263512). ALMATUR office open Mon.–Fri. 8.30 a.m.–8 p.m., Sat. 10 a.m.–6 p.m., Sun. 10 a.m.–3 p.m. Restricted hours Sept.–June Mon.–Fri. 9 a.m.–3 p.m. Even when the student hostels are not open ALMATUR may help students to find reasonably priced accommodation.

CAMPING

Expect to pay around £1 ($2; DM3) p.p. including tent.

Gromada, ul. Żwirki i Wigury (tel. 254391). Bungalows available. Bus 128, 136 or 175.

PTTK Camping, ul. Połczyńska 6a (tel. 366716). In the suburb of Wola.

Wisła, Wery-Kostrzewy 15/17 (tel. 233748). Short distance south of the bus station. Bus 154.

Zakopane (tel. code 0165)

PENSIONS

ORBIS controlled 'pensjonaty' can be booked at the reception in the Hotel Giewont (tel. 2011). Half board £8–16 ($15–30; DM23–46).

PRIVATE ROOMS

From the ORBIS office above.
  Biuro Zakwaterowańia, ul. Kościuszki 7.

IYHF HOSTEL

ul. Nowotarska 45 (tel. 4203).

CAMPING

Pod Krokiwa, ul. Żeromskiego. Open May–Aug. Opposite the foot of the ski jump.

PORTUGAL

By northern European standards accommodation is cheap here, and there are plenty of possibilities open to budget travellers. In most places it is usually quite easy to find somewhere cheap to stay, but it can be difficult on the Algarve in peak season, where it is advisable to write or telephone ahead as early as possible, for any type of accommodation.

Inexpensive and convenient options are pensions and cheap hotels. These are graded and priced by the municipal authority, albeit in a manner which at times seems quite arbitrary. Location does not affect the price, so you have the bonus of being able to stay in the town centre, or near the train station, without having to pay extra for the privilege. **Hotels** are rated from one star up to five stars, with the less expensive *pensoes* and *residencias* graded from one up to three stars. In general, three-star pensions and one-star hotels are roughly similar in price. However, it is quite possible to pay more for a very poor one-star hotel than for a comfortable three-star pension, and vice versa. Prices in one-star hotels/three-star pensions range from 2000 to 6400$ (£8.00–25.50; $15.25–48.50; DM23.25–74.00) for singles, 3300–7200$ (£6.60–14.40; $12.50–27.50; DM19.25–41.75) per person for doubles. In the lower-rated pensions singles cost around 1500–2000$ (£6–8; $11.50–15.25; DM17.50–23.25), doubles around 2500–3000$ (£5–6; $9.50–11.50; DM14.50–17.50) p.p.

In the smaller towns, seaside resorts, and areas particularly popular with tourists, **rooms in private homes** (*quartos* or *dormidas*) can be both less expensive and more comfortable than pensions. Private rooms are sometimes offered to travellers at bus and train stations. Such offers may be worth considering as private rooms are generally more difficult to find than pensions. Local Tourist Offices have lists of private rooms available in the locality. Alternatively, simply enquire at any house with a sign in the window advertising private rooms (signs are frequently written in several languages).

Hostelling can be a cheap way to see much of the country, but, especially during the peak periods, you may not feel it is worth the added effort, considering the restrictions hostelling imposes. However, hostelling can be a more attractive option in the off-season, as the hostels offer an excellent opportunity to meet other travellers, especially outside Lisbon and Oporto. There are 19 IYHF hostels and most of the main places of interest have a hostel of some sort, or can be reached on a daytrip from the nearest hostel. Standards at the hostels are high, and prices are very reasonable: depending on the standard of the hostel, the age of the user and the time of year, the overnight charge for B&B and sheets varies from 700–1250$ (£2.80–5.00; $5.25–9.50; DM8.25–14.50). Hostels are open to IYHF members only, but it is possible to buy a membership card at the hostels, though the 2100$ (£8.40; $16; DM24.50) fee is roughly twice what under 25s pay to join one of the British associations in advance. Unless the warden agrees to you staying longer, you are limited to three consecutive nights in any hostel. Curfews (midnight 1 May–30 Sept.; 11.30 p.m. at other times) can be a real nuisance, since bars and clubs stay open late, many football matches kick off at 9 p.m., and cinemas often show late films in English. The peak periods for the hostels are June to September, around Christmas, and Holy Week. At these times it is advisable to write or phone ahead to reserve a bed. As the hostel in Oporto is pitifully small considering the numbers who visit the town, to have a chance of getting a bed at any time of year you will either have to write in advance, or arrive at the hostel or phone ahead between 9.00–10.30 a.m.

In contrast to Mediterranean countries, **camping** is well worth considering in Portugal. Sites tend to be more conveniently located in and around the main towns than in Greece, Italy or neighbouring Spain. Portuguese sites are seldom more than three miles out from the town centre, and usually have a direct bus link. Nor is there any problem as regards carrying your tent around as left luggage stores are available at all train stations. Camping is a great way to meet the locals as the Portuguese themselves are enthusiastic campers. The relative unpopularity of camping with budget travellers is due to the widespread availability of other cheap accommodation, and nothing to do with the standard of the campsites, which is actually quite high. There are 97 official sites, graded from one star up to four stars, many of which require a Camping Carnet. All the sites have the basic, essential facilities – most even have a cafe and a supermarket – so bearing in mind the facilities available, prices are very reasonable. At the main site in Lisbon peak season charges are still only around 350$ (£1.40; $2.75; DM4) to pitch a tent, 250$ (£1; $1.90; DM2.90) per person. Even at some of the more expensive sites on the Algarve charges are unlikely to exceed 500$ (£2; $3.75; DM5.75) per tent and per person. **Camping outside official sites** is permitted with the consent of the landowner, but is not allowed in towns, at any spot less than one kilometre from a beach, or from an official site, or in the vicinity of a reservoir.

ADDRESSES

Portuguese YHA   Associação de Utentes das Pousadas de Juventude, Rua Andrade Corvo No 46, 1000 Lisboa (tel. 3511–571054).

Camping   Federaçao Portuguesa de Campismo, Rua Voz de Operario, Lisboa (tel. 01–862350).

Orbitur, Av. Almirante Gago Coutinho 25d, Lisboa. Orbitur operates 15 sites which are amongst the best managed, but also the most expensive, in Portugal.

A free list of the 97 official sites,
'Portugal Camping', is available from
the National Tourist Office in London
or your capital city, and from local
Tourist Offices.

Cascais (tel. code 01)

During the summer finding cheap accommodation can be difficult. There are relatively few pensions in Cascais, so consider any reasonable offer of a private room.

PENSIONS

One-star:
   Avanida, Rua da Palmeira 14–1° (tel. 2864417).
Two-star:
   Le Biarritz, Avda do Ultramar (tel. 282216).
Three-star:
   Casa Lena, Avda do Ultramar 329 (tel. 2868743).
   Italia, Rua do Poço Novo 1 (tel. 280151).
   Palma, Avda Valbom 15 (tel. 280257).

CAMPING

   Parque de Campismo do Guincho, Guincho, Areia (tel. 2851014). About 4½ miles from Cascais. Orbitur site, open year round.

Coimbra (tel. code 039)

Long-distance trains stop at the Coimbra B station on the outskirts of the town, and from there you catch a connecting train to the more central Coimbra A. The area around Coimbra A has the least expensive accommodation in town, particularly Rua da Sota and the streets running off it. While this is not the most attractive of areas the pensions are generally perfectly acceptable and safe.

HOTELS

Cheapest doubles around 1500–2000$ (£6–8; $11.50–15.20; DM17.40–23.20) p.p.

Vitoria, Rua da Sota 9 (tel. 24049).

Lorvanese, Rua da Sota 27.

Sota, Rua da Sota 41.

Flor de Coimbra, Rua da Poço 8. Good inexpensive meals available to residents. Singles 1200–1500$ (£4.80–6.00; $9.00–11.50; DM13.90–17.40).

Residencia Luis Atenas, Avda Fernão de Magalhães 68 (tel. 26412). The avenue running away to the left from the station.

Residencial Internacional de Coimbra, Avda Fernão de Magalhães (opposite the train station) (tel. 25503). Doubles around 1200$ (£4.80; $9; DM14) p.p. Prices are lower in triples and quads.

Aviz, Avda Fernão Magalhães 64 (tel. 23718).

Residencial Larbelo, Largo da Portagem (tel. 29092).

Rivoli, Praça do Comercio. Three-star pension. Doubles 1750$ (£7; $13.30; DM20.30) p.p., singles 1500$ (£6; $11.50; DM17.40).

Gouveia, Rua João de Rouão 21. Not central, but close to the station.

Jardim, Avda Emidio Navarro 65. Two-star pension. The street runs alongside the river.

Parque, Avda Emidio Navarro 42. Two-star pension.

Diogo, Praça da República 18–2°. In the university area.

Antunes, Rua Castro Matoso (tel. 23048). University quarter, beneath the aqueduct. Advance reservation advised.

IYHF HOSTEL

Rua Henriques Seco 12–14 (tel. 22955). Excellent hostel. Bus 7 from Largo da Portagem or Coimbra A to Liceu José Falcão. Also buses 8, 29 and 46. 1000$ (£4; $7.60; DM11.60) including breakfast.

CAMPING

Parque de Campismo Municipal de Coimbra, Praça 25 de
Abril (tel. 712997). 400$ (£1.60; $3; DM4.65) per tent,
including person.

Estoril (tel. code 01)

HOTELS

Two-star:
Chique do Estoril, Avda Marginal 60 (tel. 2680393).
Costa, Rua da Olivença 2–1&2° (tel. 2681699).
Maryluz, R. Maestro Lacerda 13 r/c 1° & 2° (tel. 2682740).
Three-star:
Casa Londres, Avda Fausto Figueiredo 7 (tel. 2681541).
Continental, Rua Joaquim dos Santos 2 (tel. 2680050).
Smart, Rua José Viana 3 (tel. 2682164).
São Cristóvão, Estrada Marginal (tel. 2680913).

Faro (tel. 089)

During the summer cheap accommodation can be difficult
to find in Faro unless you look early in the day. Many
people only stay one night in Faro (before flying out or
after flying in) so if you can start your search early you have
a fair chance of benefiting from this turnover of visitors.
In response to the high level of demand hoteliers often
increase their prices in July and August. The best places
to look are the streets Filipe Alistão, Alportel, Conselheiro
Bivar, Infante Dom Henrique and Vasco da Gama.

HOTELS

Expect to pay for doubles 2500–3000$ (£9–12; $17–22.80; DM26.10–34.80) p.p., and singles 1750–2300$ (£7–9.2; $13.30–25.25; DM20.30–26.70).

One-star:

Mirense, Rua Capitão Mor (tel. 22687).
Nunes, Rua Horta Machado (tel. 27876).

Two-star:
S. Filipe, Rua Infante Dom Henrique (tel. 24182).
Dany, Rua Filipe Alistão 62 (tel. 24791). Recommended.
Delfim, Rua da Alportel (tel. 22578).
Carminho, Rua da Alportel (tel. 23709).
Dina, Rua Teofilo Braga (tel. 23897).
Emilia, Rua Teixeira Guedes (tel. 23352).
Madalena, Rua Conselheiro Bivar (tel. 27284). One of the
  best.
Novo Lar, Rua Infante Dom Henrique.
Tivoli, Praça Alexandre Herculano (tel. 23350).
Tinita, Rua do Alportel (tel. 25040).

Three-star:
Algarve, Rua D. Francisco Gomes (tel. 23346).
Condado, Rua Gonçalo Barreto (tel. 22081–2).
Yorque, Rua de Berlim (tel. 23973).
Lumena, Praça Alexandre Herculano (tel. 22028).
Rest. O Faraó, Largo da Madalena (tel. 23356).
Marim, Rua Gonçalo Barreto (tel. 24063/26402).
Oceano, Travessa Ivens (tel. 23349).
Afonso III, Rua Gomes Freire (tel. 27042/27054).
Solar do Alto, Rua de Berlim (tel. 22091).
Samé, Rua do Bocage (tel. 24375/23370).
Residencial Galo, Rua Filipe Alistão 41 (tel. 26435).
  Doubles around 1500$ (£5; $9.50; DM14.50) p.p.

PRIVATE ROOMS

Turismo, Rua da Misericordia 8, by the harbour. Turismo
allocates rooms. Some are well located, others less so. In
peak season take what you get. Turismo also supplies lists
of pensions, but leave it to you to phone.

CAMPING

Parque de Campismo Municipal da Ilha de Faro, Ilha
de Faro (tel. 24876). Year-round site. Often full. Very
crowded in summer. Camping Carnet required. Bus
16 from the airport or town centre to Praia de Faro.
May–Sept. bus runs twice hourly from 7.30 a.m.–
8 p.m., hourly the rest of the year. Infrequent service
at weekends.

Lisbon (Lisboa) (tel. code 01)

At most times of the year finding a cheap room near
Rossio should be quite easy: singles 1200–1600$ (£4.80–6.40;
$8.75–12.25; DM13.25–18.50); doubles 1000–1400$ (£4.00–
5.60; $7.50–10.75; DM11.50–16.25) p.p. There are cheaper
pensions, but some of the rooms are likely to have quite a
turnover of occupants (about every half hour). Nevertheless,
most of these pensions are perfectly safe. In the summer
months, however, you may have difficulty finding accommodation at the prices quoted above as the amount of rooms
available just manages to satisfy demand. Singles become
very scarce as owners often put an extra bed in the room
during peak season. The best advice is to start looking for
a room as early as possible. If you arrive in the afternoon
be prepared to take something slightly more expensive, and
then look around early next morning. Turismo at Praça des
Restauradores will book more expensive rooms for free:
2000$ (£8; $15.25; DM23.25) plus p.p. for doubles.

HOTELS

Rossio area:
  Londres, Rossio/Praça D. Pedro V 53–1° (tel. 346 2203).
  Coimbra e Madrid, Praça de Figueira 3–3&4° (tel. 321 760).
  Evora, Rossio/Praça D. Pedro V 59–2° (tel. 346 7666).
  Do Sul, Rossio/Praça D. Pedro V 59–2° (tel. 814 7253).
  Beira Minho, Praça de Figueira 6–2° (tel. 3461846).

Baixa – the lower town; a roughly rectangular area stretching from Praça D. Pedro V & Praça de Figueira down to the River Tajus (Rio Tejo):
  Bom Conforto, Rua dos Douradores 83–3° (tel. 878 328).
  Norte, Rua dos Douradores 159–1&2° (tel. 878941).
  Santiago, Rua dos Douradores 222–3° (tel. 874353).
  Prata, Rua da Prata 71–3° (tel. 3468908). Cheap and very good.
  Rossio, Rua dos Sapateiros 173–2° (tel. 327204).
  Arco Bandeira (tel. 323478). At the end of the street near Praca D. Pedro V.
  Galiza, Rua do Crucifixio 50–5° (tel. 328430).

Around São Jorge castle and close to the Alfama:
  São João da Praça, Rua São João da Praça 97 (tel. 862591). Cheap and high quality.
  Ninho das Aguias, Rua Costa do Castelo 74 (tel. 862151). Slightly more expensive than the prices quoted above, but an excellent pension set in a garden. Highly recommended (unfortunately, by all guide books it seems).

To the west of the Baixa, around San Roque and the Rossio railway station:
  Estacio Central, Calçada do Carmo 17–21° (tel. 323308). Behind the train station.
  Henriques, Calçada do Carmo 37–11° (tel. 326886).
  Do Duque, Calçada do Duque 53 (tel. 3463444). Inexpensive and very clean.

Between Rossio and the Pombal statue – Avenida da Liberdade is the main road running between the two. Because of their location pensions on Avenida da Liberdade tend to fill quickly, despite being slightly more expensive on average than those in the areas above. Prices are lower in the streets to either side of Liberdade, and the pensions are more likely to have space.

Pembo, Avda da Liberdade 11–3° (tel. 325010).

Mucaba, Avda da Liberdade 53–2° (tel. 346567).

Lis, Avda da Liberdade 180 (tel. 521084).

Dom Sancho I, Avda da Liberdade 202–3&5° (tel. 548648).

Ritz, Avda da Liberdade 240–4° (tel. 521084).

Mansarde, Avda da Liberdade 141–5° (tel. 372963).

Do Sul, Avda da Liberdade 53 (tel. 3465647).

Modelo, Rua das Portas de Santo Antão 12 (tel. 327041). Parallel to Liberdade, on the right as you walk up from Rossio.

Flor de Baixa, Rua das Portas de Santo Antão 81–2° (tel. 323153). Good value.

Floroscente, Rua das Portas de Santo Antão 99 (tel. 326609). Inexpensive and with large capacity.

Iris, Rua da Gloria 2a–2°. Parallel to Liberdade, on the left walking up from Rossio.

Monumental, Rua da Gloria 21 (tel. 3469807).

Milanesa, Rua da Alegria 25–2° (tel. 3466456). Continues on from Rua da Gloria.

Sevilha, Praça da Alegria 11–2&3° (tel. 369579). Off Liberdade, the left turn after Rua Conceicao da Gloria.

Alegria, Praça da Alegria 12–1° (tel. 3475522).

Solar, Praça da Alegria 12–2° (tel. 322608).

Dos Restauradores, Praça dos Restauradores 13–4°. At the end of Liberdade closest to Rossio.

Imperial, Praça dos Restauradores 79 (tel. 320166).

IYHF HOSTELS

Rua Andrade Corvo 46 (tel. 532696). Metro: Picoas. Bus 1 or 45 from Rossio or Cais do Sodré. Twenty-minute walk from the centre, off Avda Fontes Pereira de Melo, in the area beyond the Pombal statue. Phone ahead to check if this hostel is open in 1992.

Lisboa-Catalazete, Estrada Marginal, OEIRAS (tel. 2430638). 11.30 p.m. curfew. Frequent trains from Cais do Sodré; 20-minute trip. On leaving the station go through the underpass, to the right beneath the Praia sign. Look for the sign pointing out the way to the hostels. It's about three-quarters of a mile and well signposted.

CAMPING

Parque de Campismo Municipal de Lisboa Monsanto (tel. 704413/708384). Bus 14 runs from Praça de Figueira. Year round site.

Parque de Campismo Municipal de Oeiras, Rua de S. Pedro do Areeiro (tel. 2430330). Train from Cais do Sodré to Oeiras. Open May–Oct.

There are six sites on the Costa da Caparica. Ask the Tourist Office which metro and/or bus you should take for the different sites. Open year round unless indicated:

Costa da Caparica, Estrada da Trafaria (tel. 2900661). Orbitur site. Bungalows available. From Praça de Espanha a bus runs right to the site, or take the metro to Palhava.

Um Lugar ao Sol, Estrada da Trafaria (tel. 2901592).

Costa Velha, Estrada da Trafaria (tel. 2900100/2900374).

C. do Concelho de Almada, Praia da Saúde (tel. 2901862).

Costa Nova, Estrada da Costa Nova (tel. 2903078). Closed Jan.

Piedense, Praia da Mata (tel. 2902004).

Oporto (Porto) (tel. code 02)

Rua do Loureiro, close to São Bento train station, has the cheapest pensions in the city, but is also the red-light area of Oporto. Most of the city's pensions are on and around Avenida dos Aliados, particularly on the western side of Aliados (on the left as you look up the street towards the Town Hall).

HOTELS

Expect to pay 1200–1750$ (£4.80–7.00; $8.75–13.25; DM14.00–20.25) p.p. for doubles. In recent years many pensions have been undergoing renovation, so finding rooms at the bottom end of this price range is likely to prove increasingly difficult.

Monumental, Avda dos Aliados 151–4° (tel. 23964). Large rooms, good value.

Next door to Monumental, above the Bel Arte, there is another good pension. Unfortunately this pension is nameless.

Norte, Rua Fernando Tomás 579. East off Aliados from the Trinidad church. The pension is at the junction with Rua Santa Catarina. Good value.

Astoria, Rua Arnaldo Gama 56 (tel. 28175). To the east of Aliados. Reserve ahead.

Vera Cruz, Rua da Ramalho Ortigão 14 (tel. 323396). The street off Aliados before the Tourist Office.

Dos Aliados, Rua Elisio de Melo 27 (tel. 24853). Off Aliados.

Novo Mundo, Rua Conde de Vizela 92 (tel. 25403). West of Aliados. Off Rua Clerigos, the street going up the hill to the Clerigos Tower.

União, Rua Conde de Vizela 62 (tel. 23078).

Duas Nações, Praça Guilherme Gomes Fernandes 59 (tel. 26807). Along Rua Carmelitas from the Clerigos Tower.

Grand Oceano, Rua da Fabrica 45 (tel. 382447). Joins Aliados on the west side near the Tourist Office.

Franco, Praça Parada de Leitão 41 (tel. 381201). To the west of Aliados.

D'Ouro, Praça Parada de Leitão 41 (tel. 381201).

San Marino, Praça Carlos Alberto 59 (tel. 325499). At the end of Rua Fabrica, the street leading out the western side of Aliados near the Tourist Office.

Estoril, Rua de Cedofeita 193 (tel. 325499). Road leading out of Praça Carlos Alberto.

Nobreza, Rua do Breyner 6 (tel. 312409). Rundown and not the cleanest of places. Rua do Breyner is on the left as you walk up Cedofeita from Praça Carlos Alberto.

Pao de Açucar, Rua do Almada 262 (tel. 922425). Parallel to Aliados, immediately to the west.

Porto Rico, Rua do Almada 262 (tel. 922425).

Europa, Rua do Almada 398 (tel. 26971). Two-star pension.

Moderna, Rua Estacão 74 (tel. 571280). A short walk from Porto Campanha train station.

IYHF HOSTEL

Rua Rodrigues Lobo 98 (tel. 65535). Very small and usually full by midday. Curfew midnight. Twenty-minute walk from the town centre. Bus 3, 19, 20 or 52 from Praça da Liberdade (at the foot of Avda dos Aliados) runs to nearby Rua Júlio Dinis.

STUDENT ACCOMMODATION

Colegio de Gaia, Rua Padua Correia 166, Vila Nova de Gaia (tel. 304007). On the other side of the River Douro from Porto. Frequent train connections, as well as local buses.

CAMPING

Parque de Campismo da Prelada, Rua Monte dos Burgos (tel. 812616). Open all year. Bus 6 from Praça da Liberdade; bus 9 from Bolhao (last bus 9 p.m.); bus 50 from Cordoaria. Closest site to the town centre, but three miles from the beach.

There are three sites in Vila Nova da Guia, closer to the beaches than Prelada. Ask the Tourist Office about the local bus service to these sites:

Salguieros-Canidelo (tel. 7810500). Open May–Sept.

Madalena, Lugar da Marinha (tel. 714162). Open June–Sept. Bus 50 from Rua Mouz, near Porto Sao Bento train station.

Marisol, Rua Alto das Chaquedas 82, Canidelo (tel. 715942).

Sintra (tel. code 01)

Sintra is close enough to Lisbon to be visited on a day trip. For railpass holders this may be the simplest option in summer because at this time finding a room can be a problem unless you arrive early in the day.

HOTELS

Cyntia Café. From the station head away from the town centre along Avda Dr. Miguel Bombarda until you see the pension.

Nova Sintra, Largo Alfonso de Albuquerque 25 (tel. 9230220). Further along from the Cyntia Café through Largo D. Manuel I.

Familiar. Past the Nova Sintra. About 10 minutes' walk from the station.

Casa Adelaide, Avda Guilherme Gomes Fernandes 11–1°
(tel. 9230873). Near the Town Hall, roughly halfway
between the train station and the Palácio Real.

Bristol. Close to the Palácio Real.

Economica. One of the cheapest. Near the Palácio Real.

PRIVATE ROOMS

Turismo in the town centre books rooms at reasonable rates.
Rooms are frequently touted by locals at the train station.

CAMPING

No really convenient site.

Capuchos convent is over six miles from Sintra. The
nearest bus stop is about three miles from the site,
with most of the remaining walk uphill.

Parque de Campismo Praia Grande (tel. 9290581/9291834)
is situated on the coast 7½ miles from Sintra, and 2½
miles from Colares. Open year round. Ask the Tourist
Office for details of the bus service. The bus stops only
50m from the site.

ROMANIA

In an effort to bolster Romania's economy, the Ceausescu regime followed a policy of consistently devaluing its hard currencies; by some 90 per cent from 1975 to 1989. This policy had a profound effect on the tourist industry, rendering most accommodation options comparable in price to their Scandinavian equivalents. Hotel prices were one striking example of this development: classified de luxe, Category I or II, in 1989 the cheapest double in a Category II hotel in Bucharest cost £25 ($47.50; DM72.50) per person. Outside Bucharest a similar room costs £20 ($38; DM58) p.p. Some sanity has returned to the pricing structure now that the Ceausescu government has been overthrown, and although this does not mean that there are any bargains to be had, as in Hungary, Czechoslovakia or Poland, at least a night in one of the cheaper hotels will not ruin your budget for days, as was the case previously.

A number of Category II **hotels** in Bucharest now offer singles for £11.50–13.25 ($21.75–25.25; DM33.50–38.25), doubles for £9.00–11.50 ($17.25–21.75; DM26.00–33.50) p.p. Outside the capital you can look for a 20–25 per cent reduction on these prices for similar accommodation. *All hotel bills must be settled in hard currency.* If these prices seem attractive to you, bear in mind that either you will have to be very fortunate to get one of these rooms on arrival, or you will have to book well in advance. During the peak season (mid June to mid September) hotels are frequently booked to near capacity by East European groups. You may be lucky enough to get one of the remaining places, or find space caused by a late cancellation, but do not expect too much help from the National Tourist Organization (ONT) in your quest for a cheap hotel room. ONT supply hotel lists and book hotels, but old habits die hard, and, especially in Bucharest, you may find they devote much of their energy to persuading you to stay in a more expensive hotel. Expect to be told that the cheaper hotels are full. If you are not pressed for time, you can try some of the hotels in person. It is possible to make hotel reservations through various private organizations in the UK before departure, but, like ONT, they are not always too receptive to enquiries regarding the cheaper hotels.

The letting of private homes was legalized in 1990. Previously Romanians were liable to severe punishment if they were found to have given lodgings to foreigners. Their guests escaped lightly: they were merely deported. Nowadays **rooms in private homes** offer budget travellers a way to avoid paying over the odds in hotels, and the efforts involved in trying to book a hostel bed. Many Romanians are keen to let rooms to earn some extra money and, as the problems besetting the country deter many people from visiting Romania, there is a plentiful supply of rooms available. Private rooms are available through ONT and prices are around £6.25 ($12; DM18.25) p.p. in Bucharest, £5.25 ($10; DM15.25) p.p. elsewhere. *Once again payment has to be made in hard currency*. Rooms offered by locals are much cheaper – rarely will their asking price reach £2.60 ($5; DM7.50) p.p., and usually it will be considerably less.

Do not be immediately suspicious of anyone offering you a room for free. This is quite a common practice. Your host may well expect some favour in return, such as exchanging money at a rate favourable to all concerned; that is, above the official rate but below the black market norm (this is still illegal). If you do decide to take up an offer of private accommodation, keep an eye on your valuables, or leave them at the station.

Youth hostels are controlled by BTT, the Romanian youth and student organization. Like other East European state tourist organizations, they have a marked preference for dealing with groups rather than with individuals. Most of the beds at the majority of youth hostels are reserved months in advance by school and youth groups. This puts the onus on you to book well ahead of your time of arrival, a major task considering the difficulties of dealing with BTT. Incredibly, when hostels have plenty of space, many simply choose to shut their doors until the next group arrives. In the later years of the Ceausescu regime the cost of BTT youth hostels spiralled dramatically. Prices remain inflated even today at around £5–9 ($9.50–17.25; DM14.50–26.50) p.p.

During the university and college summer holidays, BTT lets out **student accommodations** (*caminul de studenti*) in towns with a sizeable student population. As with youth hostels, these lodgings are frequently filled up by vacationing groups. If you do manage to get a bed, expect to pay in the region of £3–4 ($5.75–7.50; DM8.75–11.50). Many towns and university rectorates maintain a surplus capacity of student accommodation, specifically for the use of visiting foreign students. Prices are exceptionally low, at around £1.30–2.60 ($2.50–5.00; DM3.75–7.50). Such accommodation offers an excellent opportunity to meet Romanian students and you may receive offers from Romanian, African or Asian students to share their rooms. Probably the only favour they will be looking for is the chance to speak to you.

There are well over 100 **campsites,** which are very cheap. A solo traveller should pay no more than £1.60 ($3; DM4.75) to pitch a tent for one night. Cabins are available at most sites, with charges of around £2.50 ($4.75; DM7.25) p.p. being the norm, though unfortunately, these are usually full in summer. Sites are sometimes located a good distance out of town, and occasionally are none too easy to reach by public transport. Your main complaint may be the quality of the sites. Facilities are very basic, and the toilets and washrooms can be really atrocious. **Camping rough** is technically illegal, but there are few places you are likely to have any trouble once you get out into the countryside. The authorities outside the towns often ignore freelance campers, as long as you do not light fires, leave litter, or damage the natural habitat. Occasionally you may be sent on your way, but it is very rare for the statutory fine to be imposed.

In the countryside there are well in excess of 100 '*cabanas*', simple accommodations for hikers and walkers, many of which are in the more mountainous parts of the country. An ONT map, 'Cabane Turistice', shows their locations, though none too precisely. An overnight stay costs around £3 ($5.75; DM8.75). By law, cabanas are debarred from refusing entry to any hiker or climber, but it still might be sensible to reserve ahead, either through ONT, or through the Regional Tourist Office. Overnight stays are also possible at a number of **monasteries**, but it can be very difficult to gain entrance. An approach has to be made first to ONT, who will subsequently do their utmost to convince you to stay in a hotel instead. Persistence is essential on your part, but there is still no guarantee of success.

If you cannot find a bed in town, and face a night sleeping rough, do not attempt to bed down in the town, but rather head for the **train station waiting room.** If you are disturbed by the police explain that you are taking a train early in the morning. The chances are that you will have a few Romanians for company in the waiting room as this is quite a common practice amongst people setting off on an early morning train. Try to leave your pack in the left luggage store as theft is, regrettably, quite common.

As there are several long overnight train journeys in Romania it is possible to spend a few **nights on the train.** Trains are usually packed so there is little chance of you getting stretched out in a compartment, but booking a couchette gives you the chance of a good night's sleep. Prices vary according to the length of the journey, but are low by Western standards. However, couchettes have to be booked four to seven days in advance, either at an ONT office, or through a CFR (Romanian Railways) office in town (not at the station). The problem with sleeping on overnight trains is that there is a high incidence of theft from travellers on such trains.

ADDRESSES

| Hotels | booked in the UK by:
Thomas Cook, VIP Travel,
42 North Audley Street,
London, W1Y 2DU
(tel. 071–499 4221) (or your
local Thomas Cook agent)
Any branch of American
Express.
Romanian Holidays,
54 Pembroke Road,
London, W8 6NX
(tel. 071–602 7093) (London
only)
or through the Romanian
National Tourist Office in
London, or your capital
city. |
| Youth and student hostels | BTT, Onesti 6–8, Bucuresti
(tel. 140566).
BTT, 7–15 Str. Mandeleev,
Bucuresti (tel. 144200). |

Braşov (tel. code 21)

HOTELS

Carpaţi Sport, Str. Maiakovski. Cheapest in town. Not to be confused with the expensive Hotel Carpaţi on Bd Gheorghiu-Dej.

Postăvrul, Str. Republicii.

Turist, Str. Karl Marx 32. Closest to the train station.

PRIVATE ROOMS

Enquire at the ONT office in the lobby of the Hotel Carpaţi on Bd Gheorghiu-Dej. Trolleybus 4 will get you there from the train station. Open daily 10 a.m.–6 p.m.

STUDENT ACCOMMODATION

Dorm rooms available year round, at £1.30 ($2.50; DM3.75) for those with student ID. Enquire at the Rector's Office, University of Braşov. Open Mon.–Fri. 10 a.m.–5 p.m. Just along Bd Gheorghiu-Dej from the Hotel Carpaţi.

CAMPING

Zimbrul. On the road to the mountain resort of Poiana-Braşov. From Parc Central bus 20. Bus 4 links the train station to Parc Central.

Dîrste. Roughly 4½ miles from the town centre, close to the motorway to Bucharest. From the Parc Central bus 17 until it leaves Calea Bucureştilor. From here a 10-minute walk parallel to the motorway, then under the train tracks and across the river.

Bucharest (Bucereşti) (tel. code 0)

HOTELS

**Expect to pay £11.50–15.00 ($21.75–28.50; DM33.50–43.50) for singles,
£9.00–12.50 ($17.25–23.75; DM26.00–36.25) p.p. for doubles.**

Near the Gara de Nord:
   Bucegi, Str. Witing 2 (tel. 495120).
   Dunarea, Calea Griviţei 140
   Griviţa, Calea Griviţei 130 (tel. 505380).
   Oltenia, Calea Griviţei. Cheapest of the three hotels listed
     on this street.
   Marna, Str. Buzeşti.

More centrally located:
   Opera, Str. Brezoianu 37.
   Muntenia, Str. Academiei 21 (tel. 146010).
   Cişmigiu, Bd Gheorghiu-Dej 18 (tel. 147410).
   Carpaţi, Str. Matei Millo 16 (tel. 157690).
Most people arrive at the Gara de Nord. Beside the ONT office in the train station there is a board listing all the hotels in the city, with their addresses and tel. nos.

PRIVATE ROOMS

Available through ONT main office at Bd Magheru (tel. 145160). £6.25 ($12; DM18.25) p.p. Mon.–Sat. 8 a.m.–8 p.m., Sun. 8 a.m.–2 p.m.

HOSTELS/STUDENT DORMS

Expect to pay around £8 ($15; DM23) for singles, £14.75 ($28; DM 42.75) p.p. for doubles.

BTT are at Str. Mendeleev 7–15 (tel. 144200). Open
Mon.–Fri. 8 a.m.–5 p.m. Generally unwilling to help
independent travellers. You might have better luck
approaching hostels/dorms in person.

> N. Bălescu Agronomical Institute. Close to the Casa
> Şcinteii, reached by trolleybus 81 or 82. Open 1 July–
> 31 Aug.
> Institutul Politechnic. Near the Grozăveşti metro stop.
> Open 1 July–31 Aug.

Arab, African and Asian students remain at the colleges
during the summer vacation. They will probably be able
to tell you where to make enquiries regarding staying the
night. They may even offer to let you share their room.
At other times Romanian students may extend the same
hospitality.

CAMPING

> Bănasea. Twin-bedded bungalows are available, £2.65 ($5;
> DM7.75) p.p. From Gara de Nord bus 205 or trolleybus
> 81 (also trolleybus 82 from Piaţa Victoriei) to Bănasea
> airport. Bus 149 runs to the site (Sundays bus 348). Bus
> 148 lets you off about 10 minutes' walk from the site.
> Fine during the day, but the road is unlit at night.

Constanţa (tel. code 16)

Affordable accommodation in Constanţa is limited so you
may have to stay in one of the resorts nearby. Two of the
easiest to reach are Mamaia and Eforie Nord, 3¾ miles north
and 6¼ miles south respectively. Trolleybus 41 from the
station in Constanţa will take you to Mamaia, and trolleybus
11 runs from the Sud bus station to Eforie Nord. Ask the
ONT office in Constanţa about the availability of rooms in
the cheap hotels in Mamaia or Eforie Nord, or of bungalows
at the campsites.

Offices dealing with accommodation:
ONT, B-dul Tomis 46, Constanţa. Open Mon.–Sat. 8 a.m.–
6 p.m., Sun. 9 a.m.–1 p.m.
BTT, Blvd Tomis 20–24, Constanţa (tel. 16624).
Mamaia Tourist Office. In the Bucureşti B hotel (tel.
31152/31179).
Eforie Nord Tourist Office, B-dul Republicii 13 (tel. 41351).

HOTELS

Constanţa – ask ONT about rooms in the hotels below, or
at other hotels:

**Expect to pay for singles £5.75–6.85 ($11–13; DM16.75–19.75),
doubles £4.25–5.50 ($8.00–10.50; DM12.25–16.00) p.p.**

Victoria, B-dul Republicii.
Constanţa, B-dul Tomis 46. Above the Tourist Office.

Mamaia Nord:
The Tourist Office lets rooms in those hotels which have
not been block-booked by travel operators. Amongst the
cheapest in town are the Favorit and the Paloma. There are
a number of others which are only slightly more expensive,
such as the Apollo, Select, and the Caraiman I and II.

Eforie Nord:
Much the same system as in Mamaia. Hotel beds start at
around £5.75 ($11; DM16.75), so state that you are looking
for a bed around that price (quote the $11 figure).

PRIVATE ROOMS

Enquire about their availability at any of the Tourist Offices.

HOSTELS

BTT control the letting of dormitory accommodation during the summer, but are more accustomed to dealing with groups.

CAMPING

No sites in Constanţa. Just north of Mamaia is Turist, while another three miles further on is Hanul Piraţilor. There are two sites in Eforie Nord: the Şincai and the Meduza. In July and August the sites are invariably overcrowded. All four sites have bungalows for hire, and in summer these bungalows are very popular, but try to make reservations at the Tourist Offices before going to the sites and consider yourself fortunate if you are successful.

Sibiu/Hermannstädt (tel. code 24)

Despite the emigration of many of Transylvania's Germanic population in recent years, do not be surprised to hear the town referred to by its German name of Hermannstädt. The cheapest hotels are the Imperatul Romanilor, just off Piaţa Republicii on Str. N. Balcescu, and the Bulevard on Strada V. I. Lenin. Cheaper lodgings are available at the inn on Calea Dumbravii: from the bus station (adjacent to the train station on Piaţa Garii) take the bus to Pădurea Dumbrava and you'll find the inn located next to the campsite, on the left as you travel down Calea Dumbravii. For private rooms in Sibiu or the neighbouring villages contact ONT. From Piaţa Republicii walk down Str. N. Balcescu until you see the ONT office. Nearby at Str. Kornhauser 4 is the BTT office where you can enquire about the availability of dormitory accommodation. Like other BTT offices they are more used to dealing with groups, so be persistent.

Sighişoara (tel. code 23)

HOTELS
Steaua, Str. Gheorghiu-Dej. Affordable singles and doubles.

PRIVATE ROOMS
Enquire at ONT on Str. Gheorghiu-Dej.

CAMPING
There is a site on top of the hill to the rear of the train station, and bungalows are also available there. From the station walk right along Str. Liberati until you see the tunnel going under the tracks on your right. As you emerge on to Str. Primaverii go right and watch out for the path leading to the site. The Hula Danes site is located about 2½ miles from town along the road to Mediaş. Hula Danes also has bungalows for hire.

SPAIN

Although prices have risen substantially over the past decade Spain still offers the budget traveller a plentiful supply of some of the least expensive accommodation possibilities in Europe. Virtually all the various types of accommodation are inspected and categorized by the Secretaria de Estado de Turismo and maximum prices for rooms in the different categories are fixed according to the facilities available. By law these prices have to be displayed on the door of the room. With certain agreed and stipulated exceptions, it is illegal for owners to charge more than the stated price, though prices can be raised quite legally during the peak season (usually July and August). In Seville prices can actually double during Holy Week and the April Fair, as it is very much a sellers' market. However, during the quieter periods of the year (October to early March) there is no harm in trying to bargain the owner down. Understandings can be reached reasonably easily with owners who know there are plenty of rooms available just down the street, and some owners may themselves choose to offer their rooms below the official price, though this can create the impression that the whole system is a bit of a shambles; for example, you can pay more for a room in a *casa de huespedes* than for a similar room in a better category of accommodation such as a *pensión* or *hostale-residencia*.

In **hotels,** singles in the price range 900–2000ptas (£4.90–10.75; $9.25–20.50; DM14.25–31.25) are widely available, as are doubles for 800–1750ptas (£4.25–9.50; $8–18; DM12.25–27.50) per person. As a rule you are more likely to find rooms at the lower end of these price scales outside the main resorts and the more popular tourist towns. On average you can expect to pay around 1500ptas (£8; $15.25; DM23.25) for singles, 1100ptas (£6; $11.25; DM17.25) p.p. for doubles. There are some very cheap rooms available in popular places such as Madrid, Barcelona and the Andalucian cities, but these tend to fill up quickly. Phoning ahead is difficult unless you speak Spanish as very few owners speak any other language (signs outside their establishments claiming otherwise are often just a ruse to attract your attention), and in any case, owners seldom accept reservations made by phone. You can find out if rooms are available by phoning ahead, but do not be surprised if they are gone by the time you arrive in person. In this case it is handy to know what the various accommodation signs look like, and which accommodations are likely to be the cheapest. Then you will be able to spot other possibilities in the same street, or even in the same building. This is also helpful in places such as Madrid where the Tourist Office will not book the cheaper rooms that budget travellers are interested in, but merely provide you with a list to help you look on your own.

The intricacies of the rating system detailed below are intended as a rough guide to help you. For the reasons given above, do not treat them as hard and fast rules. Least expensive of all the officially categorized lodgings are *fondas*, denoted by a white 'F' on a square blue sign. Next up the scale are *casas de huespedes* (blue sign with CH), followed by *pensiónes* (P), graded from one up to three stars. Then come the infrequently seen *hospedges*. At this lower end of the market there is no point expecting anything other than basic facilities, but standards of cleanliness are usually perfectly acceptable. *Hostal-residencias* (H R) and *hostales* (H), both graded from one up to three stars, are a bit more expensive. Prices at a three-star hostale are usually roughly on a par with those of a one-star 'hotel-residencia' (HR) or a one-star *hotel* (H), but can be considerably more expensive. Hotel-residencias and hoteles are graded from one star up to five stars. With prices for a one-star double starting at around 1750ptas (£9.50; $18; DM27.50), your interest in hotels is likely to be confined to the bottom category.

Now and again you may also see *camas* (beds), *camas y*

comidas (bed and board), or *habitaciones* (rooms) advertised in bars or private homes. These can work out the least expensive accommodation option of all, with the possible bonus of good, cheap meals thrown in. As always, have a look at the room before making a firm acceptance. Again, there is probably nothing to be lost by trying to haggle the price down a bit, except in the peak periods when owners can afford to be choosy, and may just send you packing.

Hostelling is not a particularly good option in Spain as a whole. There are about 150 hostels of vastly differing quality, at which IYHF cards are obligatory. Most of the main places of interest are covered, with several notable exceptions, such as Salamanca and Santiago de Compostela. Only about 20 hostels remain open all year round, with many operating from July to September only. This means that outside these months hostel accommodation is lacking in a number of places of considerable interest. Even during the period from July to mid September independent travellers may not be able to get into the temporary hostels in places such as León, Segovia and Avila, as they are frequently filled by school and youth groups.

However, hostelling is not to be dismissed as a way of seeing the main cities, with the possible exception of Seville (with a very small hostel for so popular a city, which is usually full of local students). The question is whether prices, curfews, lack of security and the fact hostels are rarely centrally located make hostelling worthwhile. The normal hostel curfew of 10.30 p.m. in winter and 11.30 p.m. in summer is extended to 1–2 a.m. in Madrid, Barcelona and San Sebastian (no curfew at Madrid 'Richard Schirrmann' but the hostel is a long way from the centre if you miss the last metro). Even a 1 a.m. curfew is a bit early for anyone wanting to enjoy the nightlife of the cities, where things do not really begin to get going until around midnight. Charges for an overnight stay at most hostels are 550ptas (£3; $5.75; DM8.75) for under 26's. B&B 650ptas (£3.50; $6.75; DM10) (slightly more expensive for seniors). For two people travelling together, it might well be worth paying a little extra for the security of a room in one of the cheap lodgings mentioned above, plus the freedom to come and go as you wish.

Camping is not a great option either, and probably not worth considering unless you plan to travel extensively outside the main towns. Sites are frequently situated far from the town centre, and ill served by public transport. In effect, this can impose a curfew more restrictive than at any hostel. If you are keen on camping, at least the standards at the government-regulated sites are quite high, and although rating makes little difference to price, the facilities at the Class 1 sites do tend to be better than at the lesser-rated sites. Even in the sites serving the main towns you should pay no more than 400ptas (£2.15; $4; DM6.25) per person and per tent. However, to this you can add the cost of getting to the site, and, as security is a problem, the cost of leaving your luggage at the train or bus station, usually 150ptas (£0.80; $1.50; DM2.50).

Camping outside the official campgrounds is possible, provided the consent of the landowner is obtained. However, tents must not be pitched in a town; close to roads, military bases or reservoirs; in a dry river bed which may be subject to flooding; or within 1 kilometre of any official site. Camping on publicly owned land is prohibited by some local authorities.

Throughout most of the year the weather will present few problems for those **sleeping out,** but the Guardia Civil make a habit of patrolling areas which are popular and will wake up anybody they discover. Only if you are very short of money will they charge you with vagrancy. This leaves you with the same dilemma as in Belgium or the Netherlands: namely, staying within the law makes you an attractive target for muggers. Basically, sleeping out is foolhardy, especially in the cities and coastal resorts. If you are attacked it is likely to be by an organized gang, who may well become vicious if you try to resist (and sometimes even if you do not).

In the remote mountain regions, a network of cheap

refuges with bunk-bedded dormitories and basic cooking facilities is maintained by the Federacion Español de Montañismo. It may also be possible to stay in some **monasteries** in the more isolated areas. As the number of inhabitants have fallen, some monasteries have taken to letting vacant cells for about 350ptas (£1.90; $3.50; DM5.50) per night in order to supplement monastic income. Many admit visitors of either sex. Some, especially in Galicia, Catalonia, and Majorca, are located in spectacular settings. It is possible simply to enquire about staying the night on arrival, but as there may be no one about it is advisable to contact the local Tourist Office first. They will arrange a time for you to show up at the monastery.

ADDRESSES

Spanish YHA	Red Española de Albergues Juveniles, José Ortega y Gasset 71, Madrid 28006 (tel. 91–3477700).
Camping	Federacion Española de Empresarios de Campings, Gran Via 88, Madrid 28013 (tel. 91–2423168). ANCE, Principe De Vergara 85, 2° Ocha, 28006 Madrid. Maps and information on the official campsites from the above. A map is also available on request from the National Tourist Office in London or your capital city.
Mountain refuges	Federacion Español de Montañismo, Calle Alberto Aguiler 3, Madrid 15 (tel. 91–4451382).

Barcelona (tel. code 93)

HOTELS

**Cheapest doubles around 700ptas
(£3.75; $7.25; DM11) p.p.**

La Paz, Argentería 37 (tel. 3194408).
Unión, Unión 14 (tel. 3181581).

**Cheapest doubles around 900ptas
(£4.85; $9.25; DM14.25) p.p.**

La Cartuja, Tordera 43 (tel. 2133312).
Call, Arco San Ramón del Call 4 (tel. 3021123).
Catalunya 4, Pl. Catalunya 4 (tel. 3015389).
París, Cardenal Casanyes 4 (tel. 3013785).
Alberdi, Menéndez y Pelayo 95 (tel. 2173025).
Ballestero, Manuel Sancho 2 (tel. 3495053).
Coral, Calella 1 (tel. 3023120).
Florinda, Montserrat 13 (tel. 3022053).
Levante, Bajada San Miguel 2 (tel. 3179565).
Meridiana, Avda Meridiana 2 (tel. 3095125).
Plaza, Fontanella 18 (tel. 3010139).
Río, San Pablo 19 (tel. 2410651).
San Remo, Ausías March 19 (tel. 3021989).

**Cheapest doubles around 1000–1150ptas
(£5.40–6.20; $10.25–11.75; DM15.75–18.00) p.p.**

Pintor, Gignás 25 (tel. 3154708). Singles around the prices
    above. Near the Post Office.
Noya, Rambla de Canaletas 133 (tel. 3014831). Near Pl.
    Catalunya.
Canaletas, Rambla de Canaletas 133 (tel. 3015660).
Alhambra, Junqueras 13 (tel. 3171924).
Barcino, Junqueras 12 (tel. 3019020).
Clavel, Clavel 4 (tel. 2146009).
Comercio, Nueva de Zurbano 7 (tel. 3187374).

Mayoral, Pl. Real 2 (tel. 3179534).

Roma, Pl. Real 11 (tel. 3020366).

Barcelona, Rosal 40 (tel. 2425075).

Campi, Canuda 4 (tel. 3022025).

Cervantes, Cervantes 6 (tel. 3025168).

Joventut, Junta de Comercio 12 (tel. 3018499).

La Lonja, Paseo de Isabel II 14 (tel. 3193032).

Navarro, Fontanella 16 (tel. 3012496).

El Rocío, Cadena 1 (tel. 2423594).

Cheapest doubles 1150–1250ptas
(£6.20–6.75; $11.75–12.75; DM18.00–19.75) p.p.

San Medin, Carrer Gran de Gràcia 125 (tel. 2173068). On
the street linking the Fontanna and Lesseps metro
stations. Singles same price. Excellent value for money.

Bienestar, Quintona 3 (tel. 3187283). Singles at the above
doubles' prices.

Sans, Antonio de Campmany 82 (tel. 3313700).

Goya, Pau Claris 74 (tel. 3022565).

Conde Guell, Conde Guell 32 & 34 (tel. 2400257).

Fontanella, Vía Layetana 71 (tel. 3175943).

Lepanto, Raurich 10 (tel. 3020081).

Zurbano, Zurbano 8 (tel. 3177200). Rooms with showers.

Sarriá, Mayor de Sarriá 5 (tel. 2039704).

IYHF HOSTELS

Hostal de Joves, Passeig Pujades 29 (tel. 3003104). Midnight curfew. 300m from the Termino train station,
outside the Ciutadella Park.

'Mare de Deu de Montserrat', Passeig de Nostra Senyora
del Coll 41–51 (tel. 3210004). Curfew 1 a.m. Twenty-
five-minute trip from the centre. Bus 28 from Pl. de
Catalunya.

'Pere Tarres', Nunmancia 149–151 (tel. 4102309).

'Studio', Duquesa d'Orleans 58 (tel. 2050961). Open
1 July–30 Sept.

CAMPING

Barcino, Laureano Miro 50 (tel. 3728501). Open year round. In Esplugues de Llobregat, accessible by bus CO or BI from Pl. de Catalunya. Closest site to the city, and cheaper than those further out, at 460ptas (£2.50; $4.75; DM7.25) per tent and p.p.

The UC bus from Pl. Universitat dir. Castelldefels will take you to Gava, where there are two campsites with similar fees p.p. as the Barcino site, but slightly higher charge per tent:

Albatross (tel. 6622031), open May–Sept.

Tres Estrellas (tel. 6621116), open Apr.–Sept.

Córdoba (tel. code 957)

The best area to look for cheap accommodation in Códoba is the Judería, the old Jewish quarter between Plaza de las Tendillas and the River Guadalquivir. Within this district the streets around Plaza del Potro, near the cathedral, are particularly good places to look, as is Calle Rey Heredia, near the Mezquita.

HOTELS

Cheapest prices around 1000–1250ptas
(£5.40–6.75; $10.25–12.75; DM15.75–19.50)
p.p. for singles and doubles.

La Milagrosa, Calle Rey Heredia 12 (tel. 473317).

Rey Heredia, Calle Rey Heredia 26 (tel. 474182).

Las Tendillas, Jesus Maria 1 (tel. 223029).

Mari, Calle Pimentero 6–8 (tel. 479575).

Martinez Rücker, Martinez Rücker 14 (tel. 472562).

Maestre, Calle Romero Barros 16 (tel. 475395). Singles & doubles with baths are more expensive, at around 1700ptas (£9.20; $17.50; DM26.75) p.p.

**Cheapest doubles around 1300ptas
(£7; $13.25; DM20.50) p.p.**

Alhaken, Alhaken II 10 (tel. 471593).
El Cisne Verde, Pintor Greco 6 (tel. 294360).

**Cheapest doubles around 1450ptas
(£7.85; $15; DM22.75) p.p.**

Luis de Góngora, Horno de la Trinidad 7 (tel. 295399).
Mariano, Avda de Cádiz 60 (tel. 294566). If you are
travelling between Oct. and Mar. doubles with baths
are available at this price here.

**Cheapest doubles around 1750ptas
(£9.50; $18; DM27.50) p.p.**

Granada, Avda De America 17 (tel. 477000).
Seneca, Conde y Luque 7 (tel. 473324).

IYHF HOSTEL

Residencia Juvenil Cordoba, Plaza Juda Levi (tel. 290166).
Right in the middle of the Judería. Excellent hostel,
opened in 1990.

CAMPING

Campamento Municipal, Avda del Brillante 50 (tel.
472000/275048). Buses every 10 minutes to/from the
city centre. 350ptas (£1.90; $3.50; DM5.50) per tent
and per person. Grade I site, open year round.
Cerca de Lagartijo (tel. 250426). Situated two miles out
on the Madrid-Cádiz road. 260ptas (£1.40; $2.75; DM4)
per tent and p.p. Grade II site, open 1 June–30 Sept.

Granada (tel. code 958)

Two streets near the station are particularly well supplied with cheap rooms. Avenida Andaluces is opposite the station. The other is Calle San Juan de Dios. Go down Avda Andaluces, turn right along Avda de la Constitucion, then seventh on the right. The town centre is only 15 minutes' walk from the station, or take bus 4, 5, 9 or 11. Cuesta de Gomeréz, the road leading out of Plaza Nueva up to the Alhambra, has a plentiful supply of cheap accommodations.

HOTELS

Cheapest doubles around 1000ptas (£5.40; $10.25; DM15.75) p.p.

Casa Huespedes Gomeréz, Cuesta de Gomeréz 2 (tel. 226398).
Hostal Navarro Ramos (one star), Cuesta de Gomeréz 21 (tel. 221876).
Hostal Victoriano (one star), Navas 24 (tel. 225490).
Hostal-Residencia Loren (two star), Alvaro de Bazán 2 (tel. 276500).

Cheapest doubles around 1150ptas (£6.25; $11.75; DM18) p.p.

Hostal-Residencia Landázuri (two star), Cuesta de Gomeréz 24 (tel. 221406).
Hostal-Residencia Sevilla (one star), Fábrica Vieja 18 (tel. 278513).

Cheapest doubles 1250–1450ptas (£6.75–7.75; $12.75–14.75; DM19.50–22.50) p.p.

Hostal-Residencia Atenas (two star), Gran Vía 38 (tel. 278750).

Hostal California (two star), Cuesta de Gomaréz 37 (tel. 224056).

**Cheapest doubles 1500–1750ptas
(£8.10–9.50; $15.50–18.00; DM23.50–27.50) p.p.**

Hotel-Residencia Niza (one star), Navas 16 (tel. 225430).

Pension Britz (two star), Cuesta Gomaréz 1 (tel. 223652).

Hostal-Residencia Lisboa, Plaza del Carmen 27 (tel. 221413).

Pension Londres (two star), Gran Vía 29 (tel. 278034).

Hostal-Residencia Miami (two star), Camino Purchil 1 (tel. 259708).

Pension Las Nieves (two star), Sierpe Baja 5 (tel. 265311).

Hostal San Joaquin (one star), Mano de Hierro 14 (tel. 282879). Excellent.

Pension Las Cumbres (two star), Cardenal Mendoza 4 (tel. 291222).

Hotel-Residencia Zaida (one star), José Antonio 1 (tel. 229904).

IYHF HOSTEL

Camino de Ronda 171 (tel. 272638). Not far from the station. Turn left as you leave, left under the tracks. This takes you to the start of Camino de Ronda.

HOSTELS

Albergue Juvenil de Viznar, Camino de Fuente Nueva (tel. 490307).

CAMPING

There are a number of sites in and around Granada, all of which charge 275–375ptas (£1.50–2.00; $2.75–3.75; DM4.25–5.75) per person and per tent:

Sierra Nevada, Avda de Madrid 107 (tel. 270956). Grade 1 site, open 15 Mar.–15 Oct. Bus 3.

El Ultimo, Camino Huetor Vega 22 (tel. 123069). Grade 2 site, open all year.

Maria Eugenia, Carretera de Malaga (tel. 200606). Grade 2 site, open all year.

Los Alamos, Carretera Jerez-Cartagena (tel. 275743). Grade 2 site, open 1 Apr.–30 Oct.

Madrid (tel. code 910)

While Tourist Offices in Madrid will give advice on accommodation, they will not make bookings for you. A private agency called Brujula will book rooms, but not at prices you are likely to be interested in: singles start at around 2900ptas (£15.75; $29.75; DM45.50). Fortunately, Madrid has a more than adequate supply of cheap rooms, even in summer. The cheapest part of town to stay in is between the Atocha station and Puerta del Sol (some of the cheapest establishments around Puerta del Sol are used by prostitutes, and best avoided by light sleepers). Calle Fuencarral, off Gran Via, is another excellent place to look as there are scores of cheap places all along the street. Gran Via itself has an excellent supply of rooms, but prices are generally higher than in the other areas mentioned.

NB While Calle Fuencarral is a safe place to stay, you should be wary of the nearby Malasaña quarter. This area, around Plaza Dos de Mayo, is the drugs centre of Madrid, and totally unprovoked attacks on passers-by are not unknown. Do not venture through Malasaña during the day carrying cameras or rucksacks. Whether you go into the area at night is up to you. The streets are full of bars popular with young locals, and can be a great place for a night out. However, if you pick the wrong bar you could be in serious trouble.

HOTEL

**Expect to pay 1800–2500ptas
(£10.00–13.90; $19.00–26.40; DM29.00–40.30)
p.p. for double and 1000–1500ptas
(£5.50–8.30; $10.45–15.80; DM15.95–24.00)
for singles.**

La Montaña, C/ Juan Alvarez Merdizabal 44–4° (fourth
floor) (tel. 2471088).
Pinaregia, C/ Santiago 1–1° (tel. 2480819).
Conchita, Paseo de las Delicias 154 (tel. 2276958).
Leone's, C/ Nuñez de Arce 14 (tel. 5310889).
R. Albarran, Gran Via 29–9° (tel. 5319165).
R. Veguin, Calle Fuencarral 16–3°/JM Crespo (tel. 5314791).
Metro: Gran Via.
La Perla, C/ Fuencarral 10–3° (tel. 5220585). Metro: Gran
Via.
Mollo, C/ Atocha 104 (tel. 2287176).
Marrón, C/ Léon 32 (tel. 2394650).
Alonso, C/ Espozy Mina 17 (tel. 2915679).
Escadas, C/ Echegeray 5 (tel. 4296381).
Zanoran, C/ Fuencarral 18 (tel. 2322060). Metro: Gran
Via.
Sil, C/ Fuencarral 95 (tel. 4488972). Metro: Tribunal.
Serron, C/ Fuencarral 95 (tel. 4488987).
Amayo, Gran Via 12–1° (tel. 2222151).
California, Gran Via 38 (tel. 2224703).
Don José, Gran Via 38 (tel. 2321385).

**Singles around 900–1200ptas
(£5.00–6.50; $9.50–12.25; DM14.50–18.75), among the
cheapest in town. In these cheaper establishments you
will usually pay the same per person in doubles.**
Maairu, C/ Espejo 2 (tel. 2473088). Near Teatro Real.
Metro: Opera.
Mondragón, Carrera San Jerónimo 32–4° (tel. 4296816).
Near Puerta del Sol. Metro: Sol.

Jeyma, C/ Arena 124–3° (tel. 2487793). Metro: Opera.

Luceuse, C/ Nuñez de Arce 15 (tel. 5224888).

Victoriano, C/ San Bernardo 55 (tel. 5321487). Off Gran Via.

Velasco, C/ San Bernardo 55 (tel. 5214682).

Abauu, C/ San Bernardo 55–1° (tel. 5323931/5325036).

Chelo, Hortaleza 17–3° (tel. 5327033). Off Gran Via.

San Miguel, C/ Fuencarral 46–3° (tel. 5321593). Metro: Gran Via or Tribunal.

Iglesias, Plaza Cascorro 6–3° (tel. 2276635).

Coromoto, Plaza Vasquez de Mella (tel. 5327169).

Buenos Aires, Gran Via 61–2° (tel. 2478800).

In the places below singles generally cost two-thirds the price of a double room.

Cheapest doubles around 1100ptas (£6; $11.50; DM17.50) p.p.

Cruz-Sol, Plaza de Santa Cruz 6–3° (tel. 2327197). Next to Plaza Mayor.

Cheapest doubles around 1350ptas (£7.25; $13.75; DM21.25) p.p.

Paz, C/ Flora 4–1° (tel. 2473047). Off C/ Arenal near Plaza Isabel II. Metro: Opera.

Cheapest doubles 1450–1600ptas (£7.80–8.65; $15.00–16.50; DM22.75–25.00) p.p.

La Costa Verde, Gran Via 61–9° (tel. 2149141). Metro: Plaza de Espana.

Santa Cruz, Plaza de Santa Cruz 6–2° (tel. 5222441). Next to Plaza Mayor.

Regional, C/ del Principe 18 (tel. 5223373). Off Plaza de Santa Ana. Metro: Sol.

Ribadavia, C/ Fuencarral 25 (tel. 5311058). Off Gran Via. Metro: Gran Via.

Kryse, C/ Fuencarral 25 (tel. 2311512). Metro: Gran Via.
Sud-Americano, Paseo del Prado 12–6° (tel. 4292564).
Opposite the Prado. Metro: Atocha or Anton Martin.

Cheapest doubles 1700–1900ptas
(£9.25–10.25; $17.50–19.50; DM26.75–29.75) p.p.

Medieval, C/ Fuencarral 46 (tel. 5222549). Metro: Tribunal
or Gran Via.
Alcázar-Regis, Gran Via 61–5° (tel. 2473549). Metro: Plaza
de Espana.
Margarita, Gran Via 50–5° (tel. 2473549). Metro: Plaza de
Espana.

Cheapest doubles around 2300ptas
(£12.50; $23.50; DM36) p.p.

Finistere, C/ Toledo 113. With showers.

UNIVERSITY ACCOMMODATION

Available to those wishing to stay five days or more. Ask
the Tourist Office for details.

IYHF HOSTELS

Calle Santa Cruz de Mercenado 28 (tel. 2474532). Very
high risk of theft. Consider leaving your pack at the
station. Things have even been known to go missing
from the lock-up at the reception. Metro: Arguelles.
'Richard Schirrmann', Casa de Campo (tel. 4635699). No
curfew, but far from the centre if you miss the last
metro. Set in a large park within easy walking distance
of the Lago and Batan metro stops. The short cut from
Lago is along an unlit path, but it is possible to walk
along the road through the park to the hostel.

CAMPING

Osuna, Avda de Logroño (tel. 7410510). Ten miles out of the city beside the Ajalvir to Vicalvaro road. Metro to Canillejas, then bus 105.

Madrid, Iglesia de los Dominicos (tel. 2022835). Located just off the N–II, the main road to Barcelona. Metro to Plaza de Castilla, followed by bus 129.

Málaga (tel. code 952)

NB Málaga is the first (and last) stop in Spain for many travellers from the UK who take advantages of cheap flights into Málaga airport. The city is one of the most dangerous in Spain, and so, unless there is something you specifically want to see in Málaga, the best advice is probably to get out as fast as possible. In common with other cities suffering high levels of unemployment, petty theft is a problem. More worrying is the high level of violent assault, possibly associated with the relatively severe drug problems of the city. Although you may encounter people who will tell you they spent a peaceful night at Málaga train station, incidences of travellers being threatened at knife point into handing over their valuables is regrettably common. Moreover, even if you give up your belongings without a struggle, it is not unknown for assailants to inflict serious injury on their victims.

North of the Paseo del Parque and Alameda Principal there is an abundance of accommodation, but the less expensive ones tend to be run down. Streets with plenty of rooms include Calle Martinez, Calle Bolsa and Calle San Augustin.

HOTELS

Expect to pay for doubles 1800–2500ptas
(£10.00–13.90; $19.00–26.40; DM29–40.30) p.p.
and for singles 1000–1750ptas (£5.50–9.70; $10.45–18.50;
DM15.95–28.20).

Chinitas, Pasaje Chinitas 2 (tel. 214683).
Lampaerez, Calle Santa Maria 6 (tel. 219484).
Cisneros, Calle Cisneros 7–1° (first storey) (tel. 212633).
Cordoba, Calle Bolsa 9.
La Macarena, Calle San Augustin 9.
Montecarlo, Calle Trinidad Grund 23.
Trianon, Calle Trinidad Grund.
Bolivia, Calle Casas de Campos 10.
Remedios, Calle Casas de Campos 15.
El Cenachero, Calle Barroso.

CAMPING

Balneario del Carmen, Avda Juan Sebastian Ekano. Two
miles out on the road to El Palo. Bus 11.

San Sebastián/Donostia (tel. code 943)

During the summer months you may experience some
difficulty in finding a room due to this city's popularity.
Prices are generally rather higher in the old town. The
area around the cathedral is cheaper, with a good supply
of rooms; in particular Calle Loyola, C/ San Bartolemé, and
C/ Urdaneta. On the other side of the river the area behind
Plaza de Cataluna also offers many possibilities.

FONDAS

Donostia (1), C/ Fuenterrabía 19–3° (third floor) (tel.
422157).

Garate, C/ Triunfo 8 (tel. 461571).
Arsuaga, C/ Narrica 3–3° (tel. 420681).
Goi-Argi, C/ Secundino Esnaola 13–4° (tel. 278802).
Sarciada (1), C/ Fuenterrabía 48 (tel. 466020).
Vicandi, C/ Iparraguirre 1 (tel. 270795).

CASAS DE HUESPEDES

Aldazabal, C/ San Martín 36–5° (tel. 420094).
Azurmendi, Avda San Pedro 51.
Ricardo, C/ San Bartoleme 21&23–3° (tel. 461374).
Ezkurra, C/ Ametzagaña 5 (tel. 273594).
La Parisien, C/ Urdaneta 6 (tel. 464312).
Lau Aizeta, Casa Lau-Aizeta (Altza) (tel. 352445).
Vista Alegre, Casa 4 Lagun, s/n Altza (tel. 357075).

Rooms in the above accommodations should work out cheaper than in the various suggestions below, especially for singles. However, there are quirks in the pricing structure; for example, hostal-residencias that are considerably cheaper than pensions.

Cheapest doubles with shower/bath for around 1650ptas (£9; $17; DM23). During non-summer months prices fall by about 10 per cent.

Hostal-Residencia Gran Bahía (one star), Embeltrán 16 (tel. 423838).

Cheapest doubles around 2000ptas (£10.75; $20.50; DM31.50) p.p.

Hostal-Residencia Easo (one star), C/ San Bartolemé 24 (tel. 466892).
Hostal-Residencia Ozcáriz (two star), C/ Fuenterrabía 8–2&3° (tel. 425306).
Hostal Lasa (two star), C/ Vergara 15 (tel. 423052). Jan.–May rooms with a bath/shower are not much more expensive than those without.

Hostal-Residencia Comercio (two star), C/ Urdaneta 24
  (tel. 464414).
Pension Urkia (one star), C/ Urbieta 12 (tel. 424436).
Pension La Perla (one star), C/ Loyola (tel. 428123).

ONE-STAR PENSIONS

Lizaso, C/ San Vicente 7–3° (tel. 422977).
Lo Egin, C/ San Martín 16 (tel. 293423).
San Jeronimo, C/ San Jeronimo 25 (tel. 281689).
San Martin, C/ San Martín 10–1° (tel. 428714).
San Lorenzo, C/ San Lorenzo 2–1° (tel. 425516).
Ama Lur, C/ San Martín 43–2° (tel. 460861).
Amaiur, C/ 31 de Agosto 44–2° (tel. 429654).
Añorga, C/ Easo 12–1° (tel. 467945).
Aralar, C/ Easo 12–2° (tel. 470410).
Aristizabal, C/ Alfonso VIII 6 (tel. 421323).
Azurmendi, C/ Río Bidasoa 7 (tel. 427270).
Garcia, C/ Soraluce 6 (tel. 427236).
Josefina (1), C/ Easo 12 (tel. 461956).
Kaia, C/ Puerto 12–2° (tel. 290229).

IYHF HOSTELS

'Anoeta', Ciudad Deportiva Anoeta (tel. 452970). 2 a.m.
  curfew. Twenty-minute walk from the town centre.
  From Calle Urbieta, bus dir. Amara-Anoeta.
Parque Ulia s/n (tel. 293751/452970).

CAMPING

Igueldo (tel. 214502). Open May–Sept. Located about
  three miles west of the town centre on the landward
  side of Monte Igueldo. The Barrio de Igueldo bus from
  Alameda de Boulevard will get you there, but the
  service is poor. Only 13 buses per day Mon.–Sat.;
  five buses on Sun. Last bus from town 10 p.m.

Seville (Sevilla) (tel. code 954)

Normally, finding cheap accommodation in Seville is easy, even during July and August. The area around the Cordoba (Plaza de Armas) station has a large supply of cheap lodgings, especially Calle San Eloy, which probably has more fondas and casas de huespedes than any other street in the city. There are also plenty of rooms available in the Barrio Santa Cruz, the heart of the old city around the Giralda, though prices here are only slightly more expensive than in the area around the Cordoba station.

The one exception to this happy situation is the period around Easter and the April Fair, when large numbers converge on the city, and room prices can be raised quite legally. Unfortunately, 1992 may be one big fair in Seville as the city plays host to Expo 1992, and confidently expects to receive 40 million visitors. This will almost certainly ensure that competition for cheap accommodation intensifies, as even those who would not normally be regarded as budget travellers may well be happy to take any rooms available.

It remains to be seen whether the authorities will permit the raising of prices throughout much of 1992. The price guide to the accommodation below assumes that prices follow their usual patterns. The off-season for most hotels is November to February/mid March (some start earlier). Then follows the period until mid April (later at some hotels) when prices can rise sharply. The prices quoted refer to the main season, mid April to November.

NB A positive percentage figure gives a rough guide to the increase in prices around Easter and the April Fair, a negative percentage to reductions in the off-season.

HOTELS

Cheapest doubles around 900–1100ptas
(£4.90–6.00; $9.25–11.50; DM14.00–17.50) p.p.

Zaida (₧ R, three star), San Roque 26 (tel. 211138). (+90 per cent; −15 per cent.)

Capitol (₧ R, two star), Zaragoza 66 (tel. 212441). (+80 per cent; −15 per cent.)

Casa Moreno (₧ R, one star), Avda de Cádiz 15 (tel. 421460). All-year price.

Pino (₧ R, one star), Tarifa 6 (tel. 212810). (+50 per cent.)

Toledo (₧ R, one star), Santa Teresa 15 (tel. 215335). All-year price.

Herrera (₧ R, one star), Rubens 10 (tel. 384009). All year price.

Victoria (₧ R, one star), Escarpín 3 (tel. 228332). All year price.

Orellana (CH), Archeros 19 (tel. 362259).

Cheapest doubles 1200–1400ptas
(£6.50–7.50; $12.25–14.25; DM18.75–21.75) p.p.

Goya (₧ R, two star), Mateos Gagos 31 (tel. 211170). (+15 per cent.)

La Muralla (₧ R, two star), Macarena 52 (tel. 371049). All-year price.

Pino Lordelo (₧ R, two star), Quintana 29 (tel. 387905). (+50 per cent.)

Alvertos (₧ one star), Cervantes 4 (tel. 385710). All-year price.

Zahira (₧ R, two star) Zahira, San Eloy 43 (tel. 221061). All-year price.

Alcobia (P, one star), Menéndez Pelayo 51 (tel. 420370). All-year price.

Archeros (P, one star), Archeros 23 (tel. 418465). (+75 per cent; −10 per cent.) One of the best around.

El Cachorro (₧ R, one star), Castilla 38 (tel. 336146). (+35 per cent; −5 per cent.)

Espadafor (₧ R, one star), Avda Cruz del Campo 23 (tel. 573866). (+50 per cent.)

La Francesa (P, one star), Juan Rabadán 28 (tel. 383107). All-year price.

Gravina (㉐ R, one star), Gravina 46 (tel. 216414). (+100 per cent; −10 per cent.)

CH Buen Dormir, Farnesio 8 (tel. 217492).

Monreal (㉐ one star), Rodrigo Caro 8 (tel. 214166). (+300 per cent.)

Cheapest doubles 1500–1750ptas
(£8.10–9.50; $15.50–18.00; DM23.50–27.50) p.p.

Nuevo Suizo (㉐ R, two star), Azafaifo 7 (tel. 229147). (+40 per cent.)

Prado (㉐ R, two star), Avda de Málaga 6 (tel. 410011). (+55 per cent.)

Suiza (㉐ R, two star), Méndez Núñez 16 (tel. 220813). (−12.5 per cent.)

Bella Vista (㉐ R, one star), Miguel Angel 56 (tel. 690856). All-year price.

Casa Manolo (㉐ R, one star), Don Fadrique 5 (tel. 370293). (−30 per cent.)

La Castellana (㉐ one star), Gamazo 17 (tel. 220895). (+33 per cent; −15 per cent.)

Cordoba (㉐ R, one star), Farnesio 12 (tel. 227498). (+20 per cent; −25 per cent.)

Los Gabrieles (㉐ R, one star), La Legión 2 (tel. 223307). (+100 per cent.)

Guadalquivir (㉐ R, one star), Pages del Corro 53 (tel. 332100). (−35 per cent.)

Linense R (㉐ one star), Gravina 66 (tel. 229285). All-year price.

Marco de la Giralda (㉐ R, one star), Abades 30 (tel. 228324). All-year price.

La Posada (㉐ R, one star), Relator 49 (tel. 374768). (+50 per cent.)

Regente (㉐ R, one star), Amor de Dios 30 (tel. 386354). (+20 per cent; −12.5 per cent.)

Rivero (㉐ R, one star), Bailén 67 (tel. 216231). (+15 per cent.)

Union (㉐ R, one star), Tarifa 4 (tel. 229294).

**Cheapest doubles around 2500ptas
(£13.90; $26.50; DM40.25) p.p.**

Perez Montilla (ᴴ R, one star), Plaza Curidores 13 (tel.
421854). All-year price.

IYHF HOSTEL

Albergue Juvenil Fernando el Santo, Calle Isaac Peral
2 (tel. 613150). No curfew. Generally filled to near
capacity with local students. 1½ miles from the
town centre. Bus 19. Closed in 1991, probably being
renovated for 1992.

CAMPING

All three sites are accessible by the airport bus. Last bus
from town 8.45 p.m.:

Club de Campo (tel. 514379). Grade 1 site, open year
round. Ten miles out in Dos Hermanas.

Villsom (tel. 720828). Grade 2 site, open 1 Feb.–30 Nov.
Five miles out on the road to Cádiz.

Sevilla (tel. 514379). Grade 2 site, open all year. Six miles
out on the road to Madrid.

Toledo (tel. code 925)

**Cheapest rooms for under 1000ptas
(£5.50; $10.25; DM15.75) p.p.**

La Belviseña, Cuesta del Can 7 (tel. 220067). (Singles and
doubles.)

Maria Soledad, Soledad 1 (tel. 223287). (Singles and
triples.)

Rosa, Hospederia de San Bernardo 12 (tel. 225832).
(Doubles.)

Cheapest rooms for around 1100ptas
(£6; $11.50; DM17.50) p.p.

Segovia, Recoletos 2 (tel. 211124). (Doubles.)

Nuncio Viejo, Nuncio Viejo 19 (tel. 228178). (Doubles.)
Rooms with showers/baths are only slightly more
expensive.

Cheapest rooms around 1250ptas
(£6.75; $12.75; DM19.50) p.p.

Lumbreras, Juan Labrador 7 (tel. 221571). (Singles and
doubles. Triples are cheaper.)

Descalzos, Descalzos 32 (tel. 222888). (Doubles without
bath/shower.) Singles slightly more expensive. Doubles with bath/shower another 75 per cent on price
quoted above.

Cheapest rooms around 1500ptas
(£8.10; $15.50; DM23.50) p.p.

Labrador, Juan Labrador 16 (tel. 222620). (Doubles without bath/shower.) Singles 30 per cent up on price
quoted, doubles with bath/shower 20 per cent.

Amalia, Alonso Berruguete 1 (tel. 227018). (Singles and
doubles.)

San Pedro, Juan de San Pedro 2 (tel. 214734). (Singles and
doubles.)

Cheapest rooms around 1750ptas
(£9.50; $18; DM27.50) p.p.

Santa Barbara, Avda Santa Barbara 8 (tel. 220298). (Doubles.)

Las Armas, Armas 7 (tel. 221668). (Doubles.) Singles 25
per cent on quoted price.

**Cheapest doubles around 2000–2250ptas
(£10.75–12.20; $20.50–23.25; DM31.25–35.35) p.p.**

Madrid I, Marqués de Mendigorria 6&7 (tel. 221114).
Madrid II, Covarrubias 4 (tel. 221114)
Imperio, Cadenas 7 (tel. 227650).

UNIVERSITY ACCOMMODATION

For information contact the Oficina de Información Juvenil in
Calle Trinidad, between Plaza Zocodover and the cathedral.

IYHF HOSTEL

'San Servando', Castillo de San Servando (tel. 224554).
Midnight/12.30 a.m. curfew. Juniors pay slightly above
the normal price for a Spanish hostel. Those aged
26 and over can expect to pay around 1100ptas (£6;
$11.25; DM17.25). On leaving the station cross the
road. Follow the road to your right, past the shops
and houses, and round to the old Alcantara gate. Just
before the gate, turn sharp left up the hill. The hostel
is on the right. About a 15-minute walk.

CAMPING

Circo Romano, Avda Carlos III (tel. 220442). On the outskirts of the old town. 350ptas (£1.95; $3.70; DM5.65)
p.p. per tent.
El Greco (tel. 210090). A mile out of town on the N-401
road. The better of the two sites. Both charge the
same.

SWEDEN

As with the other Scandinavian countries, the best advice to the budget traveller in Sweden is to prepare for hostelling and camping. While many **hotels** cut their prices substantially during the summer, even this, unfortunately, does not bring them into our accommodation price range, as you can still expect to pay from 200kr (£19; $36; DM55) in singles, and 150kr (£14.25; $27.25; DM41.50) per person in doubles. Very occasionally you may find hotels or *pensionat* outside the main cities which charge 120–150kr (£11.50–14.25; $21.75–27.25; DM33.25–41.50) in singles, 90–120kr (£8.50–11.50; $16.25–21.75; DM24.75–33.25) each in doubles all year round. If this is within your budget, enquire at the local Tourist Office about the cheapest hotels in town. Tourist Offices will also book **private rooms** for you where these are available, costing around 125kr (£12; $22.75; DM34.50) for singles, 90kr (£8.50; $16.25; DM24.75) p.p. in doubles or larger rooms. In villages and small towns look out for the 'Rum' sign, because approaching the owner directly will save you paying the 25kr (£2.40; $4.50; DM7) booking fee charged by the Tourist Offices.

Most towns that you are likely to visit will have an IYHF hostel. Of the 280 IYHF hostels in Sweden, about 100 stay open all year round, others open only during the main tourist season (June to late August). Most of the hostels are located in the southern and central regions of the country. There are three grades of hostel: the lowest grade has cold running water only, but these are few and far between; the intermediate-grade hostels have hot running water and hot showers. By far the most common are the superior-grade hostels, which usually have hot running water in small bedrooms, hot showers, and various other special facilities. Prices vary from 56 to 85kr (£5.35–8.00; $10.25–15.25; DM15.50–23.25). Non-members are charged an extra 20kr (£1.90; $3.60; DM5.50). Outside the main towns superior-grade hostels are very popular with families, so no matter where you are headed it makes sense to book a bed in advance. If you expect to arrive after 6 p.m. you should inform the hostel, otherwise your reservation will not be held beyond that time. In university towns it is often possible to find a bed in a student hostel during the summer. The local Tourist Office will advise you about the availability of such accommodation.

Virtually every town or village of any size has a **campsite,** and quite often you will have a choice of sites. There are some 750 sites officially approved and classified by the Swedish Tourist Board and these account for most of the sites. Approved sites are rated from one star up to three stars. A one-star site has everything you would expect, while three-star sites tend to offer a whole range of facilities you will rarely use, if at all. Most sites operate with all their facilities between June and September, while in those which are also open in April and May, certain supplementary facilities may not be available. The Tourist Board boasts that the overnight charge for a family is one of the lowest in Europe, and this is hard to refute. But, as the fee for a tent is the relatively high 30–50kr (£2.75–4.75; $5.25–9.00; DM8.60–13.75), and some sites also make a nominal charge per person, this means that solo travellers do not benefit from the pricing system, whereas three or four people sharing a tent certainly do. There are very few sites at which a camping pass is not required, so unless you have an International Camping Carnet you will be obliged to buy a Swedish camping pass at the first site you visit, which costs 20kr (£1.90; $3.60; DM5.50) and is valid for the rest of the camping season. There are also 4500 cabins for rent, spread over 350 sites. Cabins sleep between two and six people, are usually equipped with a kitchen and their overnight charges vary from 60 to 100kr (£5.75–9.50; $11–18; DM16.75–27.50) per person.

Under the ancient law of Allmannsratt it is possible to **camp for free,** with certain restrictions. It is permissible to erect a tent for a day and a night on land that is not used for farming, providing you are some distance from habitations. You must obtain the consent of the landowner before pitching your tent near any dwelling place or if you are camping in a group. Avoid setting any potentially dangerous fires, and make sure you leave no rubbish behind on your departure. In more sparsely populated areas, such as the mountains, it is perfectly acceptable to stay longer than a day and a night. As with neighbouring Norway, the two problems facing campers are the cold nights and mosquitoes, so prepare yourself accordingly.

The Swedish YHA operates two other types of accommodation in the mountains. **Mountain centres** can be expensive, with the cost of a bed ranging from 70 to 350kr (£6.75–33.25; $12.75–63.25; DM19.50–96.75). **Mountain huts,** however, offer relatively cheap beds for around 75kr (£7.25; $13.50; DM20.75), in areas where any accommodation can be hard to find. These huts are normally sited far from either roads or railways, so they are likely to appeal only to those planning on doing some hiking.

ADDRESSES

Camping	Stanfords, 12–14 Long Acre, London, WC2 (tel. 071–236 1321) sell a comprehensive list. The National Tourist Board in London or your capital city supplies shorter lists free of charge.
Student hostels	SFS, Kungsgatan 4, Box 7144, Stockholm (tel. 08–234 515). For accommodation in Stockholm. SFS-Serviceverksahmet, Drottninggatan 89, 113 60 Stockholm (tel. 08–340180).

Swedish YHA	Svenska Turistföreningen (STF), Box 25, 101 20 Stockholm. Information Office, Drottninggaten 31–33, Stockholm (tel. 08–7903100).
Mountain huts and mountain centres	Contact the Swedish YHA Information Office.

Gothenburg (Göteborg) (tel. code 031)

HOTELS

Cheapest doubles around 175kr
(£16.65; $31.75; DM48.25) p.p.

Savoy, Andra Långgatan 23 (tel. 124960). 15–20 minutes' walk from the railway station. Price applies 25 June–25 Aug. only.

Cheapest doubles around 185kr
(£17.60; $33.50; DM51) p.p.

Göteborgsrasta, Parallelv. 1 (tel. 440760). Five minutes' walk from the train station in Partille. Price applies for 8 June–19 Aug. and weekends only.

Cheapest doubles around 195kr
(£18.60; $25.25; DM54) p.p.

Royal, Drottninggatan 67 (tel. 806100). Price applies from mid June to mid Aug. A few minutes' walk from the train station.

PRIVATE ROOMS

Either of the city Tourist Offices will make bookings. Expect to pay from 100kr (£9.50; $18; DM27.75) p.p. in doubles and larger rooms. A commission of 25kr (£2.40; $4.50; DM7) is charged.

IYHF HOSTELS

Studenthemmet Ostkupan, Mejerigatan 2 (tel. 254776/401050). Open 5 June–26 Aug.
Tram 1, 3 or 6 from the train station as far as Redberg, followed by bus 62 to Gräddgatan. Near the Liseberg amusement park.

Vandrarhem Partille, Landvettervägen 433, Partille (tel. 446163). About 10 miles from the centre. Bus 513 from Friggagatan, near the train station, to Åstebo. Ask the Tourist Office about directions to the hostel from Partille train station if you want to save some cash.

Torrekulla turistation, Kållered (tel. 951495). Eight miles from the centre in a nature reserve. Bus 730 from the train station.

HOSTELS

Nordengården, Stockholmsgatan 16 (tel. 196631). Open May–mid Sept. Similar prices to the IYHF hostels, more central location. Best reserved in advance. Tram 1 or 3 to Stockholmsgatan.

CAMPING

Kärralund (tel. 252761). From Brunnsparken, a few minutes' walk from the train station, tram 5 dir. Torp to Welandergatan. Near the beach. Fills quickly and is expensive for solo travellers at 80kr (£7.60; $14.50; DM22) per tent and all occupants.

Delsjö Camping (tel. 252909). Twenty-minute walk from the nearest train station.

Valhalla Idrottsplats (tel. 204185).

Kiruna (tel. code 0980)

PRIVATE ROOMS

Gult Hus (tel. 11451). Arrange the letting of houses of local people while they are on holiday, or of second homes. Singles and doubles are both about 120kr £11.40; $21.75; DM33.25) p.p., but you can pack a few more people into doubles. The organization will collect you from the station for free.

IYHF HOSTELS

Standstigen, c/o Tyyne Isaksson, Brytareg 9 (tel. 17195/ 12784). Open 13 June–31 Aug. 67kr (£6.40; $12; DM18.50) for members.

If this hostel is not open in 1992 there is the hostel below opened in 1991.

Skyttegatan 18A (tel. 17195).

CAMPING

Radhusbyn Ripan (tel. 13100). Just over a mile from the train station. 60kr (£5.75; $10.75; DM16.50) per tent and occupants. Cabins sleeping four are available for around 125kr (£12; $22.50; DM34.50) p.p.

Stockholm (tel. code 08)

From June to August finding somewhere cheap to stay in Stockholm can be difficult. If you have not booked ahead consider using one of the accommodation-finding services to look for a hostel bed, for a 10kr (£0.90; $1.75; DM2.75) commission fee. They will also find hotel rooms for twice this fee, but hopefully you will not be reduced to this option as even the cheapest hotels are outside the budget-travel category.

AGENCIES:

Hotellcentralen: At Central Station. Open daily May–Sept. from 8 a.m.–9 p.m., Oct.–Apr. Mon.–Fri. 8 a.m.–5 p.m. (tel. 240880).

Stockholm Information Service: In the Kungsträdgården on Hamngatan. Open mid June to end Aug. Mon.–Fri. 8.30 a.m.–6 p.m. Sat. and Sun. 8.30 a.m.–5 p.m. Rest of the year Mon.–Fri. 9 a.m.–5 p.m. Sat. & Sun. 9 a.m.–2 p.m.

HOTELS

Many hotels lower their prices in summer. At other times prices can be much higher.

Cheapest doubles around 160kr (£15.25; $29; DM44.25) p.p.

Residens, Kungsgatan 50 (tel. 233540). Good location, about eight minutes' walk from Central Station. Price applies 23 June–6 Aug. only.

Cheapest doubles around 170kr (£16.25; $30.75; DM47) p.p.

Jerum, Studentbacken 21 (tel. 6635380). 1 June–31 Aug. only.

Cheapest doubles around 185kr (£17.60; $33.50; DM51) p.p.

Sana, Upplandsgatan 6 (tel. 203982). 15 June–15 Aug. only. Near Central Station.

Cheapest doubles around 195kr (£18.50; $35.25; DM54) p.p.

Gustav Wasa, Västmannagatan 61 (tel. 343801). Price applies year round. Ten-minute walk from Central Station.

Gustavsvikshemmet, Västmannagatan 15 (tel. 214450). Year round price. Ten-minute walk from Central Station.

Resman, Drottninggatan 77/II (tel. 141395). Near Central Station. 22 June–11 July only.

Cheapest doubles around 210kr (£20; $38; DM58) p.p.

Pensionat Oden, Odengatan 38/2 (tel. 6124349).

**Cheapest doubles around 250kr
(£23.80; $45.25; DM69) p.p.**

Domus, Körsbärsvagen 1 (tel. 160195).

PRIVATE ROOMS

Book at the Stockholm Information Service or Hotellcentralen. Very limited supply, and not particularly
   cheap. Expect to pay from 100kr (£9.50; $18; DM27.75)
   p.p. in doubles, from 150kr (£14.30; $27; DM41.50) in
   singles, plus commission.

IYHF HOSTELS

'af Chapman', Skeppsholmen (tel. 6795015/103715). Fully
   rigged late 19th-century sailing ship. 1 a.m. curfew.
   Reserve about three months in advance, or turn up
   really early. 73kr (£7; $13.20; DM20.20) for members;
   120kr (£11.50; $21.50; DM33) non-members.
Långholmen, Kronohäktet, on Långholmen Island (tel.
   6680510). No curfew. T-bana (metro): Hornstull.
Zinken, Zinkensväg 20 (tel. 6685786). No curfew. T-bana:
   Zinkensdamm. Just in front of you right on to Horns-
   gatan, which you walk down to no. 103, then left down
   the steps at the hostel sign.
Skeppsholmen, Västra Brobänken (tel. 6795017). Located
   in the Hantverkshuset, close to the 'af Chapman'.
Botkyrka, Eriksbergsskolan, Tre Källors väg 8, Norsborg
   (tel. 0753–62105). Open 22 June–7 Aug.
Grävlingsberg, Drottningv. 15, Grävlingsberg (tel. 7478288).
   Open 1 May–15 Oct. 12½ miles from the centre. Bus 421
   from Stockholm Slussen station.

HOSTELS

Dansakademien, Döbelnsgatan 56 (tel. 6123118). Open July
   and Aug. 1 a.m. curfew. Dorms slightly cheaper than
   the IYHF hostels. Mattresses on floor 20kr (£1.90; $3.60;

DM5.50) including breakfast; sheets 25kr (£2.40; $4.50; DM7). Reception open 7 a.m.–1 p.m.; 4 p.m.–1 a.m.

YMCA Inter Rail Points. Jyllandsgatan (tel. 7526456). Open mid July–mid Aug.

Vackravägen, 4–6 Sundyberg (tel. 984753). Open mid July to first week of Aug. Similar in price to the IYHF hostels.

Frescati, Professorsslingan 13–15 (tel. 159434). Student accommodation operated as a hostel June–Aug. No curfew. Doubles 140kr (£13.35; $25.25; DM38.75) p.p. Also singles, at roughly another 50 per cent on the price p.p. in doubles. T-bana: Universitetet.

Columbus Hotell-Vandrarhjem, Tjärhovsgatan 11 (tel. 6441717). No curfew and 24-hour reception. Two- to six-bedded rooms. 105–130kr (£10.00–12.50; $19.00–23.75; DM29.00–36.25). Close to T-bana Medborgarplatsen.

Gustaf af Klint, Stadsgårdskajen 153 (tel. 6404077). In an old navy ship. 24-hour reception. 120kr (£11.50; $21.75; DM33.25). T-bana: Slussen, then a 100m walk.

Brygghuset, Norrtullsgatan 12N (tel. 312424). Open June–Aug. 2 a.m. curfew. Two- to six-bedded rooms. 110kr (£10.50; $20; DM30.50). T-bana: Odenplan.

CAMPING

Bredäng (tel. 977071). Open May–Sept. Six miles out on Lake Mälaren. T-bana: Bredang. Ten-minute walk signposted from the station.

Ångby (tel. 370420). Also on Lake Mälaren. T-ban 17 or 18.

Flaten (tel. 7730100). Open May–Sept. Bus 401 from Slussen.

Uppsala (tel. code 018)

HOTELS

**Cheapest doubles around 160kr
(£15.25; $29; DM44.25) p.p.**

Good Morning Hotels, Sylveniusgatan 9 (tel. 120390).
Price applies 22 June–12 Aug. About 2½ miles from
the train station.

IYHF HOSTEL

Sunnersta herrgård, Sunnerstavägen 24 (tel. 324220).
From Dragarbrunnsgatan, not far from St Persgatan,
bus 20 as far as Herrgardsvagen. After 6.20 p.m. and
at weekends take bus 50 instead. Short walk from the
bus stop.

HOSTEL

YMCA Inter Rail Point, Torbjörnsgatan 2 (tel. 188566).
Twenty minutes from the town centre. Bus 10 from
Stora Torget. After 6.20 p.m. bus 50 from Dragarbrunnsgatan. Price for a one-night stay is more than
for the IYHF hostel, but is cheaper thereafter.

CAMPING

Fyris (tel. 232333). Down by the river. Tents 25kr (£2.40;
$4.50; DM7). Cabins are available.

SWITZERLAND

Despite being widely regarded as one of the most expensive countries in Europe, it is quite possible both to eat well, and to sleep cheaply in Switzerland. **Hotels** are likely to be outside your budget, and probably only to be considered in emergencies. The cheapest hotels cost 30SFr (£12.50; $23.75; DM36.25) in singles, 25SFr (£10.50; $20; DM30.50) each in doubles, but such prices are rare. More typical for the lower end of the hotel market are charges of 40SFr (£16.50; $31.50; DM48) in singles, 30.00–37.50SFr (£12.50–15.50; $23.75–29.50; DM36.25–45.00) per person in doubles. In country areas B&Bs or private rooms can be more reasonable, but, in the main, your choice is between hostelling or camping. In some ways this is quite fortuitous because both of these give you the opportunity of meeting other travellers, and also vastly increases your chances of meeting young Swiss holidaymakers. In a country where the cost of a night out can limit your visits to pubs and clubs, these opportunities to make friends can be invaluable.

There are about 100 **IYHF hostels,** the vast majority of which are open to members only. While hostels in the larger towns may admit non-members (not Lucerne), this tends to incur an extra charge of 7SFr (£2.90; $5.50; DM8.50). In the main towns, hostels are open all year, except perhaps for a couple of weeks around Christmas and the New Year. Elsewhere, hostels shut for differing periods, from a few weeks to several months, at no specific time of the year. In the larger cities a midnight or 1 a.m. curfew is normal in summer, but you can expect a 10 p.m. closing time at the others. Prices vary according to the grading of the hostel: the top-rated ones cost up to 16SFr (£6.65; $12.75; DM19.25), mid-range hostels up to 13SFr (£5.40; $10.25; DM15.75), and the lower grade up to 10SFr (£4.15; $8; DM12). Facilities in the lower-grade hostels tend to be quite basic, but are perfectly adequate. In the top-rated hostels you will have no access to kitchen facilities, though these are available in many of the lesser-rated establishments. Except in the main towns, where a three-night maximum stay operates in summer, there is no limit to how long you can stay at any hostel. During the summer it is advisable to reserve hostels in the larger towns, either by letter or by phoning ahead. If you find a hostel full, you might consider staying in one in a nearby town if you have a railcard, rather than having to pay for a room in a hotel.

There is no shortage of campsites; around 1200 in all. Unfortunately, there are three camping organizations, which makes advance planning slightly more complicated. Swiss campgrounds rank amongst the best Europe has to offer, being particularly clean and well run. Prices can vary quite substantially, starting at around 3SFr (£1.25; $2.40; DM3.60) per tent and per person, but rising to the 10SFr (£4.20; DM12.25) per tent, 5.50SFr (£2.25; $4.25; DM6.50) charged at one site in Interlaken. On average a solo traveller might expect to pay around 7.50–10.00SFr (£3.10–4.20; $6–8; DM9.00–12.25) per night. One drawback to camping is that some of the large towns have no central or easily reached site, such as Berne. In other places, however, you may have a choice between two, or more, sites. In such cases, try to find out the prices of the different sites, as there can be quite a difference (one site in Interlaken works out at 7SFr (£2.90; $5.50; DM8.50) per night, more expensive for solo travellers than two other sites in town). Some campsites also offer dormitory accommodation. The local Tourist Office will advise you on the availability of such accommodation.

Tourist Offices will also have information on whether you can **camp rough** in the area. Most cantons allow freelance camping on uncultivated land, but the permission of the landowner is required on privately owned land. Camping in public places or along the roadside is expressly forbidden. Sleeping rough is not illegal, and is generally accepted in the

parks of the larger towns. Whether you camp or sleep rough
a good quality sleeping bag is recommended as it gets very
cold at night, even in summer, and especially in the more
mountainous areas. Hikers and climbers might wish to take
advantage of the chain of **mountain refuges** run by the Swiss
Alpine Club.

ADDRESSES

Hotels	Swiss Hotels Association, Montbijoustrasse 130, 3001 Bern (tel. 031–507111).
B&Bs	Bed and Breakfast Club, Case Postale 2231, 1110 Morges 2 (tel. 021–8023385).
Swiss YHA	Schweizerischer Bund für Jugendherbergen, Postfach, 3001 Bern (tel. 031–245503).
Camping	Schweizerischer Camping und Caravanning-Verband, Habsburgerstrasse 35, 6000 Luzern 4 (tel. 041–234822). Guides available from the Swiss National Tourist Office in London or your capital city. They will tell you the latest price. Expect to pay around £4 ($7.50; DM11.50).
	Touring-Club der Schweiz Division Camping, 9 rue Pierre Fatio, 1211 Genève 3 (tel. 022–7371212).
	Verband Schweizerischer Campings, Im Sydefadeli 40, 8037 Zurich. (tel. 01–2725713). Guides available, as for Schweizerischer, above.
Mountain huts	Schweizer Alpine Club (SAC), Helvetiaplatz 4, 3005 Bern (tel. 031–433611).

Basle (Basel) (tel. code 061)

HOTELS

Steinenschanze, Steinengraben 69 (tel. 235353). Students with ISIC/IUS pay 30SFr (£12.50; $23.75; DM36.25) for B&B in singles or doubles for the first three nights.

Cheapest doubles around 37.50SFr
(£15.60; $29.75; DM45.25) p.p.

Rheinfelderhof, Hammerstrasse 61 (tel. 6916656).
Stadthof, Gerbergasse 84 (tel. 258711).
Klingental Garni, Klingental 20 (tel. 6816248).
Steinenschanze (see above). Price without student discount.

If you are not keen on hostelling or camping and would prefer a hotel room but cannot afford the prices quoted above consider staying over the border in Germany or France. Mulhouse in France is about a 40-minute trip from Bâle SNCF station. The train from Paris or Calais stops in Mulhouse before reaching Basle. Local trains run from Basel Bad station to a number of small German towns. Rheinfelden is a pleasant place to stay. The Rhine divides the town in two, one part German, the other part Swiss; there are hourly trains, and it's about a 15-minute trip.

IYHF HOSTEL

St Alban Kirchrain 10 (tel. 230572). Dorms 175Fr (£7; $13.30; DM20.30). 1 a.m. curfew during the summer, midnight the rest of the year. Five minutes' walk from the town centre, 15 minutes from the station along Aeschengraben and St Alban Anlage. Tram 1 from the station to Aeschenplatz (first stop) then tram 3 to the second stop.

CAMPING

Wahldort' (tel. 766429). Cheap site for this area. Six miles out of the city in the nearby town of Reinach on Highway 18.

IYHF HOSTELS NEARBY

Route de Bâle 185, Delemont (tel. 066–222054). Regular trains, half-hour trip.

Central Culturel et de Loisirs-Auberge de Jeunesse, rue Dr. Hurst 56, St Louis (France) Hostel entrance on rue St-Exupéry (tel. 89697620). Dorms 15SFr (£6.25; $11.90; DM18.10). Fairly regular trains from Bâle SNCF station, beside Basel SBB station, 20-minute trip.

Steinenweg 40, Lörrach (Germany) (tel. 07621–47040). Ten-minute trip on the regular service from Basel Bad station. Trains from Basel SBB heading for Germany stop at Basel Bad. The station is about 15–20 minutes' walk across the Rhine from the town centre.

Berne (Bern) (tel. code 031)

HOTELS

Cheapest doubles around 37.50SFr
(£15.60; $29.75; DM45.25) p.p.

National, Hirschengraben 24 (tel. 251988). Five minutes' walk from the train station.

Bahnhof-Süd, Bümplizstrasse 189 (tel. 565111). Bus 13. Nearest train station Bern-Bümpliz.

Marthahaus-Garni, Wyttenbachstrasse 22a (tel. 424135). Bus 20. Fifteen-minute walk from the train station over the Lorrainebrücke, right down Schanzlihalde, then left.

Hospiz sur Heimat, Gerichtigkeitgasse 1 (tel. 220436). Bus 12. Fifteen-minute walk from the train station. One of the main streets of the old town following on from Spitalgasse, Marktgasse and Kramgasse. Slightly cheaper in triples and quads.

GUESTHOUSES

Around 20–30SFr (£8.35–12.50; $15.75–23.75; DM24.25–36.25) p.p. Ask at the Tourist Office. If you have a railpass you can easily travel to and from any of the small towns nearby which have a train station.

IYHF HOSTEL

'Jugendhaus', Weihergasse 4 (tel. 226316). Midnight curfew. A 10–15-minute walk from the train station. Down by the river below the Parliament building. Look for the sign pointing down the steps near the Parliament.

CAMPING

Eichholz, Strandweg 49 (tel. 542602). 2SFr (£0.85; $1.50; DM2.50) per tent, 4SFr (£1.70; $3; DM5) p.p. Also twin-bedded rooms 10SFr (£4.15; $8; DM12), plus 4SFr (£1.70; $3; DM5) p.p. Tram 9 to Wabern, the end of the line.

Eymatt (tel. 361501). Around 6SFr (£2.50; $4.75; DM7.25) per tent and per person. From the train station take the postal bus dir. Bern-Hinterkappelen to Eymatt.

IYHF HOSTELS NEARBY

Rue de l'Hopital 2, Fribourg (tel. 037–231916). Fribourg is an attractive and interesting old town on the train line between Geneva and Berne. Linked to Berne by frequent Inter-city trains, a half-hour trip.

Geneva (Genève) (tel. code 022)

HOTELS

**Cheapest doubles around 27.50SFr
(£11.50; $21.75; DM33.25) p.p.**

Pension St-Boniface, av. du Mail 14 (tel. 218844). Left
from place Cornavin in front of the station. Along bd
James-Fazy, down to the river and over the Pont de la
Coulouvrenière, bd Georges-Favon to place du Cirque.
To the right of Georges-Favon on the other side of place
du Cirque. A 15-minute walk.

**Cheapest doubles around 30SFr
(£12.50; $23.75; DM36.25) p.p.**

Hôtel de la Cloche, rue de la Cloche 6 (tel. 7329481).
Down rue des Alpes from place Cornavin, left rue
Philippe-Plantamour from place des Alpes, then right.
A 10-minute walk.

Pension Ravier, bd des Philosophes 26 (tel. 290618). Right
along rue Cornavin, left rue de Coutance, straight on
over the water, through place Neuve until you see
Philosophes on the left. A 15-minute walk.

Cheapest doubles around 34SFr (£14.15; $27; DM41) p.p.

Hôtel Paquis Fleuri, rue des Paquis 23 (tel. 7313453).
Down rue des Alpes to place des Alpes, then left. A
10-minute walk from Cornavin.

Hôtel St Gervais, rue des Corps-Saints 20 (tel. 7324572).
A continuation of rue Cornavin, to the right of place
Cornavin. Five minutes from the train station.

Hôtel Saint Victor, Rue Lefort 1 (Tranchées) (tel. 461718).
Near the centre of the Old Town. A continuation
of rue Et. Dumont which runs out of place du
Bourg-de-Four.

Hotels are cheaper in the French town of Bellegarde, just
over the border.

IYHF HOSTEL

Rue Rothschild 30 (tel. 7326260). Midnight curfew in summer, 11 p.m. at other times. Left from Cornavin along rue de Lausanne, then right. A five-minute walk. Dorms 18SFr (£7.50; $14.25; DM21.75) for IYHF members.

HOSTELS/FOYERS/STUDENT ACCOMMODATION

Home St-Pierre, Cour St-Pierre 4 (tel. 283707/286998). Women only. Dorms start at around 12SFr (£5; $9.50; DM14.50), singles around 19SFr (£7.90; $15; DM23). Doubles and triples are not much more expensive than dorms. Beneath the cathedral. Bus 5 or a 15-minute walk from Cornavin.

Foyer International des Jeunes Filles, rue Plantamour 27 (tel. 7315560). Women only. Dorms 13SFr (£5.40; $10.25; DM15.75), singles around 21SFr (£8.75; $16.50; DM25.50) p.p. Also doubles. Rue des Alpes from the station to place des Alpes, then left. A 10-minute walk.

Cité Universitaire, av. Miremont 46 (tel. 462355). Dorms 13SFr (£5.40; $10.25; DM15.75), single rooms start at around 27SFr (£11.25; $21.50; DM32.75). Open 15 July–15 Oct. From place de 22 Cantons by Cornavin station bus 3 dir. Crêts de Champel to the terminus.

Centre Masaryk, av. de la Paix 11 (tel. 7330772). Dorms similar price to the IYHF hostel. Singles 28SFr (£11.65; $22.25; DM33.75). Doubles and triples are slightly cheaper p.p. than singles. Near the United Nations building.

Evangelische Stadtmission, rue Bergalonne 7 (tel. 212611). Dorms start at around 19SFr (£8; $15; DM23). Doubles at hotel-type prices. Bus 1 to Ecole-Médecine. To the rear of the Musee d'Ethnographie.

Pension St-Boniface (see hotels/pensions). Dorms around
the same price as the IYHF hostel.

Hôtel le Grenil, av. Ste-Clotilde 7 (tel. 283055). Dorms
around 23SFr (£9.60; $18.25; DM27.75). Fifteen minutes
from Cornavin, off place du Cirque. See directions for
Pension St-Boniface above (hotels/pensions).

Foyer l'Accueil, rue Alcide-Jentzer 8 (tel. 209277). Doubles
around 24SFr (£10; $19; DM29) p.p. Singles slightly
more expensive. About 25 minutes' walk from the
Cornavin station, 15 minutes from the town centre.

Foyer St-Justin, rue du Prieuré 15–17 (tel. 7311135). Singles
start at around 27SFr (£11.25; $21.25; DM32.75). Left
from Cornavin station along rue de Lausanne, then
right. A 5–10-minute walk.

Maison des Jeunes, rue du Temple 5 (tel. 7322060).

Rue de Nant 37. In a nuclear shelter. Around 14SFr (£5.85;
$11; DM17). Bus 5 to Rive, followed by a five-minute
walk.

Cooperative du Logement, rue H. Senger 2 (tel. 292033).
Lets rooms in the four university residences.

Armée du Salut, Rue de l'Industrie 14 (tel. 7336438).
Singles 14SFr (£5.75; DM17).

CAMPING

Sylvabelle, Chemin de Conches 10 (tel. 470603). Closest
to town. Bus 3 as far as Rond Point de Rive, then bus
8 or 88,

Pointe-à-la-Bise (tel. 7521296). About five miles out. Bus 9
to Rive, then change to bus E. Open Apr.–Sept. Close
to Lac Leman (Lake Geneva).

D'Hermance, Chemin des Glerrêts (tel. 7511483). Open
Apr.–Sept. Same buses as Pointe-à-la-Bise, but take
bus E to the terminus. About 10 miles out, near Lac
Leman.

Lucerne (Luzern) (tel. code 041)

HOTELS

Cheapest doubles around 30SFr
(£12.50; $23.75; DM36.25) p.p.

Hotel Linde, Metzgerrainie 3 (tel. 513193). Between the Town Hall and Muhlenplatz.

Hotel Schlüssel, Franziskanerplatz 12 (tel. 231061). Five minutes' walk from the train station.

Cheapest doubles around 38SFr (£15.85; $30; DM46) p.p.

SSR Touristenhotel, St Karliquai 12 (tel. 512474). Fifteen minutes' walk from the station on the Old Town side of the river, past the Spreuerbrücke (the second of the covered wooden bridges).

Pension Panorama, Kapuzinerweg 9 (tel. 362298/366701).

DORMS

Available at the SSR Touristenhotel, and at Hotel Jlge, Pfistergasse 17 (tel. 220918) in the Old Town, but are more expensive than those of the IYHF hostel. See also Camping Lido.

IYHF HOSTEL

Am Rotsee, Sedelstrasse 12 (tel. 368800). Midnight curfew. Not central. A 30-minute walk from the train station. Bus 18 to Goplismoos/Friedental leaves you with a couple of minutes' walk. Last bus 7.30 p.m. The more frequent bus 1 to Schlossberg leaves you a 10-minute walk down Friedentalstrasse. Reception opens 4 p.m., and 1½ hour queues are not uncommon during the summer, with no guarantee of getting in. If possible arrive early, fill in a form and leave it with your IYHF card in the box provided, then go back

when the queue is likely to have disappeared, or at
any time before reception closes at 10 p.m.

CAMPING

Lido, Lidostrasse (tel. 312146). Near the beach and the
lake. Thirty-minute walk from the train station, over
the Seebrücke, then right along the lakeside. Bus 2
dir. Verkehrshaus. 2.50SFr (£1; $2; DM3) per tent,
5SFr (£2.10; $4; DM6) p.p. Also dorms 14SFr (£5.85;
$11; DM17). Cheapest in town. Site open Apr.–Oct.
Steinbachried (tel. 473558). Bus 20 for a 20-minute trip to
Horw Rank. 4SFr (£1.65; $3.25; DM4.75) per tent, 5SFr
(£2.10; $4; DM6) p.p. Open Apr.–Sept.

IYHF HOSTELS NEARBY

Allmeudstrasse 8, Sportstadion 'Herti', Zug (tel. 042–
215354). Frequent trains, 30-minute trip.

Zürich (tel. code 01)

HOTELS

**Cheapest doubles around 27.50SFr
(£11.50; $21.75; DM33.25) p.p.**

Justinusheim, Freudenbergstrasse 146 (tel. 3613806).
Hinterer Stern, Freieckgasse 7 (tel. 2513268).

**Cheapest doubles around 35SFr
(£14.60; $27.75; DM42.25) p.p.**

Dufour, Seefeldstrasse 188 (tel. 553655).
Hirschen, Niederdorfstrasse 13 (tel. 2514252). Over the
river from the station, on the right.
Vorderer Strenen, Bellevueplatz (tel. 2514949).

St Josef, Hirschengraben 64 (tel. 2512757). Just across the river from the station.

Schaefli, Badergasse 6 (tel. 2514144).

Foyer Hottingen, Hottingerstrasse 31 (tel. 2619315). One-star hotel run by nuns. Open to women, married couples and families only. Dorms 20SFr (£8.35; $15.75; DM24.25), singles 30SFr (£12.50; $23.75; DM36.25). Doubles work out slightly cheaper than singles. Tram 3 to Hottingerplatz from Bahnhofplatz in front of the train station. Near the centre.

Martahaus, Zähringerstrasse 36 (tel. 2514550). Doubles around 39SFr (£16.25; $31; DM47) p.p., dorms (six beds) 27SFr (£11.25; $21.25; DM32.50). Leave the station, over the River Limmat, then the right turn after Niederdorfstrasse.

Glockenhof, Sihlstrasse 33 (tel. 2213673). Men only. Ten-minute walk from the station. Singles around 30SFr (£12.50; $23.75; DM36.25).

IYHF HOSTEL

Mutschellenstrasse 114, Zürich-Wollishofen (tel. 4823544). 1 a.m. curfew. Tram 7 to Morgental, then a well-signposted five-minute walk. There is a local train station, Zürich-Wollishofen, if you have a railpass and want to save some money on transport.

CAMPING

Seestrasse 559 (tel. 4821612). Excellent site. Train to Zürich-Wollishofen, then a 10-minute walk. The site is on the Zürichsee.

IYHF HOSTELS NEARBY

Kanalstrasse 7, Baden (tel. 056–261796). Open 16 Mar.–23 Dec. Frequent trains, a half-hour trip.

Allmeudstrasse 8, Sportstadion 'Herti', Zug (tel. 042–215354). Frequent trains, a 45-minute trip.

TURKEY

As a rule, budget travellers will seldom encounter any difficulty finding suitably priced accommodation in Turkey. The one notable exception is Ankara, which, while it is not really a tourist town (and is correspondingly short on budget accommodation), seems to attract young travellers on the basis of its status as the national capital. Otherwise, it is quite easy to find a place to stay for about £1.75–2.50 ($3.50–4.50; DM5.00–7.25) along the Aegean coast, £1.50–2.50 ($3.00–4.50; 4.35–7.25DM) on its Mediterranean counterpart, or £1.25–2.25 ($2.50–4.00; DM3.50–6.50) in the east of the country.

The problem is that standards of cleanliness at establishments charging these prices can leave a lot to be desired. This is particularly true of the very cheap, ungraded, local **hotels**. However, if you are prepared to put up with the filth, the all too common bedbugs, and an unreliable water supply, most of them will be perfectly safe for you and your belongings. Standards at the hotels registered with the Tourist Board are more acceptable. These hotels, known as 'touristic', are rated from one star up to five stars. Expect to pay £4–10 ($7.50–19.00; DM11.50–29.00) per person for a double in a one-star hotel, rising to £5–10 ($9.50–19.00; DM14.50–29.00) p.p. in Istanbul. The cost of a double in a two-star hotel starts at £7.50 ($14.25; DM21.75) each.

It is not unusual for hotel touts to approach travellers at bus or train stations. Where there are several touts trying to attract custom for different hotels, there is a fair chance of bargaining them down from their initial asking price. At any hotel, make a point of seeing the room before making a firm acceptance. Again, there is nothing to be lost by haggling if the price seems to be on the high side (this is almost expected of you along the Bosphorus). Off season, it is quite normal for hoteliers to drop their prices by up to 25 per cent.

Pensions are not particularly common in Turkey, and the letting of private rooms is not officially recognized. Nonetheless, they do exist. Look for the sign 'Oda Var' indicating rooms are available (sometimes also advertised in German, 'zimmer frei'). In an attempt to attract budget travellers, pensions are sometimes advertised or touted as hostels. Quite frequently a 'pansiyon' or 'oberj' is a family-run establishment, with meals available. Those pensions registered with the Tourist Office charge from £2.50–10.00 ($4.75–19.00; DM7.25–29.00) p.p. for doubles. At others you can expect to pay around £1.50–3.00 ($2.75–5.75; DM4.25–8.75) p.p. for doubles.

There are 45 **youth hostels** in Turkey, only one of which is affiliated to the IYHF. Some student residences also serve as hostels (mainly during the months July and August only, but some operate all year round). Normally a student ID card guarantees entrance to a hostel, but it makes sense to have an IYHF card. For some strange reason even some of the non-affiliated hostels sometimes ask for an IYHF card.

Camping is popular in Turkey, and the number of sites is growing, but, on the whole, facilities are still exceptionally basic. Unless you are going to travel outside the main towns, it is probably not worth taking a tent: the sites serving the cities can be inconveniently located far out of town, and not always well served by public transport. There are quite a number of sites which charge about £1 ($1.90; DM2.90) for an overnight stay, and also a network of BP mocamps charging about £2 ($3.75; DM5.75) p.p., though these prices are increased by 20 per cent in July and August. Some campers have cast doubt on whether the latter offer good value for money. Tourist hotels may allow camping in their garden for a small charge.

Freelance camping seems to be tolerated, or cracked down upon, largely depending on which area of the country you happen to be in. Camping out in the country seldom seems to cause problems, but you can expect to be disturbed by the police if you pitch a tent somewhere in town (this is hardly safe in any case). In the east, where official sites are few and far between, it is best to choose a location to pitch your tent, and then ask the permission of the locals. If nothing else, this is likely to prevent any possible misfortune arising out of camping in a military area. Anyone (girls especially) worried about camping out in the country, but who, for any reason get stranded outside the towns, should note that petrol stations will rarely object to you pitching your tent close to the station, so affording you that little extra security. Do not consider sleeping rough in the cities, Istanbul especially. There are too many instances of mugging and rape for this to be worth the risk.

ADDRESSES

For information on youth and student travel
and accommodation contact Gençtur, Yerebatan
Caddesi 15, 3 Sultanahmet, 33410 Istanbul
(tel. 01 5136150–1).

Ankara (tel. code 04)

HOTELS

Cheapest singles £3.15–5.25 ($6–10; DM9.25–15.25), cheapest doubles £2.90–4.20 ($5.50–8.00; DM8.50–12.25) p.p.

Savaş, Altan Sok 3 (tel. 3242113).
Beyrut Palas, Denizciler Cad. 11 (tel. 3108407).
Pinar, Hisar Park 1 Cad. N° 14 Ulus (tel. 3118951).

Hotels registered with the Tourist Board:

Expect to pay from £4–10 ($7.50–19.00; DM11.50–29.00) p.p. in doubles

Safir, Denizciler Cad. 34 (tel. 3241194).
Paris, Denizciler Cad. 14 (tel. 3241283–4–5).
Efes, Denizciler Cad. 12 (tel. 324311–2). Rooms with
   baths. Singles £9 ($17; DM26), doubles £6.30 ($12;
   DM9.75) p.p.
Anit, G. Mustafa Bul. 111 (tel. 2292144).
As, Rüzgarli Cad. 4 (tel. 3103998–9).
Ergen, Karanfil Sok 48 (tel. 1175906).
Bulduk, Sanayi Cad. 26 (tel. 3104915).
Terminal, Hipodrum Cad. (tel. 3104949). Singles £5.25
   ($10; DM15.25), with bath £6.30 ($12; DM18.25);
   doubles £4 ($7.50; DM11.50), with bath £4.75 ($9;
   DM13.75) p.p. Near the bus station.
Öztürk, Talatpaşa Bul. 57 (tel. 3125186–7).
Hanecioğlu, Ulucanlar Cad. 68 (tel. 3202572).
Koyunlu, Ulucanlar Cad. 35 (tel. 3104900).
Taç, Çankiri Cad. 35 Ulus. (tel. 3243195).
Saral, Işiklar Cad. (tel. 3103488).
Olimpiyat, Rüzgarli Eşdost Sok 18 Ulus. (tel. 3243088).

YOUTH HOSTELS

Cumhuriyet Öğrenci Yurdu, Cebici (tel. 193634). Open
1 July–31 Aug.

CAMPING

Altinok. 12½ miles out on the road to Istanbul.

Antalya (tel. code 311)

HOTELS

Hotels registered with the Tourist Board:

**Expect to pay from £4–10 ($7.50–19.00; DM11.50–29.00)
p.p. in doubles.**

Büyük, Cumhuriyet Cad. 57 (tel. 11499).
Perge, Karaali Park Yani (tel. 23600).
Aras, Hüsnü Karakaş Cad. (tel. 118695).
Duru, Lara Cad. 150 (tel. 131217).

PENSIONS

Adler Pansiyon, Barbaros Mah./Civelek Sok. (tel. 117818).
Singles £3.65 ($7; DM10.75).
Aksoy Pansiyon. Next door to the Adler (tel. 126549).
Doubles £3.15 ($6; DM9.25) p.p.

The pensions below are registered with the Tourist Board:

**Expect to pay from £2.50–10.00
($4.75–19.00; DM7.25–29.00) p.p. in doubles.**

Ak-Asya, Yeni Kapi Firin Sok 5 (tel. 11404).
Holland, Lara Yolu, Bannaklar (tel. 126528).
Altun, Kaleiçi Mev 10 (tel. 16624).

Gözde, Kazim Özalp Cad. 106 Sok 3 (tel. 28656).
Anadolu, Gençlik Mah. 1311 Sok. (tel. 25938).
Türei, Çağlayan Mah. 2055 Sok 39 (tel. 20433).
Alahan, Cebesoy Cad. 29 (tel. 112591).

Ephesus (Efes)

The ruins of the city of Ephesus, one-time Roman capital of
Asia Minor, are only 10 miles from Kuşadasi, so it is quite
possible to stay there and visit Ephesus on a day trip. If
you would prefer to stay closer to Ephesus, or to stay for
a few days, then there are plenty of cheap places to stay
in the village of Selçuk (tel. code 5451), about a mile from
the ruins.

HOTELS

Tourist Board-registered hotel:

**Expect to pay £4–10 ($7.50–19.00; DM11.50–29.00)
p.p. for doubles**

Katibim, Atatürk Cad. 5 (tel. 2498). The main street of
the village.

Hotels licensed by the municipal authorities:
Hasanağa, Koçak Sok. (tel. 1317).
Aksoy, Isabey Mah. Cengiz Topel Cad. (tel. 1040).
Artemis, Atatürk Mah. 2 Pazaryeri Sok. (tel. 1191).
Güneş, Kuşadasi Cad. (tel. 1229).
Karahan, Atatürk Mah. 1 Okul Sok. (tel. 3294).
Ürkmez, Isabey Mah. Cengiz Topel Cad. (tel. 1312).
Akay, Atatürk Mah. Serin Sok 3 (tel. 3009/3172).
Atlanta, Atatürk 2ci Pazar yeri (tel. 2883).
Güven, 1002 Sok 9 (tel. 1294).
Gazi, Istasyon Meydani (tel. 1467).

PENSIONS

Expect to pay around £2.10 ($4; DM6) p.p.

Galaxi, Ataturk mah. Atatürk Cad. 21. (tel. 1304).
Evin, Isabey mah. Meydan Sok 37 (tel. 1261).
Hasan Ağa, Atatürk mah. Koçak Sok.
Sevil, Atatürk mah. Turgutreis Sok 7 (tel. 2340).
Saray, Atatürk mah. Kubilay Sok (tel. 3820).
Ferah, Atatürk mah. Karanfil Sok 5a (tel. 3814).
Buket, Isabey mah. Atatürk Cad. 6 (tel. 2378).
Australian, Zafer mah. Durak Sok 20a (tel. 1050).
Barim. Behind the Ephesus Museum (tel. 1923).

Istanbul (tel. code 01)

The best area to look for lodgings is the Sultanahmet, which
has a large number of cheap accommodation possibilities, as
well as being central and convenient to the main sights.

HOTELS

**Expect to pay £3.15–4.50 ($6.00–8.50; DM9–13) for singles;
£2.10–3.70 ($4–7; DM6.00–10.75) p.p. in doubles;
around £3.15 ($6; DM9) in dorms; and £1.85 ($3.50;
DM5.25) for a bed on the roof.**

Merih, Zeynep Sultan Cami Sok (tel. 5228522). Singles,
doubles and dorms.
Anadolu, Salkim Söğüt Sok 3 (tel. 5120135). Singles, dou-
bles and rooftop beds.
Elet, Salkim Söğüt Sok 14 (tel. 5139516). Doubles and
dorms. Price includes use of showers.
Sultan Tourist Hotel, Yerebatan Cad. (tel. 5207676).
Gögür, Divan Yolu Cad. (tel. 5262319).
Yöruk, Inçiliçavuş Sok (tel. 5276476).

Buyuk Sanid, Hudavendigar Cad. 35a (tel. 5267229). Spotless, and very safe.

Family Pansiyon, Piyerloti Cad., Kadirga Harman, Sokah No 4, Cemberlitas (tel. 5283746).

Dogan Palas, Hudavendigar Cad 44 (tel. 5264113).

Slightly more expensive:

Hotel Ema, Salkim Söğüt Sok 18. Recently opened. Singles £6.85 ($13; DM20), doubles with bath £5.75 ($11; DM16.75) p.p.

Hotels registered with the Tourist Board (all the hotels listed are in the Lâleli and Aksaray districts, adjacent to the Sultanahmet area).

Expect to pay from £5–10 ($9.50–19.00; DM14.50–29.00) p.p. for doubles.

Lâleli district:

Nobel, Aksaray Cad. 23 (tel. 5220617).

Okay, Fethibey Cad. (tel. 5112162).

Oran, Harikzadaler Sok 40 (tel. 5285813).

Uzay, Şairfitnat Sok 20 (tel. 5268776).

Tanin, Mesihpaşa Cad. 60 (tel. 5138336).

Selim, Koska Cad. 39 (tel. 5119377).

Side, Koska Cad. 33 (tel. 5267178).

Ensar, Yeşiltulumba Sok 39 (tel. 5206135).

Florida, Fevziye Cad. 38 (tel. 5281021).

Karakaş, Gençtürk Cad. 55 (tel. 5265343).

Karatay, Saitefendi Sok 42 (tel. 5265692).

Aksaray district:

Babaman, Laleli Cad. 19 (tel. 5268238).

Geçit, Aksaray Cad. 5 (tel. 5278839).

Yilmaz, Validecami Sok 79 (tel. 5867400).

Tebriz, Muratpaşa Sülüklü Sok (tel. 5244135).

Nazar, Ordu Cad. Yeşiltulumba Sok (tel. 5268060).

Pamukkale, Ordu Cad. Selimpaşa Sok (tel. 5276793).

Tahran, Mehmet Lütfişekerci Sok 21 (tel. 5214650).

IYHF HOSTEL

Yücelt Youth Hostel, Caferiya Sok 6/1 (tel. 5136150). In the Sultanahmet district, Turkey's sole IYHF hostel. Clean. Doubles £3.50 ($6.50; DM10.25) p.p.; dorms £2.50 ($4.75; DM7.25). Price includes showers. Best reserved in advance.

HOSTELS

Istanbul Youth Hostel, Cerrahpasa Cad. 63 (tel. 212455). Summer only. Aksaray district.

The four hostels below are all situated near the Topkapi Palace:

Expect to pay £2.90 ($5.50; DM8.50) p.p. in doubles, £1.10–2.20 ($2–4; DM3.00–6.25) in dorms.

Topkapi, Kutlugun Sok 1 (tel. 5272433). Dorms and doubles. Also quads £2.10 ($4; DM6) p.p.
True Blue, Akbiyik Cad. 2. Dorms and doubles.
Orient, Akbiyik Cad. 13 (tel. 5160171). Dorms and doubles.
Sultan Tourist Hostel, Cankvrtaran Akbiyik Cad. (tel. 5169260). Doubles. Also triples and quads, £2.10 ($4; DM6) p.p.

STUDENT ACCOMMODATION

Converted into temporary hostels during July and August:
Topkapi Ataturk Örenci Sitesi, Londra Asfalti, Cevizlibağ Duraği (tel. 5255032/5239488/5250280). Topkapi district.
Kadirga Öğrenci Yurdu, Cömertler Cad., Sehsuvarbey Sok (tel. 5282480–1). In the Kumpapi district.
Ortaköy Kiz Öğrenci Yurdu, Palanga Cad. 20 (tel. 1600184/1601035/1617376). In the Ortaköy district.

CAMPING

Yeşilyurt (tel. 5738408/5744230). On Sahil Yolu, close to the village of Yeşilköy.

Ataköy (tel. 5720802). Also on Sahil Yolu, near the village of Ataköy.

Florya. Accessible by the local train to Florya. Next to the beach.

Londra Mokamp. About three-quarters of a mile from the airport.

Kervansaray Kartaltepe Mokamp, Çobançeşme Mev. (tel. 5754721).

SLEEPING ROUGH

Stupidity. The risk of being a victim of theft, violent assault or rape is too high.

Izmir (tel. code 051)

HOTELS

Saray, Anafartaler Cad. 635 (tel. 136946). Singles £3.40 ($6.50; DM10), doubles £2.40 ($4.50; DM6.75) p.p.

The hotels below are registered with the Tourist Board:

Expect to pay £4–10 ($7.50–19.00; DM11.50–29.00) p.p. for doubles

Babadan, Gaziomanpaşa Bul 50 (tel. 139640–1–2–3).

Expect to pay from £7.50 ($14.25; DM21.75) p.p. for doubles.

Billur, Basmane Mey. 783 (tel. 136250).
Katipoğlu, Fevzipaşa Bul 41/2 (tel. 254122).
Kaya, Gaziomanpaşa Bul 45 (tel. 139771).
Kismet, 1377 Sok 9 (tel. 217050–1–2).

YOUTH HOSTELS

Atatürk Öğrenci Yurdu, 1888 Sokak, Inciralti (tel. 152980–1/152856). Open 1 July–31 Aug.

CAMPING

The nearest site approved by the Tourist Board is the Kervansaray Inciralti Mocamp in Balçova, about six miles out from the centre (tel. 154760).

Kuşadasi (tel. code 6361)

HOTELS

Rose (tel. 1111). Two blocks up the hill from Pansiyon Su (see below). Doubles around £3.15 ($6; DM9.25) p.p. Also beds on the roof £1.50 ($2.75; DM4.25).

The hotels below are registered with the Tourist Board:

Expect to pay £4–10 ($7.50–19.00; DM11.50–29.00) p.p. for doubles.

Aran, Kaya Aldoğan Cad. (tel. 1325).
Ekin, Kadinlar Plaji (tel. 3970).

PENSIONS

Hulya, Ileri Sok 39 (tel. 2075). £2.10 ($4; DM6) p.p. Includes use of hot showers.
Su, Aslanlar Cad. 13 (tel. 1453). £2.65 ($5; DM7.75) p.p.
Şafak (tel. 1764). A block further up the hill from Pansiyon Su. £2.50 ($4.75; DM7.25) p.p.

The pensions below are registered with the Tourist Board:

Expect to pay £2.50–10.00 ($4.75–19.00; DM7.25–29.00) p.p. for doubles.

Bahar, Cephane Sok 12 (tel. 1191).
Filiz, Yavansu Mev. (tel. 2471).
Grup, Istiklal Cad. 3 (tel. 1230).
Özer, Istiklal Cad. (tel. 1138).
Çiğdem, Istiklal Cad. 9 (tel. 1895).
Posaci, Leylak Soc. 5 (tel. 1151).
Yunus, Istiklal Cad. 7 (tel. 2268).
Nil, Ismet Inönü Bul 59 (tel. 1490).
Diamond, Yilanci Burnu Mev. (tel. 3134).

CAMPING

There are two sites located north of town, about 1½–2 miles out on the Selcuk–Izmir road.

Önder (tel. 2413) and Yat (tel. 1333). Both charge around £1.50 ($3; DM4.50) per tent, £0.80 ($1.50; DM2.25) p.p. Bungalows sleeping three are available for about £1.50 ($3; DM4.50) p.p.

UNITED KINGDOM

If, as is probable, London is your first stop in the UK, you might well wonder just how long your budget will survive, given that hostels are all around £10 ($19; DM29) at the very least, bed and breakfast (B&B) is rarely available for under £15 ($28.50; DM43.50) and the Tourist Information Centre charges a staggering £5 ($9.50; DM14.50) to find rooms that are well outside the budget category. And although you may find some comfort in the knowledge that things improve once you get outside the English capital, a trip to the UK is likely to put some strain on your budget, as there is a shortage of accommodation possibilities under £10 ($19; DM29) per night.

Camping is the best option if you want to be sure of keeping accommodation costs low. There are sites in most of the main towns of interest. Standards, and prices, vary dramatically, but it is most unusual for a solo traveller to pay more than £5 ($9.50; DM14.50) for an overnight stay. In smaller towns and villages, which have a minimal tourist trade, local farmers will usually let you pitch a tent on their land if your ask permission first. In the more remote areas there will seldom be any objection to you camping rough, provided you do not leave litter lying about, or set any potentially dangerous fires. As the nights can be very cold in the hilly parts of the country, a good-quality sleeping bag is essential, especially in the Scottish Highlands (anyone visiting the Highlands in summer would also be well advised to invest in an effective insect repellent). The one main drawback to camping is the damp climate, so be sure that your tent really is waterproof.

There are three **youth hostel** associations in the UK: the Youth Hostels Association of England and Wales, the

Youth Hostel Association of Northern Ireland, and the Scottish Youth Hostels Association (the latter were voted the best in Europe, along with An Óige hostels, in a recent survey of hostellers). Prices vary according to the standard of facilities available and the age of the user. At the Scottish and Northern Irish hostels those aged over 18 and over are referred to as 'seniors', whereas in England and Wales 'seniors' are those aged 21 and over, while visitors aged 16 to 20 are classed as 'juniors'. In the seven Northern Irish hostels, seniors pay around £6.25 ($11.75; DM18.25) during the peak season (May to September), except at the Belfast hostel which charges around £8 ($15.25; DM23.25). The most expensive hostels in Scotland, those in the cities and Inverness, charge around £6.50–7.00 ($12.25–13.25; DM18.75–20.25) for seniors, but normally seniors pay £4.75–5.25 ($9–10; DM13.75–15.25). Prices tend to be higher in English and Welsh hostels. Seniors normally pay £5–6 ($9.50–11.50; DM14.50–17.50), but there are also a fair number of hostels which charge £7–8 ($13.25–15.25; DM20.25–23.25) and the London hostels charging from £9–10 ($17–19; DM26–29) upwards. (To these prices a peak-season supplement of £1 ($2; DM3) is added at many hostels during the period June/July to August.) Advance booking in the main places of interest is advisable during the summer months. Curfews are normally 11 p.m. in England and Wales, 11.30 p.m. in Northern Ireland and 11.45 p.m. in Scotland; there are later curfews in some of. the city hostels (2 a.m. in Glasgow, Edinburgh, Aberdeen and Inverness). Although the IYHF hostel network in the UK is extensive, there are several important gaps in the network; notably some of the major English cities, such as Birmingham, Leeds, Manchester and Liverpool.

There are a number of independent hostels in the main places of interest. Standards are generally on a par with the local IYHF hostels, as are prices. The main exception is London, where some private hostels are of poor value compared to their IYHF counterparts. In cities lacking an IYHF hostel, YMCA/YWCA hostels may be your best chance of a reasonably cheap bed. Alternatively you might be lucky enough to find a room in a student residence during the Easter or summer vacations (usually mid March to mid April and July to early September). Rooms with B&B are normally available to students with ID for around £10 ($19; DM29) per person. If there are a number of you travelling together, renting a furnished student flat from a university might be better value. Many privately owned flats let to students during term-time are also rented to tourists during the summer. The Tourist Information Centre will inform you about anyone letting flats in the locality. The one hitch to renting a flat may be an insistence on a minimum stay of one week, although this is not always the case.

Bed and breakfast accommodation is available throughout the UK, with prices starting at around £10 ($19; DM29). In most towns, including popular destinations such as Edinburgh and York, you should be able to find a bed in the £10–12 ($19.00–22.75; DM29.00–34.75) price range without much difficulty, except during special events. In some of the more popular smaller cities, such as Bath and Oxford, you can consider yourself lucky if you find a room for under £14 ($26.50; DM40.75), while in London you can expect to pay £15–20 ($28.50–38.00; DM43.50–58.00). Tourist Information Centres distribute free lists of local accommodation, so unless the town is very busy you can normally find a bed quite easily by trying a few telephone numbers from the brochure. However, there is not much point in doing this if the office operates a free room-finding service. A few offices do charge for finding a room, normally £2 ($3.75; DM5.75). One really useful service provided by Tourist Information Centres is the book-a-bed-ahead service, which costs £2 ($3.75; DM5.75). This service lets you make a reservation at your next destination, and can save you a great deal of aggravation, time, and even money, especially if you are heading for a town where cheap accommodation is difficult to find, such as Edinburgh during its festival or York at weekends and Bank Holidays.

368   Cheap Sleep Guide

ADDRESSES

IYHF hostels   Youth Hostels Association of England and
                   Wales, Trevelyan House,
                   8 St Stephen's Hill,
                   St Albans, Hertfordshire, AL1 2DY
                   (tel. 0727–55215).
                Youth Hostel Association of Northern
                   Ireland, 56 Bradbury Place,
                   Belfast, BT7 1RU
                   (tel. 0232–324733).
                Scottish Youth Hostels Association,
                   7 Glebe Crescent, Stirling, FK8 2JA
                   (tel. 0786–51181).

Bath (tel. code 0225)

The popularity of the town, especially with more affluent, middle-aged tourists, means that prices in B&Bs are slightly higher than normal. Expect to pay £11–15 ($21.00–28.50; DM32.00–43.50) in the cheaper establishments, and during the peak season try to reserve a bed at least a week in advance. The Tourist Office at Colonnades (tel. 462831) finds rooms for a 10 per cent commission and distributes a free list detailing accommodation possibilities in Bath. If you arrive after the office has closed the area around the Pulteney Road is the best place to look for B&Bs (especially Pulteney Gardens). To get there cross over the river at the North Parade Bridge, then follow the North Parade Road until it joins Pulteney Road. You can also take the Badgerline bus from the bus station (bus 18 dir. University, with five buses each hour until 11 p.m.). The Wells Road also has a good supply of B&Bs.

B&Bs

The Shearns, Prior House, 3 Marlborough Lane (tel. 313587). By the Royal Victoria Park. One of the cheapest and offering excellent value. Bus 14 or 15, quarter-hourly from the bus station.

Mr and Mrs Farrar, 9 Raby Place, Bathwick Hill (tel. 464124). Left on the Pulteney Road from North Parade Road, then a sharp turn up the hill to the right.

Mrs Guy, 14 Raby Place (tel. 465120). (No smoking in the house.)

Mrs Ellis, The Limes, 1 Pulteney Road (tel. 311044). Cheap and good value. All rooms with bath and black and white television.

Mrs Rowe, 7 Widcombe Crescent (tel. 422726). Slightly more expensive than the prices quoted above.

IYHF HOSTEL

Bath Youth Hostel, Bathwick Hill (tel. 465674). Open July and Aug. Juniors £6.40 ($12.25; DM18.50), seniors £7.50 ($14.25; DM21.75). At other times prices fall slightly.

HOSTELS

YMCA International House, Broad Street Place (tel. 60471). Open to men and women. Dorms around £9.30 ($17.75; DM27), doubles around £10 ($19; DM29) p.p., singles £11 ($21; DM32). Very popular, so reserve in writing well in advance. About 300m from the Tourist Office.

CAMPING

Newton Mill Touring Centre, Newton Street Loe (tel. 333909). £4.50 ($8.50; DM13) per tent, £2.75 ($5.25; DM8) p.p. Three miles from the centre. Bus 5 from the bus station to the Newton Road.

IYHF HOSTELS NEARBY

Bristol International YHA Centre, Hayman House, 64 Prince Street, Bristol (tel. 0272–221659). Two- to six-bedded rooms. Juniors £9.40 ($17.75; DM27.25), seniors £11.20 ($21.25; DM32.50). About eight minutes' walk from Bristol Temple Meads train station. Bristol is 14 miles from Bath and the two towns are linked by frequent trains.

Belfast (tel. code 0232)

Do not be deterred from visiting Northern Ireland because of fears about your safety. Media sensationalism tends to portray the Six Counties as much more dangerous than they really are and genuinely tourists have nothing to fear outside Belfast. Even in the capital the chances of anything unpleasant happening to you are infinitesimally small and the incidence of petty crime is actually considerably lower than in mainland Britain. Belfast is an interesting and lively city, and a gateway to some of the most beautiful scenery in the UK, including the incomparable Giant's Causeway. The bulk of the accommodation is in the south of the city, around the university and the Botanic Gardens, about two miles from the centre. From City Hall take bus 69, 71, 84 or 85, all of which have frequent services. B&Bs start at around £10–11 ($19–21; DM29–32). The helpful Tourist Information Centre in River House at 48 High Street books lodgings for a £0.50 ($1; DM1.50) fee.

B&Bs

Mrs Davidson, East-Sheen Guest House, 81 Eglantine Avenue (tel. 667149). £11 ($21; DM32).

Mrs Pearl Blakely, 11 Malone Road (tel. 666145). Close to the university. £13.50 ($25.75; DM39.25).

Helga Lodge Hotel, 7 Cromwell Road (tel. 224820). Near the Botanic Gardens, off Botanic Avenue. £13.50 ($25.75; DM39.25). Rooms with showers considerably more expensive. From Donegall Square take bus 83 or 85.

STUDENT RESIDENCES

Queen's University Accomodations, 78 Malone Road (tel. 665938). Open mid June–mid Sept. No curfew. Students £6.25 ($11.75; DM18), non-students £8.50 ($16.25; DM30.75).

IYHF HOSTEL

Belfast International Youth Hostel, 'Ardmore', 11 Saint-field Road (tel. 647865). Closes for a couple of weeks around the Christmas/New Year period. Open all day during the summer. July and Aug. £8.50 ($16.25; DM30.75) for those aged 18 and over. Slightly cheaper May–June and Sept. Oct.–Apr. £7 ($13.25; DM20.25). Two miles from the centre on the Newcastle road. From Donegall Square take bus 38 or 84.

HOSTELS

YWCA, Wellesley House, 3/5 Malone Road (tel. 668347). Singles £12 ($22.75; DM34.75), doubles £10.50 ($20; DM30.50) p.p.

Cambridge (tel. code 0223)

Cambridge has a plentiful supply of rooms and so only during the peak season (late June to the end of August) are you likely to have some difficulty finding a room, and at this time it is advisable to try to reserve a bed in advance. The Tourist Information Centre in Wheeler Street, near the Market Square (tel. 322640) finds rooms for a £1 ($2; DM3) fee. They also sell a list of accommodation for £0.30 ($0.60; DM0.85), a copy of which is posted in the office window. The places to look for B&Bs are Tenison Street, near the train station, or in and around Jesus Lane, near Jesus College. Many of the establishments in the latter area are only open to visitors outside university term time, because they are filled with students during the university year.

B&Bs

Expect to pay £11–15 ($21.00–28.50; DM32.00–43.50).

Mrs French, 42 Lyndewode (tel. 316615). Off Tenison Road. Cheap and good value.
Mrs Fesenko, 15 Mill Road (tel. 329435). Cheap and good value.

Mrs Connolly, 67 Jesus Lane (tel. 61753). Around the middle of the price range above.

Mrs Bennett, 70 Jesus Lane (tel. 65497). Quite cheap.

Mrs J. Tombo, Tenison Towers, 148 Tenison Road (tel. 63924).

Mrs Day, 72 Jesus Lane (tel. 356961).

Mrs Owen, 65 Jesus Lane (tel. 60648).

Mrs Spalding, 56 Jesus Lane (tel. 353858).

The B&Bs below are slightly more expensive than the prices quoted above.

Mrs Daly, 21 Malcolm Street (tel. 65550). In between Jesus Lane and King Street.

Ellensleigh, 37 Tennyson Road (tel. 64888). Open mid June–Sept., and at Christmas and Easter.

IYHF HOSTEL

Cambridge Youth Hostel, 97 Tenison Road (tel. 354601). Open year round. Mostly four- to seven-bedded rooms. Described by the YHA England and Wales as one of their busiest hostels, so try to reserve well in advance. Juniors £7.50 ($14.25; DM21.75), seniors £8.70 ($16.50; DM25.25). In July and Aug. seniors pay an extra £1 ($2; DM3) supplement. A quarter-mile walk from the train station.

CAMPING

There is no shortage of sites in the Cambridge area (16 in all). Details of these sites are contained in the list sold by the Tourist Information Centre for a nominal fee.

Cambspeed Caravan Site, Wimpole Road, Barton. 2½ miles from town. Bus 118, 120 or 175 from Drummer Street bus station.

Highfield Farm Camping Site, Long Road, Comberton (tel. 262308). Open Apr.–Oct. Peak-season charges: £5–6 ($9.50–11.50; DM14.50–17.50); £1 ($2; DM3)

cheaper outside the peak season. Four miles out of
town on the B1046, off the A603 from Cambridge.
Accessible by Cambus 118 from the Drummer Street
bus station.

Edinburgh (Dun Eid Eann)
(tel. code 031)

Except during the Edinburgh Festival (a three-week period
in August) you should find a bed relatively easily in the
Scottish capital. The city has several hostels and student
residences open during the main tourist season from July to
early September, and more B&Bs than any other city in the
UK save London. Particularly good areas to look for B&Bs
are Bruntsfield, and the Newington/Mayfield area (between
the Royal Commonwealth Pool and Cameron Toll shopping
centre). The Tourist Information Centre in the Waverley
Market complex at 3 Princes Street (tel. 5571700) distributes a
free guide listing accommodation possibilities in the city, and
they also find rooms for a fee of £2 ($3.75; DM5.75), and you
pay 10 per cent of your bill to the Tourist Information Centre,
the remaining 90 per cent to the proprietor. At most times of
year there is little need to use the room-finding service, but
during the festival accommodation becomes very difficult to
find. It is a good idea to make use of the book-a-bed-ahead
service offered by Tourist Information Centres in other
towns to find a room before you arrive, which, if nothing
else, will save you a long wait in the queue at the Tourist
Information Centre in Edinburgh and may also save you
some money. If you do arrive without reservations and find
all the affordable accommodation gone, consider staying in
the surrounding counties of Eastlothian, Midlothian and
West Lothian for your first night, while trying to make a
reservation in the city for your second night.
NB: If you are staying in Bruntsfield, Newington or Mayfield

the tree-lined park known as The Meadows can be a useful short cut to the sights if you are on foot. The Meadows should, however, be avoided after dark. In recent years there have been a number of rapes here and numerous instances of women being subjected to severe sexual harassment. Unprovoked assaults on men by gangs of youths have also become regrettably common over the last few years.

B&Bs

Cheapest doubles £10.50 ($20; DM30.50) p.p., cheapest singles £10.50–12.00 ($20.00–22.75; DM30.50–34.75) unless shown otherwise.

Appleton House, 15 Leamington Terrace (tel. 229 3059).

The Armadillo Guest House, 5 Upper Gilmore Place (tel. 229 4669).

Bruntsfield Guest House, 55 Leamington Terrace (tel. 228 6458).

Clarin Guest House, 4 East Mayfield (tel. 667 2433).

Cree Guest House, 77 Mayfield Road (tel. 667 2524). One of the cheapest.

Falcon Crest Guest House, 70 South Trinity Road (tel. 552 5294).

Garfield Guest House, 264 Ferry Road (tel. 552 2369). Singles are expensive

Glendale Guest House, 5 Lady Road (tel. 667 6588). Singles expensive.

Hopetoun Guest House, 15 Mayfield Road (tel. 667 7691). Non-smokers only.

Kerena Guest House, 13 Hartington Gardens (tel. 229 6752).

Lorne Villa Guest House, 9 East Mayfield (tel. 667 7159).

Merlin Guest House, 14 Hartington Place (tel. 229 3864/225 3510).

Quendale Guest House, 32 Craigmillar Park (tel. 667 3171).

Mrs P. Birnie, 8 Kilmaurs Road (tel. 667 8998). Open May–Sept.

Mrs M. Carew-Stirrat, 35 Madeira St. (tel. 554 4596). Open May–Sept.

Margaret Cleland, 53 Murrayfield Gardens (tel. 337 2625). May–Sept.

Mrs V. Darlington, Borodale, 7 Argyle Place (tel. 667 5578). May–Sept.

Mr and Mrs Divine, 116 Greenbank Crescent (tel. 447 9454). May–Sept.

Joan M. Sayers, 19 Marchbank Drive (tel. 449 3095). May–Sept.

Mrs N. Shields, 178 Morrison St. (tel. 229 5943). May–Sept.

Mrs E. Sterling, 90 Liberton Brae (tel. 664 2398). May–Sept.

Mrs Elizabeth Stewart, 14 Angle Park Terrace (tel. 337 4157). One of the cheapest. Open June–Sept.

Mrs M. Hunter, 20 Primrose Bank Road (tel. 552 9442). May–Sept.

Mrs Monica Fallon, 5 Cameron Park (tel. 667 3857). May–Sept.

Mrs Marilyn Nicholl, 122 Mayfield Road (tel. 667 2526). May–Sept.

Mrs H. McKue, 1 Moat St. (tel. 443 8020).

Mrs M. Malrose, 26 Dudley Avenue (tel. 554 1915). Cheap. June–Sept.

FURNISHED FLATS WITH KITCHEN FACILITIES

Mrs M. Abbey, 7 Milton Road East (tel. 669 6900). One-bedroomed flat, sleeping four people. Min. stay one week. Weekly rate £130–220 ($250–420; DM375–640).

Mrs Donachie, 64 St John's Road (tel. 334 2860). Two–three bedrooms, sleeps five–six people. Min. stay one week. Weekly rate £160–250 ($285–475; DM465–725).

Mr J. Forbes, 10B Lauriston Park (tel. 229 0513). Four one-bedroomed flats sleeping three–five. Min. stay one week. Weekly rate £115–175 ($220–335; DM335–505).

Mr and Mrs Hepburn, No. 5, 5/7 Abercorn Terrace (tel. 669 1044). One bedroom, sleeps up to three people. Min. stay four days. Weekly rate £50–160 ($95–305; DM145–420).

Mrs C. Kent, 18 Mayfield Road (tel. 667 4650). Two-bedroomed flat sleeping five–six. Min. stay one week. Weekly rate £135–275 ($255–525; DM390–795).

C.R. McFarlane, Hospitality Services Manager, Queen Margaret College, Clerwood Terrace (tel. 317 3312). Three- to four-bedroomed flats sleeping three–four people. Min. stay one week. Open at Easter and June–Sept. Weekly rate £200–220 ($380–420; DM580–640). Student flats.

University of Edinburgh, 30 Buccleuch Place (tel. 667 0151). Three- to six-bedroomed flats sleeping four–six people. Min. stay one week. Weekly rate £235–310 ($445–590; DM680–900).

STUDENT RESIDENCES

These are expensive with most of them charging around £20 ($38; DM58), although if there are any beds which have not been pre-booked by groups, they may let them out to students with ID for about half this price. Worth a phone call.

Capital Campus, Queen Margaret College, Clerwood Terrace (tel. 317 3000). Open Apr–Sept. Singles £17 ($32.25; DM49.25; doubles £15 ($28.50; DM43.50).

Napier Polytechnic of Edinburgh, St Andrews Hall of Residence, 219 Colinton Road (tel. 444 2266, ext. 4621). Open Apr. and July–Sept. Singles and doubles £18 ($34.25; DM52.25).

Pollock Hall of Residence, 18 Holyrood Park Road (tel. 667 1971). From £20 ($38; DM58) p.p.

IYHF HOSTELS

18 Eglinton Crescent (tel. 337 1120). Curfew 2 a.m. Best reserved in advance with payment during peak months

of July–Sept. £7 ($13.25; DM20.25) A 20-minute walk from the Waverley train station but only five minutes from the Haymarket station. Trains from Glasgow and the north stop at Haymarket before Waverley. Buses 3, 4, 12, 13, 22, 26, 28, 31, 33 or 34 from Princes St run to Palmerston Place. Eglinton Crescent is off Palmerston Place. Take the bus from opposite the shops.

7 Bruntsfield Crescent (tel. 447 2994). Open 2 Feb.–1 Jan. Curfew 2 a.m. Slightly cheaper than the hostel above. Again book well in advance. Check in from 11.30 a.m. (no earlier). About 30 minutes' walk from either train station. Buses 11, 15, 16 and 17 run down Lothian Road into Bruntsfield. Lothian Road is about 10 minutes' walk from both stations.

HOSTELS

High Street Hostel, 8 Blackfriars St. (tel. 557 3984). £5.75 ($11; DM16.75). Arrive early, especially during the festival. From Waverley go out the exit the taxis use, then left up Waverley Bridge. At the mini-roundabout take the road going away to the left up the hill (Cockburn St.). Left at the top, across the road at the traffic lights, then watch for Blackfriars St. on the right past the hotel.

Cowgate Tourist Hostel, 112 The Cowgate (tel. 226 2153). Open July–21 Sept. Singles from £8.50 ($16.25; DM24.75), doubles from £7.50 ($14.25; DM21.75) p.p. If you go right down Blackfriars St. from the High St. Hostel you arrive in the Cowgate.

Christian Alliance Frances Kinnaird Hostel, 14 Coates Crescent (tel. 225 3608). Women only. Open year round. Midnight curfew, extended to 1.30 a.m. at festival time. Five-minute walk from Haymarket Station. Head for the town centre. The street is off to your left after Palmerston Place. From Waverley, walk along Princes St. into Shandwick Place, then the right turn after Stafford St. From £15 ($28.50; DM43.50) for singles, £11 ($21; DM32) p.p. for doubles.

CAMPING

Muirhouse Caravan Park, Marine Drive, Silverknowes (tel. 312 6874). Open Apr.–Oct. Two sharing a tent pay £5–6 ($9.50–11.50; DM14.50–17.50). Bus 14. Do not walk through the nearby Muirhouse or Pilton housing schemes: much of Edinburgh's reputation as the heroin and AIDS capital of Europe was built around these areas and unprovoked assaults are common.

Little France Caravan Park, 219 Old Dalkeith Road (tel. 666 2326). Two people sharing a tent pay £6–7 ($11.50–13.25; DM17.50–20.25). Maroon buses (LRT) 33, 82, or 89 from The Bridges. Green bus (SMT) 131 from the bus station or The Bridges.

Mortonhall Park Caravan Park, 38 Mortonhall Gate, Frogston Road East (tel. 664 1533). Two people sharing a tent pay £7–8 ($13.25–15.25; DM20.25–23.25). Buses (Maroon, LRT) 11, 81 or 81B run from Princes St. to Mortonhall.

Near Edinburgh:

Linlithgow (tel. code 0506)

Linlithgow is a royal burgh of Scotland and has the ruins of the royal palace by the loch to mark its glorious past. Eighteen miles out of Edinburgh, it is a short train journey away on the line to Glasgow and Falkirk. Not all trains stop at Linlithgow, but the service is frequent, and there are buses from St Andrew's Square bus station.

B&Bs

Cheapest prices around £10–11 ($19–21; DM29–32).

Mrs Findlay, 43 Clarendon Crescent (tel. 842574).
Mrs J. Gray, Meadowhead, 13 Carse Knowe (tel. 845328).
Mrs Janet McCron, Orama, 36 Baronshill Avenue (tel. 844382).
Mrs Mooney, 137 Baronshill Avenue (tel. 843903).

Musselburgh (tel. code as for Edinburgh)

The town is five miles from Edinburgh, by the coast, and its main attraction is the racecourse. There is an hourly train service to the capital, which is a 10-minute trip. The station is on the outskirts of town, 15 minutes' walk from the centre. There is also a frequent bus service from Edinburgh with Green buses (SMT) from St Andrew's Square to North Berwick, Dunbar, Haddington and Pencaitland. Only a few express buses (such as X08) do not stop in Musselburgh. Ask the driver.

B&Bs

Cheapest prices around £11 ($21; DM32).

Mrs B. Douglas, Melville House, 103a North High St. (tel. 665 5187). Main street of the Fisherrow part of town (the first part you reach coming from Edinburgh by bus).

Mrs Craven, 19 Bridge St. (tel. 665 6560). Between the Brunton Hall and the River Esk.

Mrs McGowan, 23 Linkfield Road (tel. 665 7436). By the racecourse.

Mrs C. Douglas, 5 Craighall Terrace (tel. 665 4294).

Miss Mitchell, Craigesk, 10 Albert Terrace (tel. 665 3344/665 3170).

Mrs Ross, Lochnagar, 12 Hope Place (tel. 665 2029).

North Berwick (tel. code 0620)

A royal burgh of Scotland and a pleasant seaside town, North Berwick is served by hourly trains for the 30-minute trip into Edinburgh. It is a long and expensive journey by bus. There are numerous B&Bs in this town, one of which is:

Mrs R. Lumsden, 26 Dundas Avenue (tel. 2651). Open June–Aug. From £11 ($21; DM32).

Glasgow (Glas Chu) (tel. code 041)

Glasgow has become increasingly popular in recent years, partly due to a vigorous advertising campaign aimed at altering the popular perception of Glasgow as an uninteresting and violent city (always undeserved on both counts), and partly due to the opening in the mid 1980s of the exceptional Burrell Collection. Both of these factors contributed to the city being crowned 'European City of Culture' in 1990, which brought in even larger numbers of visitors. Unfortunately the supply of rooming possibilities has failed to keep pace with the increasing demand. Although the hiatus of 1990 has now passed, you are still likely to encounter difficulties in finding a bed during the summer months (August especially). The Tourist Information Centre at 35 St Vincent Place (tel. 204 4400) will do their best to help you. They find rooms for free, and also sell a comprehensive guide to accommodation possibilities in Glasgow for £0.50 ($1; DM1.50). The office is just off George Square, a short walk from Queen Street train station and Buchanan Street bus station, and about 10 minutes' walk from the Central railway station. Glaswegians are normally happy to help out if you need directions.

B&Bs

Cheapest doubles £10–11 ($19–21; DM29–32) p.p.; singles £10.00–12.50 ($19.00–23.75; DM29.00–36.25).

   Mrs J. Briggs, 264 Langlands Road (tel. 445 1076). A short walk from Shawlands and Pollokshaws (East) rail stations. Open Apr.–Sept.

   Mrs M. Coyle, 18 Arnhall Place (tel. 882 6642). Off the Paisley Road West in the Cardonald area of the city. Open Apr.–Sept.

   Mrs J. Cunningham, 'Cathkinview', 160 Wedderlea Drive (tel. 882 4384). Off the Paisley Road West in Cardonald. Open Apr.–Sept.

   Mrs D. Shanks, 131 Brownside Road (tel. 641 3517). In Rutherglen. A 10–minute walk from the Burnside train station. Open Apr.–Sept.

   Mrs M. Williamson, 15 Kintillo Drive (tel. 959 1874). Off Queen Margaret Drive, near the Botanic Gardens.

Cheapest doubles around £12 ($22.75; DM34.75) p.p.; singles £12–13 ($22.75–24.75; DM34.75–37.75).

Mrs J. Freebairn-Smith, 14 Prospect Avenue (tel. 641 5055). Off the Glasgow Road in Cambuslang.

Linby Guest House, 29 Carmyle Avenue (tel. 763 0684). Carmyle district.

Symington Guest House, 26 Circus Drive (tel. 556 1431). Great location. To the rear of the Necropolis as you walk from St Mungo's Cathedral.

Craigpark Guest House, 33 Circus Drive (tel. 554 4160).

Mrs E. Anderson, 3 King Edward Road (tel. 954 8033). Near the Gartnavel Royal Hospital. Short walk from Anniesland train station. Open Apr.–Sept.

Mr and Mrs G. Beattie, Iona House, 18 Walmer Crescent (tel. 247 5231). Metro: Kinning Park. Just off the Paisley Road West. Short walk from Ibrox Park, home of Rangers, Scotland's most successful football team.

Mrs I. Campbell, 12 Regent Park Square (tel. 423 0727). Off the Pollokshaws Road. Short walk from Pollokshields (West) train station. Open Apr.–Sept.

Mrs J. Forsyth, 3 Blairbeth Terrace (tel. 634 4399). A few minutes' walk from Burnside train station. Open Apr.–Sept.

Mr and Mrs P. Michael, 8 Marlborough Avenue (tel. 334 5651). Just under 10 minutes' walk from Hyndland train station. Open Apr.–Sept.

Mrs C. McArdle, 171 Mount Annan Drive (tel. 632 0671). Ten minutes' walk from King's Park train station. Off the Aikenhead Road towards Hampden Park, home of Queen's Park Football Club and, until recently, the Scottish national team. Occasionally there are rock/pop concerts in the stadium.

STUDENT RESIDENCES

The University of Glasgow lets rooms in six of its halls of residence. Opening times may vary slightly from year to year, but are normally mid Mar.–mid Apr., and early July to Sept. The university administrative office is at 52 Hillhead Street (tel. 330 5385). Metro: Hillhead. The Maclay Hall (tel. 332 5056) beside the Kelvingrove Park is the most convenient to the town centre. Students £8 ($15.25; DM23.25), without breakfast. The most modern residence is the Queen Margaret Hall at 55 Bellshaugh Road (tel. 334 2192), close to Byres Road. B&B for students £11.50 ($21.75; DM33.23), non-students £18.50 ($35.25; DM53.75).

IYHF HOSTEL

11 Woodlands Terrace (tel. 332 3004). Curfew 2 a.m. £6.40 ($12.25; DM18.50) for those aged 18 and over. In summer advance reservation with payment is virtually essential. Beside the Kelvingrove Park. Metro: St George's Cross. Bus 44 from Central Station to the first stop on Woodlands Road. Bus 10, 11, 11A or 12 from the city centre. Alternatively take a low-level train from Queen Street one stop to Charing Cross, then follow the signs up the hill.

HOSTELS

YMCA Aparthotel, David Naismith Court, 33 Petershill Drive (tel. 558 6166). No curfew. B&B in singles £12 ($22.75; DM34.75), in doubles £11 ($21; DM32) p.p. From Buchanan Street bus station take bus 10 or 11. Bus 12 or 16 from Queen Street train station.

Brown's Hostel, 1 Woodlands Drive, flat 3/1 (tel. 332 1618). Small. £8 ($15.25; DM23.25). Metro: Kelvinbridge.

Glasgow Central Tourist Hostel, Balmanno Building, 81 Rottenrow East (tel. 552 2401). Great central location. Short walk from Queen Street Station and the city centre. Open in summer.

CAMPING

Kilmardinny Riding Centre, Milngavie Road, Bearsden (tel. 942 4404). Open year round, but has small capacity.

Inverness (Inbhir Nis) (tel. code 0463)

Inverness is the major transportation hub for the Highlands. The town itself offers little of interest, and is slightly shabby, but nevertheless it can be very difficult to avoid staying in Inverness as poor public transport services can make it difficult to get into, and then out of the town in the same day. Treat timetables with suspicion: rail services are unreliable, as years of government cutbacks begin to take an increasingly heavy toll on the quality of the service. Finding rooms in summer is not easy, though the excellent Tourist Information Centre at 23 Church Street (tel. 234353) finds rooms for free in establishments registered with the office. For unregistered B&Bs head across the River Ness to Kenneth Street, or try the Old Edinburgh Road (follow Castle Street from the High Street) or nearby Argyle Street.

B&Bs

Expect to pay £10.00–12.50 ($19.00–23.75; DM29.00–36.25).

Mrs J.M. Fraser, 8 Crown Street (tel. 235874). Just over half a mile from the bus and train stations. Close to Argyle Street/Old Edinburgh Road.

Mrs MacCuish, 50 Argyle Street (tel. 235150). Open Apr.–Oct.

Mrs Sheridan, 9 Old Edinburgh Road (tel. 234728).

Broadstone Lodge, 1 Broadstone Park (tel. 231822). Along St Stephen's Street from the High Street, on to Kingsmills Road, then fourth left.

IYHF HOSTEL

1 Old Edinburgh Road (tel. 231771). Ten minutes' walk from the bus and train stations. £6.40 ($12.25; DM18.50) for those aged 18 and over. Curfew 2 a.m.

HOSTELS

Inverness Student Hotel, 8 Culduthel Road (tel. 236556). Off the Old Edinburgh Road. Telephone reservations not accepted unless made by Edinburgh's High Street Hostel, but phoning ahead will allow you to check out the availability of beds. Similar price to the IYHF hostel.

CAMPING

In summer sites are frequently filled with caravans.

Bught Caravan and Camping Park (tel. 236920). Closest to the centre. Near the Ness Islands. From £1.85 ($3.50; DM5.25) p.p. On the Craig Dunain bus route.

Scaniport Caravan Park (tel. 75351). Four miles from town off the B862 towards Dores. Slightly cheaper than the site above.

The Lake District

Carlisle (tel. code 0228)

This town, with a population of just over 100,000, is a gateway to the Lake District. There are trains to and from Glasgow, Edinburgh, Newcastle, and the south of England. Trains run from Carlisle to Oxenholme, and from there a branch line takes you to Windermere, in the heart of the Lake District.

B&Bs

The Tourist Information Centre in the Old Town Hall on the Green Market (tel. 512444) books rooms in the city, and throughout Cumbria. B&B starts at around £11.50 ($21.75; DM33.25). Pay 10 per cent at the office, the remainder at the guest house.

Mrs Thompson, 19 Aglionby St. (tel. 24566). Around £12.75 ($24.25; DM37). From the train station right along Botchergate, then left along Tait St., which runs into Aglionby St.

IYHF HOSTEL

Carlisle Youth Hostel, Etterby House, Etterby (tel. 23934). Juniors £5 ($9.50; DM14.50), seniors £6 ($11.50; DM17.50). Bus 62 from the City Centre to the Red Fern Inn, then walk down Etterby Road.

Keswick (tel. code 07687)

Thirty-four miles from Carlisle, and 12 miles from Grasmere. Tourist Information Centre, Moot Hall, Market Square (tel. 72645). Book accommodation in Keswick for free, for other towns they charge a £2 ($3.75; DM5.75) fee.

B&Bs

Bridgedale, 101 Main St. (tel. 73914). £8 ($15.25; DM23.25). Breakfast is extra. By the bus station.

Mr and Mrs Nixon, Grassmoor, 10 Blencathra St. (tel. 74008). £12 ($22.75; DM34.70). Price falls by about 20 per cent out of season.

Mrs Walker, 15 Acorn St. (tel. 74165). Similar prices to above.

Mrs Peill, White House, 15 Ambleside Road (tel. 73176). Slightly cheaper than those above.

IYHF HOSTELS

Keswick YH, Station Road (tel. 72484). Off the Market Place, down towards the River Greta.

Derwentwater YH, Barrow House, Borrowdale (tel. 77246). Two miles out. Hourly Borrowdale bus CMS 79 to Seatoller.

CAMPING

Castlerigg Hall (tel. 72437). One mile out of town to the south-east.

Dalebottom Holiday Park (tel. 72176). Two miles south-east. More expensive than Castlerigg Hall.

Cockermouth (tel. code 0900)

Twenty-five miles from Carlisle, 13 miles from Keswick, and 10 miles from Buttermere.

IYHF Hostel

Cockermouth YH, Double Mills (tel. 822561). Nearest train station: Workington, eight miles away. Local buses.

Buttermere (tel. code 07687)

Keswick is 8½ miles away, and Cockermouth 10 miles.

IYHF HOSTELS

King George VI Memorial Hostel, Buttermere (tel. 70245).

Honister House YH (tel. 77267). Four miles from Buttermere. At the top of the beautiful Honister Pass.

Black Sail YH, Black Sail Hut. No telephone in this remote
YH. Located one mile up the Green Gable Hill, 3½
miles from Buttermere. To book write well in advance
to the hostel at Ennerdale, Cleator, Cumbria, CA23
3AY.

Ennerdale YH, Cat Crag, Ennerdale (tel. 0946–861237).
Three miles or seven miles from Buttermere over the
hills, depending on whether you go via Red Pike or
Scarth Gap respectively; 18 miles away by road.

Westwater YH, Wasdale Hall, Seascale (tel. 09046–222).
Eleven miles from Buttermere by mountain path; 7–8
miles from Black Sail, Ennerdale and Honister Hause,
again by mountain paths.

Boot

IYHF HOSTEL

Eskdale YH (tel. 09403–219). One mile from Boot village;
¼ mile from the Woolpack Inn; 1½ miles from the
Ravenglass to Eskdale steam railway. Seven miles
from Wastwater YH and 10 miles from Black Sail and
Coniston (Copper-mines) by mountain paths.

Grasmere (tel. code 09665)

About 5½ miles from Ambleside and 12 miles from Keswick.

B&Bs

It is expensive to stay in a local B&B as prices start around
£13.50 ($25.75; DM39.25).

IYHF HOSTELS

Butharlyp How YH (tel. 316). Just outside the village. A few minutes' walk along the road to Easedale. The hostel is on your right.

Thorney How YH (tel. 591). About a mile out. Follow the road to Easedale for about three-quarters of a mile. You will see the hostel signposted.

High Close (Langdale) YH, High Close, Loughrigg (tel. 09667–313). Two miles from Grasmere, four miles from Ambleside.

Elterwater YH (tel. 09667–245). 3½ miles from Grasmere and Ambleside.

Ambleside (tel. code 05394)

About 5½ miles from Grasmere, six miles from Hawkshead, four miles from Windermere. Tourist Information Centre, Church St. (tel. 32582). Local accommodation found for free, for which you pay 10 per cent at the office and the rest to the proprietor. They will also book rooms in other towns for a £2 ($3.75; DM5.75) fee.

B&Bs

Prices start around £12 ($22.75; DM34.75). Try Church Street or the Compston Road. The road leading out to Windermere, Lake Road, is particularly well supplied with B&Bs.

Mr and Mrs Richardson, 3 Cambridge Villas, Church St. (tel. 32307).

Raaesbec, Fair View Road (tel. 33844).

Thorneyfield, Compston Road (tel. 32464). More expensive. Prices start at around £15 ($28.50; DM43.50).

IYHF HOSTELS

Ambleside YH, Waterhead (tel. 32304). By Lake Windermere. A good deal more expensive than other Lake
District hostels. Juniors £7.50 ($14.25; DM21.75), sen-
iors £8.80 ($16.75; DM25.50) in July and Aug. Prices
fall slightly at other times.

HOSTELS

YWCA, Old Lake Road (tel. 32340). Open to men and
women. Dorms and smaller rooms from £11 ($21;
DM32).

CAMPING

Low Wray (tel. 32810). 3½ miles from town, on the road
to Hawkshead. The bus to Hawkshead stops nearby.

Windermere and Bowness
(tel. code 09662)

Four miles from Ambleside and nine miles from Hawkshead
(with ferry crossing). Another of the major gateways to the
Lake District, thanks to the town's train station. The Tourist
Information Centre is close to the railway station (tel. 6499)
and books local B&Bs for free, 10 per cent deposit, the rest
paid to the owner. Prices start around £11 ($21; DM32).

B&Bs

Mr and Mrs Austin, 'Lingmore', 7 High St. (tel. 4947).
One of the cheapest.
Mrs Graham, Brendan Chase Guest House, College Road
(tel. 5638). Around £13 ($24.75; DM37.75), falling to
£11.50 ($21.75; DM33.25) for stays of three nights and
longer.

Kirkwood, Prince's Road (tel. 3907). From around £13.50 ($25.75; DM39.25). Owners will pick you up from the train station. Down the main road to Bowness.

IYHF HOSTEL

Windermere YH, High Cross, Bridge Lane, Troutbeck (tel. 3543). £5.90 ($11.20; DM17.10) for members. Troutbeck village is two miles to the north of Windermere, off the A591. The bus to Ambleside stops in Troutbeck Bridge, about 10 minutes' walk from the hostel.

CAMPING

Park Cliffe, Birks Road (tel. 05395–31344). Open May–Oct. Off the A592 to the north of Windermere (dir. Patterdale and Penrith).

Limefitt Park (tel. 05394–32300). Mixed couples and families only. More expensive than the site above. On the A592 4½ miles south of Bowness.

Hawkshead

Ambleside 5½ miles away, Windermere nine miles (by ferry) and Grasmere 11 miles.

IYHF HOSTEL

Hawkshead YH, Esthwaite House (tel. 05394–36293/ 09666–293).

Coniston

Hawkshead five miles away, Ambleside six miles, Elterwater five miles by mountain path, Windermere 11 miles.

IYHF HOSTELS

Coniston YH, Holly How, Far End (tel. 05394–41323). £5.90 ($11.20; DM17.10) for members. Just outside Coniston village on the road to Ambleside.

Coniston Coppermines YH, Coppermines House (tel. 05394–41261). Same prices as above. 1¼ miles from the village at the top of the Coppermines Valley.

Patterdale

Ambleside 10 miles away, Grasmere nine miles by mountain path.

IYHF HOSTEL

Patterdale YH, Godrill House (tel. 07684–82394). £5.90 ($11.20; DM17.10) for members.

Glenridding

Patterdale 2½ miles away, Thirlmere four miles by path, Grasmere eight miles by path, Keswick 10 miles by path, Ambleside 12 miles.

IYHF HOSTEL

Helvellyn YH, Greenside, Glenridding (tel. 07684–82269). Same price as Patterdale. Near Ullswater. 3 miles from Aira Force, the highest waterfall in the Lake District.

Thirlmere

Keswick five miles away, Grasmere seven miles, Helvellyn four miles over the hills by path.

IYHF HOSTEL

Thirlmere YH, The Old School, Stanah Cross (tel. 05874–286). Same price as Patterdale.

Kendal (tel. code 0539)

Eleven miles from Windermere, Kendal has its train station in town and is close to the M6, so it is likely to be on your route if you are hitching up from the south.

IYHF HOSTEL

Kendal YH, Highgate (tel. 724066).

London
(tel. code 071 or 081 – use the 071 prefix unless shown otherwise)

There is a serious shortage of cheap places to stay in London, especially in the summer. It is advisable to book a bed as far in advance as you possibly can if you plan to arrive during the summer as you will struggle to find a place in a hostel, hall of residence, or one of the cheaper B&Bs on arrival. Outside the IYHF hostels and a few independent hostels it is difficult to find a bed for under £12 ($22.75; DM34.75); most halls of residence charge around £21 ($40; DM61) for a single, and doubles normally work out only slightly cheaper per person. Expect to pay from £20 ($38; DM58) for a single in a B&B, and you will do well to find a double for under £15 ($28.50; DM43.50) p.p. There are cheaper B&Bs, but they are frequently filled with homeless families, temporarily boarded by the Department of Social Security. The Tourist Information Centre Accommodation Service in Victoria train station (tel. 730 3488) locate and book rooms, but prices start at around £20 ($38; DM58), and average around £23 ($43.75; DM66.75) per person. For this service the office charges a huge £5 ($9.50; DM14.50) fee, far surpassing anywhere else in Europe to my knowledge, and over three times the charge made in Paris.

HOTELS

Many offer reduced rates in winter, or for stays of a week.
  Anne Elizabeth House Hotel, 30 Collingham Place. U: Earls Court £8–18 ($15.25–34.25; DM23.25–52.25) p.p. according to type of room, and the time of the year.

Cheapest prices for singles £17 ($32.25; DM49.25); doubles £14 ($26.50; DM40.50) p.p.

  Hyde Park Court Hotel, 41 Lancaster Gate. U: Lancaster Gate.

Cheapest prices for singles £19–23 ($36.00–43.75; DM55.00–66.75), doubles £14–17 ($26.50–32.25; DM40.50–49.25) p.p.

  Yorkshire Palace, 13–15 Argyle St. (tel. 278 8682). Also triples. U: King's Cross/St Pancras.
  Apollo, 43 Argyle St. (tel. 837 5489). Triples. U: King's Cross/St Pancras.
  Jesmond Dene Hotel, 27 Argyle St. (tel. 837 4654). Triples. U: King's Cross/St Pancras.
  Sass House Hotel, 10–11 Craven Terrace (tel. 262 2325). U: Lancaster Gate.

Cheapest prices for singles as above, doubles £17–19 ($32.25–36.00; DM40.50–55.00) p.p.

Windsor Guest House, 36 Alderney St. (tel. 828 7922). U: Victoria.

Luna House Hotel, 47 Belgrave Road (tel. 834 5897). U: Victoria or Pimlico. Bus 24 stops outside the hotel.

White House Hotel, 12 Earl's Court Gardens (tel. 373 5903). Triples. U: Earls Court.

Oxford Hotel, 24 Penywern Road (tel. 370 5162). Triples. U: Earls Court.

York House Hotel, 28 Philbeach Gardens (tel. 373 7519). Triples. At least a 25 per cent reduction for a week's stay.

Leinster Hotel Group, 7–11 Leinster Square (tel. 229 9641). Triples and quads. U: Paddington.

Melbourne House, 79 Belgrave Road (tel. 828 3516). Triples. U: Victoria or Pimlico.

More House, 53 Cromwell Road (tel. 589 8433). Triples. Weekly rate 10 per cent less. U: South Kensington.

Oakley Hotel, 73 Oakley St. (tel. 589 8433/352 6610). Triples. U: Sloane Square.

Belvedere Hotel, 52 Norfolk Square (tel. 723 8848). Triples. U: Paddington.

Cheapest prices for singles £23–25 ($43.75–47.50; DM66.75–72.50); doubles as above.

Jesmond Hotel, 63 Gower St. (tel. 636 3199). Triples. U: Goodge Street.

Repton House, 31 Bedford Place (tel. 636 7045). Triples. U: Holborn or Russell Square.

Ravna Gora, 29 Holland Park Avenue (tel. 727 7725). Triples and quads. U: Holland Park.

Hyde Park Rooms Hotel, 137 Sussex Cedars (tel. 723 0225/723 0965). Stay two nights and doubles fall in price to around £12 ($22.75; DM34.75) p.p. per night. U: Paddington.

Lords Hotel, 20–22 Leinster Square (tel. 229 8877). U: Bayswater.

Morgan House Hotel, 120 Sussex Gardens (tel. 402 7202). Triples. U: Paddington.

Cheapest prices for singles £25–30 ($47.50–57.00; DM72.50–87.00); doubles £20–23 ($38.00–43.75; DM58.00–66.75) p.p.

Arran House Hotel, 77–79 Gower St. (tel. 636 2186). Triples and quads. U: Goodge Street.

Ridgemount Hotel, 65 Gower St. (tel. 636 1141). Triples and quads. U: Goodge Street.

Regency House Hotel, 71 Gower St. (tel. 637 1804). Triples & quads. U: Goodge Street.

Garth Hotel, 69 Gower St. (tel. 636 3199). Triples and quads. U: Goodge Street.

Boka, 33–35 Eardley Crescent (tel. 373 2844). Triples. U: Earls Court.

The Beaver Hotel, 57–59 Philbeach Gardens (tel. 373 4553). Triples. U: Earls Court.

Olympic Hotel, 115 Warwick Way (tel. 828 0757). Triples. U: Victoria or Pimlico.

Oxford House, 92–94 Cambridge St. (tel. 834 6467). Triples. U: Victoria.

Flaxman House, 104–105 Oakley St. (tel. 352 0187). Triples. U: Sloane Square.

STUDENT RESIDENCES

International Lutheran Student Centre, 30 Thanet St. (tel. 388 4044). Some rooms available Christmas and Easter. More available late June–Sept. Singles around £13 ($24.75; DM37.75). Doubles slightly cheaper per person. 10 per cent surcharge for non-students. Around 30 per cent reduction for a week's stay. U: King's Cross/St Pancras.

London House, Mecklenburgh Square (tel. 837 8888). Singles £15 ($28.50; DM43.50). Doubles slightly cheaper p.p. Open to male graduates of the European Community, the British Commonwealth or the USA only, except some rooms for married couples. U: Russell Square.

William Goodenough House, Mecklenburgh Square (tel. 278 5131). The female equivalent of the London House residence. Singles only. Price as above.

Central University of Iowa Hostel, 7 Bedford Place (tel. 580 1121). Doubles £18 ($34.25; DM52.25) p.p. Slightly cheaper in quads.

Expect to pay around £20 ($38; DM58) for singles; doubles similarly priced, or slightly cheaper (open around Christmas and Easter, and July–Sept.).

Passfield Hall, 1 Endsleigh Place (tel. 387 3584/387 7743). London School of Economics (LSE) residence. U: Euston Square.

Carl Saunders Hall, 18–24 Fitzroy St. (tel. 580 6338). LSE. U: Warren Street.

Rosebery Avenue Hall, 90 Rosebery Avenue (tel. 278 3251). LSE. U: Farringdon.

John Adams Hall, 15–23 Endsleigh Place (tel. 387 4796). Univ. of London. U: Euston Square.

Connaught Hall, 36–45 Tavistock Square (tel. 636 6591). Univ. of London. U: Euston Square.

King's College Hall, Champion Hill (tel. 733 2167). King's College, Univ. of London. British Rail station: Denmark Hill.

Halliday Hall, 64–67 Clapham Common South Side (tel. 081–673 2032). King's College. U: Clapham Common.

Malcolm Gavin Hall, Beachcroft Road (tel. 081–767 3119). King's College. U: Tooting Bec.

Cheapest singles £22 ($41.75; DM63.75), doubles slightly cheaper p.p. (all King's College).

Queen Elizabeth Hall, Campden Hill Road (tel. 937 5411 extension 255). U: High Street Kensington.

Lightfoot Hall, Manresa Road (tel. 351 2488). U: Sloane
Square or South Kensington.

Ingram Court, 552 King's Road (tel. 872 3050). U: Fulham
Broadway.

Wellington Hall, Vincent Square (tel. 834 4740). U: Victoria.

King's Campus Vacation Bureau, 552 King's Road (tel. 351
6011) is the booking office for all the King's College Halls
above. Contact them as early as possible to find out about
booking procedures in 1992.

IYHF HOSTELS

Oxford Street YH, 14–18 Noel Street (tel. 734 1618). Juniors
£13.50 ($25.75; DM39.25), seniors £15.50 ($29.50; DM45).
Extra £1 ($2; DM3) charge from June. U: Oxford Circus.

Carter Lane YH, 36 Carter Lane (tel. 236 4965). Same
prices as above, though supplementary charge begins
in August. U: St Paul's.

King George VI Memorial Hostel, Holland House, Holland
Walk (tel. 937 0748). Juniors £12.50 ($23.75; DM36.25),
seniors £14.50 ($27.50; DM42). £1 ($2; DM3) surcharge
from June. U: Holland Park or High Street Kensington.

Earls Court YH, 38 Bolton Gardens (tel. 373 7083).
Juniors £11.50 ($21.75; DM33.25), senior £12.50
($23.75; DM36.25). Extra £1 ($2; DM3) charge from
June.

Hampstead Heath YH, 4 Wellgarth Road (tel. 081–458
9054/081–458 7196). Same prices as Earls Court YH,
and same supplementary charge from June.

Wood Green YH, Wood Green Halls of Residence, Brabant
Road (tel. 081–881 4432). £10.50 ($20; DM30.50) for singles
in this Middlesex Polytechnic residence converted into
a hostel mid July–mid Sept, and at Easter. U: Wood
Green.

White Hart Lane YH, All Saints Hall of Residence, White
Hart Lane (tel. 081–885 3234). Another Middlesex Poly-
technic Hall. Open mid July–Aug. Same prices as the
Wood Green Halls. U: Wood Green, then bus W3, or

walk from Seven Sisters (not the best area to walk about in at night). You can take a British Rail train to White Hart Lane from Seven Sisters, or from Liverpool Street. Mostly singles, some doubles.

Highgate Village YH, 84 Highgate West Hill (tel. 081–340 1831). Juniors £8.50 ($16.25; DM24). Seniors £10 ($19; DM29), with a supplementary charge of £1 ($2; DM3) from June. U: Archway.

HOSTELS/CHEAP HOTELS

Expect to pay in dorms £9.00–11.50 ($17.00–21.75; DM26.00–33.25).

Talbot House Hotel, Talbot Square (tel. 402 7202). Doubles, triples and quads at these prices; singles not much more expensive. U: Paddington.

Glendale Hotel, 8 Devonshire Terrace (tel. 262 1770). Triples and quads. Doubles start at around £13.50 ($25.75; DM39.25) p.p. U: Paddington.

Astor Museum Hostel, 27 Montague Street (tel. 580 5360). Slightly more expensive triples; doubles at around £15.50 ($29.50; DM45) p.p. U: Holborn, Russell Square or Tottenham Court Road. Weekly rates available.

Albert Hotel, 191 Queens Gate (tel. 584 3019). Doubles around £15.50 ($29.50; DM45), singles £20 ($38; DM58). Weekly rates. U: Gloucester Road or South Kensington.

Maranton House Hotel, 14 Barkston Gardens (tel. 373 5782). Triples and quads. Doubles similar in price to the Albert above. Expensive singles. U: Earls Court.

Quest Hotel, 45 Queensborough Terrace (tel. 229 7782). U: Lancaster Gate.

Fieldcourt House, 32 Courtfield Gardens (tel. 373 0152). Doubles £15.50 ($29.50; DM45), singles around £20 ($38; DM58). U: Gloucester Road.

Norfolk House, 54 Norfolk Square (tel. 262 3319). Singles and doubles similar in price to Fieldcourt House. U: Paddington.

Expect to pay in dorms around £14 ($26.75; DM40.75).

Curzon House Hotel 58 Courtfield Gardens (tel. 373 6745). Triples slightly more expensive; singles and doubles are on a par with the more expensive B&Bs/hotels listed above. U: Gloucester Road.

Elizabeth House (YWCA), 118 Warwick Way (tel. 630 0741). Male students accepted. Singles £20 ($38; DM58), doubles slightly cheaper p.p. U: Victoria or Pimlico.

Other hostel suggestions:

International Students House, 229 Great Portland Street (tel. 631 3223). U: Great Portland Street.

Tonbridge School Clubs. On the corner of Cromer St. and Judd St. (tel. 837 4406). Foam pads on the floor, with blankets provided. Meant for students only, but this rule is rarely enforced. £3.50 ($6.75; DM10.25). U: King's Cross/St Pancras.

CAMPING

Hackney Camping, Millfields Road, Hackney Marshes (tel. 081–985 7656). Open June–Aug. £2.50 ($4.75; DM7.25) p.p. (includes tent). Bus 38 or 55 from Victoria or Piccadilly Circus. Also bus 22 from Piccadilly.

Crystal Palace Camp Site, Crystal Palace Parade (tel. 081–778 7155). Open year round. Tent with two occupants £3.75 ($7.25; DM11). British Rail train from London Bridge to Crystal Palace.

Pickett's Lock Centre, Pickett's Lock Lane (tel. 081–803 4756). U: Seven Sisters, then bus 149, 259 or 279. Or British Rail to Angel Road, then bus W8.

Tent City, Old Oak Common Lane (tel. 081–743 5708). U: East Acton.

SLEEPING ROUGH

The embankment at Westminster Bridge, or Hyde Park are the most obvious places to try. It is not possible to sleep in the train stations, nor safe in the surrounding areas. Best avoided in London as a whole. If you must sleep rough, try to bed down beside other travellers.

Manchester (tel.code 061)

The city is a bit of a nightmare for budget travellers. There are no hostels, which means you are going to have to pay from £12 ($22.75; DM34.75) for a B&B. The Tourist Information Centre in the Town Hall Extension, Albert Square on Lloyd Street (tel. 234 3157) finds rooms for a £1 ($2; DM3) fee and some of the pubs along Chapel Street offer B&B. Apart from these, the best place to look is the Chorlton district of the city, a 15–20-minute trip from the centre by bus 85, 86, 102 or 103.

B&Bs

The Black Lion, 65 Chapel Street (tel. 834 1974). Around £14 ($26.75; DM40).

Mrs McMahon, 7 The Meade (tel. 881 2714). Four miles out from the centre. Bus 47, 82, 86 or 87 to Beech Road. From Beech Road left along Claude Road, left again on to North Meads which subsequently becomes The Meade. £12 ($22.75; DM34.75).

STUDENT RESIDENCES

University of Manchester, Wolton Hall (tel. 224 7244). Mainly singles, a few doubles. Highly popular with groups. £14 ($26.75; DM40) for B&B. Buses 40–46 and bus 49 to Owens Park.

Oxford (tel. code 0865)

Rooms (especially singles) can be at a premium in July and August in Oxford, so try to book a bed in advance if possible. You may be asked to send a deposit to confirm a booking. B&Bs are more expensive than normal and you will do well to find a double room for under £14 ($26.50; DM40.75) p.p. The Tourist Information Centre in St Aldate's Street near the Carfax Tower (tel. 726871) books rooms for a £2 ($3.75; DM5.75) fee, and it is advisable to arrive early if you want one of the cheaper rooms. The least expensive B&Bs are on Iffley Road (nos. 200–240), on Cowley Road (nos. 250–350), and on Abingdon Road.

B&Bs

Tara, 10 Holywell Street (tel. 244786/248270). Near the university colleges. Singles £20 ($38; DM58), doubles £15 ($28.50; DM43.50) p.p. Slightly cheaper in triples. Outside the June–Sept. period likely to be filled by students.

White House View, 9 White House Road (tel. 721626). Ten minutes' walk from the centre, off Abingdon Road. £15 ($28.50; DM43.50).

Gables' Guest House, 6 Cumnor Hill (tel. 862153). Near the ring road. £16 ($30.50; DM46.50) in the cheapest rooms.

Micklewood, 331 Cowley Road (tel. 247328). Singles £16 ($30.50; DM46.50); doubles £14 ($26.50; DM40.50) p.p.

Mrs Old, 58 St John Street (tel. 55454).

Newton Guest House, 82–84 Abingdon Road (tel. 240561). Just under 10 minutes' walk from the centre. Cheapest doubles £15.50 ($29.50; DM45) p.p. No singles.

King's Guest House, 363 Iffley Road (tel. 241363). No singles. £18 ($34.25; DM52.25) p.p. in doubles.

IYHF HOSTEL

Oxford Youth Hostel, Jack Straw's Lane (tel. 62997). Mar.–Oct. open daily. Closed most of December and first week of January. At other times open daily except Sunday. Juniors £5.60 ($10.75; DM16.25), seniors £6.80 ($13; DM19). July and Aug. £1 ($2; DM3) supplement for seniors. About 2½ miles from the centre. Frequent minibus service from the Job Centre (near the Tourist Information Office) or from Queen's College.

HOSTELS

YMCA, Alexandra Residential Club, 133 Woodstock Road (tel. 52021). Women aged over 16 only. Usually filled with students during term time. Best reserved a fortnight in advance during the summer vacation. 2.30 a.m. curfew Fri. and Sat., half an hour earlier the rest of the week. Around £25 ($47.50; DM72.50) per week; about a mile from the centre. Bus 420 or 423.

CAMPING

Oxford Camping International, 426 Abingdon Road (tel. 246551). Open year round. At the back of the Texaco petrol station.

Cassington Mill Caravan Site, Eynsham Road, Cassington (tel. 881081). Four miles out, off the A40 to Cheltenham. Bus 90 from the bus station. £5 ($9.50; DM14.50) for a tent and two occupants.

Stratford-upon-Avon (tel. code 0789)

Even although the town has a large number of B&Bs considering its size, rooms (especially singles) are in short supply from late June to early September. At these times try to book lodgings at least one week in advance. The Tourist Information Office at 1 High Street (tel. 293127) locates rooms, as do Guide Friday at 14 Rother Street, although the latter charge a hefty £3 ($5.75; DM8.75) fee. If you arrive in town after these offices have closed, you can pick up a list of local B&Bs at the swimming pool on Bridgequay. The best area to look for B&Bs is around Evesham Road, Evesham Place and Grove Place. To get there go down Alcester Road from the train station, then right on to Grove Road. The road runs into Evesham Place, which subsequently becomes Evesham Road. Across the river, the Shipston Road also has quite a concentration of B&Bs.

B&Bs

Expect to pay £11–15 ($21.00–28.50; DM32.00–43.50) in a B&B, or in one of the local farmhouses which let rooms.

Windfall, 118 Alcester Road (tel. 66880). One of the cheaper places.

Arrandale Guest House, 208 Evesham Road (tel. 67112). Cheap and good value, but quite far out from the centre.

The Glenavon, 6 Chestnut Walk (tel. 292588). Off Evesham Place.

Salamander Guest House, 40 Grove Road (tel. 205728).

Bradbourne Guest House, 44 Shipston Road (tel. 204178). About 10 minutes' walk from the centre.

Carlton Guesthouse, 22 Evesham Place (tel. 203548). Prices start at top of the scale quoted.

The Hollies, 16 Evesham Place (tel. 66857). No singles. Similar prices to the Carlton Guesthouse.

IYHF HOSTEL

Stratford-upon-Avon YH, Hemmingford House, Wellesbourne Road, Alveston (tel. 297093). Open mid Jan.– mid Dec. Juniors £6.40 ($12.25; DM18.50), seniors £7.50

($14.25; DM21.75). About 2½ miles from the centre: walk along the B4086 to Alveston, or take bus 518 from the Travel Shop (at the junction of Guild Street and Warwick Road). Reserve well in advance.

CAMPING

Elms, Tiddington Road (tel. 292312). On the B4056, a mile north-east of the centre. Open Apr.–Oct. Cheap at £2 ($3.75; DM5.75) for one person and a tent. Extra occupants £1 ($2; DM3) each.

Dodwell Park, Evesham Road (tel. 204957). Year-round site. Two miles out on the A439. £4 ($7.50; DM11.50) for one person and a tent. Extra occupants £1 ($2; DM3) each.

York (tel. code 0904)

Finding a cheap place to stay in York during the summer can be very difficult. At this time even campsites are best reserved in advance. The city is also highly popular with people taking weekend breaks, so try to arrive in midweek, if possible. B&Bs start at around £10 ($19; DM29), but you will have to start your search early in the day to find space in one of the cheapest B&Bs. The Tourist Information Centre in the De Grey Rooms on Exhibition Square (tel. 621756) operates a room-finding service: you pay a £1.75 ($3.25; DM5) deposit at the office and this amount is then subtracted from your bill at the B&B. When the office is closed, a list of accommodation is displayed. The Mount area of the city, (along Blossom Road beyond the train station) has a good stock of B&Bs, as has the Bootham area, also near the train station. In the latter area Bishopthorpe Road is a particularly good street to look for lodgings. If you go down to the end of Gillygate from the Tourist Information Centre, and then turn right, you will find yourself in the Haxby Road, another street with a plentiful supply of B&Bs. Alternatively take bus 2A from the city centre.

B&Bs

The Old Dairy, 10 Compton Street (tel. 623816). A 7–10-minute walk up Bootham from the train station, or take bus 5. £11 ($21; DM32).

South View Guest House, 114 Acomb Road (tel. 796512). Singles £13 ($24.75; DM37.75), doubles £12 ($22.75; DM34.75) p.p.

IYHF HOSTEL

Peter Rowntree Memorial Hostel, Haverford, Water End, Clifton (tel. 653147). Curfew 11.30 p.m. Juniors £7.50 ($14.25; DM21.75), seniors £8.80 ($16.75; DM25.50). Seniors pay an extra £1 (£2; DM3) in July and Aug. One mile from the centre, in the Clifton area of town.

HOSTELS

Bishophill House Youth Hostel, 11–13 Bishophill Senior Road (tel. 625904/630613). Dorms £5.50–7.00 ($10.50–13.25; DM16.00–20.25). Doubles slightly more expensive per person. Singles £11 ($21; DM32). Right from the train station, left along Micklegate, then right on to Trinity Lane.

International House, 33 Bootham (tel. 622874). Small dorms £5 ($9.50; DM14.50). A few minutes' walk from the train station.

Maxwell's Hotel, 54 Walmgate (tel. 624048). Dorms £8 ($15.25; DM23.25). Small rooms start at around £15 ($28.50; DM43.50) p.p.

The Racecourse Centre, Racing Stables, Dinghouses (tel. 36553 or 065381–283). Open Mar.–July. Dorms around £7.50 ($14.25; DM21.75), with breakfast. Bus 3, 3A, 3B or 4.

CAMPING

Caravan Club Site, Terry Avenue (tel. 0203–694995). Over the Skeldergate Bridge. Around £3.50 ($6.75; DM10.25) p.p. In summer generally requires three months' advance booking.

Bishopthorpe (tel. 704442). By the river in Bishopthorpe, three miles out on the A64 towards Tadcaster and Leeds. Bus 14, 15 or 15A. £3.50 ($6.75; DM10.25) for one person and tent. Not much more expensive for four sharing a tent. Open Easter–Sept.

Post Office Site (tel. 706288). Another riverside site, one mile further along the A64 than the Bishopthorpe site. Similar price for a solo traveller as the site above. Open Apr.–Oct. Any Acaster Malbis bus will get you there.

Poplar Farm (tel. 706548). Not far from the Post Office Site, but more expensive. Buses as for the site above. Also the Sykes' bus runs every two hours from Skeldergate.

IYHF HOSTELS NEARBY

Malton Youth Hostel, Derwent Bank, York Road, Malton (tel. 0653–692077). In a picturesque small town 19 miles from York. The hostel is a 10–12-minute walk from the train station. Juniors £5 ($9.50; DM14.50), seniors £6 ($11.50; DM17.50).

Beverley Friary Youth Hostel, The Friary, Friars' Lane, Beverley (tel. 0482–881751). In a market town with a beautiful minster, 30 miles from York. Same prices as the hostel in Malton.

YUGOSLAVIA

Over the last decade the Yugoslav government has raised the price of accommodation in an effort to earn hard currency to support its flagging economy. This has not (yet) resulted in a situation similar to that which prevailed in Romania, as most accommodation possibilities are still within the range of the budget traveller, but accommodation is no longer dirt cheap.

During the camping season (April to October) a tent can be a useful standby as you may encounter difficulties finding a cheap bed in some of the larger cities such as Belgrade, Zagreb and Llubljana, and also in the coastal towns and resorts, especially Split and Dubrovnik. Accommodation possibilities can be just as restricted in the off-season when the campgrounds are closed and the availability of private rooms declines dramatically. One notable exception to the general rule is Sarajevo. In summer you should have little difficulty finding suitable accommodation here, but expect difficulties in winter as Sarajevo is a major winter sports centre.

The local travel agencies will find rooms for you in hotels or private rooms, but, as these are in business to make money, they invariably try to push you towards concerns they control. If you feel they are paying little attention to your requests (especially as regards price) try to see if one of the other agencies will offer you a more acceptable deal. As well as local and regional organizations, such as Dubrovnikturist and Dalmacijaturist, there are others which operate throughout the country such as Kompas, Atlas, Putnik, Generalturist and Inex.

Hotels are graded L (de luxe), and then in descending order from A to D. There are some B- and C-class hotels in the major cities where doubles are available for around £10 ($19; DM29) p.p. but on the whole hotels are probably well outside your price range. Pensions, rated from third up to first class, are more affordable, but be wary of staying more than three days, as, after this period, pensions and hotels can legally make full-board obligatory, pushing the price up sharply. Inns are establishments which fail to meet the minimum requirements laid down for hotels and pensions: they are a good budget option with B&B in doubles from £4.50 ($8.50; DM13) per person, but are difficult to find.

More readily available, and starting from around the same price, are **rooms in private homes** (*sobe*). There is a good supply of rooms along the coast, and in the more popular tourist destinations of Macedonia, Montenegro, Serbia and the Julian Alps. Wherever you go the supply of singles is very limited, and even where singles do exist, prices approach those of doubles, so solo travellers may want to find someone to share with. Rooms are graded downwards from Category I to III. In peak season (July and Aug.) prices range from £3.50 to £10.00 ($6.75–19.00; DM10–29) p.p. for doubles depending on classification and location. At other times prices for the most expensive rooms fall to £7.50 ($14.50; DM22) p.p. for doubles.

It is possible to find rooms on your own: look out for the 'sobe' sign, or a sign showing a stylized bed, or, especially in the northern areas popular with Austrian and German holidaymakers, a sign inscribed 'zimmer'. Occasionally the owner may ask you to go into town and book the room at an agency because owners can be duty bound to do this in order that the agencies know where rooms are available. In the larger, more popular towns you are probably better to head for an agency rather than search on your own, especially during the peak season. When booking through an agency you will find that they generally add a surcharge of up to 30 per cent for stays of less than four days. In the popular coastal towns travellers are often approached at bus and train stations, and at ferry terminals, by locals offering rooms. These are no great bargains, as the asking price will normally be on a par with prices at the local agencies, but the bonus for you is the convenience of getting a room virtually on arrival and unless there is a high ratio of travellers to touts they can usually be talked down from their initial asking price, but do not expect anything more than a 20–25 per cent reduction. Have a look at the room before committing yourself. If the room is not nearby leave your pack at the station while you go and have a look.

There are about 40 **IYHF hostels** in Yugoslavia, covering many of the major places of interest, with the notable exceptions of Split and Mostar. In theory IYHF cards are obligatory, but most hostels will settle for adding a small surcharge for non-members. Very few hostels remain open all year round, while in peak season you will struggle to find a bed unless you have reserved in advance. Hostels are not particularly good value for money, costing between £3.10 and £6.20 ($6–12; DM9–18). Not only are inflexible early curfews common, but also many hostels are not clean and lack hot running water.

A more pleasant alternative, and not much more expensive, are studentski domovi, or **student dormitories**, which are converted into hostels during July and August. They are aimed particularly at young Yugoslav holidaymakers and their popularity means that they are often full, but they are still well worth enquiring about. Try to reserve ahead where possible. Studentski domovi cost around £4.25–5.25 ($8–10; DM12.25–15.25) for B&B in small rooms. Unlike the IYHF hostels studentski domovi do offer good value for money. They can be found in most towns with a university, notably Llubljana, Zagreb, Split, Sarajevo and Skopje. The youth and travel organization Yugotours-Narom operate several International Youth Centres, including one in Dubrovnik. For more information on these centres, and to make reservations, contact the head office of Yugotours-Narom.

There are few of the towns of major interest that do not have a **campsite**. There are roughly 300 official sites, with concentrations along the coast, and in the Slovene mountains. Sites open for varying periods of time during the camping season and as a rule they are large, and frequently crowded. Most are equipped with leisure facilities and shops, the latter of which can be a godsend as they are often open when the local shops are closed. Camping is inexpensive, usually costing a solo traveller from £2.75 to £3.75 ($5.25–7.25; DM8–11). Occasionally this can rise to £4.50 ($8.50; DM13) in exceptionally popular places such as Dubrovnik. Camping rough is strictly illegal unless you have been granted a permit by the local authority. The authorities invariably take strong action against anyone caught flouting the law by imposing hefty fines. The same applies to anyone caught sleeping rough, especially in town parks, or along the beaches of the Adriatic.

ADDRESSES

Yugoslav YHA	Ferijalni savez Jugoslavije, Mose Pijade 12/V, 11000 Beograd (tel. 011–339802).
International Youth Centres	Yugotours-Narom, Dure Dakoviča 31, 11000 Beograd (tel. 011–764622).
Youth hostels, travel, and accommodation	International Youth Travel Centre, FSJ/FSH, Trg žrtava fasizma 13, 41000 Zagreb (tel. 041–415038).
	International Information Centre, FS Srbija, Mladost-turist-Beograd, Terazije 3, Beograd (tel. 011–322131).
Camping	Maps and lists of organizations booking private rooms are available from the National Tourist Office in London or your capital city.

Dubrovnik (tel. code 050)

In the peak season (July to September) hotels are very
expensive. Even C-class hotels such as the Stadion and the
Dubravka charge around £14.50 ($27.50; DM42) per person
at this time. Prices at hotels are lower in May and June, but
only if you are travelling in April or October are there more
than a handful of hotels with affordable rooms.

HOTELS

Peak season:
  Gruž, Gruška obala 25 (tel. 24777). Half board £15.25 ($29;
    DM44.25) p.p.

May and June:

Expect to pay around £11 ($21; DM32) p.p. for doubles.

  Dubravka (tel. 26284).
  Stadion (tel. 23449).

April and October:

**Expect to pay around £9.50 ($18; DM27.50)
p.p. for doubles.**

  Neptun (B class) (tel. 23755).
  Sumratin (B), I.L. Ribara 27 (tel. 24722).
  Jadran (B) (tel. 23322/23276).
  Bellevue (B), P. Čingrije 7 (tel. 25077).
  Adriatic (B) (tel. 24144).
  Lapad (B), Lapadska obala 37 (tel. 23473).
  Dubravka and Stadion. Tel. nos as above.
  Gruž. At this time of year half board here costs around
    £8 ($15; DM23.25) p.p.

PRIVATE ROOMS

Can be booked at various offices in town. In July and August prices p.p. in doubles are: Category I £6.90–9.50 ($13–18; DM20.00–27.50); Category II £5.70–7.60 ($10.75–14.50; DM16.50–22.00); Category III £4.50–5.70 ($8.50–10.75; DM13.00–16.50). At other times prices are: Category I £5.70–7.60 ($10.75–14.50; DM16.50–22.00); Category II £4.50–5.70 ($8.50–10.75; DM13.00–16.50); Category III £3.45–4.50 ($6.50–8.50; DM10–13).

Atlas, Pile 1 (tel. 27333).
Dalmacijaturist, M. Pracata 7 (tel. 29367/24077/24078).
Dubrovnikturist, Put Republike 5 (tel. 32108/29679).
Generalturist, F. Supila 29 (tel. 23554–5–6).
Kvarner-Express, Gručka obala 69 (tel. 22772).
Putnik, F. Supila 7 (tel. 26650/26651/26398).
Razvitakturist, U Pilama 2 (tel. 26677/26111).
Unisturist, Masarykov put 9 (tel. 25594).
Sunturist, F. Supila 8 (tel. 24965/23843).
Turisticki Informativni centar, P. Miličevića 1
   (tel. 26354–5/23746).

IYHF HOSTELS

Oktobarske revolucije 17/Vinka Sagrastena 3 (tel. 23241). For information contact FSH-Zagreb, Trg žrtava fašizma 13, Zagreb (tel. 041–415038). Open 15 Apr.–15 Oct. 1 a.m. curfew. Around £4.75 ($9; DM13.75). A 10-minute walk from the bus station.

HOSTELS

International Youth and Student Center Dvorac Rašica, Ivanska 14 (tel. 23841/23241). Bus 2 or 4 from the bus station of ferry terminal, or walk up Od Batale on to Ivanska. Open July–Oct. Advance reservation essential July and Aug. Contact Ferijalni savez, Mose Pijade 12/1, PO Box 374, 11000 Beograd, or Yugotours-Narom.

CAMPING

Solitudo (tel. 20770). Open 1 Apr.–31 Oct. Roughly two miles west of the bus station. Bus 6 from the Old Town, or from near the bus station. £2.10 ($4; DM6) per tent, £3.10 ($6; DM9) p.p.

There is another site in Kupari, about five miles out of Dubrovnik, accessible by bus 10 (tel. 486020). Open 15 Apr.–15 Oct. £1.20 ($2.25; DM3.50) per tent, £1.50 ($3; DM4.50) p.p.

SLEEPING ROUGH

There is virtually no chance of you getting away with sleeping on the beach as the police make regular patrols. You can take a chance and bed down in the terraced park overlooking the sea below Marsala Tita, but if you are caught you can expect a steep fine. If you really are stuck, head for the campsites: even if you have to pay the price for one person and a tent, it is far better than being fined.

Llubljana (tel. code 061)

HOTELS

**Cheapest singles around £7 ($13; DM20),
doubles around £5.25 ($9.75; DM15) p.p.**

Grandovec Inn (tel. 666350/666449).

Cheapest doubles around £9.25 ($17.75; DM27) p.p.

Park Hotel, Tabor 9 (tel. 316777). Also triples.
Primraku Hotel (tel. 223412).
Zajčja Dobrava Inn (tel. 442108).
Dom učencev Tabor, Vidovdanska 7 (tel. 321067). Ask the
   Tourist Office if this hotel has re-opened.

Cheapest doubles around £11.25 ($21.25; DM32.50) p.p.

Ilirija Hotel (tel. 551162).
Pension Lieber (tel. 374080).

PRIVATE ROOMS

Turistično-Informacijski center, Titova II (tel. 215412/
224222). Price p.p. in doubles: Category I £5.35
($10.25; DM15.50). Category II £4.50 ($8.50; DM13).
Category III £3.80 ($7.20; DM11). Singles range from
£5 to £6 ($9.50–11.50; DM14.50–17.50). Same price
year round, but there's a limited supply of rooms.

IYHF HOSTEL

Bežigrad, Kardeljeva ploščad 28 (tel. 312185/321897).
Open 25 June–28 Aug. For information contact Mladi
turist, Celovška 49, Llubljana. Bus 6 from Titova Cesta
to Stadion. Walk a short distance, then go right on to
Dimičeva, then left.

HOSTELS

Zvezni Center, Kardeljeva ploščad 27 (tel. 342626). £7
($13.25; DM20.25), price includes sheets and showers.
Dijaški Dom Ivana Cankarja, Poljanska 26–28 (tel. 318948).
Bus 11 from the train station. Alternatively walk down
Resljeva, then go left on Poljanska. Take the path
between nos. 24 and 26. At the foot of the path go
left.
Ask the Turistično-Informacijski center at Titova II (tel.
215412/224222) about the current location of the International
Student Hostel as it tends to change annually. Open from
July–Sept. They will also book you doubles in student
residences at £7 ($13.25; DM20.25) p.p.

CAMPING

Ježica, Titova Cesta 260a (tel. 372901). Bus 6 from the
train station. £2.10 ($4; DM6) per tent and p.p. Also
twin-bedded bungalows with showers, £11.20 ($21.25;
DM32.50) p.p.

Split (tel. code 058)

HOTELS

Hotels in Split are very expensive: for example, the D-class
Central (tel. 41132) charges £13.75 ($26; DM39.75) p.p. for
doubles with showers during the peak season of June to
September. At other times prices fall to around £11 ($21;
DM32) p.p. The Slavija (tel. 47053) has doubles which
are slightly more expensive, but these rooms lack private
showers.

PRIVATE ROOMS

Let by the Tourist Office: OOUR Turist biro, Titova obala 12 (tel. 42142/42544). In July and Aug. prices p.p. in doubles are: Category I £7.60–9.15 ($14.50–17.25; DM22.00–26.50), Category II £6.50 ($12.50; DM19), Category III £5.35 ($10.25; DM15.50). At other times: Category I £6.00–7.25 ($11.50–13.75; DM17.50–21.00), Category II £5 ($9.50; DM14.50), Category III £4.25 ($8; DM12).

HOSTELS

Studencki Dom, Maleśina 66 (tel. 551774). B&B in triples £5 ($9.50; DM14.50) p.p. Close to Proleterskin Brigada. Reached by bus 18 from the open-air market.

CAMPING

Trstenik, Put Trstenika (tel. 521971). Open 1 May–1 Oct. Not the greatest of sites, but preferable to being fined for sleeping rough.

SLEEPING ROUGH

Probably your best chance of remaining undetected is to bed down deep in the woods of Marjan Park. The risk is yours.

Zagreb (tel. code 041)

HOTELS

Cheapest doubles around £10.35 ($19.75; DM30) p.p.

Park (tel. 233422).
Jadran (tel. 414600).
Tomislavov Dom (tel. 449821).
Šumski Dvor (tel. 275892/272195).

PRIVATE ROOMS

Expect to pay p.p. in doubles all year round: Category II £4.30 ($8.25; DM12.50), Category III £3.45 ($6.50; DM10).

Generalturist, Zrinjevac 18 (tel. 425566/427723).
Turističko društvo Novi Zagreb, 33 divizije 15 (tel. 529426).

IYHF HOSTEL

Omladinski Hotel, Petrijnska 77 (tel. 434964). Dorms around £4 ($7.50; DM11.50), doubles and triples around £10 ($19; DM29) p.p. Turn right on leaving the station, walk one block and you will see Petrijnska on your left. Fills quickly.

HOSTELS

Studentski Centar, Savska 25 (tel. 274674). Dorms £5.50 ($10.50; DM16) mid July–Sept. From Trg Republike tram 14 to the junction of Vodnikova and Savska.

CAMPING

Plitvice, Zagreb/Lučko (tel. 522230/529882). £1.70 ($3.30; DM5) per tent, plus £2.25 ($4.25; DM6.50) p.p. Open 1 May–1 Oct. Six miles out on the road to Maribor. Tram 4, 14 or 17 to Savski Most, then bus 112 or 167 to Lucko, followed by a two-mile walk.

Index